Guy Mannering

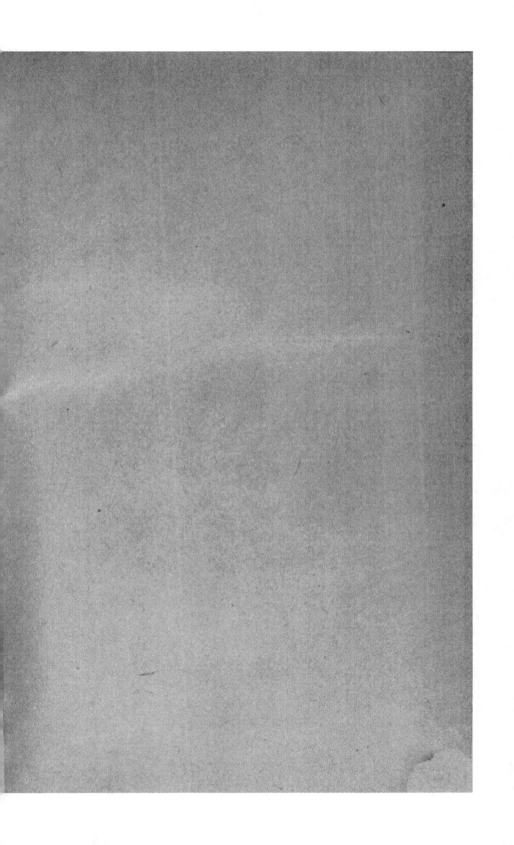

Pocahontas

Published by James and Taylor New York 18?

WAVERLEY NOVELS.

HOUSEHOLD EDITION.

PEVERIL OF THE PEAK.

II.

BOSTON:
TICKNOR AND FIELDS.
M DCCC LVIII.

RIVERSIDE, CAMBRIDGE
STEREOTYPED AND PRINTED BY
H. O. HOUGHTON AND COMPANY.

35552

PEVERIL OF THE PEAK.

" If my readers should at any time remark that I am particularly dull, they
may be assured there is a design under it."

BRITISH ESSAYIST.

PEVERIL OF THE PEAK.

CHAPTER XXIII.

The Gordon then his bugle blew,
And said, awa, awa;
The House of Rhodes is all on flame,
I hauld it time to ga'.

OLD BALLAD.

WHEN Julian awakened the next morning, all was still
and vacant in the apartment. The rising sun, which
shone through the half-closed shutters, showed some
relics of the last night's banquet, which his confused
and throbbing head assured him had been carried into a
debauch.

Without being much of a boon companion, Julian, like
other young men of the time, was not in the habit of
shunning wine, which was then used in considerable
quantities; and he could not help being surprised, that
the few cups he had drank over night had produced on
his frame the effects of excess. He rose up, adjusted his
dress, and sought in the apartment for water to perform
his morning ablutions, but without success. Wine there
was on the table; and beside it one stool stood, and
another lay, as if thrown down in the heedless riot of the
evening. "Surely," he thought to himself, "the wine

must have been very powerful, which rendered me insensible to the noise my companions must have made ere they finished their carouse."

With momentary suspicion he examined his weapons, and the packet which he had received from the Countess, and kept in a secret pocket of his upper coat, bound close about his person. All was safe; and the very operation reminded him of the duties which lay before him. He left the apartment where they had supped, and went into another, wretched enough, where, in a truckle-bed, were stretched two bodies, covered with a rug, the heads belonging to which were amicably deposited upon the same truss of hay. The one was the black shock-head of the groom; the other, graced with a long thrum night-cap, showed a grizzled pate, and a grave caricatured countenance, which the hook-nose and lantern-jaws proclaimed to belong to the Gallic minister of good cheer, whose praises he had heard sung forth on the preceding evening. These worthies seemed to have slumbered in the arms of Bacchus as well as of Morpheus, for there were broken flasks on the floor; and their deep snoring alone showed that they were alive.

Bent upon resuming his journey, as duty and expedience alike dictated, Julian next descended the trap-stair, and essayed a door at the bottom of the steps. It was fastened within. He called—no answer was returned. It must be, he thought, the apartment of the revellers, now probably sleeping as soundly as their dependants still slumbered, and as he himself had done a few minutes before. Should he awake them?—To what purpose? They were men with whom accident had involved him against his own will; and situated as he was, he thought it wise to take the earliest opportunity of breaking off from society which was suspicious, and might be perilous. Ruminating thus, he essayed another door, which admitted him to a bedroom, where lay another harmonious slumberer. The mean utensils, pewter measures, empty cans and casks, with which this room was lumbered, proclaimed it that of the host, who slept surrounded by his professional implements of hospitality and stock in trade.

This discovery relieved Peveril from some delicate embarrassment which he had formerly entertained. He put upon the table a piece of money, sufficient, as he judged, to pay his share of the preceding night's reckoning; not caring to be indebted for his entertainment to the strangers, whom he was leaving without the formality of an adieu.

His conscience cleared of this gentleman-like scruple, Peveril proceeded with a light heart, though somewhat a dizzy head, to the stable, which he easily recognised among a few other paltry out-houses. His horse, refreshed with rest, and perhaps not unmindful of his services the evening before, neighed as his master entered the stable; and Peveril accepted the sound as an omen of a prosperous journey. He paid the augury with a sieveful of corn; and, while his palfrey profited by his attention, walked into the fresh air to cool his heated blood, and consider what course he should pursue in order to reach the Castle of Martindale before sunset. His acquaintance with the country in general, gave him confidence that he could not have greatly deviated from the nearest road; and with his horse in good condition, he conceived he might easily reach Martindale before nightfall.

Having adjusted his route in his mind, he returned into the stable to prepare his steed for the journey, and soon led him into the ruinous court-yard of the inn, bridled, saddled, and ready to be mounted. But as Peveril's hand was upon the mane, and his left foot in the stirrup, a hand touched his cloak, and the voice of Ganlesse said, " What, Master Peveril, is this your foreign breeding? or have you learned in France to take French leave of your friends ? "

Julian started like a guilty thing, although a moment's reflection assured him that he was neither wrong nor in danger. " I cared not to disturb you," he said, "although I did come as far as the door of your chamber. I supposed your friend and you might require, after our last night's revel, rather sleep than ceremony. I left my own bed, though a rough one, with more reluctance than usual; and as my occasions oblige me to be an early traveller, I thought it best to depart without leave-taking. I have left a token for mine host, on the table of his apartment."

" It was unnecessary," said Ganlesse; " the rascal is already overpaid.—But are you not rather premature in your purpose of departing? My mind tells me that Master Julian Peveril had better proceed with me to London, than turn aside for any purpose whatever. You may see already that I am no ordinary person, but a master-spirit of the time. For the cuckoo I travel with, and whom I indulge in his prodigal follies, he also has his uses. But you are of a different cast; and I not only would serve you, but even wish you, to be my own."

Julian gazed on this singular person when he spoke. We have already said his figure was mean and slight, with very ordinary and unmarked features, unless we were to distinguish the lightnings of a keen gray eye, which corresponded in its careless and prideful glance, with the haughty superiority which the stranger assumed in his conversation. It was not till after a momentary pause, that Julian replied, " Can you wonder, sir, that in my circumstances—if they are indeed known to you so well as they seem—I should decline unnecessary confidence on the affairs of moment which have called me hither, or refuse the company of a stranger, who assigns no reason for desiring mine ? "

" Be it as you list, young man," answered Ganlesse ; " only remember hereafter, you had a fair offer—it is not every one to whom I would have made it. If we should meet hereafter, on other, and on worse terms, impute it to yourself and not to me."

" I understand not your threat," answered Peveril, " if a threat be indeed implied. I have done no evil—I feel no apprehension—and I cannot, in common sense, conceive why I should suffer for refusing my confidence to a stranger, who seems to require that I should submit me blindfold to his guidance."

" Farewell, then, Sir Julian of the Peak,—that may soon be," said the stranger, removing the hand which he had as yet left carelessly on the horse's bridle.

" How mean you by that phrase ? " said Julian ; " and why apply such a title to me ? "

The stranger smiled, and only answered, " Here our conference ends. The way is before you. You will find it longer and rougher than that by which I would have guided you."

So saying, Ganlesse turned his back and walked toward the house. On the threshold he turned about once more, and seeing that Peveril had not yet moved from the spot, he again smiled and beckoned to him, but Julian

recalled by that sign to recollection, spurred his horse and
set forward on his journey.

It was not long ere his local acquaintance with the
country enabled him to regain the road to Martindale,
from which he had diverged on the preceding evening
for about two miles. But the roads, or rather the paths,
of this wild country, so much satirized by their native
poet, Cotton, were so complicated in some places, so difficult to be traced in others, and so unfit for hasty travelling in almost all, that, in spite of Julian's utmost exertions, and though he made no longer delay upon the journey than was necessary to bait his horse at a small hamlet
through which he passed at noon, it was nightfall ere he
reached an eminence, from which, an hour sooner, the
battlements of Martindale Castle would have been visible;
and where when they were hid in night, their situation was
indicated by a light constantly maintained in a lofty tower,
called the Warder's Turret; and which domestic beacon
had acquired, through all the neighbourhood, the name of
Peveril's Polestar.

This was regularly kindled at curfew toll, and supplied
with as much wood and charcoal as maintained the light
till sunrise; and at no period was the ceremonial omitted,
saving during the space intervening between the death of
a Lord of the Castle and his interment. When this last
event had taken place, the nightly beacon was rekindled
with some ceremony, and continued till fate called the
successor to sleep with his fathers. It is not known from
what circumstance the practice of maintaining this light
originally sprung. Tradition spoke of it doubtfully.
Some thought it was the signal of general hospitality.
which, in ancient times, guided the wandering knight, or
the weary pilgrim, to rest and refreshment. Others spoke

of it as a " love-lighted watchfire," by which the provi-
dent anxiety of a former lady of Martindale guided her
husband homeward through the terrors of a midnight
storm. The less favourable construction of unfriendly
neighbours of the dissenting persuasion, ascribed the origin and continuance of this practice, to the assuming pride
of the family of Peveril, who thereby chose to intimate
their ancient *suzerainté* over the whole country, in the
manner of the admiral who carries the lantern in the
poop, for the guidance of the fleet. And in the former
times, our old friend, Master Solsgrace, dealt from the
pulpit many a hard hit against Sir Geoffrey, as he that
had raised his horn, and set up his candlestick on high.
Certain it is, that all the Peverils, from father to son, had
been especially attentive to the maintenance of this custom, as something intimately connected with the dignity
of their family ; and in the hands of Sir Geoffrey the
observance was not likely to be omitted.

Accordingly, the polar-star of Peveril had continued to
beam more or less brightly during all the vicissitudes of
the Civil War; and glimmered, however faintly, during
the subsequent period of Sir Geoffrey's depression. But
he was often heard to say, and sometimes to swear, that
while there was a perch of woodland left to the estate,
the old beacon-grate should not lack replenishing. All
this his son Julian well knew; and therefore it was with
no ordinary feelings of surprise and anxiety, that, looking
in the direction of the Castle, he perceived that the light
was not visible. He halted—rubbed his eyes—shifted his
position—and endeavoured, in vain, to persuade himself
that he had mistaken the point from which the polar-star
of his house was visible, or that some newly intervening
obstacle, the growth of a plantation, perhaps, or the erec-

tion of some building, intercepted the light of the beacon.
But a moment's reflection assured him, that from the high
and free situation which Martindale Castle bore in reference to the surrounding country, this could not have taken
place ; and the inference necessarily forced itself upon his
mind, that Sir Geoffrey, his father, was either deceased,
or that the family must have been disturbed by some
strange calamity, under the pressure of which, their
wonted custom and solemn usage had been neglected.

Under the influence of undefinable apprehension, young
Peveril now struck the spurs into his jaded steed, and
forcing him down the broken and steep path, at a pace
which set safety at defiance, he arrived at the village of
Martindale-Moultrassie, eagerly desirous to ascertain the
cause of this ominous eclipse.   The street, through which
his tired horse paced slow and reluctantly, was now
deserted and empty ; and scarcely a candle twinkled from
a casement, except from the latticed window of the little
inn, called the Peveril Arms, from which a broad light
shone, and several voices were heard in rude festivity.

Before the door of this inn, the jaded palfrey, guided
by the instinct or experience which makes a hackney
well acquainted with the outside of a house of entertainment, made so sudden and determined a pause, that, notwithstanding his haste, the rider thought it best to dis-
mount, expecting to be readily supplied with a fresh horse
by Roger Raine, the landlord, the ancient dependent of
his family.   He also wished to relieve his anxiety, by
inquiring concerning the state of things at the Castle,
when he was surprised to hear, bursting from the taproom
of the loyal old host, a well-known song of the Com-
monwealth time, which some puritanical wag had written in reprehension of the Cavaliers, and their dissolute

courses, and in which his father came in for a lash of the satirist.

"Ye thought in the world there was no power to tame ye,
So you tippled and drabb'd till the saints overcame ye;
'Forsooth,' and 'Ne'er stir,' sir, have vanquish'd 'G— d—n me,'
     Which nobody can deny.

"There was bluff old Sir Geoffrey loved brandy and mum well,
And to see a beer-glass turned over the thumb well;
But he fled like the wind, before Fairfax and Cromwell,
     Which nobody can deny."

Some strange revolution, Julian was aware, must have taken place, both in the village and in the Castle, ere these sounds of unseemly insult could have been poured forth in the very inn which was decorated with the armorial bearings of his family; and not knowing how far it might be advisable to intrude on these unfriendly revellers, without the power of repelling or chastising their insolence, he led his horse to a back-door, which, as he recollected, communicated with the landlord's apartment, having determined to make private inquiry of him concerning the state of matters at the Castle. He knocked repeatedly, and as often called on Roger Raine with an earnest but stifled voice. At length a female voice replied by the usual inquiry, "Who is there?"

"It is I, Dame Raine—I, Julian Peveril—tell your husband to come to me presently."

"Alack, and a well-a-day, Master Julian, if it be really you—you are to know my poor goodman has gone where he can come to no one; but, doubtless, we shall all go to him, as Matthew Chamberlain says."

"He is dead, then?" said Julian. "I am extremely sorry"——

"Dead six months and more, Master Julian; and let

me tell you, it is a long time for a lone woman, as Matt Chamberlain says."

" Well, do you or your chamberlain undo the door. I want a fresh horse; and I want to know how things are at the Castle."

" The Castle—lack-a-day !—Chamberlain—Matthew Chamberlain—I say, Matt! "

Matt Chamberlain apparently was at no great distance, for he presently answered her call; and Peveril, as he stood close to the door, could hear them whispering to each other, and distinguish in a great measure what they said. And here it may be noticed, that Dame Raine, accustomed to submit to the authority of old Roger, who vindicated as well the husband's domestic prerogative, as that of the monarch in the state, had, when left a buxom widow, been so far incommoded by the exercise of her newly acquired independence, that she had recourse, upon all occasions, to the advice of Matt Chamberlain; and as Matt began no longer to go slipshod, and in a red night-cap, but wore Spanish shoes, and a high-crowned beaver, (at least of a Sunday,) and moreover was called Master Matthew by his fellow-servants, the neighbours in the village argued a speedy change of the name on the sign-post; nay, perhaps, of the very sign itself, for Matthew was a bit of a Puritan, and no friend to Peveril of the Peak.

" Now counsel me, an you be a man, Matt Chamberlain," said Widow Raine; " for never stir, if here be not Master Julian's own self, and he wants a horse, and what not, and all as if things were as they wont to be."

" Why, dame, an ye will walk by my counsel," said the Chamberlain, " e'en shake him off—let him be jogging while his boots are green. This is no world for folks to scald their fingers in other folks' broth."

" And that is well spoken, truly," answered Dame
Raine ; " but then look you, Matt, we have eaten their
bread, and, as my poor goodman used to say "———

" Nay, nay, dame, they that walk by the counsel of the
dead, shall have none of the living ; and so you may do
as you list ; but if you will walk by mine, drop latch, and
draw bolt, and bid him seek quarters farther—that is my
counsel."

" I desire nothing of you, sirrah," said Peveril, " save
but to know how Sir Geoffrey and his lady do ? "

" Lack-a-day !—lack-a-day ! " in a tone of sympathy,
was the only answer he received from the landlady ; and
the conversation betwixt her and her chamberlain was
resumed, but in a tone too low to be overheard.

At length Matt Chamberlain spoke aloud, and with a
tone of authority : " We undo no doors at this time of
night, for it is against the Justices' orders, and might
cost us our license ; and for the Castle, the road up to
it lies before you, and I think you know it as well as
we do."

" And I know you," said Peveril, remounting his wearied horse, " for an ungrateful churl, whom, on the first
opportunity, I will assuredly cudgel to a mummy."

To this menace Matthew made no reply, and Peveril
presently heard him leave the apartment, after a few
earnest words betwixt him and his mistress.

Impatient at this delay, and at the evil omen implied
in these people's conversation and deportment, Peveril,
after some vain spurring of his horse, which positively
refused to move a step farther, dismounted once more,
and was about to pursue his journey on foot, notwithstanding the extreme disadvantage under which the high
riding-boots of the period laid those who attempted to

walk with such encumbrances, when he was stopped by a
gentle call from the window.

Her counsellor was no sooner gone, than the good-
nature and habitual veneration of the dame for the house
of Peveril, and perhaps some fear for her counsellor's
bones, induced her to open the casement, and cry, but in
a low and timid tone, "Hist! hist! Master Julian—be
you gone?"

"Not yet, dame," said Julian; "though it seems my
stay is unwelcome."

"Nay, but good young master, it is because men counsel so differently; for here was my poor old Roger Raine
would have thought the chimney corner too cold for you;
and here is Matt Chamberlain thinks the cold court-yard
is warm enough."

"Never mind that, dame," said Julian; "do but only
tell me what has happened at Martindale Castle? I see
the beacon is extinguished."

"Is it in troth?—ay, like enough—then good Sir
Geoffrey has gone to heaven with my old Roger Raine!"

"Sacred Heaven!" exclaimed Peveril; "when was
my father taken ill?"

"Never, as I knows of," said the dame; "but, about
three hours since, arrived a party at the Castle, with buff-
coats and bandoleers, and one of the Parliament's folks,
like in Oliver's time. My old Roger Raine would have
shut the gates of the inn against them, but he is in the
churchyard, and Matt says it is against law; and so they
came in and refreshed men and horses, and sent for
Master Bridgenorth, that is at Moultrassie-Hall even
now; and so they went up to the Castle, and there was a
fray, it is like, as the old Knight was no man to take nap-
ping, as poor Roger Raine used to say. Always the

officers had the best on't; and reason there is, since they had law of their side, as our Matthew says. But since the polestar of the Castle is out, as your honour says, why, doubtless, the old gentleman is dead."

"Gracious Heaven!—Dear dame, for love or gold, let me have a horse to make for the Castle!"

"The Castle?" said the dame; "the Roundheads, as my poor Roger called them, will kill you as they have killed your father! Better creep into the woodhouse, and I will send Bett with a blanket and some supper—Or stay—my old Dobbin stands in the little stable beside the hencoop—e'en take him, and make the best of your way out of the country, for there is no safety here for you. Hear what songs some of them are singing at the tap!—so take Dobbin, and do not forget to leave your own horse instead."

Peveril waited to hear no farther, only, that just as he turned to go off to the stable, the compassionate female was heard to exclaim,—"O Lord! what will Matthew Chamberlain say?" but instantly added, "Let him say what he will, I may dispose of what's my own."

With the haste of a double-fee'd hostler did Julian exchange the equipments of his jaded brute with poor Dobbin, who stood quietly tugging at his rackful of hay, without dreaming of the business which was that night destined for him. Notwithstanding the darkness of the place, Julian succeeded marvellous quickly in preparing for his journey; and leaving his own horse to find its way to Dobbin's rack by instinct, he leaped upon his new acquisition, and spurred him sharply against the hill, which rises steeply from the village to the Castle. Dobbin, little accustomed to such exertions, snorted, panted, and trotted as briskly as he could, until at length he brought his rider before the entrance-gate of his father's ancient seat.

The moon was now rising, but the portal was hidden from its beams, being situated, as we have mentioned elsewhere, in a deep recess betwixt two large flanking towers. Peveril dismounted, turned his horse loose, and advanced to the gate, which, contrary to his expectation, he found open. He entered the large court-yard; and could then perceive that lights yet twinkled in the lower part of the building, although he had not before observed them, owing to the height of the outward walls. The main door, or great hall-gate, as it was called, was, since the partially decayed state of the family, seldom opened, save on occasions of particular ceremony. A smaller postern door served the purpose of ordinary entrance; and to that Julian now repaired. This also was open— a circumstance which would of itself have alarmed him, had he not already had so many causes for apprehension. His heart sunk within him as he turned to the left, through a small outward hall, towards the great parlour, which the family usually occupied as a sitting apartment; and his alarm became still greater, when, on a nearer approach, he heard proceeding from thence the murmur of several voices. He threw the door of the apartment wide; and the sight which was thus displayed, warranted all the evil bodings which he had entertained.

In front of him stood the old Knight, whose arms were strongly secured, over the elbows, by a leathern belt drawn tight round them, and made fast behind; two ruffianly-looking men, apparently his guards, had hold of his doublet. The scabbardless sword which lay on the floor, and the empty sheath which hung by Sir Geoffrey's side, showed the stout old Cavalier had not been reduced to this state of bondage without an attempt at resistance. Two or three persons, having their backs turned towards Julian, sat round a table, and appeared engaged in writing—the voices which he had heard were theirs, as they murmured to each other. Lady Peveril—the emblem of death, so pallid was her countenance—stood at the distance of a yard or two from her husband, upon whom her eyes were fixed with an intenseness of gaze, like that of one who looks her last on the object which she loves the best. She was the first to perceive Julian; and she exclaimed, "Merciful Heaven!—my son!—the misery of our house is complete!"

"My son!" echoed Sir Geoffrey, starting from the sullen state of dejection, and swearing a deep oath—"thou art come in the right time, Julian. Strike me one good blow—cleave me that traitorous thief from the crown to the brisket! and that done, I care not what comes next."

The sight of his father's situation made the son forget the inequality of the contest which he was about to provoke.

"Villains," he said, "unhand him!" and rushing on the guards with his drawn sword, compelled them to let go Sir Geoffrey, and stand on their own defence.

Sir Geoffrey, thus far liberated, shouted to his lady. "Undo the belt, dame, and we will have three good blows for it yet—they must fight well that beat both father and son."

But one of those men who had started up from the writing-table when the fray commenced, prevented Lady Peveril from rendering her husband this assistance; while another easily mastered the hampered Knight, though not without receiving several severe kicks from his heavy boots—his condition permitting him no other mode of defence. A third, who saw that Julian, young, active, and animated with the fury of a son who fights for his parents, was compelling the two guards to give ground, seized on his collar, and attempted to master his sword. Suddenly dropping that weapon, and snatching one of his pistols, Julian fired it at the head of the person by whom he was thus assailed. He did not drop, but, staggering back as if he had received a severe blow, showed Peveril, as he sunk into a chair, the features of old Bridgenorth, blackened with the explosion, which had even set fire to a part of his gray hair. A cry of astonishment escaped from Julian ; and in the alarm and horror of the moment, he was easily secured and disarmed by those with whom he had been at first engaged.

"Heed it not, Julian," said Sir Geoffrey ; "heed it not, my brave boy—that shot has balanced all accompts! —but how—what the devil—he lives !—Was your pistol loaded with chaff? or has the foul fiend given him proof against lead ? "

There was some reason for Sir Geoffrey's surprise, since, as he spoke, Major Bridgenorth collected himself— sat up in the chair as one who recovers from a stunning blow—then rose, and wiping with his handkerchief the marks of the explosion from his face, he approached Julian, and said, in the same cold unaltered tone in which he usually expressed himself, "Young man, you have reason to bless God, who has this day saved you from the commission of a great crime."

"Bless the devil, ye crop-eared knave ! " exclaimed Sir Geoffrey ; "for nothing less than the father of all fanatics saved your brains from being blown about like the rinsings of Beelzebub's porridge pot ! "

"Sir Geoffrey," said Major Bridgenorth, "I have already told you, that with you I will hold no argument; for to you I am not accountable for any of my actions."

"Master Bridgenorth," said the lady, making a strong effort to speak, and to speak with calmness, "whatever revenge your Christian state of conscience may permit you to take on my husband—I—I, who have some right to experience compassion at your hand, for most sincerely did I compassionate you when the hand of Heaven was heavy on you—I implore you not to involve my son in our common ruin!—Let the destruction of the father and mother, with the ruin of our ancient house, satisfy your resentment for any wrong which you have ever received at my husband's hand."

"Hold your peace, housewife," said the Knight, "you speak like a fool, and meddle with what concerns you not. —Wrong at *my* hand? The cowardly knave has ever had but even too much right. Had I cudgelled the cur soundly when he first bayed at me, the cowardly mongrel had been now crouching at my feet, instead of flying at my throat. But if I get through this action, as I have got through worse weather, I will pay off old scores as far as tough crab-tree and cold iron will bear me out."

"Sir Geoffrey," replied Bridgenorth, "if the birth you boast of has made you blind to better principles, it might have at least taught you civility. What do you complain of? I am a magistrate; and I execute a warrant, addressed to me by the first authority in the state. I am a creditor also of yours; and law arms me with powers to recover my own property from the hands of an improvident debtor."

"You a magistrate!" said the Knight; "much such a magistrate as Noll was a monarch. Your heart is up, I warrant, because you have the King's pardon; and are replaced on the bench, forsooth, to persecute the poor Papist. There was never turmoil in the state, but knaves had their vantage by it—never pot boiled, but the scum was cast uppermost."

"For God's sake, my dearest husband," said Lady Peveril, "cease this wild talk! It can but incense Master Bridgenorth, who might otherwise consider, that in common charity"——

"Incense him!" said Sir Geoffrey, impatiently interrupting her; "God's-death, madam, you will drive me mad! Have you lived so long in this world, and yet expect consideration and charity from an old starved wolf like that? And if he had it, do you think that I, or you, madam, as my wife, are subjects for his charity? —Julian, my poor fellow, I am sorry thou hast come so unluckily, since thy petronel was not better loaded—but thy credit is lost for ever as a marksman."

This angry colloquy passed so rapidly on all sides, that Julian, scarce recovered from the extremity of astonishment with which he was overwhelmed at finding himself suddenly plunged into a situation of such extremity, had no time to consider in what way he could most effectually act for the succour of his parents. To speak Bridgenorth fair, seemed the more prudent course; but to this his pride could hardly stoop; yet he forced himself to say, with as much calmness as he could assume, "Master Bridgenorth, since you act as a magistrate, I desire to be treated according to the laws of England; and demand to know of what we are accused, and by whose authority we are arrested?"

" Here is another howlet for ye!" exclaimed the impetuous old Knight; "his mother speaks to a Puritan of
charity; and thou must talk of law to a roundheaded
rebel, with a wannion to you! What warrant hath he,
think ye, beyond the Parliament's or the devil's?"

" Who speaks of the Parliament?" said a person entering, whom Peveril recognised as the official person
whom he had before seen at the horse-dealer's, and who
now bustled in with all the conscious dignity of plenary
authority,—" Who talks of the Parliament?" he exclaimed. " I promise you, enough has been found in this
house to convict twenty plotters—Here be arms, and
that good store. Bring them in, Captain."

" The very same," exclaimed the Captain, approaching,
" which I mention in my printed Narrative of Information, lodged before the Honourable House of Commons;
they were commissioned from old Vander Huys of Rot-
terdam, by orders of Don John of Austria, for the service
of the Jesuits."

" Now, by this light," said Sir Geoffrey, "They are the
pikes, musketoons, and pistols, that have been hidden in
the garret ever since Naseby fight!"

" And here," said the Captain's yoke-fellow, Everett,
" are proper priest's trappings—antiphoners, and missals,
and copes, I warrant you—ay, and proper pictures, too,
for Papists to mutter and bow over."

" Now plague on thy snuffling whine," said Sir Geoffrey;
" here is a rascal will swear my grandmother's old farth-
ingale to be priest's vestments, and the story book of
Owlenspiegel, a Popish missal!"

" But how's this, Master Bridgenorth?" said Topham,
addressing the magistrate; " your honour has been as
busy as we have; and you have caught another knave
while we recovered these toys."

"I think, sir," said Julian, "if you look into your warrant, which, if I mistake not, names the persons whom you are directed to arrest, you will find you have no title to apprehend me."

"Sir," said the officer, puffing with importance, "I do not know who you are; but I would you were the best man in England, that I might teach you the respect due to the warrant of the House. Sir, there steps not the man within the British seas, but I will arrest him on authority of this bit of parchment; and I do arrest you accordingly.—What do you accuse him of, gentlemen?"

Dangerfield swaggered forward, and peeping under Julian's hat, "Stop my vital breath," he exclaimed, "but I have seen you before, my friend, an I could but think where; but my memory is not worth a bean, since I have been obliged to use it so much of late, in the behalf of the poor state. But I do know the fellow; and I have seen him amongst the Papists—I'll take that on my assured damnation."

"Why, Captain Dangerfield," said the Captain's smoother, but more dangerous associate,—"verily, it is the same youth whom we saw at the horse-merchant's yesterday; and we had matter against him then, only Master Topham did not desire us to bring it out."

"Ye may bring out what ye will against him now," said Topham, "for he hath blasphemed the warrant of the House. I think ye said ye saw him somewhere."

"Ay, verily," said Everett, "I have seen him amongst the seminary pupils at Saint Omer's—he was who but he with the regents there."

"Nay, Master Everett, collect yourself," said Topham; "for, as I think, you said you saw him at a consult of the Jesuits in London."

"It was I said so, Master Topham," said the undaunted Dangerfield; "and mine is the tongue that will swear it."

"Good Master Topham," said Bridgenorth, "you may suspend farther inquiry at present, as it doth but fatigue and perplex the memory of the King's witnesses."

"You are wrong, Master Bridgenorth—clearly wrong. It doth but keep them in wind—only breathes them like greyhounds before a coursing match."

"Be it so," said Bridgenorth, with his usual indifference of manner; "but at present this youth must stand committed upon a warrant, which I will presently sign, of having assaulted me while in discharge of my duty as a magistrate, for the rescue of a person legally attached. Did you not hear the report of a pistol?"

"I will swear to it," said Everett.

"And I," said Dangerfield. "While we were making search in the cellar, I heard something very like a pistol-shot; but I conceived it to be the drawing of a long-corked bottle of sack, to see whether there were any Popish relics in the inside on't."

"A pistol-shot!" exclaimed Topham; "here might have been a second Sir Edmondsbury Godfrey's matter. —Oh, thou real spawn of the red old dragon! for he too would have resisted the House's warrant, had we not taken him something at unawares.—Master Bridgenorth, you are a judicious magistrate, and a worthy servant of the state—I would we had many such sound Protestant justices. Shall I have this young fellow away with his parents—what think you?—or will you keep him for re-examination?"

"Master Bridgenorth," said Lady Peveril, in spite of her husband's efforts to interrupt her, "for God's sake, if ever you knew what it was to love one of the many children you have lost, or her who is now left to you, do not pursue your vengeance to the blood of my poor boy! I will forgive you all the rest—all the distress you have wrought—all the yet greater misery with which you threaten us; but do not be extreme with one who never can have offended you! Believe, that if your ears are shut against the cry of a despairing mother, those which are open to the complaint of all who sorrow, will hear my petition and your answer!"

The agony of mind and of voice with which Lady Peveril uttered these words, seemed to thrill through all present, though most of them were but too much inured to such scenes. Every one was silent, when, ceasing to speak, she fixed on Bridgenorth her eyes, glistening with tears, with the eager anxiety of one whose life or death seemed to depend upon the answer to be returned. Even Bridgenorth's inflexibility seemed to be shaken; and his voice was tremulous, as he answered, "Madam, I would to God I had the present means of relieving your great distress, otherwise than by recommending to you a reliance upon Providence; and that you take heed to your spirit, that it murmur not under this crook in your lot. For me, I am but as a rod in the hand of the strong man, which smites not of itself, but because it is wielded by the arm of him who holds the same."

"Even as I and my black rod are guided by the Commons of England," said Master Topham, who seemed marvellously pleased with the illustration.

Julian now thought it time to say something in his own behalf; and he endeavoured to temper it with as much composure as it was possible for him to assume. "Master Bridgenorth," he said, "I neither dispute your authority, nor this gentleman's warrant"——

" You do not ? " said Topham. " O, ho, master youngster, I thought we should bring you to your senses presently ! "

" Then, if you so will it, Master Topham," said Bridgenorth, " thus it shall be. You shall set out with early day, taking with you, towards London, the persons of Sir Geoffrey and Lady Peveril ; and that they may travel according to their quality, you will allow them their coach, sufficiently guarded."

" I will travel with them myself," said Topham ; " for these rough Derbyshire roads are no easy riding ; and my very eyes are weary with looking on these bleak hills. In the coach I can sleep as sound as if I were in the House, and Master Bodderbrains on his legs."

" It will become you so to take your ease, Master Topham," answered Bridgenorth. " For this youth, I will take him under my charge, and bring him up myself."

" I may not be answerable for that, worthy Master Bridgenorth," said Topham, " since he comes within the warrant of the House."

" Nay, but," said Bridgenorth, " he is only under custody for an assault, with the purpose of a rescue ; and I counsel you against meddling with him, unless you have stronger guard. Sir Geoffrey is now old and broken, but this young fellow is in the flower of his youth, and hath at his beck all the debauched young Cavaliers of the neighbourhood—You will scarce cross the country without a rescue."

Topham eyed Julian wistfully, as a spider may be supposed to look upon a stray wasp which has got into his web, and which he longs to secure, though he fears the consequences of attempting him.

Julian himself replied, " I know not if this separation

be well or ill meant on your part, Master Bridgenorth;
but on mine, I am only desirous to share the fate of my
parents; and therefore I will give my word of honour to
attempt neither rescue nor escape, on condition you do
not separate me from them."

"Do not say so, Julian," said his mother; "abide with
Master Bridgenorth—my mind tells me he cannot mean
so ill by us as his rough conduct would now lead us to
infer."

"And I," said Sir Geoffrey, "know, that between the
doors of my father's house and the gates of hell, there
steps not such a villain on the ground! And if I wish
my hands ever to be unbound again, it is because I hope
for one downright blow at a gray head, that has hatched
more treason than the whole Long Parliament."

"Away with thee," said the zealous officer; "is Parliament a word for so foul a mouth as thine?—Gentlemen," he added, turning to Everett and Dangerfield,
"you will bear witness to this."

"To his having reviled the House of Commons—by
G—d, that I will!" said Dangerfield; "I will take it on
my damnation."

"And verily," said Everett, "as he spoke of Parliament generally, he hath contemned the House of Lords
also."

"Why, ye poor insignificant wretches," said Sir Geoffrey, "whose very life is a lie—and whose bread is perjury—would you pervert my innocent words almost as
soon as they have quitted my lips? I tell you the country
is well weary of you; and should Englishmen come to
their senses, the jail, the pillory, the whipping-post, and
the gibbet, will be too good preferment for such base
blood-suckers.—And now, Master Bridgenorth, you and

they may do your worst; for I will not open my mouth
to utter a single word while I am in the company of such
knaves."

"Perhaps, Sir Geoffrey," answered Bridgenorth, "you
would better have consulted your own safety in adopting
that resolution a little sooner—the tongue is a little member, but it causes much strife.—You, Master Julian, will
please to follow me, and without remonstrance or resistance; for you must be aware that I have the means of
compelling."

Julian was, indeed, but too sensible, that he had no
other course but that of submission to superior force; but
ere he left the apartment, he kneeled down to receive his
father's blessing, which the old man bestowed not without
a tear in his eye, and in the emphatic words, "God bless
thee, my boy; and keep thee good and true to Church
and King, whatever wind shall bring foul weather!"

His mother was only able to pass her hand over his
head, and to implore him, in a low tone of voice, not to
be rash or violent in any attempt to render them assistance. "We are innocent," she said, "my son—we are
innocent—and we are in God's hands. Be the thought
our best comfort and protection."

Bridgenorth now signed to Julian to follow him, which
he did, accompanied, or rather conducted, by the two
guards who had first disarmed him. When they had
passed from the apartment, and were at the door of the
outward hall, Bridgenorth asked Julian whether he
should consider him as under parole; in which case, he
said, he would dispense with all other security but his
own promise.

Peveril, who could not help hoping somewhat from the
favourable and unresentful manner in which he was

treated by one whose life he had so recently attempted, replied, without hesitation, that he would give his parole for twenty-four hours, neither to attempt to escape by force nor by flight.

"It is wisely said," replied Bridgenorth; "for though you might cause bloodshed, be assured that your utmost efforts could do no service to your parents.—Horses there—horses to the court-yard!"

The trampling of the horses was soon heard; and in obedience to Bridgenorth's signal, and in compliance with his promise, Julian mounted one which was presented to him, and prepared to leave the house of his fathers, in which his parents were now prisoners, and to go, he knew not whither, under the custody of one known to be the ancient enemy of his family. He was rather surprised at observing, that Bridgenorth and he were about to travel without any other attendants.

When they were mounted, and as they rode slowly towards the outer gate of the court-yard, Bridgenorth said to him, "It is not every one who would thus unreservedly commit his safety, by travelling at night, and unaided, with the hot-brained youth who so lately attempted his life."

"Master Bridgenorth," said Julian, "I might tell you truly, that I knew you not at the time when I directed my weapon against you; but I must also add, that the cause in which I used it, might have rendered me, even had I known you, a slight respecter of your person. At present, I do know you; and have neither malice against your person, nor the liberty of a parent to fight for. Besides, you have my word; and when was a Peveril known to break it?"

"Ay," replied his companion, "a Peveril—a Peveril

of the Peak!—a name which has long sounded like a
war-trumpet in the land; but which has now perhaps
sounded its last loud note. Look back, young man, on
the darksome turrets of your father's house, which up-
lift themselves as proudly on the brow of the hill, as their
owners raised themselves above the sons of their people.
Think upon your father, a captive—yourself in some sort
a fugitive—your light quenched—your glory abased—
your estate wrecked and impoverished. Think that
Providence has subjected the destinies of the race of
Peveril to one, whom, in their aristocratic pride, they
held as a plebeian upstart. Think of this; and when
you again boast of your ancestry, remember, that he who
raiseth the lowly can also abase the high in heart."

Julian did indeed gaze for an instant, with a swelling
heart, upon the dimly seen turrets of his paternal mansion, on which poured the moonlight, mixed with long
shadows of the towers and trees. But while he sadly
acknowledged the truth of Bridgenorth's observation, he
felt indignant at his ill-timed triumph. "If fortune had
followed worth," he said, "the Castle of Martindale, and
the name of Peveril, had afforded no room for their
enemy's vainglorious boast. But those who have stood
high on Fortune's wheel, must abide by the consequence
of its revolutions. Thus much I will at least say for my
father's house, that it has not stood unhonoured; nor will
it fall—if it is to fall—unlamented. Forbear, then, if
you are indeed the Christian you call yourself, to exult
in the misfortunes of others, or to confide in your own
prosperity. If the light of our house be now quenched,
God can rekindle it in his own good time."

Peveril broke off in extreme surprise; for as he spoke
the last words, the bright red beams of the family beacon

began again to glimmer from its wonted watch-tower, checkering the pale moonbeam with a ruddier glow. Bridgenorth also gazed on this unexpected illumination with surprise, and not, as it seemed, without disquietude. "Young man," he resumed, "it can scarcely be but that Heaven intends to work great things by your hand, so singularly has that augury followed on your words."

So saying, he put his horse once more in motion; and looking back, from time to time, as if to assure himself that the beacon of the Castle was actually rekindled, he led the way through the well-known paths and alleys, to his own house of Moultrassie, followed by Peveril, who, although sensible that the light might be altogether accidental, could not but receive as a good omen an event so intimately connected with the traditions and usages of his family.

They alighted at the hall-door, which was hastily opened by a female; and while the deep tone of Bridgenorth called on the groom to take their horses, the well-known voice of his daughter Alice was heard to exclaim in thanksgiving to God, who had restored her father in safety.

CHAPTER XXIV.

We meet, as men see phantoms in a dream,
Which glide, and sigh, and sign, and move their lips,
But make no sound; or, if they utter voice,
'Tis but a low and undistinguish'd moaning,
Which has nor word nor sense of utter'd sound.

THE CHIEFTAIN.

WE said, at the conclusion of the last chapter, that a female form appeared at the door of Moultrassie-Hall; and that the well-known accents of Alice Bridgenorth were heard to hail the return of her father, from what she naturally dreaded as a perilous visit to the Castle of Martindale.

Julian, who followed his conductor with a throbbing heart into the lighted hall, was therefore prepared to see her whom he best loved, with her arms thrown around her father. The instant she had quitted his paternal embrace, she was aware of the unexpected guest who had returned in his company. A deep blush, rapidly succeeded by deadly paleness, and again by a slighter suffusion, showed plainly to her lover that his sudden appearance was any thing but indifferent to her. He bowed profoundly—a courtesy which she returned with equal formality, but did not venture to approach more nearly, feeling at once the delicacy of his own situation and of hers.

Major Bridgenorth turned his cold, fixed, gray, melan-

choly glance, first on the one of them and then on the
other. "Some," he said, gravely, "would, in my case,
have avoided this meeting; but I have confidence in you
both, although you are young, and beset with the snares
incidental to your age. There are those within who
should not know that ye have been acquainted. Wherefore, be wise, and be as strangers to each other."

Julian and Alice exchanged glances as her father
turned from them, and lifting a lamp which stood in the
entrance-hall, led the way to the interior apartment.
There was little of consolation in this exchange of looks;
for the sadness of Alice's glance was mingled with fear,
and that of Julian clouded by an anxious sense of doubt.
The look also was but momentary; for Alice, springing
to her father, took the light out of his hand, and, stepping
before him, acted as the usher of both into the large
oaken parlour, which has been already mentioned as the
apartment in which Bridgenorth had spent the hours of
dejection which followed the death of his consort and
family. It was now lighted up as for the reception of
company; and five or six persons sat in it, in the plain,
black, stiff dress, which was affected by the formal Puritans of the time, in evidence of their contempt of the
manners of the luxurious Court of Charles the Second;
amongst whom, excess of extravagance in apparel, like
excess of every other kind, was highly fashionable.

Julian at first glanced his eyes but slightly along the
range of grave and severe faces which composed this society—men, sincere, perhaps, in their pretensions to a
superior purity of conduct and morals, but in whom that
high praise was somewhat chastened by an affected austerity in dress and manners, allied to those Pharisees of
old, who made broad their phylacteries, and would be

seen of men to fast, and to discharge with rigid punctuality the observances of the law. Their dress was almost uniformly a black cloak and doublet, cut straight and close, and undecorated with lace or embroidery of any kind, black Flemish breeches and hose, square-toed shoes, with large roses made of serge ribbon. Two or three had large loose boots of calf-leather, and almost every one was begirt with a long rapier, which was suspended by leathern thongs, to a plain belt of buff, or of black leather. One or two of the elder guests, whose hair had been thinned by time, had their heads covered with a skull-cap of black silk or velvet, which, being drawn down betwixt the ears and the skull, and permitting no hair to escape, occasioned the former to project in the ungraceful manner which may be remarked in old pictures, and which procured for the Puritans the term of "prick-eared Roundheads," so unceremoniously applied to them by their contemporaries.

These worthies were ranged against the wall, each in his ancient high-backed, long-legged chair; neither looking towards, nor apparently discoursing with each other; but plunged in their own reflections, or awaiting, like an assembly of Quakers, the quickening power of divine inspiration.

Major Bridgenorth glided along this formal society with noiseless step, and a composed severity of manner, resembling their own. He paused before each in succession, and apparently communicated, as he passed, the transactions of the evening, and the circumstances under which the heir of Martindale Castle was now a guest at Moultrassie-Hall. Each seemed to stir at his brief detail, like a range of statues in an enchanted hall, starting into something like life, as a talisman is applied to them successively. Most of them, as they heard the narrative of their host, cast upon Julian a look of curiosity, blended with haughty scorn and the consciousness of spiritual superiority; though, in one or two instances, the milder influences of compassion were sufficiently visible.—Peveril would have undergone this gauntlet of eyes with more impatience, had not his own been for the time engaged in following the motions of Alice, who glided through the apartment; and only speaking very briefly, and in whispers, to one or two of the company who addressed her, took her place beside a treble-hooded old lady, the only female of the party, and addressed herself to her in such earnest conversation, as might dispense with her raising her head, or looking at any others in the company.

Her father put a question, to which she was obliged to return an answer—" Where was Mistress Debbitch?"

" She had gone out," Alice replied, " early after sunset, to visit some old acquaintances in the neighbourhood, and she was not yet returned."

Major Bridgenorth made a gesture indicative of displeasure; and, not content with that, expressed his determined resolution that Dame Deborah should no longer remain a member of his family. " I will have those," he said aloud, and without regarding the presence of his guests, " and those only, around me, who know to keep within the sober and modest bounds of a Christian family. Who pretends to more freedom, must go out from among us, as not being of us."

A deep and emphatic humming noise, which was at that time the mode in which the Puritans signified their applause, as well of the doctrines expressed by a favourite divine in the pulpit, as of those delivered in private society, ratified the approbation of the assessors, and

seemed to secure the dismission of the unfortunate governante, who stood thus detected of having strayed out of
bounds. Even Peveril, although he had reaped considerable advantages, in his early acquaintance with Alice,
from the mercenary and gossiping disposition of her gov-
erness, could not hear of her dismissal without approbation, so much was he desirous, that, in the hour of
difficulty, which might soon approach, Alice might have
the benefit of countenance and advice from one of her
own sex, of better manners and less suspicious probity,
than Mistress Debbitch.

Almost immediately after this communication had taken
place, a servant in mourning showed his thin, pinched,
and wrinkled visage in the apartment, announcing, with
a voice more like a passing bell than the herald of a banquet, that refreshments were provided in an adjoining
apartment. Gravely leading the way, with his daughter
on one side, and the puritanical female whom we have
distinguished on the other, Bridgenorth himself ushered
his company, who followed, with little attention to order
or ceremony, into the eating-room, where a substantial
supper was provided.

In this manner, Peveril, although entitled according to
ordinary ceremonial, to some degree of precedence—a
matter at that time considered of much importance, although now little regarded—was left among the last of
those who quitted the parlour ; and might indeed have
brought up the rear of all, had not one of the company,
who was himself late in the retreat, bowed and resigned
to Julian the rank in the company which had been
usurped by others.

This act of politeness naturally induced Julian to examine the features of the person who had offered him

this civility; and he started to observe, under the pinched velvet cap, and above the short band-strings, the countenance of Ganlesse, as he called himself—his companion on the preceding evening. He looked again and again, especially when all were placed at the supper board, and when, consequently, he had frequent opportunities of observing this person fixedly, without any breach of good manners. At first he wavered in his belief, and was much inclined to doubt the reality of his recollection; for the difference of dress was such as to effect a considerable change of appearance; and the countenance itself, far from exhibiting any thing marked or memorable, was one of those ordinary visages which we see almost without remarking them, and which leave our memory so soon as the object is withdrawn from our eyes. But the impression upon his mind returned, and became stronger, until it induced him to watch with peculiar attention the manners of the individual who had thus attracted his notice.

During the time of a very prolonged grace before meat, which was delivered by one of the company—who, from his Geneva band and serge doublet, presided, as Julian supposed, over some dissenting congregation—he noticed that this man kept the same demure and severe cast of countenance usually affected by the Puritans, and which rather caricatured the reverence unquestionably due upon such occasions. His eyes were turned upward, and his huge penthouse hat, with a high crown and broad brim, held in both hands before him, rose and fell with the cadences of the speaker's voice; thus marking time, as it were, to the periods of the benediction. Yet when the slight bustle took place which attends the adjusting of chairs, &c., as men sit down to table, Julian's eye encoun-

tered that of the stranger; and as their looks met, there
glanced from those of the latter, an expression of satirical humour and scorn, which seemed to intimate internal
ridicule of the gravity of his present demeanour.

Julian again sought to fix his eye, in order to ascertain
that he had not mistaken the tendency of this transient
expression, but the stranger did not allow him another
opportunity. He might have been discovered by the
tone of his voice; but the individual in question spoke
little, and in whispers, which was indeed the fashion of
the whole company, whose demeanour at table resembled
that of mourners at a funeral feast.

The entertainment itself was coarse, though plentiful;
and must, according to Julian's opinion, be distasteful to
one so exquisitely skilled in good cheer, and so capable
of enjoying, critically and scientifically, the genial preparations of his companion, Smith, as Ganlesse had shown
himself on the preceding evening. Accordingly, upon
close observation, he remarked that the food which he
took upon his plate, remained there unconsumed; and
that his actual supper consisted only of a crust of bread,
with a glass of wine.

The repast was hurried over with the haste of those
who think it shame, if not sin, to make mere animal en-
joyments the means of consuming time, or of receiving
pleasure; and when men wiped their mouths and mustaches, Julian remarked, that the object of his curiosity
used a handkerchief of the finest cambric—an article
rather inconsistent with the exterior plainness, not to say
coarseness, of his appearance. He used also several of
the more minute refinements, then only observed at tables
of the higher rank; and Julian thought he could discern,
at every turn, something of courtly manners and gestures,

under the precise and rustic simplicity of the character which he had assumed.*

But if this were indeed that same Ganlesse with whom Julian had met on the preceding evening, and who had boasted the facility with which he could assume any character which he pleased to represent for the time, what could be the purpose of his present disguise? He was, if his own words could be credited, a person of some importance, who dared to defy the danger of those officers and informers, before whom all ranks at that time trembled; nor was he likely, as Julian conceived, without some strong purpose, to subject himself to such a masquerade as the present, which could not be otherwise than irksome to one whose conversation proclaimed him of light life and free opinions. Was his appearance here for good or for evil? Did it respect his father's house, or his own person, or the family of Bridgenorth? Was the real character of Ganlesse known to the master of the house, inflexible as he was in all which concerned morals as well as religion? If not, might not the machinations of a brain so subtle, affect the peace and happiness of Alice Bridgenorth?

These were questions which no reflection could enable Peveril to answer. His eyes glanced from Alice to the stranger; and new fears, and undefined suspicions, in which the safety of that beloved and lovely girl was implicated, mingled with the deep anxiety which already occupied his mind, on account of his father, and his father's house.

He was in this tumult of mind, when, after a thanks-

* A Scottish gentleman, *in hiding*, as it was emphatically termed, for some concern in a Jacobite insurrection or plot, was discovered among a number of ordinary persons, by the use of his toothpick.

giving as long as the grace, the company arose from table, and were instantly summoned to the exercise of family worship. A train of domestics, grave, sad, and melancholy as their superiors, glided in to assist at this act of devotion, and ranged themselves at the lower end of the apartment. Most of these men were armed with long tucks, as the straight stabbing swords, much used by Cromwell's soldiery, were then called. Several had large pistols also; and the corselets or cuirasses of some were heard to clank, as they seated themselves to partake in this act of devotion. The ministry of him whom Julian had supposed a preacher, was not used on this occasion. Major Bridgenorth himself read and expounded a chapter of Scripture, with much strength and manliness of expression, although so as not to escape the charge of fanaticism. The nineteenth chapter of Jeremiah was the portion of Scripture which he selected; in which, under the type of breaking a potter's vessel, the prophet presages the desolation of the Jews. The lecturer was not naturally eloquent; but a strong, deep, and sincere conviction of the truth of what he said, supplied him with language of energy and fire, as he drew a parallel between the abominations of the worship of Baal, and the corruptions of the Church of Rome—so favourite a topic with the Puritans of that period; and denounced against the Catholics, and those who favoured them, that hissing and desolation which the prophet directed against the city of Jerusalem. His hearers made a yet closer application than the lecturer himself suggested; and many a dark proud eye intimated, by a glance on Julian, that on his father's house were already, in some part, realized these dreadful maledictions.

The lecture finished, Bridgenorth summoned them to

unite with him in prayer; and on a slight change of
arrangements amongst the company, which took place as
they were about to kneel down, Julian found his place
next to the single-minded and beautiful object of his
affection, as she knelt, in her loveliness, to adore her
Creator. A short time was permitted for mental devotion; during which, Peveril could hear her half-breathed
petition for the promised blessings of peace on earth, and
good-will towards the children of men.

The prayer which ensued was in a different tone. It
was poured forth by the same person who had officiated
as chaplain at the table; and was in the tone of a
Boanerges, or Son of Thunder—a denouncer of crimes—
an invoker of judgments—almost a prophet of evil and
of destruction. The testimonies and the sins of the day
were not forgotten—the mysterious murder of Sir Edmondsbury Godfrey was insisted upon—and thanks and
praise were offered, that the very night on which they
were assembled, had not seen another offering of a
Protestant magistrate, to the bloodthirsty fury of the
revengeful Catholics.

Never had Julian found it more difficult, during an act
of devotion, to maintain his mind in a frame befitting the
posture and the occasion; and when he heard the speaker
return thanks for the downfall and devastation of his
family, he was strongly tempted to have started upon his
feet, and charged him with offering a tribute, stained with
falsehood and calumny, at the throne of truth itself. He
resisted, however, an impulse which it would have been
insanity to have yielded to, and his patience was not
without its reward; for when his fair neighbour arose
from her knees, the lengthened and prolonged prayer
being at last concluded, he observed that her eyes were

streaming with tears; and one glance with which she
looked at him in that moment, showed more of affectionate interest for him in his fallen fortunes and precarious condition, than he had been able to obtain from
her when his worldly estate seemed so much the more
exalted of the two.

Cheered and fortified with the conviction that one
bosom in the company, and that in which he most eagerly
longed to secure an interest, sympathized with his distress, he felt strong to endure whatever was to follow,
and shrunk not from the stern still smile with which, one
by one, the meeting regarded him, as, gliding to their
several places of repose, they indulged themselves at
parting with a look of triumph on one, whom they considered as their captive enemy.

Alice also passed by her lover, her eyes fixed on the
ground, and answered his low obeisance without raising
them. The room was now empty, but for Bridgenorth,
and his guest, or prisoner; for it is difficult to say in
which capacity Peveril ought to regard himself. He
took an old brazen lamp from the table, and, leading the
way, said, at the same time, "I must be the uncourtly
chamberlain, who am to usher you to a place of repose,
more rude, perhaps, than you have been accustomed to
occupy."

Julian followed him, in silence, up an old-fashioned
winding staircase, within a turret. At the landing-place
on the top, was a small apartment, where an ordinary
pallet bed, two chairs, and a small stone table, were the
only furniture. "Your bed," continued Bridgenorth, as
if desirous to prolong their interview, "is not of the
softest; but innocence sleeps as sound upon straw as on
down."

" Sorrow, Major Bridgenorth, finds little rest on either," replied Julian. " Tell me, for you seem to await some question from me, what is to be the fate of my parents, and why you separate me from them? "

Bridgenorth, for answer, indicated with his finger the mark which his countenance still showed from the explosion of Julian's pistol.

" That," replied Julian, " is not the real cause of your proceedings against me. It cannot be, that you, who have been a soldier, and are a man, can be surprised or displeased by my interference in the defence of my father. Above all, you cannot, and I must needs say you do not, believe that I would have raised my hand against you personally, had there been a moment's time for recognition."

" I may grant all this," said Bridgenorth ; " but what the better are you for my good opinion, or for the ease with which I can forgive you the injury which you aimed at me? You are in my custody as a magistrate, accused of abetting the foul, bloody, and heathenish plot, for the establishment of Popery, the murder of the King, and the general massacre of all true Protestants."

" And on what grounds, either of fact or suspicion, dare any one accuse me of such a crime? " said Julian. " I have hardly heard of the plot, save by the mouth of common rumour, which, while it speaks of nothing else, takes care to say nothing distinctly even on that subject."

" It may be enough for me to tell you," replied Bridgenorth, " and perhaps it is a word too much—that you are a discovered intriguer—a spied spy—who carries tokens and messages betwixt the Popish Countess of Derby, and the Catholic party in London. You have not con-

ducted your matters with such discretion, but that this is
well known, and can be sufficiently proved. To this
charge, which you are well aware you cannot deny, these
men, Everett and Dangerfield, are not unwilling to add,
from the recollection of your face, other passages, which
will certainly cost you your life when you come before a
Protestant jury."

"They lie like villains," said Peveril, "who hold me
accessory to any plot either against the King, the nation, or
the state of religion ; and for the Countess, her loyalty
has been too long.and too highly proved, to permit her
being implicated in such injurious suspicions."

"What she has already done," said Bridgenorth, his
face darkening as he spoke, "against the faithful champions of pure religion, hath sufficiently shown of what she
is capable. She hath betaken herself to her rock, and
sits, as she thinks, in security, like the eagle reposing
after his bloody banquet. But the arrow of the fowler
may yet reach her—the shaft is whetted—the bow is
bended—and it will be soon seen whether Amalek or
Israel shall prevail. But for thee, Julian Peveril—why
should I conceal it from thee?—my heart yearns for thee
as a woman's for her first-born. To thee I will give, at
the expense of my own reputation—perhaps at the risk
of personal suspicion—for who, in these days of doubt,
shall be exempted from it—to thee, I say, I will give
means of escape, which else were impossible to thee.
The staircase of this turret descends to the gardens—the
postern-gate is unlatched—on the right hand lie the stables, where you will find your own horse—take it, and
make for Liverpool—I will give you credit with a friend
under the name of Simon Simonson, one persecuted by
the prelates ; and he will expedite your passage from the
kingdom."

"Major Bridgenorth," said Julian, "I will not deceive you. Were I to accept your offer of freedom, it would be to attend to a higher call than that of mere self-preservation. My father is in danger—my mother in sorrow —the voices of religion and nature call me to their side. I am their only child—their only hope—I will aid them, or perish with them!"

"Thou art mad," said Bridgenorth—"aid them thou canst not—perish with them thou well mayst, and even accelerate their ruin ; for, in addition to the charges with which thy unhappy father is loaded, it·would be no slight aggravation, that while he meditated arming and calling together the Catholics and High Churchmen of Cheshire and Derbyshire, his son should prove to be the confidential agent of the Countess of Derby, who aided her in making good her stronghold against the Protestant commissioners, and was despatched by her to open secret communication with the Popish interest in London."

"You have twice stated me as such an agent," said Peveril, resolved that his silence should not be construed into an admission of the charge, though he felt that it was in some degree well founded—"What reason have you for such an allegation ? "

"Will it suffice for a proof of my intimate acquaintance with your mystery," replied Bridgenorth, "if I should repeat to you the last words which the Countess used to you when you left the Castle of that Amalekitish woman ? Thus she spoke : ' I am now a forlorn widow,' she said, ' whom sorrow has made selfish.' "

Peveril started, for these were the very words the Countess had used ; but he instantly recovered himself, and replied, " Be your information of what nature it will, I deny, and I defy it, so far as it attaches aught like guilt to me. There lives not a man more innocent of a disloyal thought, or of a traitorous purpose. What I say for myself, I will, to the best of my knowledge, say and maintain, on account of the noble Countess, to whom I am indebted for nurture."

"Perish, then, in thy obstinacy!" said Bridgenorth; and turning hastily from him, he left the room, and Julian heard him hasten down the narrow staircase, as if distrusting his own resolution.

With a heavy heart, yet with that confidence in an overruling Providence which never forsakes a good and brave man, Peveril betook himself to his lowly place of repose.

CHAPTER XXV.

The course of human life is changeful still,
As is the fickle wind and wandering rill;
Or, like the light dance which the wild-breeze weaves
Amidst the fated race of fallen leaves:
Which now its breath bears down, now tosses high,
Beats to the earth, or wafts to middle sky.
Such, and so varied, the precarious play,
Of fate with man, frail tenant of a day!

ANONYMOUS.

WHILST, overcome with fatigue, and worn out by anxiety, Julian Peveril slumbered as a prisoner in the house
of his hereditary enemy, Fortune was preparing his re-
lease by one of those sudden frolics with which she loves
to confound the calculations and expectancies of humanity; and as she fixes on strange agents for such purposes,
she condescended to employ, on the present occasion, no
less a personage than Mistress Deborah Debbitch.

Instigated, doubtless, by the pristine reminiscences of
former times, no sooner had that most prudent and con-
siderate dame found herself in the vicinity of the scenes
of her earlier days, than she bethought herself of a visit
to the ancient housekeeper of Martindale Castle, Dame
Ellesmere by name, who, long retired from active service,
resided at the keeper's lodge, in the west thicket, with her
nephew, Lance Outram, subsisting upon the savings of
her better days, and on a small pension allowed by Sir
Geoffrey to her age and faithful services.

Now Dame Ellesmere and Mistress Deborah had not by any means been formerly on so friendly a footing, as this haste to visit her might be supposed to intimate. But years had taught Deborah to forget and forgive; or perhaps she had no special objection, under cover of a visit to Dame Ellesmere, to take the chance of seeing what changes time had made on her old admirer the keeper. Both inhabitants were in the cottage, when, after having seen her master set forth on his expedition to the Castle, Mistress Debbitch, dressed in her very best gown, footed it through gutter, and over stile, and by pathway green, to knock at their door, and to lift the latch at the hospitable invitation which bade her come in.

Dame Ellesmere's eyes were so dim, that, even with the aid of spectacles, she failed to recognise, in the portly and mature personage who entered their cottage, the tight well-made lass, who, presuming on her good looks and flippant tongue, had so often provoked her by insubordination; and her former lover, the redoubted Lance, not being conscious that ale had given rotundity to his own figure, which was formerly so slight and active, and that brandy had transferred to his nose the colour which had once occupied his cheeks, was unable to discover that Deborah's French cap, composed of sarsenet and Brussels lace, shaded the features which had so often procured him a rebuke from Dr. Dummerar, for suffering his eyes, during the time of prayers, to wander to the maid-servants' bench.

In brief, the blushing visiter was compelled to make herself known; and when known, was received by aunt and nephew with the most sincere cordiality.

The home-brewed was produced; and, in lieu of more vulgar food, a few slices of venison presently hissed in the frying-pan, giving strong room for inference that Lance Outram, in his capacity of keeper, neglected not his own cottage when he supplied the larder at the Castle. A modest sip of the excellent Derbyshire ale, and a taste of the highly-seasoned hash, soon placed Deborah entirely at home with her old acquaintance.

Having put all necessary questions, and received all suitable answers, respecting the state of the neighbourhood, and such of her own friends as continued to reside there, the conversation began rather to flag, until Deborah found the art of again renewing its interest, by communicating to her friends the dismal intelligence that they must soon look for deadly bad news from the Castle; for that her present master, Major Bridgenorth, had been summoned, by some great people from London, to assist in taking her old master, Sir Geoffrey; and that all Master Bridgenorth's servants, and several other persons whom she named, friends and adherents of the same interest, had assembled a force to surprise the Castle; and that as Sir Geoffrey was now so old, and gouty withal, it could not be expected he should make the defence he was wont; and then he was known to be so stout-hearted, that it was not to be supposed that he would yield up without stroke of sword; and then if he was killed, as he was like to be, amongst them that liked never a bone of his body, and now had him at their mercy, why, in that case, she, Dame Deborah, would look upon Lady Peveril as little better than a dead woman; and undoubtedly there would be a general mourning through all that country, where they had such great kin; and silks were likely to rise on it, as Master Lutestring, the mercer of Chesterfield, was like to feel in his purse bottom. But for her part, let matters wag how they would, an if Master Julian

Peveril was to come to his own, she could give as near a guess as e'er another who was likely be Martindale.

The text of this lecture, or, in other words, the fact that Bridgenorth was gone with a party to attack Sir Geoffrey Peveril in his own Castle of Martindale, sounded so stunningly strange in the ears of those old retainers of his family, that they had no power either to attend to Mistress Deborah's inferences, or to interrupt the velocity of speech with which she poured them forth. And when at length she made a breathless pause, all that poor Dame Ellesmere could reply, was the emphatic' question, " Bridgenorth brave Peveril of the Peak !—Is the woman mad ? "

" Come, come, dame," said Deborah, " woman me no more than I woman you. I have not been called Mistress at the head of the table for so many years, to be woman'd here by you. And for the news, it is as true as that you are sitting there in a white hood, who will wear a black one ere long."

" Lance Outram," said the old woman, " make out, if thou be'st a man, and listen about if aught stirs up at the Castle."

" If there should," said Outram, " I am even too long here ; " and he caught up his crossbow, and one or two arrows, and rushed out of the cottage.

" Well-a-day ! " said Mistress Deborah, " see if my news have not frightened away Lance Outram too, whom they used to say nothing could start. But do not take on so, dame ; for I dare say if the Castle and the lands pass to my new master, Major Bridgenorth, as it is like they will—for I have heard that he has powerful debts over the estate—you shall have my good word with him, and I promise you he is no bad man; something precise about preaching and praying, and about the dress which one should wear, which, I must own, beseems not a gentleman, as, to be sure, every woman knows best what becomes her. But for you, dame, that wear a prayer-book at your girdle, with your housewife-case, and never change the fashion of your white hood, I dare say he will not grudge you the little matter you need, and are not able to win."

"Out, sordid jade!" exclaimed Dame Ellesmere, her very flesh quivering betwixt apprehension and anger, "and hold your peace this instant, or I will find those that shall flay the very hide from thee with dog-whips. Hast thou eat thy noble master's bread, not only to betray his trust, and fly from his service, but wouldst thou come here, like an ill-omened bird as thou art, to triumph over his downfall?"

"Nay, dame," said Deborah, over whom the violence of the old woman had obtained a certain predominance; "it is not I that say it—only the warrant of the Parliament folks."

"I thought we had done with their warrants ever since the blessed twenty-ninth of May," said the old housekeeper of Martindale Castle; "but this I tell thee, sweetheart, that I have seen such warrants crammed, at the sword's point, down the throats of them that brought them; and so shall this be, if there is one true man left to drink of the Dove."

As she spoke, Lance Outram re-entered the cottage. "Naunt," he said in dismay, "I doubt it is true what she says. The beacon tower is as black as my belt. No Polestar of Peveril. What does that betoken?"

"Death, ruin, and captivity," exclaimed old Ellesmere. "Make for the Castle, thou knave. Thrust in thy

great body. Strike for the house that bred thee and fed
thee ; and if thou art buried under the ruins, thou diest a
man's death."

" Nay, naunt, I shall not be slack," answered Outram.
" But here come folks that I warrant can tell us more
on't."

One or two of the female servants, who had fled from
the Castle during the alarm, now rushed in with various
reports of the case ; but all agreeing that a body of armed
men were in possession of the. Castle, and that Major
Bridgenorth had taken young Master Julian prisoner, and
conveyed him down to Moultrassie-Hall, with his feet tied
under the belly of the nag—a shameful sight to be seen—
and he so well born and so handsome.

Lance scratched his head ; and though feeling the duty
incumbent upon him as a faithful servant, which was indeed specially dinned into him by the cries and exclamations of his aunt, he seemed not a little dubious how to
conduct himself.

" I would to God, naunt," he said at last, "that old
Whitaker were alive now, with his long stories about
Marston-moor and Edge-hill, that made us all yawn our
jaws off their hinges, in spite of broiled rashers and
double beer ! When a man is missed, he is moaned, as
they say ; and I would rather than a broad piece he had
been here to have sorted this matter, for it is clean out of
my way as a woodsman, that have no skill of war. But
dang it, if old Sir Geoffrey go to the wall without a knock
for it !—Here you, Nell "—(speaking to one of the fugitive maidens from the Castle)—" but, no—you have not
the heart of a cat, and are afraid of your own shadow by
moonlight—But, Cis, you are a stout-hearted wench, and
know a buck from a bullfinch. Hark thee, Cis, as you

would wish to be married, get up to the Castle, again,
and get thee in—thou best knowest where—for thou hast
oft gotten out of postern to a dance or junketing, to my
knowledge—Get thee back to the Castle, as ye hope to be
married—See my lady—they cannot hinder thee of that
—my lady has a head worth twenty of ours—If I am to
gather force, light up the beacon for a signal; and spare
not a tar barrel on't. Thou mayst do it safe enough. I
warrant the Roundheads busy with drink and plunder.—
And, hark thee, say to my lady I am gone down to the
miners' houses at Bonadventure. The rogues were mu-
tinying for their wages but yesterday; they will be all
ready for good or bad. Let her send orders down to me;
or do you come yourself, your legs are long enough."

"Whether they are or not, Master Lance, (and you
know nothing of the matter,) they shall do your errand
to-night, for love of the old knight and his lady."

So Cisly Sellok, a kind of Derbyshire Camilla, who
had won the smock at the foot-race at Ashbourne, sprung
forward towards the Castle with a speed which few could
have equalled.

"There goes a mettled wench," said Lance; "and now,
naunt, give me the old broadsword—it is above the bed-
head—and my wood-knife; and I shall do well enough."

"And what is to become of me?" bleated the unfortunate Mistress Deborah Debbitch.

"You must remain here with my aunt, Mistress Deb;
and, for old acquaintance' sake, she will take care no
harm befalls you; but take heed how you attempt to
break bounds."

So saying, and pondering in his own mind the task
which he had undertaken, the hardy forester strode down
the moonlight glade, scarcely hearing the blessings and

cautions which Dame Ellesmere kept showering after
him. His thoughts were not altogether warlike. "What
a tight ankle the jade hath!—she trips it like a doe in
summer over the dew. Well, but here are the huts—Let
us to this gear.—Are ye all asleep, ye dammers, sinkers,
and drift-drivers? turn out, ye subterranean badgers.
Here is your master, Sir Geoffrey, dead, for aught you
know or care. Do not you see the beacon is unlit, and
you sit there like so many asses?"

"Why," answered one of the miners, who now began
to come out of their huts,

> "An he be dead,
> He will eat no more bread."

"And you are like to eat none neither," said Lance;
"for the works will be presently stopped, and all of you
turned off."

"Well, and what of it, Master Lance? As good play
for nought as work for nought. Here is four weeks we
have scarce seen the colour of Sir Geoffrey's coin; and
you ask us to care whether he be dead or in life? For
you, that goes about, trotting upon your horse, and doing
for work what all men do for pleasure, it may be well
enough; but it is another matter to be leaving God's
light, and burrowing all day and night in darkness, like a
toad in a hole—that's not to be done for nought, I trow;
and if Sir Geoffrey is dead, his soul will suffer for't; and
if he's alive, we'll have him in the Barmoot Court."

"Hark ye, gaffer," said Lance, "and take notice, my
mates, all of you," for a considerable number of these
rude and subterranean people had now assembled to hear
the discussion—"Has Sir Geoffrey, think you, ever put
a penny in his pouch out of this same Bonadventure
mine?"

"I cannot say as I think he has," answered old Ditchley, the party who maintained the controversy.

"Answer on your conscience, though it be but a leaden one. Do not you know that he hath lost a good penny?"

"Why, I believe he may," said Gaffer Ditchley. "What then!—lose to-day, win to-morrow—the miner must eat in the meantime."

"True; but what will you eat when Master Bridgenorth gets the land, that will not hear of a mine being wrought on his own ground? Will he work on at dead loss, think ye?" demanded trusty Lance.

"Bridgenorth?—he of Moultrassie-Hall, that stopped the great Felicity Work, on which his father laid out, some say, ten thousand pounds, and never got in a penny? Why, what has he to do with Sir Geoffrey's property down here at Bonadventure? It was never his, I trow."

"Nay, what do I know?" answered Lance, who saw the impression he had made. "Law and debt will give him half Derbyshire, I think, unless you stand by old Sir Geoffrey."

"But if Sir Geoffrey be dead," said Ditchley, cautiously, "what good will our standing by do to him?"

"I did not say he was dead, but only as bad as dead; in the hands of the Roundheads—a prisoner up yonder, at his own castle," said Lance; "and will have his head cut off, like the good Earl of Derby's, at Bolton-le-Moors."

"Nay, then, comrades," said Gaffer Ditchley, "an it be as Master Lance says, I think we should bear a hand for stout old Sir Geoffrey, against a low-born mean-spirited fellow like Bridgenorth, who shut up a shaft had cost thousands, without getting a penny profit on't. So

hurra for Sir Geoffrey, and down with the Rump! But
hold ye a blink—hold "—(and the waving of his hand
stopped the commencing cheer)—" Hark ye, Master
Lance, it must be all over, for the beacon is as black as
night; and you know yourself that marks the Lord's
death."

" It will kindle again in an instant," said Lance; internally adding, " I pray to God it may!—It will kindle in
an instant—lack of fuel, and the confusion of the family."

"Ay, like enow, like enow," said Ditchley; " but I
winna budge till I see it blazing."

" Why then, there a-goes!" said Lance, " Thank thee,
Cis—thank thee, my good wench.—Believe your own
eyes, my lads, if you will not believe me; and now hurra
for Peveril of the Peak—the King and his friends—and
down with Rumps and Roundheads!"

The sudden rekindling of the beacon had all the effect
which Lance could have desired upon the minds of his
rude and ignorant hearers, who, in their superstitious
humour, had strongly associated the Polar-star of Peveril with the fortunes of the family. Once moved, according to the national character of their countrymen,
they soon became enthusiastic; and Lance found himself
at the head of thirty stout fellows and upwards, armed
with their pick-axes, and ready to execute whatever task
he should impose on them.

Trusting to enter the Castle by the postern, which had
served to accommodate himself and other domestics upon
an emergency, his only anxiety was to keep his march
silent; and he earnestly recommended to his followers to
reserve their shouts for the moment of the attack. They
had not advanced far on their road to the Castle, when
Cisly Sellok met them, so breathless with haste, that the

poor girl was obliged to throw herself into Master Lance's arms.

"Stand up, my mettled wench," said he, giving her a sly kiss at the same time, "and let us know what is going on up at the Castle."

"My lady bids you, as you would serve God and your master, not to come up to the Castle, which can but make bloodshed; for she says Sir Geoffrey is lawfully in hand, and that he must bide the issue; and that he is innocent of what he is charged with, and is going up to speak for himself before King and Council, and she goes up with him. And besides, they have found out the postern, the Roundhead rogues; for two of them saw me when I went out of door, and chased me; but I showed them a fair pair of heels."

"As ever dashed dew from the cowslip," said Lance. "But what the foul fiend is to be done? for if they have secured the postern, I know not how the dickens we can get in."

"All is fastened with bolt and staple, and guarded with gun and pistol, at the Castle," quoth Cisly; "and so sharp are they, that they nigh caught me coming with my lady's message, as I told you. But my lady says, if you could deliver her son, Master Julian, from Bridgenorth, that she would hold it good service."

"What!" said Lance, "is young master at the Castle? I taught him to shoot his first shaft. But how to get in!"

"He was at the Castle in the midst of the ruffle, but old Bridgenorth has carried him down prisoner to the hall," answered Cisly. "There was never faith nor courtesy in an old Puritan who never had pipe and tabor in his house since it was built."

"Or who stopped a promising mine," said Ditchley, "to save a few thousand pounds, when he might have made himself as rich as the Lord of Chatsworth, and fed a hundred good fellows all the whilst."

"Why, then," said Lance, "since you are all of a mind, we will go draw the cover for the old badger; and I promise you that the Hall is not like one of your real houses of quality, where the walls are as thick as whinstone-dikes, but foolish brick-work, that your pick-axes will work through as if it were cheese. Huzza one more for Peveril of the Peak! down with Bridgenorth, and all upstart cuckoldy Roundheads!"

Having indulged the throats of his followers with one buxom huzza, Lance commanded them to cease their clamours, and proceeded to conduct them, by such paths as seemed the least likely to be watched, to the court-yard of Moultrassie-Hall. On the road they were joined by several stout yeomen farmers, either followers of the Peveril family, or friends to the High Church and Cavalier party; most of whom, alarmed by the news which began to fly fast through the neighbourhood, were armed with sword and pistol.

Lance Outram halted his party, at the distance, as he himself described it, of a flight-shot from the house, and advanced alone, and in silence, to reconnoitre; and having previously commanded Ditchley and his subterranean allies to come to his assistance whenever he should whistle, he crept cautiously forward, and soon found that those whom he came to surprise, true to the discipline which had gained their party such decided superiority during the Civil War, had posted a sentinel, who paced through the court-yard, piously chanting a psalm-tune, while his arms, crossed on his bosom, supported a gun of formidable length.

"Now, a true soldier," said Lance Outram to himself,
"would put a stop to thy snivelling ditty, by making a
broad arrow quiver in your heart, and no great alarm
given. But, dang it, I have not the right spirit for a
soldier—I cannot fight a man till my blood's up; and for
shooting him from behind a wall, it is cruelly like to
stalking a deer. I'll e'en face him, and try what to
make of him."

With this doughty resolution, and taking no farther
care to conceal himself, he entered the court-yard boldly
and was making forward to the front door of the hall, as
a matter of course. But the old Cromwellian, who was
on guard, had not so learned his duty. "Who goes
there?—Stand, friend—stand; or, verily, I will shoot
thee to death!" were challenges which followed each
other quick, the last being enforced by the levelling and
presenting the said long-barrelled gun with which he was
armed.

"Why, what a murrain!" answered Lance. "Is it
your fashion to go a-shooting at this time o' night? Why,
this is but a time for bat-fowling."

"Nay, but hark thee, friend," said the experienced
sentinel, "I am none of those who do this work negligently. Thou canst not snare me with thy crafty speech,
though thou wouldst make it to sound simple in mine ear.
Of a verity I will shoot, unless thou tell thy name and
business."

"Name!" said Lance; "why, what a dickens should
it be but Robin Round—honest Robin of Redham; and
for business, an you must need know, I come on a message from some Parliament man, up yonder at the Castle,
with letters for worshipful Master Bridgenorth of Moultrassie-Hall; and this be the place as I think; though

why ye be marching up and down at his door, like the
sign of a Red Man, with your old firelock there, I cannot
so well guess."

"Give me the letters, my friend," said the sentinel, to
whom this explanation seemed very natural and probable,
"and I will cause them forthwith to be delivered into his
worship's own hand."

Rummaging in his pockets, as if to pull out the letters
which never existed, Master Lance approached within the
sentinel's piece, and, before he was aware, suddenly seized
him by the collar, whistled sharp and shrill, and exerting
his skill as a wrestler, for which he had been distinguished
in his youth, he stretched his antagonist on his back—the
musket for which they struggled going off in the fall.

The miners rushed into the court-yard at Lance's
signal; and, hopeless any longer of prosecuting his design
in silence, Lance commanded two of them to secure the
prisoner, and the rest to cheer loudly, and attack the door
of the house. Instantly the court-yard of the mansion
rang with the cry of "Peveril of the Peak for ever!"
with all the abuse which the Royalists had invented to
cast upon the Roundheads, during so many years of contention; and at the same time, while some assailed the
door with their mining implements, others directed their
attack against the angle, where a kind of porch joined to
the main front of the building; and there, in some degree
protected by the projection of the wall, and of a balcony
which overhung the porch, wrought in more security, as
well as with more effect, than the others; for the doors
being of oak, thickly studded with nails, offered a more
effectual resistance to violence than the brick-work.

The noise of this hubbub on the outside, soon excited
wild alarm and tumult within. Lights flew from window

to window, and voices were heard demanding the cause
of the attack ; to which the party cries of those who were
in the court-yard afforded a sufficient, or at least the only
answer, which was vouchsafed. At length the window
of a projecting staircase opened, and the voice of Bridgenorth himself demanded authoritatively what the tumult
meant, and commanded the rioters to desist, upon their
own proper and immediate peril.

"We want our young master, you canting old thief,"
was the reply; "and if we have him not instantly, the
topmost stone of your house shall lie as low as the
foundation."

"We will try that presently," said Bridgenorth ; "for
if there is another blow struck against the walls of my
peaceful house, I will fire my carabine among you, and
your blood be upon your own head. I have a score of
friends, well armed with musket and pistol, to defend
my house ; and we have both the means and heart,
with Heaven's assistance, to repay any violence you can
offer."

"Master Bridgenorth," replied Lance, who, though no
soldier, was sportsman enough to comprehend the advantage which those under cover, and using fire-arms, must
necessarily have over his party, exposed to their aim, in
a great measure, and without means of answering their
fire,—"Master Bridgenorth, let us crave parley with you,
and fair conditions. We desire to do you no evil, but
will have back our young master; it is enough that you
have got our old one and his lady. It is foul chasing to
kill hart, hind, and fawn ; and we will give you some
light on the subject in an instant."

This speech was followed by a great crash amongst the
lower windows of the house, according to a new species

of .attack which had been suggested by some of the assailants.

"I would take the honest fellow's word, and let young Peveril go," said one of the garrison, who, carelessly yawning, approached on the inside the post at which Bridgenorth had stationed himself.

"Are you mad?" said Bridgenorth; "or do you think me poor enough in spirit to give up the advantages I now possess over the family of Peveril, for the awe of a parcel of boors, whom the first discharge will scatter like chaff before the whirlwind?"

"Nay," answered the speaker, who was the same individual that had struck Julian by his resemblance to the man who called himself Ganlesse, "I love a dire revenge, but we shall buy it somewhat too dear if these rascals set the house on fire, as they are like to do, while you are parleying from the window. They have thrown torches or fire-brands into the hall; and it is all our friends can do to keep the flame from catching the wainscoting, which is old and dry."

"Now, may Heaven judge thee for thy lightness of spirit," answered Bridgenorth; "one would think mischief was so properly thy element, that to thee it was indifferent whether friend or foe was the sufferer."

So saying, he ran hastily down stairs towards the hall, into which, through broken casements, and betwixt the iron bars, which prevented human entrance, the assailants had thrust lighted straw, sufficient to excite much smoke and some fire, and to throw the defenders of the house into great confusion; insomuch, that of several shots fired hastily from the windows, little or no damage followed to the besiegers, who, getting warm in the onset, answered the hostile charges with loud shouts of "Peveril for ever!" and had already made a practicable breach through the brick-wall of the tenement, through which Lance, Ditchley, and several of the most adventurous among their followers, made their way into the hall.

The complete capture of the house remained, however, as far off as ever. The defenders mixed with much coolness and skill, that solemn and deep spirit of enthusiasm which sets life at less than nothing, in comparison to real or supposed duty. From the half open doors which led into the hall, they maintained a fire which began to grow fatal. One miner was shot dead; three or four were wounded; and Lance scarce knew whether he should draw his forces from the house, and leave it a prey to the flames, or, making a desperate attack on the posts occupied by the defenders, try to obtain unmolested possession of the place. At this moment, his course of conduct was determined by an unexpected occurrence, of which it is necessary to trace the cause.

Julian Peveril had been, like other inhabitants of Moultrassie Hall on that momentous night, awakened by the report of the sentinel's musket, followed by the shouts of his father's vassals and followers; of which he collected enough to guess that Bridgenorth's house was attacked with a view to his liberation. Very doubtful of the issue of such an attempt, dizzy with the slumber from which he had been so suddenly awakened, and confounded with the rapid succession of events to which he had been lately a witness, he speedily put on a part of his clothes, and hastened to the window of his apartment. From this he could see nothing to relieve his anxiety, for it looked towards a quarter different from that on which the attack was made. He attempted his door; it was locked on the outside; and his perplexity and anxiety became extreme, when suddenly the lock was turned, and in an undress, hastily assumed in the moment of alarm, her hair streaming on her shoulders, her eyes gleaming betwixt fear and resolution, Alice Bridgenorth rushed into his apartment, and seized his hand with the fervent exclamation, "Julian, save my father !"

The light which she bore in her hand served to show those features which could rarely have been viewed by any one without emotion, but which bore an expression irresistible to a lover.

"Alice," he said, "what means this ? What is the danger ? Where is your father ?"

" Do not stay to question," she answered ; "but if you would save him, follow me !"

At the same time she led the way, with great speed, half way down the turret staircase which led to his room, thence turning through a side door, along a long gallery, to a larger and wider stair, at the bottom of which stood her father, surrounded by four or five of his friends, scarce discernible through the smoke of the fire which began to take hold in the hall, as well as that which arose from the repeated discharge of their own fire-arms.

Julian saw there was not a moment to be lost, if he meant to be a successful mediator. He rushed through Bridgenorth's party ere they were aware of his approach, and throwing himself amongst the assailants who occupied the hall in considerable numbers, he assured them of his personal safety, and conjured them to depart.

" Not without a few more slices at the Rump, master," answered Lance. " I am principally glad to see you safe and well ; but here is Joe Rimegap shot as dead as a buck in season, and more of us are hurt ; and we'll have revenge, and roast the Puritans like apples for lambs-wool!"

"Then you shall roast me along with them," said Julian; "for I vow to God, I will not leave the hall, being bound by parole of honour to abide with Major Bridgenorth till lawfully dismissed."

"Now out on you, an you wère ten times a Peveril!" said Ditchley; "to give so many honest fellows loss and labour on your behalf, and to show them no kinder countenance.—I say, beat up the fire, and burn all together!"

"Nay, nay; but peace, my masters, and hearken to reason," said Julian; "we are all here in evil condition, and you will only make it worse by contention. Do you help to put out this same fire, which will else cost us all dear. Keep yourselves under arms. Let Master Bridgenorth and me settle some grounds of accommodation, and I trust all will be favourably made up on both sides; and if not, you shall have my consent and countenance to fight it out; and come on it what will, I will never forget this night's good service."

He then drew Ditchley and Lance Outram aside, while the rest stood suspended at his appearance and words, and expressing the utmost thanks and gratitude for what they had already done, urged them, as the greatest favour which they could do towards him and his father's house, to permit him to negotiate the terms of his emancipation from thraldom; at the same time, forcing on Ditchley five or six gold pieces, that the brave lads of Bonadventure might drink his health; whilst to Lance he expressed the warmest sense of his active kindness, but protested he could only consider it as good service to his house, if he was allowed to manage the matter. after his own fashion.

" Why," answered Lance, " I am well out on it, Master Julian ; for it is matter beyond my mastery. All that I stand to is, that I will see you safe out of this same Moultrassie Hall ; for our old Naunt Ellesmere will else give me but cold comfort when I come home. Truth is, I began unwillingly ; but when I saw the poor fellow Joe shot beside me, why, I thought we should have some amends. But I put it all in your Honour's hands."

During this colloquy both parties had been amicably employed in extinguishing the fire, which might otherwise have been fatal to all. It required a general effort to get it under ; and both parties agreed on the necessary labour, with as much unanimity, as if the water they brought in leathern buckets from the well to throw upon the fire, had had some effect in slaking their mutual hostility.

CHAPTER XXVI.

Necessity—thou best of peacemakers,
As well as surest prompter of invention—
Help us to composition !
ANONYMOUS.

WHILE the fire continued, the two parties laboured in
active union, like the jarring factions of the Jews during
the siege of Jerusalem, when compelled to unite in resisting an assault of the besiegers. But when the last
bucket of water had hissed on the few embers that continued to glimmer—when the sense of mutual hostility,
hitherto suspended by a feeling of common danger, was
in its turn rekindled—the parties, mingled as they had
hitherto been in one common exertion, drew off from
each other, and began to arrange themselves at opposite
sides of the hall, and handle their weapons, as if for a
renewal of the fight.

Bridgenorth interrupted any farther progress of this
menaced hostility. " Julian Peveril," he said, " thou art
free to walk thine own path, since thou wilt not walk
with me that road which is more safe, as well as more
honourable. But if you do by my counsel, you will get
soon beyond the British seas."

" Ralph Bridgenorth," said one of his friends, " this is
but evil and feeble conduct on thine own part. Wilt
thou withhold thy hand from the battle, to defend, from
these sons of Belial, the captive of thy bow and of thy

spear? Surely we are enow to deal with them in the
security of our good old cause; nor should we part with
this spawn of the old serpent, until we essay whether
the Lord will not give us victory therein."

A hum of stern assent followed; and had not Ganlesse
now interfered, the combat would probably have been
renewed. He took the advocate for war apart into one
of the window recesses, and apparently satisfied his objections; for as he returned to his companions, he said to
them, " Our friend hath so well argued this matter, that,
verily, since he is of the same mind with the worthy
Major Bridgenorth, I think the youth may be set at liberty."

As no farther objection was offered, it only remained
with Julian to thank and reward those who had been
active in his assistance. Having first obtained from
Bridgenorth a promise of indemnity to them for the riot
they had committed, a few kind words conveyed his sense
of their services; and some broad pieces, thrust into the
hand of Lance Outram, furnished the means for affording
them a holiday. They would have remained to protect
him, but, fearful of farther disorder, and relying entirely
on the good faith of Major Bridgenorth, he dismissed
them all excepting Lance, whom he detained to attend
upon him for a few minutes, till he should depart from
Moultrassie. But ere leaving the Hall, he could not repress his desire to speak with Bridgenorth in secret; and
advancing towards him, he expressed such a desire.

Tacitly granting what was asked of him, Bridgenorth
led the way to a small summer saloon adjoining to the
Hall, where, with his usual gravity and indifference of
manner, he seemed to await in silence what Peveril had
to communicate.

Julian found it difficult, where so little opening was
afforded him, to find a tone in which to open the subjects
he had at heart, that should be at once dignified and con-
ciliating. "Major Bridgenorth," he said at length, "you
have been a son, and an affectionate one—You may conceive my present anxiety—My father!—What has been
designed for him?"

"What the law will," answered Bridgenorth. "Had
he walked by the counsels which I procured to be given
to him, he might have dwelt safely in the house of his
ancestors. His fate is now beyond my control—far beyond yours. It must be with him as his country shall
decide."

"And my mother?" said Peveril.

"Will consult, as she has ever done, her own duty;
and create her own happiness by doing so," replied
Bridgenorth. "Believe, my designs towards your family
are better than they may seem through the mist which
adversity has spread around your house. I may triumph
as a man; but as a man I must also remember, in my
hour, that mine enemies have had theirs.—Have you
aught else to say? he added, after a momentary pause.
"You have rejected once, yea, and again, the hand I
stretched out to you. Methinks little more remains between us."

These words, which seemed to cut short farther discussion, were calmly spoken; so that though they appeared to discourage farther question, they could not
interrupt that which still trembled on Julian's tongue.
He made a step or two towards the door; then suddenly
returned. "Your daughter?" he said—"Major Bridgenorth—I should ask—I *do* ask forgiveness for mentioning
her name—but may I not inquire after her?—May I not
express my wishes for her future happiness?"

"Your interest in her is but too flattering," said Bridgenorth; "but you have already chosen your part; and you must be, in future, strangers to each other. I may have wished it otherwise, but the hour of grace is passed during which your compliance with my advice might—I will speak it plainly—have led to your union. For her happiness—if such a word belongs to mortal pilgrimage—I shall care for it sufficiently. She leaves this place to-day, under the guardianship of a sure friend."

"Not of——?" exclaimed Peveril, and stopped short; for he felt he had no right to pronounce the name which came to his lips.

"Why do you pause?" said Bridgenorth; "a sudden thought is often a wise, almost always an honest one. With whom did you suppose I meant to intrust my child, that the idea called forth so anxious an expression?"

"Again I should ask your forgiveness," said Julian, "for meddling where I have little right to interfere. But I saw a face here that is known to me—the person calls himself Ganlesse—Is it with him that you mean to intrust your daughter?"

"Even to the person who calls himself Ganlesse," said Bridgenorth, without expressing either anger or surprise.

"And do you know to whom you commit a charge so precious to all who know her, and so dear to yourself?" said Julian.

"Do *you* know, who ask me the question?" answered Bridgenorth.

"I own I do not," answered Julian; "but I have seen him in a character so different from what he now wears, that I feel it my duty to warn you, how you intrust the charge of your child to one who can alternately play the profligate or the hypocrite, as it suits his own interest or humour."

Bridgenorth smiled contemptuously. "I might be angry," he said, "with the officious zeal which supposes that its green conceptions can instruct my gray hairs; but, good Julian, I do but only ask from you the liberal construction, that I, who have had much converse with mankind, know with whom I trust what is dearest to me. He of whom thou speakest, hath one visage to his friends, though he may have others to the world, living amongst those before whom honest features should be concealed under a grotesque vizard; even as in the sinful sports of the day, called maskings and mummeries, where the wise, if he show himself at all, must be contented to play the apish and fantastic fool."

"I would only pray your wisdom to beware," said Julian, "of one, who, as he has a vizard for others, may also have one which can disguise his real features from you yourself."

"This is being over careful, young man," replied Bridgenorth, more shortly than he had hitherto spoken; "if you would walk by my counsel, you will attend to your own affairs, which, credit me, deserve all your care, and leave others to the management of theirs."

This was too plain to be misunderstood; and Peveril was compelled to take his leave of Bridgenorth, and of Moultrassie-Hall, without farther parley or explanation. The reader may imagine how oft he looked back, and tried to guess, amongst the lights which continued to twinkle in various parts of the building, which sparkle it was that gleamed from the bower of Alice. When the road turned into another direction, he sunk into a deep reverie, from which he was at length roused by the voice

of Lance, who demanded where he intended to quarter·
for the night. He was unprepared to answer the question, but the honest keeper himself prompted a solution
of the problem, by requesting that he would occupy a
spare bed in the Lodge; to which Julian willingly agreed.
The rest of the inhabitants had retired to rest when they
entered; but Dame Ellesmere, apprized by a messenger
of her nephew's hospitable intent, had every thing in the
best readiness she could, for the son of her ancient patron.
Peveril betook himself to rest; and, notwithstanding so
many subjects of anxiety, slept soundly till the morning
was far advanced.

His slumbers were first broken by Lance, who had
been long up, and already active in his service. He informed him, that his horse, arms, and small cloak-bag,
had been sent from the Castle by one of Major Bridgenorth's servants, who brought a letter, discharging from
the Major's service the unfortunate Deborah Debbitch,
and prohibiting her return to the Hall. The officer of
the House of Commons, escorted by a strong guard, had
left Martindale Castle that morning early, travelling in
Sir Geoffrey's carriage—his lady being also permitted to
attend on him. To this he had to add, that the property
at the Castle was taken possession of by Master Win-the-
fight, the attorney, from Chesterfield, with other officers
of law, in name of Major Bridgenorth, a large creditor
of the unfortunate knight.

Having told these Job's tidings, Lance paused; and,
after a moment's hesitation, declared he was resolved to
quit the country, and go up to London along with his
young master. Julian argued the point with him; and
insisted he had better stay to take charge of his aunt, in
case she should be disturbed by these strangers. Lance

replied, " She would have one with her, who would protect her well enough ; for there was wherewithal to buy
protection amongst them. But for himself, he was resolved to follow Master Julian to the death."

Julian heartily thanked him for his love.

" Nay, it is not altogether out of love neither," said
Lance, " though I am as loving as another; but it is, as
it were, partly out of fear, lest I be called over the coals
for last night's matter; for as for the miners, they will
never trouble them, as the creatures only act after their
kind."

" I will write in your behalf to Major Bridgenorth,
who is bound to afford you protection, if you have such
fear," said Julian.

" Nay, for that matter, it is not altogether fear, more
than altogether love," answered the enigmatical keeper,
" although it hath a tasting of both in it. And, to speak
plain truth, thus it is—Dame Debbitch and Naunt Ellesmere have resolved to set up their horses together, and
have made up all their quarrels. And of all ghosts in
the world, the worst is, when an old true-love comes back
to haunt a poor fellow like me. Mistress Deborah,
though distressed enow for the loss of her place, has been
already speaking of a broken sixpence, or some such
token, as if a man could remember such things for so
many years, even if she had not gone over seas, like a
woodcock, in the meanwhile."

Julian could scarce forbear laughing. " I thought you
too much of a man, Lance, to fear a woman marrying
you whether you would or no."

" It has been many an honest man's luck, for all that,"
said Lance ; " and a woman in the very house has so
many deuced opportunities. And then there would be

two upon one; for Naunt, though high enough when any of *your* folks are concerned, hath some look to the main chance; and it seems Mistress Deb is as rich as a Jew."

"And you, Lance," said Julian, "have no mind to marry for cake and pudding."

"No, truly, master," answered Lance, "unless I knew of what dough they were baked. How the devil do I know how the jade came by so much? And then if she speaks of tokens and love-passages, let her be the same tight lass I broke the six-pence with, and I will be the same true lad to her. But I never heard of true love lasting ten years; and hers, if it lives at all, must be nearer twenty."

"Well, then, Lance," said Julian, "since you are resolved on the thing, we will go to London together; where, if I cannot retain you in my service, and if my father recovers not these misfortunes, I will endeavour to promote you elsewhere."

"Nay, nay," said Lance, "I trust to be back to bonny Martindale before it is long, and to keep the greenwood, as I have been wont to do; for, as to Dame Debbitch, when they have not me for their common butt, Naunt and she will soon bend bows on each other. So here comes old Dame Ellesmere with your breakfast. I will but give some directions about the deer to Rough Ralph, my helper, and saddle my forest pony, and your honour's horse, which is no prime one, and we will be ready to trot."

Julian was not sorry for this addition to his establishment; for Lance had shown himself, on the preceding evening, a shrewd and bold fellow, and attached to his master. He therefore set himself to reconcile his aunt to parting with her nephew for some time. Her unlimited devotion for "the family," readily induced the old lady to acquiesce in his proposal, though not without a gentle sigh over the ruins of a castle in the air, which was founded on the well-saved purse of Mistress Deborah Debbitch. "At any rate," she thought, "it was as well that Lance should be out of the way of that bold, long-legged, beggarly trollop, Cis Sellok." But to poor Deb herself, the expatriation of Lance, whom she had looked to as a sailor to a port under his lee, for which he can run, if weather becomes foul, was a second severe blow, following close on her dismissal from the profitable service of Major Bridgenorth.

Julian visited the disconsolate damsel, in hopes of gaining some light upon Bridgenorth's projects regarding his daughter—the character of this Ganlesse—and other matters, with which her residence in the family might have made her acquainted; but he found her by far too much troubled in mind to afford him the least information. The name of Ganlesse she did not seem to recollect—that of Alice rendered her hysterical—that of Bridgenorth, furious. She numbered up the various services she had rendered in the family—and denounced the plague of swartness to the linen—of leanness to the poultry—of dearth and dishonour to the housekeeping—and of lingering sickness and early death to Alice ;—all which evils, she averred, had only been kept off by her continued, watchful, and incessant cares.—Then again turning to the subject of the fugitive Lance, she expressed such a total contempt of that mean-spirited fellow, in a tone between laughing and crying, as satisfied Julian it was not a topic likely to act as a sedative ; and that, therefore, unless he made a longer stay than the urgent state of his affairs permitted, he was not likely to find

Mistress Deborah in such a state of composure as might enable him to obtain from her any rational or useful information.

Lance, who good-naturedly took upon himself the whole burden of Dame Debbitch's mental alienation, or " taking on," as such fits of *passio hysterica* are usually termed in the country, had too much feeling to present himself before the victim of her own sensibility, and of his obduracy. He therefore intimated to Julian, by his assistant Ralph, that the horses stood saddled behind the Lodge, and that all was ready for their departure.

Julian took the hint, and they were soon mounted, and clearing the road, at a rapid trot, in the direction of London; but not by the most usual route. Julian calculated that the carriage in which his father was transported would travel slowly; and it was his purpose, if possible, to get to London before it should arrive there, in order to have time to consult with the friends of his family, what measures should be taken in his father's behalf.

In this manner, they advanced a day's journey towards London; at the conclusion of which, Julian found his resting-place in a small inn upon the road. No one came, at the first call, to attend upon the guests and their horses, although the house was well lighted up; and there was a prodigious chattering in the kitchen, such as can only be produced by a French cook when his mystery is in the very moment of projection. It instantly occurred to Julian—so rare was the ministry of these Gallic artists at that time—that the clamour he heard must necessarily be produced by the Sieur Chaubert, on whose *plats* he had lately feasted, along with Smith and Ganlesse.

One, or both of these, were therefore probably in the

little inn; and if so, he might have some opportunity to discover their real purpose and character. How to avail himself of such a meeting, he knew not; but chance favoured him more than he could have expected.

"I can scarce receive you, gentlefolks," said the landlord, who at length appeared at the door; "here be a sort of quality in my house to-night, whom less than all will not satisfy; nor all neither, for that matter."

"We are but plain fellows, landlord," said Julian; "we are bound for Moseley-market, and can get no farther to-night. Any hole will serve us, no matter what."

"Why," said the honest host, "if that be the case, I must e'en put one of you behind the bar, though the gentlemen have desired to be private; the other must take heart of grace and help me at the tap."

"The tap for me," said Lance, without waiting his master's decision. "It is an element which I could live and die in."

"The bar, then, for me," said Peveril; and stepping back, whispered to Lance to exchange cloaks with him, desirous, if possible, to avoid being recognised.

The exchange was made in an instant; and presently afterwards the landlord brought a light; and as he guided Julian into his hostelry, cautioned him to sit quiet in the place where he should stow him; and if he was discovered, to say that he was one of the house, and leave him to make it good. "You will hear what the gallants say," he added; "but I think thou wilt carry away but little on it; for when it is not French, it is Court gibberish; and that is as hard to construe."

The bar, into which our hero was inducted on these conditions, seemed formed, with respect to the public room, upon the principle of a citadel, intended to observe

and bridle a rebellious capital.   Here sat the host on the
Saturday evenings, screened from the observation of his
guests, yet with the power of observing both their wants
and their behaviour, and also that of overhearing their
conversation—a practice which he was much addicted to,
being one of that numerous class of philanthropists, to
whom their neighbours' business is of as much consequence, or rather more, than their own.

Here he planted his new guest, with a repeated caution
not to disturb the gentlemen by speech or motion ; and a
promise that he should be speedily accommodated with a
cold buttock of beef, and a tankard of home-brewed.
And here he left him with no other light than that which
glimmered from the well-illuminated apartment within,
through a sort of shuttle which accommodated the landlord with a view into it.

This situation, inconvenient enough in itself, was, on
the present occasion, precisely what Julian would have
selected.   He wrapped himself in the weather-beaten
cloak of Lance Outram, which had been stained, by age
and weather, into a thousand variations of its original
Lincoln green ; and with as little noise as he could, set
himself to observe the two inmates, who had engrossed to
themselves the whole of the apartment, which was usually
open to the public.   They sat by a table well covered
with such costly rarities, as could only have been procured by much forecast, and prepared by the exquisite
Mons. Chaubert ; to which both seemed to do much
justice.

Julian had little difficulty in ascertaining, that one of
the travellers was, as he had anticipated, the master of
the said Chaubert, or, as he was called by Ganlesse,
Smith ; the other, who faced him, he had never seen

before. This last was dressed like a gallant of the first
order.   His periwig, indeed, as he travelled on horseback, did not much exceed in size the barwig of a modern
lawyer; but then the essence which he shook from it with
every motion, impregnated a whole apartment, which was
usually only perfumed by that vulgar herb, tobacco. His
riding-coat was laced in the newest and most courtly
style; and Grammont himself might have envied the
embroidery of his waistcoat, and the peculiar cut of his
breeches, which buttoned above the knee, permitting the
shape of a very handsome leg to be completely seen.
This, by the proprietor thereof, had been stretched out
upon a stool, and he contemplated its proportions, from
time to time, with infinite satisfaction.

The conversation between these worthies was so interesting, that we propose to assign to it another chapter.

CHAPTER XXVII.

—— This is some creature of the elements,
Most like your sea-gull. He can wheel and whistle
His screaming song, e'en when the storm is loudest—
Take for his sheeted couch the restless foam
Of the wild wave-crest—slumber in the calm,
And dally with the storm. Yet 'tis a gull,
An arrant gull, with all this.
                                    THE CHIEFTAIN.

" AND here is to thee," said the fashionable gallant whom we have described, " honest Tom; and a cup of welcome to thee out of Looby-land. Why, thou hast been so long in the country, that thou hast got a bump-kinly clod-compelling sort of look thyself. That greasy doublet fits thee as if it were thy reserved Sunday's apparel; and the points seem as if they were stay-laces bought for thy true-love Marjory. I marvel thou canst still relish a ragout. Methinks now, to a stomach bound in such a jacket, eggs and bacon were a diet more conforming."

" Rally away, my good lord, while wit lasts," answered his companion; " yours is not the sort of ammunition which will bear much expenditure. Or rather, tell me news from Court, since we have met so opportunely."

" You would have asked me these an hour ago," said the lord, " had not your very soul been under Chaubert's covered dishes. You remembered King's affairs will keep cool, and *entre-mets* must be eaten hot."

" Not so, my lord; I only kept common talk whilst that eavesdropping rascal of a landlord was in the room; so that, now the coast is clear once more, I pray you for news from Court."

" The Plot is nonsuited," answered the courtier—" Sir George Wakeman acquitted*—the witnesses discredited by the jury—Scroggs, who ranted on one side, is now ranting on t'other."

" Rat the Plot, Wakeman, witnesses, Papists, and Protestants, all together!   Do you think I care for such trash as that?—Till the Plot comes up the Palace back-stair, and gets possession of old Rowley's own imagination, I care not a farthing who believes or disbelieves.   I hang by him will bear me out."

" Well, then," said my lord, " the next news is Rochester's disgrace."

" Disgraced!—How, and for what?   The morning I came off, he stood as fair as any one."

" That's over—the epitaph † has broken his neck—and

---

* The first check received by Doctor Oates and his colleagues in the task of supporting the Plot by their testimony, was in this manner:—After a good deal of prevarication, the prime witness at length made a direct charge against Sir George Wakeman, the Queen's physician, of an attempt to poison the King, and even connected the Queen with this accusation, whom he represented as Wakeman's accomplice.   This last piece of effrontery recalled the King to some generous sentiments.   " The villains," said Charles, " think I am tired of my wife; but they shall find I will not permit an innocent woman to be persecuted."   Scroggs, the Lord Chief-Justice, accordingly received instructions to be favourable to the accused; and, for the first time, he was so.   Wakeman was acquitted, but thought it more for his safety to retire abroad.   His acquittal, however, indicated a turn of the tide, which had so long set in favour of the Plot, and of the witnesses by whom it had hitherto been supported.

† The epitaph alluded to is the celebrated epigram made by Roch-

now he may write one for his own Court favour, for it is
dead and buried."

"The epitaph!" exclaimed Tom ; "why, I was by
when it was made; and it passed for an excellent good
jest with him whom it was made upon."

"Ay, so it did amongst ourselves," answered his companion ; "but it got abroad, and had a run like a mill-
race. It was in every coffee-house, and in half the
diurnals. Grammont translated it into French too ; and
there is no laughing at so sharp a jest, when it is dinned
into your ears on all sides. So, disgraced is the author ;
and but for his Grace of Buckingham, the Court would
be as dull as my Lord Chancellor's wig."

"Or as the head it covers.—Well, my lord, the fewer
at Court, there is the more room for those that can bustle
there. But there are two mainstrings of Shaftesbury's
fiddle broken—the Popish Plot fallen into discredit—and
Rochester disgraced. Changeful times—but here is to
the little man who shall mend them."

"I apprehend you," replied his lordship; "and meet
your health with my love. Trust me, my lord loves you,
and longs for you.—Nay, I have done you reason.—By
your leave, the cup is with me. Here is to his buxom
Grace of Bucks."

"As blithe a peer," said Smith, "as ever turned night
to day. Nay, it shall be an overflowing bumper, an you

ester on Charles II. It was composed at the King's request, who nevertheless resented its poignancy.

The lines are well known:—

> "Here lies our sovereign lord the King,
>   Whose word no man relies on,
> Who never said a foolish thing,
>   And never did a wise one."

will; and I will drink it *super naculum.*—And how stands the great Madam?" *

"Stoutly against all change," answered my lord— "Little Anthony † can make nought of her."

"Then he shall bring her influence to nought. Hark in thine ear. Thou knowest "—(Here he whispered so low that Julian could not catch the sound.)

"Know him?" answered the other—"Know Ned of the Island?—To be sure I do."

"He is the man that shall knot the great fiddle-strings that have snapped. Say I told you so; and thereupon I give thee his health."

"And thereupon I pledge thee," said the young nobleman, "which on any other argument I were loath to do— thinking of Ned as somewhat the cut of a villain."

"Granted, man—granted," said the other,—"a very thorough-paced rascal; but able, my lord, able and necessary; and, in this plan, indispensable.—Pshaw!—This champagne turns stronger as it gets older, I think."

"Hark, mine honest fellow," said the courtier; "I would thou wouldst give me some item of all this mystery. Thou hast it, I know; for whom do men intrust but trusty Chiffinch?"

"It is your pleasure to say so, my lord," answered Smith, (whom we shall hereafter call by his real name of Chiffinch,) with much drunken gravity, for his speech had become a little altered by his copious libations in the course of the evening,—"few men know more, or say less, than I do; and it well becomes my station. *Conti-*

* The Duchess of Portsmouth, Charles II.'s favourite mistress; very unpopular at the time of the Popish Plot, as well from her religion as her country, being a Frenchwoman and a Catholic.

† Anthony Ashley Cooper, Earl of Shaftesbury, the politician and intriguer of the period.

cuere omnes, as the grammar hath it—all men should
learn to hold their tongue."

"Except with a friend, Tom—except with a friend.
Thou wilt never be such a dogbolt as to refuse a hint to
a friend? Come, you get too wise and statesman-like for
your office.—The ligatures of thy most peasantly jacket
there are like to burst with thy secret. Come, undo a
button, man; it is for the health of thy constitution—Let
out a reef; and let thy chosen friend know what is meditating. Thou knowest I am as true as thyself to little
Anthony, if he can but get uppermost."

"*If,* thou lordly infidel!" said Chiffinch—"talk'st thou
to me of *ifs?*—There is neither *if* nor *and* in the matter.
The great Madam shall be pulled a peg down—the great
Plot screwed a peg or two up. Thou knowest Ned?—
Honest Ned had a brother's death to revenge."

"I have heard so," said the nobleman; "and that his
persevering resentment of that injury was one of the few
points which seemed to be a sort of heathenish virtue in
him."

"Well," continued Chiffinch, "in manœuvring to bring
about this revenge, which he hath laboured at many a
day, he hath discovered a treasure."

"What!—In the Isle of Man?" said his companion.

"Assure yourself of it.—She is a creature so lovely,
that she needs but be seen to put down every one of the
favourites, from Portsmouth and Cleveland down to that
threepenny baggage, Mistress Nelly."

"By my word, Chiffinch," said my lord, "that is a reinforcement after the fashion of thine own best tactics. But
bethink thee, man! To make such a conquest, there
wants more than a cherry-cheek and a bright eye—there
must be wit—wit, man, and manners, and a little sense
besides, to keep influence when it is gotten."

"Pshaw! will you tell me what goes to this vocation?" said Chiffinch. "Here, pledge me her health in a brimmer.—Nay, you shall do it on knees, too.—Never such a triumphant beauty was seen—I went to church on purpose, for the first time these ten years—Yet I lie, it was not to church neither—it was to chapel."

"To chapel!—What the devil, is she a Puritan?" exclaimed the other courtier.

"To be sure she is. Do you think I would be accessory to bringing a Papist into favour in these times, when, as my good Lord said in the House, there should not be a Popish man-servant, nor a Popish maid-servant, not so much as dog or cat, left to bark or mew about the King!"*

"But consider, Chiffie, the dislikelihood of her pleasing," said the noble courtier.—"What! old Rowley, with his wit, and love of wit—his wildness, and love of wildness—he form a league with a silly, scrupulous, unidea'd Puritan!—Not if she were Venus."

"Thou knowest nought of the matter," answered Chiffinch. "I tell thee, the fine contrast between the seeming saint and falling sinner will give zest to the old gentleman's inclinations. If I do not know him, who does?—Her health, my lord, on your bare knee, as you would live to be of the bedchamber."

"I pledge you most devoutly," answered his friend. "But you have not told me how the acquaintance is to be made; for you cannot, I think, carry her to Whitehall."

"Aha, my dear lord, you would have the whole secret! but that I cannot afford—I can spare a friend a peep at my ends, but no one must look on the means by which

* Such was the extravagance of Shaftesbury's eloquence.

they are achieved."—So saying, he shook his drunken head most wisely.

The villainous design which this discourse implied, and which his heart told him was designed against Alice Bridgenorth, stirred Julian so extremely, that he involuntarily shifted his posture, and laid his hand on his sword hilt.

Chiffinch heard a rustling, and broke off, exclaiming, " Hark !—Zounds, something moved—I trust I have told the tale to no ears but thine."

" I will cut off any which have drunk in but a syllable of thy words," said the nobleman ; and raising a candle, he took a hasty survey of the apartment. Seeing nothing that could incur his menaced resentment, he replaced the light and continued :—" Well, suppose the Belle Louise de Querouaille * shoots from her high station in the firmament, how will you rear up the downfallen Plot again— for without that same Plot, think of it as thou wilt, we have no change of hands—and matters remain as they were, with a Protestant courtezan instead of a Papist— Little Anthony can but little speed without that Plot of his—I believe, in my conscience, he begot it himself." †

" Whoever begot it," said Chiffinch, " he hath adopted it ; and a thriving babe it has been to him. Well, then, though it lies out of my way, I will play Saint Peter again—up with t' other key, and unlock t' other mystery."

" Now thou speakest like a good fellow ; and I will, with my own hands, unwire this fresh flask, to begin a brimmer to the success of thy achievement."

* Charles's principal mistress *en titre*. She was created Duchess of Portsmouth.

† Shaftesbury himself is supposed to have said that he knew not who was the inventor of the Plot, but that he himself had all the advantage of the discovery.

" Well, then," continued the communicative Chiffinch,
"thou knowest that they have long had a nibbling at the
old Countess of Derby.—So Ned was sent down—he
owes her an old accompt, thou knowest—with private
instructions to possess himself of the island, if he could,
by help of some of his old friends. He hath ever kept
up spies upon her; and happy man was he, to think his
hour of vengeance was come so nigh. But he missed his
blow; and the old girl being placed on her guard, was
soon in a condition to make Ned smoke for it. Out of the
island he came with little advantage for having entered
it; when, by some means—for the devil, I think, stands
ever his friend—he obtained information concerning a
messenger, whom her old Majesty of Man had sent to
London to make party in her behalf. Ned stuck himself
to this fellow—a raw, half-bred lad, son of an old blundering Cavalier of the old stamp, down in Derbyshire—
and so managed the swain, that he brought him to the
place where I was waiting, in anxious expectation of the
pretty one I told you of. By Saint Anthony, for I will
swear by no meaner oath, I stared when I saw this great
lout—not that the fellow is so ill-looked neither—I stared
like—like—good now, help me to a simile."

" Like Saint Anthony's pig, an it were sleek," said the
young lord; "your eyes, Chiffie, have the very blink of
one. But what hath all this to do with the Plot? Hold,
I have had wine enough."

" You shall not baulk me," said Chiffinch; and a
jingling was heard, as if he were filling his comrade's
glass with a very unsteady hand. " Hey—What the
devil is the matter?—I used to carry my glass steady—
very steady."

" Well, but this stranger? "

"Why, he swept at game and ragout as he would at spring beef or summer mutton. Never saw so unnurtured a cub—Knew no more what he eat than an infidel—I cursed him by my gods when I saw Chaubert's chef-d'œuvres glutted down so indifferent a throat. We took the freedom to spice his goblet a little, and ease him of his packet of letters; and the fool went on his way the next morning with a budget artificially filled with gray paper. Ned would have kept him, in hopes to have made a witness of him, but the boy was not of that mettle."

"How will you prove your letters?" said the courtier.

"La you there, my lord," said Chiffinch; "one may see with half an eye, for all your laced doublet, that you have been of the family of Furnival's, before your brother's death sent you to Court. How prove the letters?—Why, we have but let the sparrow fly with a string round his foot.—We have him again so soon as we list."

"Why, thou art turned a very Machiavel, Chiffinch," said his friend. "But how if the youth proved restive?—I have heard these Peak men have hot heads and hard hands."

"Trouble not yourself—that was cared for, my lord," said Chiffinch—"his pistols might bark, but they could not bite."

"Most exquisite Chiffinch, thou art turned micher as well as padder—Canst both rob a man and kidnap him!"

"Micher and padder—what terms be these?" said Chiffinch. "Methinks these are sounds to lug out upon. You will have me angry to the degree of falling foul—robber and kidnapper!"

"You mistake verb for noun-substantive," replied his lordship; "I said *rob* and *kidnap*—a man may do either once and away without being professional."

" But not without spilling a little foolish noble blood, or some such red-coloured gear," said Chiffinch, starting up.

" O yes," said his lordship; " all this may be without these direful consequences, and so you will find to-morrow, when you return to England; for at present you are in the land of Champagne, Chiffie; and that you may continue so, I drink thee this parting cup to line thy nightcap."

" I do not refuse your pledge," said Chiffinch; " but I drink to thee in dudgeon and in hostility—It is a cup of wrath, and a gage of battle. To-morrow, by dawn, I will have thee at point of fox, wert thou the last of the Savilles.—What the devil! think you I fear you because you are a lord?"

" Not so, Chiffinch," answered his companion. " I know thou fearest nothing but beans and bacon, washed down with bumpkin-like beer.—Adieu, sweet Chiffinch—to bed —Chiffinch—to bed."

So saying, he lifted a candle, and left the apartment. And Chiffinch, whom the last draught had nearly overpowered, had just strength enough left to do the same, muttering, as he staggered out, " Yes, he shall answer it. —Dawn of day? D—n me—It is come already—Yonder's the dawn—No, d—n me, 'tis the fire glancing on the cursed red lattice—I am whistled drunk, I think— This comes of a country inn—It is the smell of the brandy in this cursed room—It could not be the wine—Well, old Rowley shall send me no more errands to the country again—Steady, steady."

So saying, he reeled out of the apartment, leaving Peveril to think over the extraordinary conversation he had just heard.

The name of Chiffinch, the well-known minister of

Charles's pleasures, was nearly allied to the part which he seemed about to play in the present intrigue; but that Christian, whom he had always supposed a Puritan as strict as his brother-in-law, Bridgenorth, should be associated with him in a plot so infamous, seemed alike unnatural and monstrous. The near relationship might blind Bridgenorth, and warrant him in confiding his daughter to such a man's charge; but what a wretch he must be, that could coolly meditate such an ignominious abuse of his trust! In doubt whether he could credit for a moment the tale which Chiffinch had revealed, he hastily examined his packet, and found that the sealskin case in which it had been wrapt up, now only contained an equal quantity of waste paper. If he had wanted further confirmation, the failure of the shot which he had fired at Bridgenorth, and of which the wadding only struck him, showed that his arms had been tampered with. He examined the pistol which still remained charged, and found that the ball had been drawn. "May I perish," said he to himself, "amid these villainous intrigues, but thou shalt be more surely loaded, and to better purpose! The contents of these papers may undo my benefactress —their having been found on me, may ruin my father— that I have been the bearer of them, may cost, in these fiery times, my own life—that I care least for—they form a branch of the scheme laid against the honour and happiness of a creature so innocent, that it is almost sin to think of her within the neighbourhood of such infamous knaves. I will recover the letters at all risks—But how? —that is to be thought on.—Lance is stout and trusty; and when a bold deed is once resolved upon, there never yet lacked the means of executing it."

His host now entered, with an apology for his long

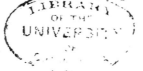

absence; and after providing Peveril with some refreshments, invited him to accept, for his night-quarters, the accommodation of a remote hay-loft, which he was to share with his comrade; professing, at the same time, he could hardly have afforded them this courtesy, but out of deference to the exquisite talents of Lance Outram, as assistant at the tap; where, indeed, it seems probable that he, as well as the admiring landlord, did that evening contrive to drink nearly as much liquor as they drew.

But Lance was a seasoned vessel, on whom liquor made no lasting impression; so that when Peveril awaked that trusty follower at dawn, he found him cool enough to comprehend and enter into the design which he expressed, of recovering the letters which had been abstracted from his person.

Having considered the whole matter with much attention, Lance shrugged, grinned, and scratched his head; and at length manfully expressed his resolution. " Well, my naunt speaks truth in her old saw,—

' He that serves Peveril munna be slack,
Neither for weather, nor yet for wrack.'

And then again, my good dame was wont to say, that whenever Peveril was in a broil, Outram was in a stew; so I will never bear a base mind, but even hold a part with you as my fathers have done with yours, for four generations, whatever more."

" Spoken like a most gallant Outram," said Julian; "and were we but rid of that puppy lord and his retinue, we two could easily deal with the other three."

" Two Londoners and a Frenchman?" said Lance,— " I would take them in mine own hand. And as for my Lord Saville, as they call him, I heard word last night

that he and all his men of gilded gingerbread
at an honest fellow like me, as if they were the ore and I
the dross—are all to be off this morning to some races,
or such like junketings, about Tutbury.   It was that
brought him down here, where he met this other civet-
cat by accident."

In truth, even as Lance spoke, a trampling was heard
of horses in the yard; and from the hatch of their hay-
loft they beheld Lord Saville's attendants mustered, and
ready to set out so soon as he should make his appearance.

"So ho, Master Jeremy," said one of the fellows, to a
sort of principal attendant, who just came out of the
house, "methinks the wine has proved a sleeping cup to
my lord this morning."

"No," answered Jeremy, "he hath been up before
light writing letters for London; and to punish thy ir-
reverence, thou, Jonathan, shalt be the man to ride back
with them."

"And so to miss the race?" said Jonathan, sulkily;
"I thank you for this good turn, good Master Jeremy;
and hang me if I forget it."

Further discussion was cut short by the appearance
of the young nobleman, who, as he came out of the inn,
said to Jeremy, "These be the letters.   Let one of the
knaves ride to London for life and death, and deliver
them as directed; and the rest of them get to horse and
follow me."

Jeremy gave Jonathan the packet with a malicious
smile; and the disappointed groom turned his horse's
head sullenly towards London, while Lord Saville, and
the rest of his retinue, rode briskly off in an opposite
direction pursued by the benedictions of the host and his

family, who stood bowing and courtesying at the door, in gratitude, doubtless, for the receipt of an unconscionable reckoning.

It was full three hours after their departure, that Chiffinch lounged into the room in which they had supped, in a brocade nightgown, and green velvet cap, turned up with the most costly Brussels lace. He seemed but half awake; and it was with drowsy voice that he called for a cup of cold small beer. His manner and appearance were those of a man who had wrestled hard with Bacchus on the preceding evening, and had scarce recovered the effects of his contest with the jolly god. Lance, instructed by his master, to watch the motions of the courtier, officiously attended with the cooling beverage he called for, pleading, as an excuse to the landlord, his wish to see a Londoner in his morning-gown and cap.

No sooner had Chiffinch taken his morning draught, than he inquired after Lord Saville.

"His lordship was mounted and away by peep of dawn," was Lance's reply.

"What, the devil!" exclaimed Chiffinch; "why, this is scarce civil.—What! off for the races with his whole retinue?"

"All but one," replied Lance, "whom his lordship sent back to London with letters."

"To London with letters!" said Chiffinch. "Why, I am for London, and could have saved his express a labour.—But stop—hold—I begin to recollect—d——n, can I have blabbed?—I have—I have—I remember it all now—I have blabbed; and to the very weazel of the Court, who sucks the yelk out of every man's secret. Furies and fire—that my afternoons should ruin my mornings thus!—I must turn boon companion and good

fellow in my cups—and have my confidences and my
quarrels—my friends and my enemies, with a plague to
me, as if any one could do a man much good or harm but
his own self. His messenger must be stopped, though—
I will put a spoke in his wheel.—Hark ye, drawer-fellow
—call my groom hither—call Tom Beacon."

Lance obeyed; but failed not, when he had introduced
the domestic, to remain in the apartment, in order to hear
what should pass betwixt him and his master.

"Hark ye, Tom," said Chiffinch, " here are five pieces
for you."

" What's to be done now, I trow?" said Tom, without
even the ceremony of returning thanks, which he was
probably well aware would not be received even in part
payment of the debt he was incurring.

" Mount your fleet nag, Tom—ride like the devil—
overtake the groom whom Lord Saville despatched to
London this morning—lame his horse—break his bones
—fill him as drunk as the Baltic sea; or do whatever
may best and most effectually stop his journey.—Why
does the lout stand there without answering me? Dost
understand me?"

" Why, ay, Master Chiffinch," said Tom; "and so I am
thinking doth this honest man here, who need not have
heard quite so much of your counsel, and it had been
your will."

" I am bewitched this morning," said Chiffinch to himself, " or else the champagne runs in my head still. My
brain has become the very lowlands of Holland—a gill-
cup would inundate it—Hark thee, fellow," he added,
addressing Lance, "keep my counsel—there is a wager
betwixt Lord Saville and me, which of us shall first have
a letter in London. Here is to drink my health, and

bring luck on my side. Say nothing of it.; but help Tom to his nag.—Tom, ere thou startest come for thy credentials—I will give thee a letter to the Duke of Bucks, that may be evidence thou wert first in town."

Tom Beacon ducked and exit; and Lance, after having made some show of helping him to horse, ran back to tell his master the joyful intelligence, that a lucky accident had abated Chiffinch's party to their own number.

Peveril immediately ordered his horses to be got ready; and, so soon as Tom Beacon was despatched towards London, on a rapid trot, had the satisfaction to observe Chiffinch, with his favourite Chaubert, mount to pursue the same journey, though at a more moderate rate. He permitted them to attain such a distance, that they might be dogged without suspicion; then paid his reckoning, mounted his horse, and followed, keeping his men carefully in view, until he should come to a place proper for the enterprise which he meditated.

It had been Peveril's intention, that when they came to some solitary part of the road, they should gradually mend their pace, until they overtook Chaubert—that Lance Outram should then drop behind, in order to assail the man of spits and stoves, while he himself spurring onwards, should grapple with Chiffinch. But this scheme presupposed that the master and servant should travel in the usual manner—the latter riding a few yards behind the former. Whereas, such and so interesting were the subjects of discussion betwixt Chiffinch and the French cook, that, without heeding the rules of etiquette, they rode on together, amicably abreast, carrying on a conversation on the mysteries of the table, which the ancient Comus, or a modern gastronome, might have listened to with pleasure. It was therefore necessary to venture on them both at once.

For this purpose, when they saw a long tract of road before them, unvaried by the least appearance of man, beast, or human habitation, they began to mend their pace, that they might come up to Chiffinch, without giving him any alarm, by a sudden and suspicious increase of haste. In this manner they lessened the distance which separated them till they were within about twenty yards, when Peveril, afraid that Chiffinch might recognise him at a nearer approach, and so trust to his horse's heels, made Lance the signal to charge.

At the sudden increase of their speed, and the noise with which it was necessarily attended, Chiffinch looked around, but had time to do no more, for Lance, who had pricked his pony (which was much more speedy than Julian's horse) into full gallop, pushed, without ceremony, betwixt the courtier and his attendant; and ere Chaubert had time for more than one exclamation, he upset both horse and Frenchman,—*mortbleu!* thrilling from his tongue as he rolled on the ground amongst the various articles of his occupation, which, escaping from the budget in which he bore them, lay tumbled upon the highway in strange disorder; while Lance, springing from his palfrey, commanded his foeman to be still, under no less a penalty than that of death, if he attempted to rise.

Before Chiffinch could avenge his trusty follower's downfall, his own bridle was seized by Julian, who presented a pistol with the other hand, and commanded him to stand or die.

Chiffinch, though effeminate, was no coward. He stood still as commanded, and said, with firmness, "·Rogue, you have taken me at surprise. If you are a highwayman, there is my purse. Do us no bodily harm, and spare the budget of spices and sauces."

"Look you, Master Chiffinch," said Peveril, "this is no time for dallying. I am no highwayman, but a man of honour. Give me back that packet which you stole from me the other night; or, by all that is good, I will send a brace of balls through you, and search for it at leisure."

"What night?—What packet?" answered Chiffinch, confused; yet willing to protract the time for the chance of assistance, or to put Peveril off his guard. "I know nothing of what you mean. If you are a man of honour, let me draw my sword, and I will do you right, as a gentleman should do to another."

"Dishonourable rascal!" said Peveril, "you escape not in this manner. You plundered me when you had me at odds; and I am not the fool to let my advantage escape, now that my turn is come. Yield up the packet; and then, if you will, I will fight you on equal terms. But first," he reiterated, "yield up the packet, or I will instantly send you where the tenor of your life will be hard to answer for."

The tone of Peveril's voice, the fierceness of his eye, and the manner in which he held the loaded weapon, within a hand's-breadth of Chiffinch's head, convinced the last there was neither room for compromise, nor time for trifling. He thrust his hand into a side-pocket of his cloak, and with visible reluctance, produced those papers and dispatches with which Julian had been intrusted by the Countess of Derby.

"They are five in number," said Julian; "and you have given me only four. Your life depends on full restitution."

"It escaped from my hand," said Chiffinch, producing the missing document—"There it is. Now, sir, your

pleasure is fulfilled, unless," he added sulkily, " you design either murder or farther robbery."

" Base wretch!" said Peveril, withdrawing his pistol,
yet keeping a watchful eye on Chiffinch's motions, " thou
art unworthy any honest man's sword; and yet, if you
dare draw your own, as you proposed but now, I am
willing to give you a chance upon fair equality of terms."

" Equality!" said Chiffinch, sneeringly; " yes, a proper
equality—sword and pistol against single rapier, and two
men upon one, for Chaubert is no fighter. No, sir; I
shall seek amends upon some more fitting occasion, and
with more equal weapons."

" By backbiting, or by poison, base pander!" said
Julian; " these are thy means of vengeance. But mark
me—I know your vile purpose respecting a lady who is
too worthy that her name should be uttered in such a
worthless ear. Thou hast done me one injury, and thou
see'st I have repaid it. But prosecute this farther villainy, and be assured I will put thee to death like a foul
reptile, whose very slaver is fatal to humanity. Rely
upon this, as if Machiavel had sworn it; for so surely as
you keep your purpose, so surely will I prosecute my
revenge.—Follow me, Lance, and leave him to think on
what I have told him."

Lance had, after the first shock, sustained a very easy
part in this rencontre; for all he had to do, was to point
the butt of his whip, in the manner of a gun, at the intimidated Frenchman, who, lying on his back, and gazing
at random on the skies, had as little the power or purpose
of resistance, as any pig which had ever come under his
own slaughter-knife.

Summoned by his master from the easy duty of guard-
ing such an unresisting prisoner, Lance remounted his

horsè, and they both rode off, leaving their discomfited antagonists to console themselves for their misadventure as they best could. But consolation was hard to come by in the circumstances. The French artist had to lament the dispersion of his spices, and the destruction of his magazine of sauces—an enchanter despoiled of his magic wand and talisman, could scarce have been in more desperate extremity. Chiffinch had to mourn the downfall of his intrigue, and its premature discovery; "To this fellow, at least," he thought, "I can have bragged none—here my evil genius alone has betrayed me. With this infernal discovery, which may cost me so dear on all hands, champagne had nought to do. If there be a flask left unbroken, I will drink it after dinner, and try if it may not even yet suggest some scheme of redemption and of revenge."

With this manly resolution, he prosecuted his journey to London.

CHAPTER XXVIII.

A man so various, that he seem'd to be
Not one, but all mankind's epitome;
Stiff in opinions—always in the wrong—
Was every thing by starts, but nothing long;
Who, in the course of one revolving moon,
Was chemist, fiddler, statesman, and buffoon;
Then, all for women, painting, fiddling, drinking,
Besides a thousand freaks that died in thinking.

DRYDEN.

WE must now transport the reader to the magnificent hotel in —— Street, inhabited at this time by the celebrated George Villiers, Duke of Buckingham, whom Dryden has doomed to a painful immortality by the few lines which we have prefixed to this chapter. Amid the gay and the licentious of the laughing Court of Charles, the Duke was the most licentious and most gay; yet, while expending a princely fortune, a strong constitution, and excellent talents, in pursuit of frivolous pleasures, he nevertheless nourished deeper and more extensive designs; in which he only failed from want of that fixed purpose and regulated perseverance essential to all important enterprises, but particularly in politics.

It was long past noon; and the usual hour of the Duke's levee—if any thing could be termed usual where all was irregular—had been long past. His hall was filled with lackeys and footmen, in the most splendid liveries; the interior apartments, with the gentlemen and

pages of his household, arrayed as persons of the first
quality, and, in that respect, rather exceeding than falling short of the Duke in personal splendour.   But his
antechamber, in particular, might be compared to a
gathering of eagles to the slaughter, were not the simile
too dignified to express that vile race, who, by a hundred
devices all tending to one common end, live upon the
wants of needy greatness, or administer to the pleasures
of summer-teeming luxury, or stimulate the wild wishes
of lavish and wasteful extravagance, by devising new
modes and fresh motives of profusion.   There stood the
projector, with his mysterious brow, promising unbounded
wealth to whomsoever might choose to furnish the small
preliminary sum necessary to change egg-shells into the
great *arcanum*.   There was Captain Seagull, undertaker
for a foreign settlement, with the map under his arm of
Indian or American kingdoms, beautiful as the primitive
Eden, waiting the bold occupants, for whom a generous
patron should equip two brigantines and a fly-boat.
Thither came, fast and frequent, the gamesters, in their
different forms and calling.   This, light, young, gay in
appearance, the thoughtless youth of wit and pleasure—
the pigeon rather than the rook—but at heart the same
sly, shrewd, cold-blooded calculator, as yonder old hard-
featured professor of the same science, whose eyes are
grown dim with watching the dice at midnight; and
whose fingers are even now assisting his mental compu-
tation of chances and of odds.   The fine arts, too—I
would it were otherwise—have their professors amongst
this sordid train.   The poor poet, half ashamed, in spite
of habit, of the part which he is about to perform, and
abashed by consciousness at once of his base motive and
his shabby black coat, lurks in yonder corner for the

favourable moment to offer his dedication. Much better attired, the architect presents his splendid vision of front and wings, and designs a palace, the expense of which may transfer his employer to a jail. But uppermost of all, the favourite musician, or singer, who waits on my lord to receive, in solid gold, the value of the dulcet sounds, which solaced the banquet of the preceding evening.

Such, and many such like, were the morning attendants of the Duke of Buckingham—all genuine descendants of the daughter of the horse-leech, whose cry is " Give, give."

But the levee of his Grace contained other and very different characters ; and was indeed as various as his own opinions and pursuits. Besides many of the young nobility and wealthy gentry of England, who made his Grace the glass at which they dressed themselves for the day, and who learned from him how to travel, with the newest and best grace, the general Road to Ruin ; there were others of a graver character—discarded statesmen, political spies, opposition orators, servile tools of administration, men who met not elsewhere, but who regarded the Duke's mansion as a sort of neutral ground ; sure, that if he was not of their opinion to-day, this very circumstance rendered it most likely he should think with them to-morrow. The Puritans themselves did not shun intercourse with a man whose talents must have rendered him formidable, even if they had not been united with high rank and an immense fortune. Several grave personages, with black suits, short cloaks, and band-strings of a formal cut, were mingled, as we see their portraits in a gallery of paintings, among the gallants who ruffled in silk and embroidery. It is true, they escaped the scandal of being thought intimates of the Duke, by their business being supposed to refer to money matters. Whether these grave and professing citizens mixed politics with money-lending, was not known; but it had been long observed, that the Jews, who in general confine themselves to the latter department, had become for some time faithful attendants at the Duke's levee.

It was high-tide in the antechamber, and had been so for more than an hour, ere the Duke's gentleman in ordinary ventured into his bedchamber, carefully darkened, so as to make midnight at noon-day, to know his Grace's pleasure. His soft and serene whisper, in which he asked whether it were his Grace's pleasure to rise, was briefly and sharply answered by the counter questions, " Who waits?—What's o'clock?"

" It is Jerningham, your Grace," said the attendant. " It is one, afternoon; and your Grace appointed some of the people without at eleven."

" Who are they?—What do they want?"

" A message from Whitehall, your Grace."

" Pshaw! it will keep cold. Those who make all others wait, will be the better of waiting in their turn. Were I to be guilty of ill-breeding, it should rather be to a King than a beggar."

" The gentlemen from the city."

" I am tired of them—tired of their all cant, and no religion—all Protestantism, and no charity. Tell them to go to Shaftesbury—to Aldersgate Street with them— that's the best market for their wares."

" Jockey, my lord, from Newmarket."

" Let him ride to the devil—he has horse of mine, and spurs of his own. Any more?"

" The whole antechamber is full, my lord—knights and squires, doctors and dicers."

"The dicers, with their doctors * in their pockets, I presume."

"Counts, captains, and clergymen."

"You are alliterative, Jerningham," said the Duke; "and that is a proof you are poetical. Hand me my writing things."

Getting half out of bed—thrusting one arm into a brocade nightgown, deeply furred with sables, and one foot into a velvet slipper, while the other pressed in primitive nudity the rich carpet—his Grace, without thinking farther on the assembly without, began to pen a few lines of a satirical poem; then suddenly stopped—threw the pen into the chimney—exclaimed that the humour was past—and asked his attendant if there were any letters. Jerningham produced a huge packet.

"What the devil!" said his Grace, "do you think I will read all these? I am like Clarence, who asked a cup of wine, and was soused into a butt of sack. I mean, is there any thing which presses?"

"This letter, your Grace," said Jerningham, "concerning the Yorkshire mortgage."

"Did I not bid thee carry it to old Gatheral, my steward?"

"I did, my lord," answered the other; "but Gatheral says there are difficulties."

"Let the usurers foreclose, then—there is no difficulty in that; and out of a hundred manors I shall scarce miss one," answered the Duke. "And hark ye, bring me my chocolate."

"Nay, my lord, Gatheral does not say it is impossible —only difficult."

"And what is the use of him, if he cannot make it

* Doctor, a cant name for false dice.

easy? But you are all born to make difficulties," replied
the Duke.

"Nay, if your Grace approves the terms in this
schedule, and pleases to sign it, Gatheral will undertake
for the matter," answered Jerningham.

"And could you not have said so at first, you blockhead?" said the Duke, signing the paper without looking
at the contents—"What other letters? And remember,
I must be plagued with no more business."

"Billets-doux, my lord—five or six of them. This left
at the porter's lodge by a vizard mask."

"Pshaw!" answered the Duke, tossing them over,
while his attendant assisted in dressing him—"an acquaintance of a quarter's standing."

"This given to one of the pages by my Lady ——'s
waiting-woman."

"Plague on it—a Jeremiade on the subject of perjury
and treachery, and not a single new line to the old tune,"
said the Duke, glancing over the billet. "Here is the
old cant—*cruel man—broken vows—Heaven's just revenge.* Why, the woman is thinking of murder—not of
love. No one should pretend to write upon so threadbare a topic without having at least some novelty of expression. *The despairing Araminta*—Lie there, fair
desperate. And this—how comes it?"

"Flung into the window of the hall, by a fellow who
ran off at full speed," answered Jerningham.

"This is a better text," said the Duke; "and yet it is
an old one too—three weeks old at least—The little
Countess with the jealous lord—I should not care a
farthing for her, save for that same jealous lord—
Plague on't, and he's gone down to the country—*this
evening—in silence and safety—written with a quill*

pulled from the wing of Cupid—Your ladyship has left him pen-feathers enough to fly away with—better clipped his wings when you had caught him, my lady—And *so confident of her Buckingham's faith,*—I hate confidence in a young person—She must be taught better—I will not go."

"Your Grace will not be so cruel!" said Jerningham.

"Thou art a compassionate fellow, Jerningham; but conceit must be punished."

"But if your lordship should resume your fancy for her?"

"Why, then, you must swear the billet-doux miscarried," answered the Duke. "And stay, a thought strikes me—it shall miscarry in great style. Hark ye—Is—what is the fellow's name—the poet—is he yonder?"

"There are six gentlemen, sir, who, from the reams of paper in their pocket, and the threadbare seams at their elbows, appear to wear the livery of the Muses."

"Poetical once more, Jerningham. He, I mean, who wrote the last lampoon," said the Duke.

"To whom your Grace said you owed five pieces and a beating?" replied Jerningham.

"The money for his satire, and the cudgel for his praise—Good—find him—give him the five pieces, and thrust the Countess's billet-doux—Hold—take Araminta's and the rest of them—thrust them all into his portfolio—All will come out at the Wit's Coffee-house; and if the promulgator be not cudgelled into all the colours of the rainbow, there is no spite in woman, no faith in crabtree, or pith in heart of oak—Araminta's wrath alone would overburden one pair of mortal shoulders."

" But, my Lord Duke," said his attendant, " this Settle * is so dull a rascal, that nothing he can write will take."

" Then as we have given him steel to head the arrow," said the Duke, " we will give him wings to waft it with— wood, he has enough of his own to make a shaft or bolt of. Hand me my own unfinished lampoon—give it to him with the letters—let him make what he can of them all."

" My Lord Duke—I crave pardon—but your Grace's style will be discovered; and though the ladies' names are not at the letters, yet they will be traced."

" I would have it so, you blockhead. Have you lived with me so long, and cannot discover that the eclat of an intrigue is, with me, worth all the rest of it ? "

" But the danger, my Lord Duke ? " replied Jerning-ham. " There are husbands, brothers, friends, whose revenge may be awakened."

" And beaten to sleep again," said Buckingham haughtily. " I have Black Will and his cudgel for plebeian grumblers ; and those of quality I can deal with myself. I lack breathing and exercise of late." †

---

* Elkana Settle, the unworthy scribbler whom the envy of Rochester and others tried to raise to public estimation, as a rival to Dryden; a circumstance which has been the means of elevating him to a very painful species of immortality.

† It was the unworthy distinction of men of wit and honour about town, to revenge their own quarrels with inferior persons by the hands of bravoes. Even in the days of chivalry, the knights, as may be learned from Don Quixote, turned over to the chastisement of their squires such adversaries as were not dubb'd; and thus it was not unusual for men of quality in Charles II.'s time, to avenge their wrongs by means of private assassination. Rochester writes composedly concerning a satire imputed to Dryden, but in reality composed by Mulgrave. " If he falls upon me with the blunt, which is

" But yet your Grace "——

" Hold your peace, fool ! I tell you that your poor
dwarfish spirit cannot measure the scope of mine.   I tell
thee I would have the course of my life a torrent—I am
weary of easy achievements, and wish for obstacles, that
I can sweep before my irresistible course."

Another gentleman now entered the apartment.   " I
humbly crave your Grace's pardon," he said ; " but Master Christian . is so importunate for admission instantly,
that I am obliged to take your Grace's pleasure."

" Tell him to call three hours hence.   Damn his politic
pate, that would make all men dance after his pipe ! "

" I thank you for the compliment, my Lord Duke,"
said Christian, entering the apartment in somewhat a
more courtly garb, but with the same unpretending and
undistinguished mien, and in the same placid and indifferent manner with which he had accosted Julian Peveril
upon different occasions during his journey to London.
" It is precisely my present object to pipe to you ; and
you may dance to your own profit, if you will."

" On my word, Master Christian," said the Duke,
haughtily, " the affair should be weighty, that removes
ceremony so entirely from betwixt us.   If it relates to
the subject of our last conversation, I must request our
interview be postponed to some farther opportunity.   I
am engaged in an affair of some weight."   Then turning
his back on Christian, he went on with his conversation
with Jerningham.   " Find the person you wot of, and

his very good weapon in wit, I will forgive him, if you please, and
leave the repartee to Black Will with a cudgel."   And, in conformity
with this cowardly and brutal intimation, that distinguished poet was
waylaid and beaten severely in Rose Street, Covent Garden, by ruffians who could not be discovered, but whom all concluded to be the
agents of Rochester's mean revenge.

give him the papers; and hark ye, give him this gold to pay for the shaft of his arrow—the steel-head and peacock's wing we have already provided."

"This is all well, my lord," said Christian, calmly, and taking his seat at the same time in an easy-chair at some distance; "but your Grace's levity is no match for my equanimity. It is necessary I should speak with you; and I will await your Grace's leisure in the apartment."

"*Very* well, sir, said the Duke, peevishly; "if an evil is to be undergone, the sooner it is over the better—I can take measures to prevent its being renewed. So let me hear your errand without farther delay."

"I will wait till your Grace's toilette is completed," said Christian, with the indifferent tone which was natural to him. "What I have to say must be between ourselves."

"Begone, Jerningham; and remain without till I call. Leave my doublet on the couch.—How now, I have worn this cloth of silver a hundred times."

"Only twice, if it please your Grace," replied Jerningham.

"As well twenty times—keep it for yourself, or give it to my valet, if you are too proud of your gentility."

"Your Grace has made better men than me wear your cast clothes," said Jerningham, submissively.

"Thou art sharp, Jerningham," said the Duke—"in one sense I have, and I may again. So now, that pearl-coloured thing will do with the ribbon and George. Get away with thee.—And now that he is gone, Master Christian, may I once more crave your pleasure?"

"My Lord Duke," said Christian, "you are a worshipper of difficulties in state affairs, as in love matters."

"I trust you have been no eavesdropper, Master Christian," replied the Duke ; " it scarce argues the respect due to me, or to my roof."

" I know not what you mean, my lord," replied Christian.

" Nay, I care not if the whole world heard what I said but now to Jerningham. But to the matter," replied the Duke of Buckingham.

" Your Grace is so much occupied with conquests over the fair and over the witty, that you have perhaps forgotten what a stake you have in the little Island of Man."

" Not a whit, Master Christian. I remember well enough that my roundheaded father-in-law, Fairfax, had the island from the Long Parliament; and was ass enough to quit hold of it at the Restoration, when, if he had closed his clutches, and held fast, like a true bird of prey, as he should have done, he might have kept it for him and his. It had been a rare thing to have had a little kingdom—made laws of my own—had my Chamberlain with his white staff—I would have taught Jerningham, in half a day, to look as wise, walk as stiffly, and speak as sillily, as Harry Bennet." *

" You might have done this, and more, if it had pleased your Grace."

" Ay, and if it had pleased my Grace, thou, Ned

* Bennet, Earl of Arlington, was one of Charles's most attached courtiers during his exile. After the Restoration, he was employed in the ministry, and the name of Bennet supplies its initial B to the celebrated word Cabal, but the King was supposed to have lost respect for him; and several persons at Court took the liberty to mimic his person and behaviour, which was stiff and formal. Thus it was a common jest for some courtier to put a black patch on his nose, and strut about with a white staff in his hand, to make the King merry. But, notwithstanding, he retained his office of Lord Chamberlain and his seat in the Privy Council, till his death in 1685.

Christian, shouldst have been the Jack Ketch of my dominions."

"*I* your Jack Ketch, my lord?" said Christian, more in a tone of surprise than of displeasure.

"Why, ay ; thou hast been perpetually intriguing against the life of yonder poor old woman. It were a kingdom to thee to gratify thy spleen with thy own hands."

" I only seek justice against the Countess," said Christian.

" And the end of justice is always a gibbet," said the Duke.

" Be it so," answered Christian. " Well, the Countess is in the Plot."

" The devil confound the Plot, as I believe he first invented it ! " said the Duke of Buckingham ; " I have heard of nothing else for months. If one must go to hell, I would it were by some new road, and in gentlemen's company. I should not like to travel with Oates, Bedlow, and the rest of that famous cloud of witnesses."

" Your Grace is then resolved to forego all the advantages which may arise? If the House of Derby fall under forfeiture, the grant to Fairfax, now worthily represented by your Duchess, revives, and you become the Lord and Sovereign of Man."

" In right of a woman," said the Duke ; " but, in troth, my godly dame owes me some advantage for having lived the first year of our marriage with her and old Black Tom, her grim, fighting, puritanic father. A man might as well have married the Devil's daughter, and set up house-keeping with his father-in-law." *

* Mary, daughter of Thomas, Lord Fairfax, was wedded to the

"I understand you are willing, then, to join your interest for a heave at the House of Derby, my Lord Duke?"

"As they are unlawfully possessed of my wife's kingdom, they certainly can expect no favour at my hand. But thou knowest there is an interest at Whitehall predominant over mine."

"That is only by your Grace's sufferance," said Christian.

"No, no; I tell thee a hundred times, no," said the Duke, rousing himself to anger at the recollection. "I tell thee that base courtezan, the Duchess of Portsmouth, hath impudently set herself to thwart and contradict me; and Charles has given me both cloudy looks and hard words before the Court. I would he could but guess what is the offence between her and me! I would he knew but that! But I will have her plumes plucked, or my name is not Villiers. A worthless French fille-de-joie to brave me thus!—Christian, thou art right; there is no passion so spirit-stirring as revenge. I will patronize the Plot, if it be but to spite her, and make it impossible for the King to uphold her."

As the Duke spoke, he gradually wrought himself into a passion, and traversed the apartment with as much vehemence as if the only object he had on earth was to deprive the Duchess of her power and favour with the King. Christian smiled internally to see him approaching the state of mind in which he was most easily worked upon, and judiciously kept silence, until the Duke called out to him, in a pet, "Well, Sir Oracle, you that have laid so many schemes to supplant this she-wolf of Gaul,

Duke of Buckingham, whose versatility made him capable of rendering himself for a time as agreeable to his father-in-law, though a rigid Presbyterian, as to the gay Charles II.

where are all your contrivances now?—Where is the exquisite beauty who was to catch the Sovereign's eye at the first glance?—Chiffinch, hath he seen her?—and what does he say, that exquisite critic in beauty and blanc-mange, women and wine?"

"He has *seen* and approves, but has not yet heard her; and her speech answers to all the rest. We came here yesterday; and to-day I intend to introduce Chiffinch to her, the instant he arrives from the country; and I expect him every hour. I am but afraid of the damsel's peevish virtue, for she hath been brought up after the fashion of our grandmothers—our mothers had better sense."

"What! so fair, so young, so quick-witted, and so difficult?" said the Duke. "By your leave, you shall introduce me as well as Chiffinch."

"That your Grace may cure her of her intractable modesty?" said Christian.

"Why," replied the Duke, "it will but teach her to stand in her own light. Kings do not love to court and sue; they should have their game run down for them."

"Under your Grace's favour," said Christian, "this cannot be—*Non omnibus dormio*—Your Grace knows the classic allusion. If this maiden become a Prince's favourite, rank gilds the shame and the sin. But to any under Majesty, she must not vail topsail."

"Why, thou suspicious fool, I was but in jest," said the Duke. "Do you think I would interfere to spoil a plan so much to my own advantage as that which you have laid before me?"

Christian smiled and shook his head. "My lord," he said, "I know your Grace as well, or better, perhaps, than you know yourself. To spoil a well-concerted

intrigue by some cross stroke of your own, would give
you more pleasure, than to bring it to a successful termination according to the plans of others. But Shaftesbury,
and all concerned, have determined that our scheme shall
at least have fair play. We reckon, therefore, on your
help; and—forgive me when I say so—we will not permit
ourselves to be impeded by your levity and fickleness of
purpose."

"Who?—I light and fickle of purpose?" said the
Duke. "You see me here as resolved as any of you, to
dispossess the mistress, and to carry on the plot; these
are the only two things I live for in this world. No one
can play the man of business like me, when I please, to
the very filing and labelling of my letters. I am regular
as a scrivener."

"You have Chiffinch's letter from the country; he told
me he had written to you about some passages betwixt
him and the young Lord Saville."

"He did so—he did so," said the Duke, looking among
his letters; "but I see not his letter just now—I scarcely
noted the contents—I was busy when it came—but I have
it safely."

"You should have acted on it," answered Christian.
"The fool suffered himself to be choused out of his secret,
and prayed you to see that my lord's messenger got not
to the Duchess with some despatches which he sent up
from Derbyshire, betraying our mystery."

The Duke was now alarmed, and rang the bell hastily.
Jerningham appeared. "Where is the letter I had from
Master Chiffinch some hours since?"

"If it be not amongst those your Grace has before you,
I know nothing of it," said Jerningham. "I saw none
such arrive."

" You lie, you rascal," said Buckingham ; " have you
a right to remember better than I do ? "

" If your Grace will forgive me reminding you, you
have scarce opened a letter this week," said his gentleman.

" Did you ever hear such a provoking rascal ? " said
the Duke. " He might be a witness in the Plot. He
has knocked my character for regularity entirely on the
head with his damned counter-evidence."

" Your Grace's talent and capacity will at least remain
unimpeached," said Christian ; " and it is those that must
serve yourself and your friends. If I might advise, you
will hasten to Court, and lay some foundation for the impression we wish to make. If your Grace can take the
first word, and throw out a hint. to crossbite Saville, it
will be well. But above all, keep the King's ear employed, which no one can do so well as you. Leave
Chiffinch to fill his heart with a proper object. Another
thing is, there is a blockhead of an old Cavalier, who must
needs be a bustler in the Countess of Derby's behalf—he
is fast in hold, with the whole tribe of witnesses at his
haunches."

" Nay, then, take him, Topham."

" Topham has taken him already, my lord," said
Christian ; " and there is, besides, a young gallant, a son
of the said Knight, who was bred in the household of
the Countess of Derby, and who has brought letters
from her to the Provincial of the Jesuits, and others in
London."

" What are their names ? " said the Duke, dryly.

" Sir Geoffrey Peveril of Martindale Castle, in Derbyshire, and his son Julian."

" What ! Peveril of the Peak ? " said the Duke,—" a

stout old Cavalier as ever swore an oath—A Worcester-
man, too—and, in truth, a man of all work, when blows
were going. I will not consent to his ruin, Christian.
These fellows must be flogged off such false scents—
flogged in every sense, they must, and will be, when the
nation comes to its eye-sight again."

"It is of more than the last importance, in the meantime, to the furtherance of our plan," said Christian, "that
your Grace should stand for a space between them and
the King's favour. The youth hath influence with the
maiden, which we should find scarce favourable to our
views; besides, her father holds him as high as he can
any one who is no such puritanic fool as himself."

"Well, most Christian Christian," said the Duke, "I
have heard your commands at length. I will endeavour
to stop the earths under the throne, that neither the lord,
knight, nor squire in question, shall find it possible to
burrow there. For the fair one, I must leave Chiffinch
and you to manage her introduction to her high destinies,
since I am not to be trusted. Adieu, most Christian
Christian."

He fixed his eyes on him, and then exclaimed, as he
shut the door of the apartment,—"Most profligate and
damnable villain ! And what provokes me most of all,
is the knave's composed insolence. Your Grace will do
this—and your Grace will condescend to do that—A
pretty puppet I should be, to play the second part, or
rather the third, in such a scheme ! No, they shall all
walk according to my purpose, or I will cross them.
I will find this girl out in spite of them, and judge if
their scheme is likely to be successful. If so, she shall
be mine—mine entirely, before she becomes the King's;
and I will command her who is to guide Charles.—

Jerningham," * (his gentleman entered,) " cause Christian
to be dogged wherever he goes, for the next four-and-

---

* The application of the very respectable old English name of Jerningham to the valet-de-chambre of the Duke of Buckingham, has
proved of force sufficient to wake the resentment of the dead, who
had in early days won that illustrious surname,—for the author
received by post the following expostulation on the subject:—

" *To the learned Clerk and Worshipful Knight, Sir Walter Scott, give
these:*

" Mye mortal frame has long since mouldered into dust, and the
young saplinge that was planted on the daye of mye funeral, is now a
doddered oak, standinge hard bye the mansion of the familie. The
windes doe whistle thro' its leaves, moaninge among its moss-covered
branches, and awakeninge in the soules of mye descendants, that pen-
sive melancholy which leads back to the contemplating those that are
gone!—I, who was once the courtly dame, that held high revelry in
these gaye bowers, am now light as the blast!

" If I essaye, from vain affection, to make my name be thought of
by producing the noise of rustlinge silkes, or the slow tread of a midnight foot along the chapel floor, alas! I only scare the simple maidens,
and my wearie efforts (how wearie none alive can tell) are derided and
jeered at by knightlie descendants. Once indeed—but it boots not to
burthen your ear with this particular, nor why I am still sad and
aching, between earth and heaven! Know only, that I still walk this
place (as mye playmate, your great-grandmother, does hers.) I sit in
my wonted chair, tho' now it stands in a dusty garret. I frequent my
ladye's room, and I have hushed her wailinge babes, when all the cunning of the nurse has failed. I sit at the window where so long a succession of honorable dames have presided their daye, and are passed
away! But in the change that centuries brought, honor and truth
have remained; and, as adherents to King Harry's eldest daughter, as
true subjects to her successors, as faithful followers of the unfortunate
Charles and his posteritie, and as loyal and attached servauntes of the
present royal stock, the name of *Jerningham* has ever remained un-
sullied in honor, and uncontaminated in aught unfitting its ancient
knightlie origin. You, noble and learned sir, whose quill is as the
trumpet arousinge the slumberinge soule to feelings of loftie chivalrie,
—you, Sir Knight, who feel and doe honor to your noble lineage,
wherefore did you say, in your chronicle or historie of the brave
knight, Peveril of the Peake, that my Lord of Buckingham's servaunte

twenty hours, and find out where he visits a female newly
come to town.—You smile, you knave?"

"I did but suspect a fresh rival to Araminta and the
little Countess," said Jerningham.

"Away to your business, knave," said the Duke, "and
let me think of mine.—To subdue a Puritan in Esse—a
King's favourite in Posse—the very muster of western
beauties—that is point first. The impudence of this
Manx mongrel to be corrected—the pride of Madame
la Duchesse to be pulled down—an important state intrigue to be furthered, or baffled, as circumstances render
most to my own honour and glory—I wished for business
but now, and I have got enough of it. But Buckingham
will keep his own steerage-way through shoal and through
weather."

was a Jerningham!!! a vile varlet to a viler noble! Many honorable
families have, indeed, shot and spread from the parent stock into wilde
entangled mazes, and reached perchance beyond the confines of gentle
blood: but it so pleased Providence, that mye worshipful husband,
good Sir Harry's line, has flowed in one confined, but clear deep
stream, down to my well-beloued son, the present Sir George Jerningham (by just claim Lorde Stafforde;) and if any of your courtly ancestors that hover round your bed, could speak, they would tell you
that the Duke's valet was not Jerningham, but Sayer or Sims.—Act
as you shall think mete hereon, but defend the honored names of those
whose champion you so well deserve to be.   J. JERNINGHAM."

Having no mode of knowing how to reply to this ancient dignitary,
I am compelled to lay the blame of my error upon wicked example,
which has misled me; and to plead that I should never have been
guilty of so great a misnomer, but for the authority of one Oliver
Goldsmith, who, in an elegant dialogue between the Lady Blarney and
Miss Carolina Wilelmina Amelia Skeggs, makes the former assure
Miss Skeggs as a fact, that the next morning my lord called out three
times to his valet-de-chambre, "Jernigan, Jernigan, Jernigan! bring
me my garters!" Some inaccurate recollection of this passage has
occasioned the offence rendered, for which I make this imperfect, yet
respectful apology.

CHAPTER XXIX.

—— Mark you this, Bassanio—
The devil can quote Scripture for his purpose.
MERCHANT OF VENICE.

AFTER leaving the proud mansion of the Duke of Buckingham, Christian, full of the deep and treacherous schemes which he meditated, hastened to the city, where, in a decent inn, kept by a person of his own persuasion, he had been unexpectedly summoned to meet with Ralph Bridgenorth of Moultrassie. He was not disappointed— the Major had arrived that morning, and anxiously expected him. The usual gloom of his countenance was darkened into a yet deeper shade of anxiety, which was scarcely relieved, even while, in answer to his inquiry after his daughter, Christian gave the most favourable account of her health and spirits, naturally and unaffectedly intermingled with such praises of her beauty and her disposition, as were likely to be most grateful to a father's ear.

But Christian had too much cunning to expatiate on this theme, however soothing. He stopped short exactly at the point where, as an affectionate relative, he might be supposed to have said enough. " The lady," he said, " with whom he had placed Alice, was delighted with her aspect and manners, and undertook to be responsible for her health and happiness. He had not, he said, deserved

so little confidence at the hand of his brother, Bridgenorth, as that the Major should, contrary to his purpose,
and to the plan which they had adjusted together, have
hurried up from the country, as if his own presence were
necessary for Alice's protection."

"Brother Christian," said Bridgenorth in reply, "I
must see my child—I must see this person with whom
she is intrusted."

"To what purpose?" answered Christian. "Have
you not often confessed that the over excess of the carnal
affection which you have entertained for your daughter,
hath been a snare to you?—Have you not, more than
once, been on the point of resigning those great designs
which should place righteousness as a counsellor beside
the throne, because you desired to gratify your daughter's
girlish passion for this descendant of your old persecutor
—this Julian Peveril?"

"I own it," said Bridgenorth; "and worlds would I
have given, and would yet give, to clasp that youth to my
bosom, and call him my son. The spirit of his mother
looks from his eye, and his stately step is as that of his
father, when he daily spoke comfort to me in my distress,
and said, 'The child liveth.'"

"But the youth walks," said Christian, "after his own
lights, and mistakes the meteor of the marsh for the
Polar star. Ralph Bridgenorth, I will speak to thee in
friendly sincerity. Thou must not think to serve both
the good cause and Baal. Obey, if thou wilt, thine own
carnal affections, summon this Julian Peveril to thy house,
and let him wed thy daughter—But mark the reception
she will meet with from the proud old knight, whose spirit
is now, even now, as little broken with his chains, as
after the sword of the Saints had prevailed at Worcester.

Thou wilt see thy daughter spurned from his feet like an outcast."

"Christian," said Bridgenorth, interrupting him, "thou dost urge me hard; but thou dost it in love, my brother, and I forgive thee—Alice shall never be spurned.—But this friend of thine—this lady—thou art my child's uncle; and after me, thou art next to her in love and affection—Still, thou art not her father—hast not her father's fears. Art thou sure of the character of this woman to whom my child is intrusted?"

"Am I sure of my own?—Am I sure that my name is Christian—yours Bridgenorth?—Is it a thing I am likely to be insecure in?—Have I not dwelt for many years in this city?—Do I not know this Court?—And am I likely to be imposed upon? For I will not think you can fear my imposing upon you."

"Thou art my brother," said Bridgenorth—"the blood and bone of my departed Saint—and I am determined that I will trust thee in this matter."

"Thou dost well," said Christian; "and who knows what reward may be in store for thee?—I cannot look upon Alice, but it is strongly borne in on my mind, that there will be work for a creature so excellent beyond ordinary women. Courageous Judith freed Bethulia by her valour, and the comely features of Esther made her a safeguard and a defence to her people in the land of captivity, when she found favour in the sight of King Ahasuerus."

"Be it with her as Heaven wills," said Bridgenorth; "and now tell me what progress there is in the great work."

"The people are weary of the iniquity of this Court," said Christian; "and if this man will continue to reign, it must be by calling to his councils men of another stamp. The alarm excited by the damnable practices of the Papists has called up men's souls, and awakened their eyes, to the dangers of their state.—He himself—for he will give up brother and wife to save himself—is not averse to a change of measures; and though we cannot at first see the Court purged as with a winnowing fan, yet there will be enough of the good to control the bad— enough of the sober party to compel the grant of that universal toleration, for which we have sighed so long, as a maiden for her beloved. Time and opportunity will lead the way to more thorough reformation; and that will be done without stroke of sword, which our friends failed to establish on a sure foundation, even when their victorious blades were in their hands."

"May God grant it!" said Bridgenorth; "for I fear me I should scruple to do aught which should once more unsheath the civil sword; but welcome all that comes in a peaceful and parliamentary way."

"Ay," said Christian, "and which will bring with it the bitter amends, which our enemies have so long merited at our hands. How long hath our brother's blood cried for vengeance from the altar!—Now shall that cruel Frenchwoman find that neither lapse of years, nor her powerful friends, nor the name of Stanley, nor the Sovereignty of Man, shall stop the stern course of the pursuer of blood. Her name shall be struck from the noble, and her heritage shall another take."

"Nay, but, brother Christian," said Bridgenorth, "art thou not over eager in pursuing this thing?—It is thy duty as a Christian to forgive thine enemies."

"Ay, but not the enemies of Heaven—not those who shed the blood of the saints," said Christian, his eyes kindling with that vehement and fiery expression which at times gave to his uninteresting countenance the only character of passion which it ever exhibited. " No, Bridgenorth," he continued, " I esteem this purpose of revenge holy—I account it a propitiatory sacrifice for what may have been evil in my life. I have submitted to be spurned by the haughty—I have humbled myself to be as a servant; but in my breast was the proud thought, I who do this—do it that I may avenge my brother's blood."

" Still, my brother," said Bridgenorth, " although I participate thy purpose, and have aided thee against this Moabitish woman, I cannot but think thy revenge is more after the law of Moses than after the law of love."

" This comes well from thee, Ralph Bridgenorth," answered Christian ; " from thee, who hast just smiled over the downfall of thine own enemy."

" If you mean Sir Geoffrey Peveril," said Bridgenorth, " I smile not on his ruin. It is well he is abased ; but if it lies with me, I may humble his pride, but will never ruin his house."

" You know your purpose best," said Christian ; " and I do justice, brother Bridgenorth, to the purity of your principles ; but men who see with but worldly eyes, would discern little purpose of mercy in the strict magistrate and severe creditor—and such have you been to Peveril."

" And, brother Christian," said Bridgenorth, his colour rising as he spoke, " neither do I doubt your purpose, nor deny the surprising address with which you have procured such perfect information concerning the purposes of yonder woman of Ammon. But it is free to me to think, that in your intercourse with the Court, and with courtiers, you may, in your carnal and worldly policy, sink the value of those spiritual gifts, for which you were once so much celebrated among the brethren."

"Do not apprehend it," said Christian, recovering his temper, which had been a little ruffled by the previous discussion. "Let us but work together as heretofore; and I trust each of us shall be found doing the work of a faithful servant to that good old cause for which we have heretofore drawn the sword."

So saying, he took his hat, and bidding Bridgenorth farewell, declared his intention of returning in the evening.

"Fare thee well!" said Bridgenorth, "to that cause wilt thou find me ever a true and devoted adherent. I will act by that counsel of thine, and will not even ask thee—though it may grieve my heart as a parent—with whom, or where, thou hast intrusted my child. I will try to cut off, and cast from me, even my right hand, and my right eye; but for thee, Christian, if thou dost deal otherwise than prudently and honestly in this matter, it is what God and man will require at thy hand."

"Fear not me," said Christian, hastily, and left the place, agitated by reflections of no pleasant kind.

"I ought to have persuaded him to return," he said, as he stepped out into the street. "Even his hovering in this neighbourhood may spoil the plan on which depends the rise of my fortunes—ay, and of his child's. Will men say I have ruined her, when I shall have raised her to the dazzling height of the Duchess of Portsmouth, and perhaps máde her mother to a long line of princes? Chiffinch hath vouched for opportunity; and the voluptuary's fortune depends upon his gratifying the taste of his master for variety. If she makes an impression, it must be a deep one; and once seated in his affections, I fear

not her being supplanted.—What will her father say?
Will he, like a prudent man, put his shame in his pocket,
because it is well gilded? or will he think it fitting to
make a display of moral wrath and parental frenzy? I
fear the latter—He has ever kept too strict a course to
admit his conniving at such license. But what will his
anger avail?—I need not be seen in the matter—those
who are will care little for the resentment of a country
Puritan. And after all, what I am labouring to bring
about is best for himself, the wench, and, above all, for
me, Edward Christian."

With such base opiates did this unhappy wretch stifle
his own conscience, while anticipating the disgrace of his
friend's family, and the ruin of a near relative, committed
in confidence to his charge. The character of this man
was of no common description; nor was it by an ordinary
road that he had arrived at the present climax of unfeel-
ing and infamous selfishness.

Edward Christian, as the reader is aware, was the
brother of that William Christian, who was the principal
instrument in delivering up the Island of Man to the Re-
public, and who became the victim of the Countess of Derby's revenge on that account. Both had been educated
as Puritans, but William was a soldier, which somewhat
modified the strictness of his religious opinions; Edward,
a civilian, seemed to entertain these principles in the utmost rigour. But it was only seeming. The exactness
of deportment, which procured him great honour and influence among the *sober party*, as they were wont to term
themselves, covered a voluptuous disposition, the gratification of which was sweet to him as stolen waters, and
pleasant as bread eaten in secret. While, therefore, his
seeming godliness brought him worldly gain, his secret

pleasures compensated for his outward austerity; until
the Restoration, and the Countess's violent proceedings
against his brother, interrupted the course of both. He
then fled from his native island, burning with the desire
of revenging his brother's death—the only passion foreign
to his own gratification which he was ever known to
cherish, and which was also, at least, partly selfish, since it
concerned the restoration of his own fortunes.

He found easy access to Villiers, Duke of Buckingham, who, in right of his Duchess, claimed such of the
Derby estate as had been bestowed by the Parliament on
his celebrated father-in-law, Lord Fairfax. His influence
at the Court of Charles, where a jest was a better plea
than a long claim of faithful service, was so successfully
exerted, as to contribute greatly to the depression of that
loyal and ill-rewarded family. But Buckingham was incapable, even for his own interest, of pursuing the steady
course which Christian suggested to him; and his vacil-
lation probably saved the remnant of the large estates of
the Earl of Derby.

Meantime, Christian was too useful a follower to be dismissed. From Buckingham, and others of that stamp,
he did not affect to conceal the laxity of his morals; but,
towards the numerous and powerful party to which he
belonged, he was able to disguise them by a seeming gravity of exterior, which he never laid aside. Indeed, so
wide and absolute was then the distinction betwixt the
Court and the city, that a man might have for some time
played two several parts, as in two different spheres, without its being discovered in the one that he exhibited himself in a different light in the other. Besides, when a
man of talent shows himself an able and useful partisan,
his party will continue to protect and accredit him, in

spite of conduct the most contradictory to their own principles.   Some facts are, in such cases, denied—some are
glossed over—and party zeal is permitted to cover at
least as many defects as ever doth charity.   ·

Edward Christian had often need of the partial indulgence of his friends; but he experienced it, for he was
eminently useful.   Buckingham, and other courtiers of the
same class, however dissolute in their lives, were desirous
of keeping some connexion with the Dissenting or Puritanic party, as it was termed? thereby to strengthen themselves against their opponents at Court.   In such intrigues,
Christian was a notable agent; and at one time had nearly procured an absolute union between a class which
professed the most rigid principles of religion and morality, and the latitudinarian courtiers, who set all principle
at defiance.

Amidst the vicissitudes of a life of intrigue, during
which Buckingham's ambitious schemes, and his own,
repeatedly sent him across the Atlantic, it was Edward
Christian's boast that he never lost sight of his principal
object,—revenge on the Countess of Derby.   He maintained a close and intimate correspondence with his native
island, so as to be perfectly informed of whatever took
place there; and he stimulated, on every favourable
opportunity, the cupidity of Buckingham to possess himself of this petty kingdom, by procuring the forfeiture of
its present Lord.   It was not difficult to keep his patron's
wild wishes alive on this topic, for his own mercurial
imagination attached particular charms to the idea of
becoming a sort of sovereign even in this little island;
and he was, like Catiline, as covetous of the property of
others, as he was profuse of his own.

But it was not until the pretended discovery of the

Papist Plot that the schemes of Christian could be
brought to ripen; and then, so odious were the Catholics
in the eyes of the credulous people of England, that,
upon the accusation of the most infamous of mankind,
common informers, the scourings of jails, and the refuse
of the whipping-post, the most atrocious charges against
persons of the highest rank and fairest character, were
readily received and credited.

This was a period which Christian did not fail to improve. He drew close his intimacy with Bridgenorth,
which had indeed never been interrupted, and readily
engaged him in his schemes, which, in the eyes of his
brother-in-law, were alike honourable and patriotic. But,
while he flattered Bridgenorth with the achieving a complete reformation in the state—checking the profligacy
of the Court—relieving the consciences of the Dissenters
from the pressure of the penal laws—amending, in fine,
the crying grievances of the time—while he showed him
also, in prospect, revenge upon the Countess of Derby,
and a humbling dispensation on the house of Peveril,
from whom Bridgenorth had suffered such indignity,
Christian did not neglect, in the meanwhile, to consider
how he could best benefit himself by the confidence reposed in him by his unsuspicious relation.

The extreme beauty of Alice Bridgenorth—the great
wealth which time and economy had accumulated on her
father—pointed her out as a most desirable match to
repair the wasted fortunes of some of the followers of the
Court; and he flattered himself that he could conduct
such a negotiation so as to be in a high degree conducive
to his own advantage. He found there would be little
difficulty in prevailing on Major Bridgenorth to intrust
him with the guardianship of his daughter. That unfor-

tunate gentleman had accustomed himself, from the very period of her birth, to regard the presence of his child as a worldly indulgence too great to be allowed to him; and Christian had little trouble in convincing him that the strong inclination which he felt to bestow her on Julian Peveril, provided he could be brought over to his own political opinions, was a blameable compromise with his more severe principles. Late circumstances had taught him the incapacity and unfitness of Dame Debbitch for the sole charge of so dear a pledge; and he readily and thankfully embraced the kind offer of her maternal uncle, Christian, to place Alice under the protection of a lady of rank in London, whilst he himself was to be engaged in the scenes of bustle and blood, which, in common with all good Protestants, he expected was speedily to take place on a general rising of the Papists, unless prevented by the active and energetic measures of the good people of England. He even confessed his fears, that his partial regard for Alice's happiness might enervate his efforts in behalf of his country; and Christian had little trouble in eliciting from him a promise, that he would forbear to inquire after her for some time.

Thus certain of being the temporary guardian of his niece for a space long enough, he flattered himself, for the execution of his purpose, Christian endeavoured to pave the way by consulting Chiffinch, whose known skill in Court policy qualified him best as an adviser on this occasion. But this worthy person, being, in fact, a purveyor for his Majesty's pleasures, and on that account high in his good graces, thought it fell within the line of his duty to suggest another scheme than that on which Christian consulted him. A woman of such exquisite beauty as Alice was described, he deemed more worthy to be a partaker of the affections of the merry Monarch, whose taste in female beauty was so exquisite, than to be made the wife of some worn-out prodigal of quality. And then, doing perfect justice to his own character, he felt it would not be one whit impaired, while his fortune would be, in every respect, greatly amended, if, after sharing the short reign of the Gwyns, the Davises, the Robertses, and so forth, Alice Bridgenorth should retire from the state of a royal favourite, into the humble condition of Mrs. Chiffinch.

After cautiously sounding Christian, and finding that the near prospect of interest to himself effectually prevented his starting at this iniquitous scheme, Chiffinch detailed it to him fully, carefully keeping the final termination out of sight, and talking of the favour to be acquired by the fair Alice as no passing caprice, but the commencement of a reign as long and absolute as that of the Duchess of Portsmouth, of whose avarice and domineering temper Charles was now understood to be much tired, though the force of habit rendered him unequal to free himself of her yoke.

Thus chalked out, the scene prepared was no longer the intrigue of a Court pander, and a villainous resolution for the ruin of an innocent girl, but became a state intrigue, for the removal of an obnoxious favourite, and the subsequent change of the King's sentiments upon various material points, in which he was at present influenced by the Duchess of Portsmouth. In this light it was exhibited to the Duke of Buckingham, who, either to sustain his character for daring gallantry, or in order to gratify some capricious fancy, had at one time made love to the reigning favourite, and experienced a repulse which he had never forgiven.

But one scheme was too little to occupy the active and
enterprising spirit of the Duke. An appendix of the
Popish Plot was easily so contrived as to involve the
Countess of Derby, who, from character and religion,
was precisely the person whom the credulous part of the
public were inclined to suppose the likely accomplice of
such a conspiracy. Christian and Bridgenorth undertook
the perilous commission of attacking her even in her own
little kingdom of Man, and had commissions for this purpose, which were only to be produced in case of their
scheme taking effect.

It miscarried, as the reader is aware, from the Countess's alert preparations for defence; and neither Christian
nor Bridgenorth held it sound policy to practise openly,
even under parliamentary authority, against a lady so little
liable to hesitate upon the measures most likely to secure
her feudal sovereignty; wisely considering that even
the omnipotence, as it has been somewhat too largely
styled, of Parliament, might fail to relieve them from the
personal consequences of a failure.

On the continent of Britain, however, no opposition
was to be feared; and so well was Christian acquainted
with all the motions in the interior of the Countess's little
court, or household, that Peveril would have been arrested the instant he set foot on shore, but for the gale of
wind, which obliged the vessel, in which he was a pas-
senger, to run for Liverpool. Here Christian, under the
name of Ganlesse, unexpectedly met with him, and preserved him from the fangs of the well-breathed witnesses
of the Plot, with the purpose of securing his dispatches,
or, if necessary, his person also, in such a manner as to
place him at his own discretion—a narrow and perilous
game, which he thought it better, however, to undertake,

than to permit these subordinate agents, who were always
ready to mutiny against all in league with them, to obtain
the credit which they must have done by the seizure of the
Countess of Derby's dispatches. It was, besides, essential to Buckingham's schemes that these should not pass
into the hands of a public officer like Topham, who, however pompous and stupid, was upright and well-inten-
tioned, until they had undergone the revisal of a private
committee, where something might have probably been
suppressed, even supposing that nothing had been added.
In short, Christian, in carrying on his own separate and
peculiar intrigue, by the agency of the Great Popish
Plot, as it was called, acted just like an engineer, who
derives the principle of motion which turns his machinery, by means of a steam-engine, or large water-wheel,
constructed to drive a separate and larger engine. Accordingly, he was determined that, while he took all the
advantage he could from their supposed discoveries, no
one should be admitted to tamper or interfere with his
own plans of profit and revenge.

Chiffinch, who, desirous of satisfying himself with his
own eyes of that excellent beauty which had been so
highly extolled, had gone down to Derbyshire on purpose, was infinitely delighted, when, during the course of
a two hours' sermon at the dissenting chapel in Liverpool,
which afforded him ample leisure for a deliberate survey,
he arrived at the conclusion that he had never seen a
form or face more captivating. His eyes having confirmed what was told him, he hurried back to the little
inn which formed their place of rendezvous, and there
awaited Christian and his niece, with a degree of confidence in the success of their project which he had not before
entertained ; and with an apparatus of luxury, calculated,

as he thought, to make a favourable impression on the mind of a rustic girl. He was somewhat surprised, when, instead of Alice Bridgenorth, to whom he expected that night to have been introduced, he found that Christian was accompanied by Julian Peveril. It was indeed a severe disappointment, for he had prevailed on his own indolence to venture thus far from the Court, in order that he might judge, with his own paramount taste, whether Alice was really the prodigy which her uncle's praises had bespoken her, and, as such, a victim worthy of the fate to which she was destined.

A few words betwixt the worthy confederates determined them on the plan of stripping Peveril of the Countess's despatches; Chiffinch absolutely refusing to take any share in arresting him, as a matter of which his Master's approbation might be very uncertain.

Christian had also his own reasons for abstaining from so decisive a step. It was by no means likely to be agreeable to Bridgenorth, whom it was necessary to keep in good humour;—it was not necessary, for the Countess's despatches were of far more importance than the person of Julian. Lastly, it was superfluous in this respect also, that Julian was on the road to his father's castle, where it was likely he would be seized, as a matter of course, along with the other suspicious persons who fell under Topham's warrant, and the denunciations of his infamous companions. He, therefore, far from using any violence to Peveril, assumed towards him such a friendly tone, as might seem to warn him against receiving damage from others, and vindicate himself from having had any share in depriving him of his charge. This last manœuvre was achieved by an infusion of a strong narcotic into Julian's wine; under the influence of which he slumbered so soundly, that the confederates were easily able to accomplish their inhospitable purpose.

The events of the succeeding days are already known to the reader. Chiffinch set forward to return to London, with the packet, which it was desirable should be in Buckingham's hands as soon as possible; while Christian went to Moultrassie, to receive Alice from her father, and convey her safely to London—his accomplice agreeing to defer his curiosity to see more of her until they should have arrived in that city.

Before parting with Bridgenorth, Christian had exerted his utmost address to prevail on him to remain at Moultrassie; he had even overstepped the bounds of prudence, and, by his urgency, awakened some suspicions of an indefinite nature, which he found it difficult to allay. Bridgenorth, therefore, followed his brother-in-law to London; and the reader has already been made acquainted with the arts which Christian used to prevent his farther interference with the destinies of his daughter, or the unhallowed schemes of her ill-chosen guardian. Still Christian, as he strode along the street in profound reflection, saw that his undertaking was attended with a thousand perils; and the drops stood like beads on his brow when he thought of the presumptuous levity and fickle temper of Buckingham—the frivolity and intemperance of Chiffinch—the suspicions of the melancholy and bigoted, yet sagacious and honest Bridgenorth. " Had I," he thought, " but tools fitted, each to their portion of the work, how easily could I heave asunder and disjoint the strength that opposes me! But with these frail and insufficient implements, I am in daily, hourly, momentary danger, that one lever or other gives way, and that the whole ruin recoils on my own head. And yet, were it not for those failings I complain of, how were it possible for me to have acquired that power over them all which constitutes them my passive tools, even when they seem most to exert their own free will? Yes, the bigots have some right when they affirm that all is for the best."

It may seem strange, that, amidst the various subjects of Christian's apprehension, he was never visited by any long or permanent doubt that the virtue of his niece might prove the shoal on which his voyage should be wrecked. But he was an arrant rogue, as well as a hardened libertine; and, in both characters, a professed disbeliever in the virtue of the fair sex.

CHAPTER XXX.

As for John Dryden's Charles, I own that King
Was never any very mighty thing;
And yet he was a devilish honest fellow—
Enjoy'd his friend and bottle, and got mellow.

DR. WOLCOT.

LONDON, the grand central point of intrigues of every description, had now attracted within its dark and shadowy region the greater number of the personages whom we have had occasion to mention.

Julian Peveril, amongst others of the dramatis personæ, had arrived, and taken up his abode in a remote inn in the suburbs. His business, he conceived, was to remain incognito until he should have communicated in private with the friends who were most likely to lend assistance to his parents, as well as to his patroness, in their present situation of doubt and danger. Amongst these, the most powerful was the Duke of Ormond, whose faithful services, high rank, and acknowledged worth and virtue, still preserved an ascendency in that very Court, where, in general, he was regarded as out of favour. Indeed, so much consciousness did Charles display in his demeanour towards that celebrated noble, and servant of his father, that Buckingham once took the freedom to ask the King whether the Duke of Ormond had lost his Majesty's favour, or his Majesty the Duke's? since, whenever they chanced to meet, the King appeared the more embarrassed of the two. But it was not Peveril's good fortune to obtain the advice or countenance of this distinguished person. His Grace of Ormond was not at that time in London.

The letter, about the delivery of which the Countess had seemed most anxious after that to the Duke of Ormond, was addressed to Captain Barstow, (a Jesuit, whose real name was Fenwicke,) to be found, or at least to be heard of, in the house of one Martin Christal in the Savoy. To this place hastened Peveril, upon learning the absence of the Duke of Ormond. He was not ignorant of the danger which he personally incurred, by thus becoming a medium of communication betwixt a Popish priest and a suspected Catholic. But when he undertook the perilous commission of his patroness, he had done so frankly, and with the unreserved resolution of serving her in the manner in which she most desired her affairs to be conducted. Yet he could not forbear some secret apprehension, when he felt himself engaged in the labyrinth of passages and galleries, which led to different obscure sets of apartments in the ancient building termed the Savoy.

This antiquated and almost ruinous pile occupied a part of the site of the public offices in the Strand, commonly called Somerset-House. The Savoy had been formerly a palace, and took its name from an Earl of Savoy, by whom it was founded. It had been the habitation of John of Gaunt, and various persons of distinction—had become a convent, an hospital, and finally, in Charles II.'s time, a waste of dilapidated buildings and ruinous apartments, inhabited chiefly by those who had some connexion with, or dependence upon, the neighbouring palace of Somerset-House, which, more fortunate

than the Savoy, had still retained its royal title, and was
the abode of a part of the Court, and occasionally of the
King himself, who had apartments there.

It was not without several inquiries, and more than one
mistake, that, at the end of a long and dusky passage,
composed of boards so wasted by time that they threatened to give way under his feet, Julian at length found
the name of Martin Christal, broker and appraiser, upon
a shattered door. He was about to knock, when some
one pulled his cloak; and looking round, to his great
astonishment, which indeed almost amounted to fear, he
saw the little mute damsel, who had accompanied him for
a part of the way on his voyage from the Isle of Man.
"Fenella!" he exclaimed, forgetting that she could
neither hear nor reply,—"Fenella! Can this be you?"

Fenella, assuming the air of warning and authority,
which she had heretofore endeavoured to adopt towards
him, interposed betwixt Julian and the door at which he
was about to knock—pointed with her finger towards it
in a prohibiting manner, and at the same time bent her
brows, and shook her head sternly.

After a moment's consideration, Julian could place but
one interpretation upon Fenella's appearance and conduct, and that was, by supposing her lady had come up
to London, and had dispatched this mute attendant, as a
confidential person, to apprize him of some change of
her intended operations, which might render the delivery
of her letters to Barstow, *alias* Fenwicke, superfluous, or
perhaps dangerous. He made signs to Fenella, demanding to know whether she had any commission from the
Countess. She nodded. "Had she any letter?" he
continued, by the same mode of inquiry. She shook her
head impatiently, and, walking hastily along the passage,

made a signal to him to follow. He did so, having little doubt that he was about to be conducted into the Countess's presence; but his surprise, at first excited by Fenella's appearance, was increased by the rapidity and ease with which she seemed to track the dusky and decayed mazes of the dilapidated Savoy, equal to that with which he had seen her formerly lead the way through the gloomy vaults of Castle Rushin, in the Isle of Man.

When he recollected, however, that Fenella had accompanied the Countess on a long visit to London, it appeared not improbable that she might then have acquired this local knowledge which seemed so accurate. Many foreigners, dependent on the Queen or Queen Dowager, had apartments in the Savoy. Many Catholic priests also found refuge in its recesses, under various disguises, and in defiance of the severity of the laws against Popery. What was more likely, than that the Countess of Derby, a Catholic and a Frenchwoman, should have had secret commissions amongst such people; and that the execution of such should be intrusted, at least occasionally, to Fenella?

Thus reflecting, Julian continued to follow her light and active footsteps as she glided from the Strand to Spring-Garden, and thence into the Park.

It was still early in the morning, and the Mall was untenanted, save by a few walkers, who frequented these shades for the wholesome purposes of air and exercise. Splendour, gaiety, and display, did not come forth, at that period, until noon was approaching. All readers have heard that the whole space where the Horse Guards are now built, made, in the time of Charles II., a part of St. James's Park; and that the old building,

now called the Treasury, was a part of the ancient
Palace of Whitehall, which was thus immediately connected with the Park. The canal had been constructed,
by the celebrated Le Notre, for the purpose of draining
the Park; and it communicated with the Thames by a
decoy, stocked with a quantity of the rarer waterfowl.
It was towards this decoy that Fenella bent her way with
unabated speed; and they were approaching a group of
two or three gentlemen, who sauntered by its banks,
when, on looking closely at him who appeared to be the
chief of the party, Julian felt his heart beat uncommonly
thick, as if conscious of approaching some one of the
highest consequence.

The person whom he looked upon was past the middle
age of life, of a dark complexion, corresponding with the
long, black, full-bottomed periwig, which he wore instead
of his own hair. His dress was plain black velvet, with
a diamond star, however, on his cloak, which hung carelessly over one shoulder. His features, strongly lined,
even to harshness, had yet an expression of dignified
good-humour; he was well and strongly built, walked
upright and yet easily, and had upon the whole the air
of a person of the highest consideration. He kept rather
in advance of his companions, but turned and spoke to
them, from time to time, with much affability, and probably with some liveliness, judging by the smiles, and
sometimes the scarce restrained laughter, by which some
of his sallies were received by his attendants. They also
wore only morning dresses; but their looks and manner
were those of men of rank, in presence of one in station
still more elevated. They shared the attention of their
principal in common with seven or eight little black
curly-haired spaniels, or rather, as they are now called,

cockers, which attended their master as closely, and perhaps with as deep sentiments of attachment, as the bipeds of the group; and whose gambols, which seemed to afford him much amusement, he sometimes checked, and sometimes encouraged. In addition to this pastime, a lackey, or groom, was also in attendance, with one or two little baskets and bags, from which the gentleman we have described took, from time to time, a handful of seeds, and amused himself with throwing them to the waterfowl.

This, the King's favourite occupation, together with his remarkable countenance, and the deportment of the rest of the company towards him, satisfied Julian Peveril that he was approaching, perhaps indecorously, near to the person of Charles Stewart, the second of that unhappy name.

While he hesitated to follow his dumb guide any nearer, and felt the embarrassment of being unable to communicate to her his repugnance to farther intrusion, a person in the royal retinue touched a light and lively air on the flageolet, at a signal from the King, who desired to have some tune repeated which had struck him in the theatre on the preceding evening. While the good-natured monarch marked time with his foot, and with the motion of his hand, Fenella continued to approach him, and threw into her manner the appearance of one who was attracted, as it were in spite of herself, by the sounds of the instrument.

Anxious to know how this was to end, and astonished to see the dumb girl imitate so accurately the manner of one who actually heard the musical notes, Peveril also drew near, though at somewhat greater distance.

The King looked good-humouredly at both, as if he

admitted their musical enthusiasm as an excuse for their intrusion; but his eyes became riveted on Fenella, whose face and appearance, although rather singular than beautiful, had something in them wild, fantastic, and, as being so, even captivating, to an eye which had been gratified perhaps to satiety with the ordinary forms of female beauty. She did not appear to notice how closely she was observed; but, as if acting under an irresistible impulse, derived from the sounds to which she seemed to listen, she undid the bodkin round which her long tresses were winded, and flinging them suddenly over her slender person, as if using them as a natural veil, she began to dance, with infinite grace and agility, to the tune which the flageolet played.

Peveril lost almost his sense of the King's presence, when he observed with what wonderful grace and agility Fenella kept time to notes, which could only be known to her by the motions of the musician's fingers. He had heard, indeed, among other prodigies, of a person in Fenella's unhappy situation, acquiring, by some unaccountable and mysterious tact, the power of acting as an instrumental musician, nay, becoming so accurate a performer as to be capable of leading a musical band; and he had also heard of deaf and dumb persons dancing with sufficient accuracy, by observing the motions of their partner. But Fenella's performance seemed more wonderful than either, since the musician was guided by his written notes, and the dancer by the motions of the others; whereas Fenella had no intimation, save what she seemed to gather, with infinite accuracy, by observing the motion of the artist's fingers on his small instrument.

As for the King, who was ignorant of the particular circumstances which rendered Fenella's performance

almost marvellous, he was contented, at her first commencement, to authorize what seemed to him the frolic
of this singular-looking damsel, by a good-humoured
smile, but when he perceived the exquisite truth and
justice, as well as the wonderful combination of grace
and agility, with which she executed to his favourite air
a dance which was perfectly new to him, Charles turned
his mere acquiescence into something like enthusiastic
applause.   He bore time to her motions with the movement of his foot—applauded with head and with hand—
and seemed, like herself, carried away by the enthusiasm
of the gestic art.

After a rapid yet graceful succession of *entrechats*,
Fenella introduced a slow movement, which terminated
the dance; then dropping a profound courtesy, she continued to stand motionless before the King, her arms
folded on her bosom, her head stooped, and her eyes cast
down, after the manner of an Oriental slave; while
through the misty veil of her shadowy locks, it might be
observed, that the colour which exercise had called to
her cheeks was dying fast away, and resigning them to
their native dusky hue.

" By my honour," exclaimed the King, " she is like a
fairy who trips it in moonlight.   There must be more of
air and fire than of earth in her composition.   It is well
poor Nelly Gwyn saw her not, or she would have died of
grief and envy.—Come, gentlemen, which of you contrived this pretty piece of morning pastime?"

The courtiers looked at each other, but none of them
felt authorized to claim the merit of a service so agreeable.

"We must ask the quick-eyed nymph herself then,"
said the King; and, looking at Fenella, he added, "Tell

us, my pretty one, to whom we owe the pleasure of seeing you?—I suspect the Duke of Buckingham; for this is exactly a *tour de son métier.*"

Fenella, on observing that the King addressed her, bowed low, and shook her head, in signal that she did not understand what he said. "Oddsfish, that is true," said the King; "she must perforce be a foreigner—her complexion and agility speak it. France or Italy has had the moulding of these elastic limbs, dark cheek, and eye of fire." He then put to her in French, and again in Italian, the question, "By whom she had been sent hither?"

At the second repetition, Fenella threw back her veiling tresses, so as to show the melancholy which sat on her brow; while she sadly shook her head, and intimated by imperfect muttering, but of the softest and most plaintive kind, her organic deficiency.

"Is it possible Nature can have made such a fault?" said Charles. "Can she have left so curious a piece as thou art without the melody of voice, while she has made thee so exquisitely sensible to the beauty of sound?— Stay: what means this? and what young fellow are you bringing up there? O, the master of the show, I suppose.—Friend," he added, addressing himself to Peveril, who, on the signal of Fenella, stepped forward almost instinctively, and kneeled down, "we thank thee for the pleasure of this morning.—My Lord Marquis, you rooked me at piquet last night; for which disloyal deed thou shalt now atone, by giving a couple of pieces to this honest youth, and five to the girl."

As the nobleman drew out his purse and came forward to perform the King's generous commission, Julian felt some embarrassment ere he was able to explain, that he had no title to be benefited by the young person's performance, and that his Majesty had mistaken his character.

"And who art thou, then, my friend?" said Charles; "but, above all, and particularly, who is this dancing nymph, whom thou standest waiting on like an attendant fawn?"

"The young person is a retainer of the Countess-Dowager of Derby, so please your Majesty," said Peveril, in a low tone of voice; "and I am "——

"Hold, hold," said the King; "this is a dance to another tune, and not fit for a place so public. Hark thee, friend; do thou and the young woman follow Empson where he will conduct thee.—Empson, carry them—hark in thy ear."

"May it please your Majesty, I ought to say," said Peveril, "that I am guiltless of any purpose of intrusion "——

"Now a plague on him who can take no hint," said the King, cutting short his apology. "Oddsfish, man, there are times when civility is the greatest impertinence in the world. Do thou follow Empson, and amuse thyself for an half hour's space with the fairy's company, till we shall send for you."

Charles spoke this not without casting an anxious eye around, and in a tone which intimated apprehension of being overheard. Julian could only bow obedience, and follow Empson, who was the same person that played so rarely on the flageolet.

When they were out of sight of the King and his party, the musician wished to enter into conversation with his companions, and addressed himself first to Fenella with a broad compliment of, "By the mass, ye dance rarely—ne'er a slut on the board shows such a shank! I would

be content to play to you till my throat were as dry as
my whistle. Come, be a little free—old Rowley will not
quit the Park till nine. I will carry you to Spring Gardens, and bestow sweet-cakes and a quart of Rhenish on
both of you; and we'll be cameradoes.—What the devil?
no answer?—How's this, brother?—Is this neat wench
of yours deaf or dumb, or both? I should laugh at that,
and she trip it so well to the flageolet."

To rid himself of this fellow's discourse, Peveril answered him in French, that he was a foreigner, and spoke
no English; glad to escape, though at the expense of a
fiction, from the additional embarrassment of a fool, who
was likely to ask more questions than his own wisdom
might have enabled him to answer.

" *Étranger*—that means stranger," muttered their
guide; "more French dogs and jades come to lick the
good English butter off our bread, or perhaps an Italian
puppet-show. Well, if it were not that they have a
mortal enmity to the whole *gamut*, this were enough to
make any honest fellow turn Puritan. But if I am to
play to her at the Duchess's, I'll be d—d but I put her
out in the tune, just to teach her to have the impudence
to come to England, and to speak no English.

Having muttered to himself this truly British resolution, the musician walked briskly on towards a large
house near the bottom of St. James's Street, and entered
the court, by a grated door, from the Park, of which the
mansion commanded an extensive prospect.

Peveril finding himself in front of a handsome portico,
under which opened a stately pair of folding-doors, was
about to ascend the steps that led to the main entrance,
when his guide seized him by the arm, exclaiming,
" Hold, Mounseer! What! you'll lose nothing, I see, for

want of courage; but you must keep the back way, for all your fine doublet. Here it is not, knock and it shall be opened; but may be instead, knock and you shall be knocked."

Suffering himself to be guided by Empson, Julian deviated from the principal door, to one which opened, with less ostentation, in an angle of the court-yard. On a modest tap from the flute-player, admittance was afforded him and his companions by a footman, who conducted them through a variety of stone-passages, to a very handsome summer parlour, where a lady, or something resembling one, dressed in a style of extra elegance, was trifling with a play-book while she finished her chocolate. It would not be easy to describe her, but by weighing her natural good qualities against the affectations which counterbalanced them. She would have been handsome, but for rouge and *minauderie*—would have been civil, but for overstrained airs of patronage and condescension—would have had an agreeable voice, had she spoken in her natural tone—and fine eyes, had she not made such desperate hard use of them. She could only spoil a pretty ankle by too liberal display; but her shape, though she could not yet be thirty years old, had the embonpoint which might have suited better with ten years more advanced. She pointed Empson to a seat with the air of a Duchess, and asked him, languidly, how he did this age, that she had not seen him? and what folks these were he had brought with him?

"Foreigners, madam; d—d foreigners," answered Empson; "starving beggars, that our old friend has picked up in the Park this morning—the wench dances, and the fellow plays on the Jew's trump, I believe. On my life, madam, I begin to be ashamed of old Rowley;

I must discard him, unless he keeps better company in future."

"Fie, Empson," said the lady; "consider it is our duty to countenance him, and keep him afloat; and indeed I always make a principle of it. Hark ye, he comes not hither this morning?"

"He will be here," answered Empson, "in the walking of a minuet."

"My God!" exclaimed the lady, with unaffected alarm; and starting up with utter neglect of her usual airs of graceful languor, she tripped as swiftly as a milk-maid into an adjoining apartment, where they heard presently a few words of eager and animated discussion.

"Something to be put out of the way, I suppose," said Empson. "Well for madam I gave her the hint. There he goes, the happy swain."

Julian was so situated, that he could, from the same casement through which Empson was peeping, observe a man in a laced roquelaure, and carrying his rapier under his arm, glide from the door by which he had himself entered, and out of the court, keeping as much as possible under the shade of the buildings.

The lady re-entered at this moment, and observing how Empson's eyes were directed, said with a slight appearance of hurry, "A gentleman of the Duchess of Portsmouth's with a billet; and so tiresomely pressing for an answer, that I was obliged to write without my diamond pen. I have daubed my fingers, I dare say," she added, looking at a very pretty hand, and presently after dipping her fingers in a little silver vase of rose-water. "But that little exotic monster of yours, Empson, I hope she really understands no English?—On my life she coloured.—Is she such a rare dancer?—I must see her dance, and hear him play on the Jew's harp."

" Dance ! " replied Empson; " she danced well enough when *I* played to her. I can make any thing dance. Old Counsellor Clubfoot danced when he had a fit of the gout; you have seen no such pas seul in the theatre. I would engage to make the Archbishop of Canterbury dance the hays like a Frenchman. There is nothing in dancing; it all lies in the music. Rowley does not know that now. He saw this poor wench dance; and thought so much on't, when it was all along of me. I would have defied her to sit still. And Rowley gives her the credit of it, and five pieces to boot; and I have only two for my morning's work ! "

" True, Master Empson," said the lady; " but you are of the family, though in a lower station; and you ought to consider "—— " By G—, madam," answered Empson, " all I consider is, that I play the best flageolet in England; and that they can no more supply my place, if they were to discard me, than they could fill Thames from Fleet-Ditch."

" Well, Master Empson, I do not dispute but you are a man of talents," replied the lady; " still I say, mind the main chance—you please the ear to-day—another has the advantage of you to-morrow."

" Never, mistress, while ears have the heavenly power of distinguishing one note from another."

" Heavenly power, say you, Master Empson ? " said the lady.

" Ay, madam, heavenly; for some very neat verses which we had at our festival say,

' What know we of the blest above,
But that they sing and that they love ? '

It is Master Waller wrote them, as I think; who, upon
my word, ought to be encouraged."

"And so should you, my dear Empson," said the dame,
yawning, "were it only for the honour you do to your
own profession. But in the meantime, will you ask these
people to have some refreshment?—and will you take
some yourself?—the chocolate is that which the Ambas-
sador Portuguese fellow brought over to the Queen."

"If it be genuine," said the musician.

"How, sir," said the fair one, half rising from her pile
of cushions—"Not genuine, and in this house!—Let me
understand you, Master Empson—I think, when I first
saw you, you scarce knew chocolate from coffee."

"By G—, madam," answered the flageolet-player,
"you are perfectly right. And how can I show better
how much I have profited by your ladyship's excellent
cheer, except by being critical?"

"You stand excused, Master Empson," said the petite
maitresse, sinking gently back on the downy couch, from
which a momentary irritation had startled her—"I think
the chocolate will please you, though scarce equal to what
we had from the Spanish resident Mendoza.—But we
must offer these strange people something. Will you ask
them if they would have coffee and chocolate, or cold
wild-fowl, fruit, and wine? They must be treated, so as
to show them where they are, since here they are."

"Unquestionably, madam," said Empson; "but I have
just at this instant forgot the French for chocolate, hot
bread, coffee, game, and drinkables."

"It is odd," said the lady; "and I have forgot my
French and Italian at the same moment. But it signifies
little—I will order the things to be brought, and they will
remember the names of them themselves."

Empson laughed loudly at this jest, and pawned his soul that the cold sirloin which entered immediately after, was the best emblem of roast-beef all the world over. Plentiful refreshments were offered to all the party, of which both Fenella and Peveril partook.

In the meanwhile, the flageolet-player drew closer to the side of the lady of the mansion—their intimacy was cemented, and their spirits set afloat, by a glass of liqueur, which gave them additional confidence in discussing the characters, as well of the superior attendants of the Court, as of the inferior rank, to which they themselves might be supposed to belong.

The lady, indeed, during this conversation, frequently exerted her complete and absolute superiority over Master Empson; in which that musical gentleman humbly acquiesced whenever the circumstance was recalled to his attention, whether in the way of blunt contradiction, sarcastic insinuation, downright assumption of higher importance, or in any of the other various modes by which such superiority is usually asserted and maintained. But the lady's obvious love of scandal was the lure which very soon brought her again down from the dignified port which for a moment she assumed, and placed her once more on a gossiping level with her companion.

Their conversation was too trivial, and too much allied to petty Court intrigues, with which he was totally unacquainted, to be in the least interesting to Julian. As it continued for more than an hour, he soon ceased to pay the least attention to a discourse consisting of nicknames, patchwork, and innuendo; and employed himself in reflecting on his own complicated affairs, and the probable issue of his approaching audience with the King, which had been brought about by so singular an agent, and by means so unexpected. He often looked to his guide, Fenella; and observed that she was, for the greater part of the time, drowned in deep and abstracted meditation. But three or four times—and it was when the assumed airs and affected importance of the musician and their hostess rose to the most extravagant excess—he observed that Fenella dealt askance on them some of those bitter and almost blighting elfin looks, which in the Isle of Man were held to imply contemptuous execration. There was something in all her manner so extraordinary, joined to her sudden appearance, and her demeanour in the King's presence, so oddly, yet so well contrived to procure him a private audience—which he might, by graver means, have sought in vain—that it almost justified the idea, though he smiled at it internally, that the little mute agent was aided in her machinations by the kindred imps, to whom, according to Manx superstition, her genealogy was to be traced.

Another idea sometimes occurred to Julian, though he rejected the question, as being equally wild with those doubts which referred Fenella to a race different from that of mortals—" Was she really afflicted with those organical imperfections which had always seemed to sever her from humanity?—If not, what could be the motives of so young a creature practising so dreadful a penance for such an unremitted term of years? And how formidable must be the strength of mind which could condemn itself to so terrific a sacrifice—How deep and strong the purpose for which it was undertaken!"

But a brief recollection of past events enabled him to dismiss this conjecture as altogether wild and visionary. He had but to call to memory the various stratagems practised by his light-hearted companion, the young Earl of Derby, upon this forlorn girl—the conversations held in her presence, in which the character of a creature so irritable and sensitive upon all occasions, was freely, and sometimes satirically discussed, without her expressing the least acquaintance with what was going forward, to convince him that so deep a deception could never have been practised for so many years, by a being of a turn of mind so peculiarly jealous and irascible.

He renounced, therefore, the idea, and turned his thoughts to his own affairs, and his approaching interview with his Sovereign; in which meditation we propose to leave him, until we briefly review the changes which had taken place in the situation of Alice Bridgenorth.

CHAPTER XXXI.

I fear the devil worst when gown and cassock,
Or, in the lack of them, old Calvin's cloak,
Conceals his cloven hoof.

ANONYMOUS.

JULIAN PEVERIL had scarce set sail for Whitehaven, when Alice Bridgenorth and her governante, at the hasty command of her father, were embarked with equal speed and secrecy on board of a bark bound for Liverpool. Christian accompanied them on their voyage, as the friend to whose guardianship Alice was to be consigned during any future separation from her father, and whose amusing conversation, joined to his pleasing though cold manners, as well as his near relationship, induced Alice, in her forlorn situation, to consider her fate as fortunate in having such a guardian.

At Liverpool, as the reader already knows, Christian took the first overt step in the villainy which he had contrived against the innocent girl, by exposing her at a meeting-house to the unhallowed gaze of Chiffinch, in order to convince him she was possessed of such uncommon beauty as might well deserve the infamous promotion to which they meditated to raise her.

Highly satisfied with her personal appearance, Chiffinch was no less so with the sense and delicacy of her conversation, when he met her in company with her uncle afterwards in London. The simplicity, and at the same time the spirit of her remarks, made him regard her as his scientific attendant the cook might have done a newly invented sauce, sufficiently *piquante* in its qualities to awaken the jaded appetite of a cloyed and gorged epicure. She was, he said and swore, the very corner-stone on which, with proper management, and with his instructions, a few honest fellows might build a Court fortune.

That the necessary introduction might take place, the confederates judged fit she should be put under the charge of an experienced lady, whom some called Mistress Chiffinch, and others Chiffinch's mistress—one of those obliging creatures who are willing to discharge all the duties of a wife, without the inconvenient and indissoluble ceremony.

It was one, and not perhaps the least prejudicial consequence of the license of that ill-governed time, that the bounds betwixt virtue and vice were so far smoothed down and levelled, that the frail wife, or the tender friend who was no wife, did not necessarily lose their place in society ; but, on the contrary, if they moved in the higher circles, were permitted and encouraged to mingle with women whose rank was certain, and whose reputation was untainted.

A regular *liaison*, like that of Chiffinch and his fair one, inferred little scandal ; and such was his influence, as prime minister of his master's pleasures, that, as Charles himself expressed it, the lady whom we introduced to our readers in the last chapter, had obtained a brevet commission to rank as a married woman. And to do the gentle dame justice, no wife could have been more attentive to forward his plans, or more liberal in disposing of his income.

She inhabited a set of apartments called Chiffinch's—the scene of many an intrigue, both of love and politics; and where Charles often held his private parties for the evening, when, as frequently happened, the ill-humour of the Duchess of Portsmouth, his reigning Sultana, prevented his supping with her. The hold which such an arrangement gave a man like Chiffinch, used as he well knew how to use it, made him of too much consequence to be slighted even by the first persons in the state, unless they stood aloof from all manner of politics and Court intrigue.

In the charge of Mistress Chiffinch, and of him whose name she bore, Edward Christian placed the daughter of his sister, and of his confiding friend, calmly contemplating her ruin as an event certain to follow; and hoping to ground upon it his own chance of a more assured fortune, than a life spent in intrigue had hitherto been able to procure for him.

The innocent Alice, without being able to discover what was wrong either in the scenes of unusual luxury with which she was surrounded, or in the manners of her hostess, which, both from nature and policy, were kind and caressing—felt nevertheless an instinctive apprehension that all was not right—a feeling in the human mind, allied, perhaps, to that sense of danger which animals exhibit when placed in the vicinity of the natural enemies of their race, and which makes birds cower when the hawk is in the air, and beasts tremble when the tiger is abroad in the desert. There was a heaviness at her heart which she could not dispel; and the few hours which she had already spent at Chiffinch's were like those passed in a prison by one unconscious of the cause or event of his captivity. It was the third morning after her arrival

in London, that the scene took place which we now recur
to.

The impertinence and vulgarity of Empson, which was
permitted to him as an unrivalled performer upon his
instrument, were exhausting themselves at the expense
of all other musical professors, and Mrs. Chiffinch was
listening with careless indifference, when some one was
heard speaking loudly, and with animation, in the inner
apartment.

"Oh, gemini and gilliflower water!" exclaimed the
damsel, startled out of her fine airs into her natural vulgarity of exclamation, and running to the door of communication—"if he has not come back again after all!—
and if old Rowley"——

A tap at the farther and opposite door here arrested
her attention—she quitted the handle of that which she
was about to open as speedily as if it had burnt her fingers, and, moving back towards her couch, asked, "Who
is there?"

"Old Rowley himself, madam," said the King, entering
the apartment with his usual air of easy composure.

"O crimini!—your Majesty!—I thought"——

"That I was out of hearing, doubtless," said the King;
"and spoke of me as folk speak of absent friends.
Make no apology. I think I have heard ladies say of
their lace, that a rent is better than a darn.—Nay, be
seated.—Where is Chiffinch?"

"He is down at York-House, your Majesty," said the
dame, recovering, though with no small difficulty, the
calm affectation of her usual demeanour. "Shall I send
your Majesty's commands?"

"I will wait his return," said the King.—"Permit me
to taste your chocolate."

" There is some fresh frothed in the office," said the lady ; and using a little silver call, or whistle, a black boy, superbly dressed, like an Oriental page, with gold bracelets on his naked arms, and a gold collar around his equally bare neck, attended with the favourite beverage of the morning, in an apparatus of the richest china.

While he sipped his cup of chocolate, the King looked round the apartment, and observing Fenella, Peveril, and the musician, who remained standing beside a large Indian screen, he continued, addressing Mistress Chiffinch, though with polite indifference, " I sent you the fiddles this morning—or rather the flute—Empson, and a fairy elf whom I met in the Park, who dances divinely. She has brought us the very newest saraband from the Court of Queen Mab, and I sent her here, that you may see it at leisure."

" Your Majesty does me by far too much honour," said Chiffinch, her eyes properly cast down, and her accents minced into becoming humility.

" Nay, little Chiffinch," answered the King, in a tone of as contemptuous familiarity as was consistent with his good-breeding, " it was not altogether for thine own private ear, though quite deserving of all sweet sounds ; but I thought Nelly had been with thee this morning."

" I can send Bajazet for her, your Majesty," answered the lady.

" Nay, I will not trouble your little heathen sultan to go so far. Still it strikes me that Chiffinch said you had company—some country cousin, or such a matter—Is there not such a person ? "

" There is a young person from the country," said Mistress Chiffinch, striving to conceal a considerable portion of embarrassment ; " but she is unprepared for such an honour as to be admitted into your Majesty's presence, and "——

"And therefore the fitter to receive it, Chiffinch. There is nothing in nature so beautiful as the first blush of a little rustic between joy and fear, and wonder and curiosity. It is the down on the peach—pity it decays so soon!—the fruit remains, but the first high colouring and exquisite flavour are gone.—Never put up thy lip for the matter, Chiffinch, for it is as I tell you; so pray let us have *la belle cousine.*"

Mistress Chiffinch, more embarrassed than ever, again advanced towards the door of communication, which she had been in the act of opening when his Majesty entered. But just as she coughed pretty loudly, perhaps as a signal to some one within, voices were again heard in a raised tone of altercation—the door was flung open, and Alice rushed out of the inner apartment, followed to the door of it by the enterprising Duke of Buckingham, who stood fixed with astonishment on finding his pursuit of the flying fair one had hurried him into the presence of the King.

Alice Bridgenorth appeared too much transported with anger to permit her to pay attention to the rank or character of the company into which she had thus suddenly entered. "I remain no longer here, madam," she said to Mrs. Chiffinch, in a tone of uncontrollable resolution; "I leave instantly a house where I am exposed to company which I detest, and to solicitations which I despise."

The dismayed Mrs. Chiffinch could only implore her, in broken whispers, to be silent; adding, while she pointed to Charles, who stood with his eyes fixed rather on his audacious courtier than on the game which he pursued, "The King—the King!"

" If I am in the King's presence," said Alice, aloud,
and in the same torrent of passionate feeling, while her
eye sparkled through tears of resentment and insulted
modesty, " it is the better—it is his Majesty's duty to protect me ; and on his protection I throw myself."

These words, which were spoken aloud, and boldly, at
once recalled Julian to himself, who had hitherto stood, as
it were, bewildered. He approached Alice, and, whispering in her ear that she had beside her one who would
defend her with his life, implored her to trust to his guardianship in this emergency.

Clinging to his arm in all the ecstasy of gratitude and
joy, the spirit which had so lately invigorated Alice in her
own defence, gave way in a flood of tears, when she saw
herself supported by him whom perhaps she most wished
to recognise as her protector. She permitted Peveril
gently to draw her back towards the screen before which
he had been standing ; where, holding by his arm, but at
the same time endeavouring to conceal herself behind
him, they waited the conclusion of a scene so singular.

The King seemed at first so much surprised at the
unexpected apparition of the Duke of Buckingham, as to
pay little or no attention to Alice, who had been the
means of thus unceremoniously introducing his Grace into
the presence at a most unsuitable moment. In that intriguing Court, it had not been the first time that the
Duke had ventured to enter the lists of gallantry in rivalry of his Sovereign, which made the present insult the
more intolerable. His purpose of lying concealed in these
private apartments was explained by the exclamations of
Alice ; and Charles, notwithstanding the placidity of his
disposition, and his habitual guard over his passions, resented the attempt to seduce his destined mistress, as an

Eastern Sultan would have done the insolence of a vizier, who anticipated his intended purchases of captive beauty in the slave market. The swarthy features of Charles reddened, and the strong lines on his dark visage seemed to become inflated, as he said, in a voice which faltered with passion, "Buckingham, you dared not have thus insulted your equal! To your master you may securely offer any affront, since his rank glues his sword to the scabbard."

The haughty Duke did not brook this taunt unanswered. "My sword," he said, with emphasis, "was never in the scabbard, when your Majesty's service required it should be unsheathed."

"Your Grace means, when its service was required for its master's interest," said the King; "for you could only gain the coronet of a Duke by fighting for the royal crown. But it is over—I have treated you as a friend—a companion—almost an equal—you have repaid me with insolence and ingratitude."

"Sire," answered the Duke, firmly, but respectfully, "I am unhappy in your displeasure; yet thus far fortunate, that while your words can confer honour, they cannot impair or take it away.—It is hard," he added, lowering his voice, so as only to be heard by the King,—"It is hard that the squall of a peevish wench should cancel the services of so many years!"

"It is harder," said the King, in the same subdued tone, which both preserved through the rest of the conversation, "that a wench's bright eyes can make a nobleman forget the decencies due to his Sovereign's privacy."

"May I presume to ask your Majesty what decencies are those?" said the Duke.

Charles bit his lip to keep himself from smiling.

"Buckingham," he said, "this is a foolish business ; and we must not forget, (as we have nearly done,) that we have an audience to witness this scene, and should walk the stage with dignity. I will show you your fault in private."

"It is enough that your Majesty has been displeased, and that I have unhappily been the occasion," said the Duke, kneeling ; "although quite ignorant of any purpose beyond a few words of gallantry ; and I sue thus low for your Majesty's pardon."

So saying, he kneeled gracefully down. "Thou hast it, George," said the placable Prince. "I believe thou wilt be sooner tired of offending than I of forgiving."

"Long may your Majesty live to give the offence, with which it is your royal pleasure at present to charge my innocence," said the Duke.

"What mean you by that, my lord?" said Charles, the angry shade returning to his brow for a moment.

"My Liege," replied the Duke, "you are too honourable to deny your custom of shooting with Cupid's birdbolts in other men's warrens. You have ta'en the royal right of free-forestry over every man's park. It is hard that you should be so much displeased at hearing a chance arrow whizz near your own pales."

"No more on't," said the King ; "but let us see where the dove has harboured."

"The Helen has found a Paris while we were quarrelling," replied the Duke.

"Rather an Orpheus," said the King ; "and what is worse, one that is already provided with a Eurydice— She is clinging to the fiddler."

"It is mere fright," said Buckingham, "like Rochester's, when he crept into the bass-viol to hide himself from Sir Dermot O'Cleaver."

"We must make the people show their talents," said
the King, " and stop their mouths with money and civility, or we shall have this foolish encounter over half the
town."

The King then approached Julian, and desired him to
take his instrument, and cause his female companion to
perform a saraband.

" I had already the honour to inform your Majesty,"
said Julian, " that I cannot contribute to your pleasure in
the way you command me; and that this young person
is "——

" A retainer of the Lady Powis," said the King, upon
whose mind things not connected with his pleasures made
a very slight impression. " Poor lady, she is in trouble
about the lords in the Tower."

" Pardon me, sir," said Julian, " she is a dependent of
the Countess of Derby."

" True, true," answered Charles ; " it is indeed of Lady
Derby, who hath also her own distresses in these times.
Do you know who taught the young person to dance?
Some of her steps mightily resemble Le Jeune's of
Paris."

" I presume she was taught abroad, sir," said Julian ;
"for myself, I am charged with some weighty business
by the Countess, which I would willingly communicate to
your Majesty."

" We will send you to our Secretary of State," said the
King. " But this dancing envoy will oblige us once
more, will she not?—Empson, now that I remember, it
was to your pipe that she danced—Strike up, man, and
put mettle into her feet."

Empson began to play a well-known measure ; and, as
he had threatened, made more than one false note, until the

King, whose ear was very accurate, rebuked him with, "Sirrah, art thou drunk at this early hour, or must thou too be playing thy slippery tricks with me? Thou thinkest thou art born to beat time, but I will have time beat into thee."

The hint was sufficient, and Empson took good care so to perform his air as to merit his high and deserved reputation. But on Fenella it made not the slightest impression. She rather leant than stood against the wall of the apartment; her countenance as pale as death, her arms and hands hanging down as if stiffened, and her existence only testified by the sobs which agitated her bosom, and the tears which flowed from her half-closed eyes.

"A plague on it," said the King, "some evil spirit is abroad this morning; and the wenches are all bewitched, I think. Cheer up, my girl. What, in the devil's name, has changed thee at once from a Nymph to a Niobe? If thou standest there longer, thou wilt grow to the very marble wall—Or—oddsfish, George, have you been bird-bolting in this quarter also?"

Ere Buckingham could answer to this charge, Julian again kneeled down to the King, and prayed to be heard, were it only for five minutes. "The young woman," he said, "had been long in attendance on the Countess of Derby. She was bereaved of the faculties of speech and hearing."

"Oddsfish, man, and dances so well?" said the King. "Nay, all Gresham College shall never make me believe that."

"I would have thought it equally impossible, but for what I to-day witnessed," said Julian; "but only permit me, sir, to deliver the petition of my lady the Countess."

"And who art thou thyself, man?" said the Sovereign;

"for though every thing which wears bodie and breast-knot has a right to speak to a King, and be answered, I know not that they have a title to audience through an envoy extraordinary.".

"I am Julian Peveril of Derbyshire," answered the supplicant, "the son of Sir Geoffrey Peveril of Martin-dale Castle, who "——

"Body of me—the old Worcester man?" said the King. "Oddsfish, I remember him well—some harm has happened to him, I think—Is he not dead, or very sick at least?"

"Ill at ease, and it please your Majesty, but not ill in health. He has been imprisoned on account of an alleged accession to this Plot."

"Look you there," said the King; "I knew he was in trouble; and yet how to help the stout old Knight, I can hardly tell. I can scarce escape suspicion of the Plot myself, though the principal object of it is to take away my own life. Were I to stir to save a plotter, I should certainly be brought in as an accessary.—Buckingham, thou hast some interest with those who built this fine state engine, or at least who have driven it on—be good-natured for once, though it is scarcely thy wont, and in-terfere to shelter our old Worcester friend, Sir Godfrey. You have not forgot him?"

"No, Sir," answered the Duke; "for I never heard the name."

"It is Sir Geoffrey his Majesty would say," said Julian.

"And if his Majesty *did* say Sir Geoffrey, Master Peveril, I cannot see of what use I can be to your father," replied the Duke, coldly. "He is accused of a heavy crime; and a British subject so accused, can have no shelter either from prince or peer, but must stand to the award and deliverance of God and his country."

"Now, Heaven forgive thee thy hypocrisy, George," said the King, hastily. "I would rather hear the devil preach religion than thee teach patriotism. Thou knowest as well as I, that the nation is in a scarlet fever for fear of the poor Catholics, who are not two men to five hundred; and that the public mind is so harassed with new narrations of conspiracy, and fresh horrors every day, that people have as little real sense of what is just or unjust, as men who talk in their sleep of what is sense or nonsense. I have borne, and borne with it—I have seen blood flow on the scaffold, fearing to thwart the nation in its fury—and I pray to God that I or mine be not called on to answer for it. I will no longer swim with the torrent, which honour and conscience call upon me to stem—I will act the part of a Sovereign, and save my people from doing injustice, even in their own despite."

Charles walked hastily up and down the room as he expressed these unwonted sentiments, with energy equally unwonted. After a momentary pause, the Duke answered him gravely, "Spoken like a Royal King, sir, but —pardon me—not like a King of England."

Charles paused, as the Duke spoke, beside a window which looked full on Whitehall, and his eye was involuntarily attracted by the fatal window of the Banqueting House out of which his unhappy father was conducted to execution. Charles was naturally, or, more properly, constitutionally brave; but a life of pleasure, together with the habit of governing his course rather by what was expedient than by what was right, rendered him unapt to dare the same scene of danger or of martyrdom, which had closed his father's life and reign; and the thought came over his half-formed resolution, like the rain upon a kindling beacon. In another man, his perplexity would have seemed almost ludicrous; but Charles could not lose, even under these circumstances, the dignity and grace, which were as natural to him as his indifference and his good humour. " Our council must decide in this matter," he said, looking to the Duke; " and be assured, young man," he added, addressing Julian, " your father shall not want an intercessor in his King, so far as the laws will permit my interference in his behalf."

Julian was about to retire, when Fenella, with a marked look, put into his hand a slip of paper, on which she had hastily written, " The packet—give him the packet."

After a moment's hesitation, during which he reflected that Fenella was the organ of the Countess's pleasure, Julian resolved to obey. " Permit me, then, Sire," he said, " to place in your royal hands this packet, intrusted to me by the Countess of Derby. The letters have already been once taken from me; and I have little hope that I can now deliver them as they are addressed. I place them, therefore, in your royal hands, certain that they will evince the innocence of the writer."

The King shook his head as he took the packet reluctantly. " It is no safe office you have undertaken, young man. A messenger has sometimes his throat cut for the sake of his dispatches—But give them to me; and, Chiffinch, give me wax and a taper." He employed himself in folding the Countess's packet in another envelope. " Buckingham," he said, " you are evidence that I do not read them till the Council shall see them."

Buckingham approached, and offered his services in folding the parcel, but Charles rejected his assistance ; and having finished his task, he sealed the packet with his own signet-ring. The Duke bit his lip and retired.

"And now, young man," said the King, "your errand is sped, so far as it can at present be forwarded."

Julian bowed deeply, as to take leave at these words, which he rightly interpreted as a signal for his departure. Alice Bridgenorth still clung to his arm, and motioned to withdraw along with him. The King and Buckingham looked at each other in conscious astonishment, and yet not without a desire to smile, so strange did it seem to them that a prize, for which, an instant before, they had been mutually contending, should thus glide out of their grasp, or rather be borne off by a third and very inferior competitor.

"Mistress Chiffinch," said the King, with a hesitation which he could not disguise, "I hope your fair charge is not about to leave you ?"

"Certainly not, your Majesty," answered Chiffinch. "Alice, my love—you mistake—that opposite door leads to your apartments."

"Pardon me, madam," answered Alice; "I have indeed mistaken my road, but it was when I came hither."

"The errant damozel," said Buckingham, looking at Charles with as much intelligence as etiquette permitted him to throw into his eye, and then turning it towards Alice, as she still held by Julian's arm, "is resolved not to mistake her road a second time. She has chosen a sufficient guide."

"And yet stories tell that such guides have led maidens astray," said the King."

Alice blushed deeply, but instantly recovered her composure so soon as she saw that her liberty was likely to depend upon the immediate exercise of resolution. She quitted, from a sense of insulted delicacy, the arm of Julian, to which she had hitherto clung; but as she spoke, she continued to retain a slight grasp of his cloak "I have indeed mistaken my way," she repeated, still addressing Mrs. Chiffinch, "but it was when I crossed this threshold. The usage to which I have been exposed in your house, has determined me to quit it instantly."

"I will not permit that, my young mistress," answered Mrs. Chiffinch, "until your uncle, who placed you under my care, shall relieve me of the charge of you."

"I will answer for my conduct, both to my uncle, and, what is of more importance, to my father," said Alice. "You must permit me to depart, madam; I am free-born, and you have no right to detain me."

"Pardon me, my young madam," said Mistress Chiffinch, "I have a right, and I will maintain it too."

"I will know that before quitting this presence," said Alice, firmly; and, advancing a step or two, she dropped on her knee before the King. "Your Majesty," said she, "if indeed I kneel before King Charles, is the father of your subjects."

"Of a good many of them," said the Duke of Buckingham, apart.

"I demand protection of you, in the name of God, and of the oath your Majesty swore when you placed on your head the crown of this kingdom!"

"You have my protection," said the King, a little confused by an appeal so unexpected and so solemn. "Do but remain quiet with this lady, with whom your parents have placed you; neither Buckingham nor any one else shall intrude on you."

"His Majesty," added Buckingham, in the same tone, and speaking from the restless and mischief-making spirit of contradiction, which he never could restrain, even when indulging it was most contrary, not only to propriety, but to his own interest,—"His Majesty will protect you, fair lady, from all intrusion save what must not be termed such."

Alice darted a keen look on the Duke, as if to read his meaning; another on Charles, to know whether she had guessed it rightly. There was a guilty confession on the King's brow, which confirmed Alice's determination to depart. "Your Majesty will forgive me," she said; "it is not here that I can enjoy the advantage of your royal protection. I am resolved to leave this house. If I am detained, it must be by violence, which I trust no one dare offer me in your Majesty's presence. This gentleman, whom I have long known, will conduct me to my friends."

"We make but an indifferent figure in this scene, methinks," said the King, addressing the Duke of Buckingham, and speaking in a whisper; "but she must go—I neither will, nor dare, stop her from returning to her father."

"And if she does," swore the Duke internally, "I would, as Sir Andrew Smith saith, I might never touch fair lady's hand." And stepping back, he spoke a few words with Empson the musician, who left the apartment, for a few minutes, and presently returned.

The King seemed irresolute concerning the part he should act under circumstances so peculiar. To be foiled in a gallant intrigue, was to subject himself to the ridicule of his gay court; to persist in it by any means which approached to restraint, would have been tyrannical; and, what perhaps he might judge as severe an imputation, it would have been unbecoming a gentleman. " Upon my honour, young lady," he said, with an emphasis, " you have nothing to fear in this house. But it is improper, for your own sake, that you should leave it in this abrupt manner. If you will have the goodness to wait but a quarter of an hour, Mistress Chiffinch's coach will be placed at your command, to transport you where you will. Spare yourself the ridicule, and me the pain of seeing you leave the house of one of my servants, as if you were escaping from a prison."

The King spoke in good-natured sincerity, and Alice was inclined for an instant to listen to his advice; but recollecting that she had to search for her father and uncle, or, failing them, for some suitable place of secure residence, it rushed on her mind that the attendants of Mistress Chiffinch were not likely to prove trusty guides or assistants in such a purpose. Firmly and respectfully she announced her purpose of instant departure. She needed no other escort, she said, than what this gentleman, Master Julian Peveril, who was well known to her father, would willingly afford her; nor did she need that farther than until she had reached her father's residence.

" Farewell, then, lady, a God's name! " said the King; " I am sorry so much beauty should be wedded to so many shrewish suspicions.—For you, Master Peveril, I should have thought you had enough to do with your own affairs without interfering with the humours of the fair sex. The duty of conducting all strayed damsels into the right path, is, as matters go in this good city, rather too weighty an undertaking for your youth and inexperience."

Julian, eager to conduct Alice from a place of which he began fully to appreciate the perils, answered nothing to this taunt, but bowing reverently, led her from the apartment. Her sudden appearance, and the animated scene which followed, had entirely absorbed, for the moment, the recollection of his father, and of the Countess of Derby; and while the dumb attendant of the latter remained in the room, a silent, and, as it were, stunned spectator of all that had happened, Peveril had become, in the predominating interest of Alice's critical situation, totally forgetful of her presence. But no sooner had he left the room, without noticing or attending to her, than Fenella, starting, as from a trance, drew herself up, and looked wildly around, like one waking from a dream, as if to assure herself that her companion was gone, and gone without paying the slightest attention to her. She folded her hands together, and cast her eyes upwards, with an expression of such agony as explained to Charles (as he thought) what painful ideas were passing in her mind. " This Peveril is a perfect pattern of successful perfidy," said the King; " he has not only succeeded at first sight in carrying off this Queen of the Amazons, but he has left us, I think, a disconsolate Ariadne in her place.—But weep not, my princess of pretty movements," he said, addressing himself to Fenella; " if we cannot call in Bacchus to console you, we will commit you to the care of Empson, who shall drink with *Liber Pater* for a thousand pounds, and I will say done first."

As the King spoke these words, Fenella rushed past him with her wonted rapidity of step, and, with much less courtesy than was due to the royal presence, hurried down stairs, and out of the house, without attempting to open any communication with the Monarch. He saw her abrupt departure with more surprise than displeasure; and presently afterwards, bursting into a fit of laughter, he said to the Duke, "Oddsfish, George, this young spark might teach the best of us how to manage the wenches. I have had my own experience, but I could never yet contrive either to win or lose them with so little ceremony."

"Experience, sir," replied the Duke, "cannot be acquired without years."

"True, George; and you would, I suppose, insinuate," said Charles, "that the gallant who acquires it, loses as much in youth as he gains in art? I defy your insinuation, George. You cannot overreach your master, old as you think him, either in love or politics. You have not the secret *plumer la poule sans la faire crier*, witness this morning's work. I will give you odds at all games—ay, and at the Mall, too, if thou darest accept my challenge. —Chiffinch, what for dost thou convulse thy pretty throat and face with sobbing and hatching tears, which seem rather unwilling to make their appearance?"

"It is for fear," whined Chiffinch, "that your Majesty should think—that you should expect "——

"That I should expect gratitude from a courtier, or faith from a woman?" answered the King, patting her at the same time under the chin, to make her raise her face —"Tush! chicken, I am not so superfluous."

"There it is now," said Chiffinch, continuing to sob the more bitterly, as she felt herself unable to produce any tears; "I see your Majesty is determined to lay all the blame on me, when I am innocent as an unborn babe—I will be judged by his Grace."

"No doubt, no doubt, Chiffie," said the King. "His Grace and you will be excellent judges in each other's cause, and as good witnesses in each other's favour. But to investigate the matter impartially, we must examine our evidence apart.—My Lord Duke, we meet at the Mall at noon, if your Grace dare accept my challenge."

His Grace of Buckingham bowed, and retired.

CHAPTER XXXII.

But when the bully with assuming pace,
Cocks his broad hat, edged round with tarnish'd lace,
Yield not the way—defy his strutting pride,
And thrust him to the muddy kennel's side,
Yet rather bear the shower and toils of mud,
Than in the doubtful quarrel risk thy blood.

GAY'S TRIVIA.

JULIAN PEVERIL, half-leading, half-supporting, Alice Bridgenorth, had reached the middle of Saint James's Street ere the doubt occurred to him which way they should bend their course. .He then asked Alice whither he should conduct her, and learned, to his surprise and embarrassment, that, far from knowing where her father was to be found, she had no certain knowledge that he was in London, and only hoped that he had arrived, from the expressions which he had used at parting. She mentioned her uncle Christian's address, but it was with doubt and hesitation, arising from the hands in which he had already placed her; and her reluctance to go again under his protection was strongly confirmed by her youthful guide, when a few words had established to his conviction the identity of Ganlesse and Christian.—What then was to be done?

"Alice," said Julian, after a moment's reflection, "you must seek your earliest and best friend—I mean my mother. She has now no castle in which to receive you

—she has but a miserable lodging, so near the jail in which my father is confined, that it seems almost a cell of the same prison. I have not seen her since my coming hither; but thus much have I learned by inquiry. We will now go to her apartment; such as it is, I know she will share it with one so innocent and so unprotected as you are."

"Gracious Heaven!" said the poor girl, "am I then so totally deserted, that I must throw myself on the mercy of her who, of all the world, has most reason to spurn me from her?—Julian, can you advise me to this? —Is there none else who will afford me a few hours' refuge, till I can hear from my father?—No other protectress but her whose ruin has, I fear, been accelerated by——Julian, I dare not appear before your mother! she must hate me for my family, and despise me for my meanness. To be a second time cast on her protection, when the first has been so evil repaid—Julian, I dare not go with you."

"She has never ceased to love you, Alice," said her conductor, whose steps she continued to attend, even while declaring her resolution not to go with him, "she never felt any thing but kindness towards you, nay, towards your father; for though his dealings with us have been harsh, she can allow much for the provocation which he has received. Believe me, with her you will be safe as with a mother—perhaps it may be the means of reconciling the divisions by which we have suffered so much."

"Might God grant it!" said Alice. "Yet how shall I face your mother? And will she be able to protect me against these powerful men—against my uncle Christian? Alas, that I must call him my worst enemy!"

"She has the ascendency which honour hath over infamy, and virtue over vice," said Julian; "and to no human power but your father's will she resign you, if you consent to choose her for your protectress. Come, then, with me, Alice; and "——

Julian was interrupted by some one, who, laying an unceremonious hold of his cloak, pulled it with so much force as compelled him to stop and lay his hand on his sword. He turned at the same time, and, when he turned, beheld Fenella. The cheek of the mute glowed like fire; her eyes sparkled, and her lips were forcibly drawn together, as if she had difficulty to repress those wild screams which usually attended her agonies of passion, and which, uttered in the open street, must instantly have collected a crowd. As it was, her appearance was so singular, and her emotion so evident, that men gazed as they came on, and looked back after they had passed, at the singular vivacity of her gestures; while, holding Peveril's cloak with one hand, she made with the other the most eager and imperious signs that he should leave Alice Bridgenorth and follow her. She touched the plume in her bonnet, to remind him of the Earl—pointed to her heart, to imitate the Countess—raised her closed hand, as if to command him in their name—and next moment folded both, as if to supplicate him in her own; while pointing to Alice with an expression at once of angry and scornful derision, she waved her hand repeatedly and disdainfully, to intimate that Peveril ought to cast her off, as something undeserving his protection.

Frightened, she knew not why, at these wild gestures, Alice clung closer to Julian's arm than she had at first dared to do: and this mark of confidence in his protection seemed to increase the passion of Fenella.

Julian was dreadfully embarrassed; his situation was sufficiently precarious, even before Fenella's ungovernable passions threatened to ruin the only plan which he had been able to suggest. What she wanted with him—how far the fate of the Earl and Countess might depend on his following her, he could not even conjecture; but be the call how peremptory soever, he resolved not to comply with it until he had seen Alice placed in safety. In the meantime, he determined not to lose sight of Fenella; and disregarding her repeated, disdainful, and impetuous rejection of the hand which he offered her, he at length seemed so far to have soothed her, that she seized upon his right arm, and, as if despairing of his following *her* path, appeared reconciled to attend him on that which he himself should choose.

Thus, with a youthful female clinging to each arm, and both remarkably calculated to attract the public eye, though from very different reasons, Julian resolved to make the shortest road to the water-side, and there to take boat for Blackfriars, as the nearest point of landing to Newgate, where he concluded that Lance had already announced his arrival in London to Sir Geoffrey, then inhabiting that dismal region, and to his lady, who, so far as the jailer's rigour permitted, shared and softened his imprisonment.

Julian's embarrassment in passing Charing-Cross and Northumberland-House was so great as to excite the attention of the passengers; for he had to compose his steps so as to moderate the unequal and rapid pace of Fenella to the timid and faint progress of his left-hand companion; and while it would have been needless to address himself to the former, who could not comprehend him, he dared not speak himself to Alice, for fear of awakening into frenzy the jealousy, or at least the impatience of Fenella.

Many passengers looked at them with wonder, and some with smiles; but Julian remarked that there were two who never lost sight of them, and to whom his situation, and the demeanour of his companions, seemed to afford matter of undisguised merriment. These were young men, such as may be seen in the same precincts in the present day, allowing for the difference in the fashion of their apparel. They abounded in periwig, and fluttered with many hundred yards of ribbon, disposed in bow-knots, upon their sleeves, their breeches, and their waistcoats, in the very extremity of the existing mode. A quantity of lace and embroidery made their habits rather fine than tasteful. In a word, they were dressed in that caricature of the fashion, which sometimes denotes a harebrained man of quality who has a mind to be distinguished as a fop of the first order, but is much more frequently the disguise of those who desire to be esteemed men of rank on account of their dress, having no other pretension to the distinction.

These two gallants passed Peveril more than once, linked arm in arm, then sauntered, so as to oblige him to pass them in turn, laughing and whispering during these manœuvres—staring broadly at Peveril and his female companions—and affording them, as they came into contact, none of those facilities of giving place which are required on such occasions by the ordinary rules of the pavé.

Peveril did not immediately observe their impertinence; but when it was too gross to escape his notice, his gall began to arise; and, in addition to all the other embarrassments of his situation, he had to combat the longing desire which he felt to cudgel handsomely the two coxcombs who seemed thus determined on insulting him. Patience and sufferance were indeed strongly imposed on him by circumstances ; but at length it became scarcely possible to observe their dictates any longer.

When, for the third time, Julian found himself obliged, with his companions, to pass this troublesome brace of fops, they kept walking close behind him, speaking so loud as to be heard, and in a tone of perfect indifference whether he listened to them or not.

" This is bumpkin's best luck," said the taller of the two, (who was indeed a man of remarkable size, alluding to the plainness of Peveril's dress, which was scarce fit for the streets of London)—" Two such fine wenches, and under guard of a gray frock and an oaken riding-rod ! "

" Nay, Puritan's luck rather, and more than enough of it," said his companion. " You may read Puritan in his pace and in his patience."

" Right as a pint bumper, Tom," said his friend— " Issachar is an ass that stoopeth between two burdens."

" I have a mind to ease long-eared Laurence of one of his encumbrances," said the shorter fellow. " That black-eyed sparkler looks as if she had a mind to run away from him."

"Ay," answered the taller, "and the blue-eyed trembler looks as if she would fall behind into my loving arms."

At these words, Alice, holding still closer by Peveril's arm than formerly, mended her pace almost to running, in order to escape from men whose language was so alarming; and Fenella walked hastily forward in the same manner, having perhaps caught, from the men's gestures and demeanour, that apprehension which Alice had taken from their language.

Fearful of the consequences of a fray in the streets, which must necessarily separate him from these unprotected females, Peveril endeavoured to compound betwixt the prudence necessary for their protection and his own rising resentment; and as this troublesome pair of attendants endeavoured again to pass them close to Hungerford Stairs, he said to them with constrained calmness, " Gentlemen, I owe you something for the attention you have bestowed on the affairs of a stranger. If you have any pretension to the name I have given you, you will tell me where you are to be found."

"And with what purpose," said the taller of the two, sneeringly, " does your most rustic gravity, or your most grave rusticity, require of us such information ? "

So saying, they both faced about, in such a manner as to make it impossible for Julian to advance any farther.

" Make for the stairs, Alice," he said ; " I will be with you in an instant." Then freeing himself with difficulty from the grasp of his companions, he cast his cloak hastily round his left arm, and said, sternly, to his opponents, " Will you give me your names, sirs ; or will you be pleased to make way ? "

" Not till we know for whom we are to give place ? " said one of them.

" For one who will else teach you what you want— good manners," said Peveril, and advanced as if to push between them.

They separated, but one of them stretched forth his foot before Peveril, as if he meant to trip him. The blood of his ancestors was already boiling within him ; he struck the man on the face with the oaken rod which he had just sneered at, and throwing it from him, instantly unsheathed his sword. Both the others drew, and pushed at once; but he caught the point of the one rapier in his cloak, and parried the other thrust with his own weapon. He might have been less lucky in the second close, but a cry arose among the watermen, of "Shame, shame! two upon one!"

"They are men of the Duke of Buckingham's," said one fellow—"there's no safe meddling with them."

"They may be the devil's men, if they will," said an ancient Triton, flourishing his stretcher; "but I say fair play, and old England for ever; and, I say, knock the gold-laced puppies down, unless they will fight turn about with gray jerkin, like honest fellows. One down—t'other come on."

The lower orders of London have in all times been remarkable for the delight which they have taken in club-law, or fist-law; and for the equity and impartiality with which they see it administered. The noble science of defence was then so generally known, that a bout at single rapier excited at that time as much interest and as little wonder as a boxing-match in our own days. The bystanders, experienced in such affrays, presently formed a ring, within which Peveril and the taller and more forward of his antagonists were soon engaged in close combat with their swords, whilst the other, overawed by the spectators, was prevented from interfering.

"Well done the tall fellow!"—"Well thrust, long-legs!"—"Huzza for two ells and a quarter!" were the sounds with which the fray was at first cheered; for Peveril's opponent not only showed great activity and skill in fence, but had also a decided advantage, from the anxiety with which Julian looked out for Alice Bridge-north; the care for whose safety diverted him in the beginning of the onset from that which he ought to have

exclusively bestowed on the defence of his own life. A
slight flesh-wound in the side at once punished, and
warned him of, his inadvertence ; when, turning his whole
thoughts on the business in which he was engaged, and
animated with anger against his impertinent intruder, the
rencontre speedily began to assume another face, amidst
cries of " Well done, gray jerkin ! "—" Try the metal of
his gold doublet ! "—" Finely thrust ! "—" Curiously parried ! "—" There went another eyelet-hole to his broidered
jerkin ! "—" Fairly pinked, by G—d ! "   In fact, the last
exclamation was uttered amid a general roar of applause,
accompanying a successful and conclusive lounge, by
which Peveril ran his gigantic antagonist through the
body. He looked at his prostrate foe for a moment ;
then, recovering himself, called loudly to know what had
become of the lady.

" Never mind the lady, if you be wise," said one of the
watermen ; " the constable will be here in an instant.
I'll give your honour a cast across the water in a moment.
It may be as much as your neck's worth. Shall only
charge a Jacobus."

" You be d—d ! " said one of his rivals in profession,
" as your father was before you ; for a Jacobus, I'll set
the gentleman into Alsatia, where neither bailiff nor constable dare trespass."

" The lady, you scoundrels, the lady ! " exclaimed
Peveril—" Where is the lady ? "

" I'll carry your honour where you shall have enough
of ladies, if that be your want," said the old Triton ; and
as he spoke, the clamour amongst the watermen was
renewed, each hoping to cut his own profit out of the
emergency of Julian's situation.

"A sculler will be least suspected, your honour," said
one fellow.

"A pair of oars will carry you through the water like a wild-duck," said another.

" But you have got never a tilt, brother," said a third. " Now I can put the gentleman as snug as if he were under hatches."

In the midst of the oaths and clamour attending this aquatic controversy for his custom, Peveril at length made them understand that he would bestow a Jacobus, not on him whose boat was first oars, but on whomsoever should inform him of the fate of the lady.

" Of which lady?" said a sharp fellow; " for, to my thought, there was a pair on them."

" Of both, of both," answered Peveril; " but first of the fair-haired lady?"

"Ay, ay, that was she that shrieked so when gold-jacket's companion handed her into No. 20."

" Who—what—who dared to hand her?" exclaimed Peveril.

" Nay, master, you have heard enough of my tale without a fee," said the waterman.

"Sordid rascal!" said Peveril, giving him a gold piece, " speak out, or I'll run my sword through you!"

" For the matter of that, master," answered the fellow, "not while I can handle this trunnion—but a bargain's a bargain; and so I'll tell you, for your gold piece, that the comrade of the fellow forced one of your wenches, her with the fair hair, will she nill she, into Tickling Tom's wherry; and they are far enough up Thames by this time, with wind and tide."

"Sacred Heaven, and I stand here!" exclaimed Julian.

"Why, that is because your honour will not take a boat."

" You are right, my friend—a boat—a boat instantly ! "

" Follow me, then, squire.—Here, Tom, bear a hand—
the gentleman is our fare."

A volley of water language was exchanged betwixt the
successful candidate for Peveril's custom and his disappointed brethren, which concluded by the ancient Triton's
bellowing out, in a tone above them all, " that the gentleman was in a fair way to make a voyage to the isle of
gulls, for that sly Jack was only bantering him—No. 20
had rowed for York-Buildings."

" To the isle of gallows," cried another; " for here
comes one who will mar his trip up Thames, and carry
him down to Execution-Dock."

In fact, as he spoke the word, a constable, with three
or four of his assistants, armed with the old-fashioned
brown bills, which were still used for arming those guardians of the peace, cut off our hero's farther progress to
the water's edge, by arresting him in the King's name.
To attempt resistance would have been madness, as he
was surrounded on all sides ; so Peveril was disarmed,
and carried before the nearest Justice of the Peace, for
examination and committal.

The legal sage before whom Julian was taken, was a
man very honest in his intentions, very bounded in his
talents, and rather timid in his disposition. Before the
general alarm given to England, and to the city of London in particular, by the notable discovery of the Popish
Plot, Master Maulstatute had taken serene and undisturbed pride and pleasure in the discharge of his duties
as a Justice of the Peace, with the exercise of all its hon-
orary privileges and awful authority. But the murder
of Sir Edmondsbury Godfrey had made a strong, nay, an
indelible impression on his mind ; and he walked the

Courts of Themis with fear and trembling after that memorable and melancholy event.

Having a high idea of his official importance, and rather an exalted notion of his personal consequence, his honour saw nothing from that time but cords and daggers before his eyes, and never stepped out of his own house, which he fortified, and in some measure garrisoned, with half a dozen tall watchmen and constables, without seeing himself watched by a Papist in disguise, with a drawn sword under his cloak. It was even whispered, that, in the agonies of his fears, the worshipful Master Maulstatute mistook the kitchen-wench with a tinder-box, for a Jesuit with a pistol; but if any one dared to laugh at such an error, he would have done well to conceal his mirth, lest he fell under the heavy inculpation of being a banterer and stifler of the Plot—a crime almost as deep as that of being himself a plotter. In fact, the fears of the honest Justice, however ridiculously exorbitant, were kept so much in countenance by the outcry of the day, and the general nervous fever, which afflicted every good Protestant, that Master Maulstatute was accounted the bolder man and the better magistrate, while, under the terror of the air-drawn dagger which fancy placed continually before his eyes, he continued to dole forth justice in the recesses of his private chamber, nay, occasionally to attend Quarter-Sessions, when the hall was guarded by a sufficient body of the militia. Such was the wight, at whose door, well chained and doubly bolted, the constable who had Julian in custody now gave his important and well-known knock.

Notwithstanding this official signal, the party was not admitted until the clerk, who acted the part of high-warder, had reconnoitred them through a grated wicket;

for who could say whether the Papists might not have made themselves master of Master Constable's sign, and have prepared a pseudo watch to burst in and murder the Justice, under pretence of bringing a criminal before him ? —Less hopeful projects had figured in the Narrative of the Popish Plot.

All being found right, the key was turned, the bolts were drawn, and the chain unhooked, so as to permit entrance to the constable, the prisoner, and the assistants ; and the door was then as suddenly shut against the witnesses, who, as less trustworthy persons, were requested (through the wicket) to remain in the yard, until they should be called in their respective turns.

Had Julian been inclined for mirth, as was far from being the case, he must have smiled at the incongruity of the clerk's apparel, who had belted over his black buckram suit a buff baldric, sustaining a broadsword, and a pair of huge horse-pistols ; and, instead of the low flat hat, which, coming in place of the city cap, completed the dress of a scrivener, had placed on his greasy locks a rusted steel-cap, which had seen Marston-Moor ; across which projected his well-used quill, in the guise of a plume—the shape of the morion not admitting of its being stuck, as usual, behind his ear.

This whimsical figure conducted the constable, his assistants, and the prisoner, into the low hall, where his principal dealt forth justice ; who presented an appearance still more singular than that of his dependant.

Sundry good Protestants, who thought so highly of themselves as to suppose they were worthy to be distinguished as objects of Catholic cruelty, had taken to defensive arms on the occasion. But it was quickly found that a breast-plate and back-plate of proof, fastened together with iron clasps, was no convenient enclosure for a man who meant to eat venison and custard ; and that a buff-coat or shirt of mail, was scarcely more accommodating to the exertions necessary on such active occasions. Besides, there were other objections, as the alarming and menacing aspects which such warlike habiliments gave to the Exchange, and other places, where merchants most do congregate ; and excoriations were bitterly complained of by many, who, not belonging to the artillery company, or trained bands, had no experience in bearing defensive armour.

To obviate these objections, and, at the same time, to secure the persons of all true Protestant citizens against open force or privy assassinations on the part of the Papists, some ingenious artist, belonging, we may presume, to the worshipful Mercers' Company, had contrived a species of armour, of which neither the horse-armory in the Tower, nor Gwynnap's Gothic Hall, no, nor Dr. Meyrick's invaluable collection of ancient arms, has preserved any specimen. It was called silk-armour,* being com-

* Roger North gives us a ridiculous description of these warlike habiliments, when talking of the Whig Club in Fuller's Rents: " The conversation and ordinary discourse of the club was chiefly on the subject of bravery in defending the cause of liberty and property, and what every Protestant Englishman ought to venture and do, rather than be overrun with Popery and slavery. There was much recommendation of silk armour, and the prudence of being provided with it, against the time that Protestants were to be massacred; and accordingly there were abundance of these silken backs, breasts, and pots, [i. e., head pieces,] made and sold, which were pretended to be pistol proof, in which any man dressed up was as safe as in a house; for it was impossible any one could go to strike him for laughing, so ridiculous was the figure, as they say, of hogs in armour—an image of derision insensible but to the view, as I have had it, [viz. that none can imagine without seeing it as I have.] This was armour of defence, but our sparks were not altogether so tame as to carry their provisions

posed of a doublet and breeches of quilted silk, so closely
stitched, and of such thickness, as to be proof against
either bullet or steel; while a thick bonnet of the same
materials, with ear-flaps attached to it, and on the whole,
much resembling a night-cap, completed the equipment,
and ascertained the security of the wearer from the head
to the knee.

Master Maulstatute, among other worthy citizens, had
adopted this singular panoply, which had the advantage
of being soft, and warm, and flexible, as well as safe.
And he now sat in his judicial elbow-chair—a short, rotund
figure, hung round, as it were, with cushions, for such was
the appearance of the quilted garments ; and with a nose
protruded from under the silken casque, the size of which,
together with the unwieldiness of the whole figure, gave
his worship no indifferent resemblance to the sign of the
Hog in Armour, which was considerably improved by the
defensive garment being of a dusty orange-colour, not
altogether unlike the hue of those half-wild swine which
are to be found in the forests of Hampshire.

Secure in these invulnerable envelopments, his worship

no farther; for truly they intended to be assailants upon fair occasion,
and had for that end recommended to them a certain pocket weapon,
which, for its design and efficacy, had the honour to be called a Protestant flail. It was for street and crowd work, and the instrument,
lurking *perdue* in a coat-pocket, might readily sally out to execution,
and by clearing a great hall, piazza, or so, carry an election, by a
choice way of polling called ' knocking down.' The handle resembled
a farrier's blood-stick, and the fall was joined to the end by a strong
nervous ligature, that in its swing fell short of the hand, and was
made of *lignum-vitœ*, or rather, as the poet termed it, *mortis.*"—*Examen*, p. 173.

This last weapon will remind the reader of the blood-stick so cruelly used, as was alleged, in a murder committed in England some
years ago, and for a participation in which two persons were tried and
acquitted at the assizes of autumn, 1830.

had rested content, although severed from his own death-
doing weapons, of rapier, poniard, and pistols, which were
placed, nevertheless, at no great distance from his chair.
One offensive implement, indeed, he thought it prudent to
keep on the table beside his huge Coke upon Lyttleton.
This was a sort of pocket-flail, consisting of a piece of
strong ash, about eighteen inches long, to which was
attached a swinging club of *lignum-vitæ*, nearly twice as
long as the handle, but jointed so as to be easily folded
up. This instrument, which bore at that time the singular name of the Protestant flail, might be concealed under
the coat, until circumstances demanded its public appearance. A better precaution against surprise than his
arms, whether offensive or defensive, was a strong iron
grating, which, crossing the room in front of the justice's
table, and communicating by a grated door, which was
usually kept locked, effectually separated the accused
party from his judge.

Justice Maulstatute, such as we have described him,
chose to hear the accusation of the witnesses before calling on Peveril for his defence. The detail of the affray
was briefly given by the bystanders, and seemed deeply
to touch the spirit of the examinator. He shook his
silken casque emphatically, when he understood that, after
some language betwixt the parties, which the witnesses
did not quite understand, the young man in custody struck
the first blow, and drew his sword before the wounded
party had unsheathed his weapon. Again he shook his
crested head yet more solemnly, when the result of the
conflict was known; and yet again, when one of the witnesses declared, that, to the best of his knowledge, the
sufferer in the fray was a gentleman belonging to the
household of his Grace the Duke of Buckingham.

" A worthy peer," quoth the armed magistrate—" a true Protestant, and a friend to his country. Mercy on us, to what a height of audacity hath this age arisen! We see well, and could, were we as blind as a mole, out of what quiver this shaft hath been drawn."

He then put on his spectacles, and having desired Julian to be brought forward, he glared upon him awfully with those glazen eyes, from under the shade of his quilted turban.

" So young," he said, "and so hardened—lack-a-day! —and a Papist, I'll warrant."

Peveril had time enough to recollect the necessity of his being at large, if he could possibly obtain his freedom, and interposed here a civil contradiction of his worship's gracious supposition. "He was no Catholic," he said, "but an unworthy member of the Church of England."

" Perhaps but a lukewarm Protestant, notwithstanding," said the sage Justice; "there are those amongst us who ride tantivy to Rome, and have already made out half the journey—ahem!"

Peveril disowned his being any such.

" And who art thou, then?" said the Justice; "for, friend, to tell you plainly, I like not your visage— ahem!"

These short and emphatic coughs were accompanied each by a succinct nod, intimating the perfect conviction of the speaker that he had made the best, the wisest, and the most acute observation, of which the premises admitted.

Julian, irritated by the whole circumstances of his detention, answered the Justice's interrogation in rather a lofty tone. "My name is Julian Peveril!"

" Now, Heaven be around us!" said the terrified

Justice—"the son of that black-hearted Papist and traitor, Sir Geoffrey Peveril, now in hands, and on the verge of trial!"

"How, sir!" exclaimed Julian, forgetting his situation, and, stepping forward to the grating, with a violence which made the bars clatter, he so startled the appalled Justice, that, snatching his Protestant flail, Master Maul-statute aimed a blow at his prisoner, to repel what he apprehended was a premeditated attack. But whether it was owing to the Justice's hurry of mind, or inexperience in managing the weapon, he not only missed his aim, but brought the swinging part of the machine round his own skull, with such a severe counter-buff, as completely to try the efficacy of his cushioned helmet, and, in spite of its defence, to convey a stunning sensation, which he rather hastily imputed to the consequence of a blow received from Peveril.

His assistants did not indeed directly confirm the opinion which the Justice had so unwarrantably adopted; but all with one voice agreed, that, but for their own active and instantaneous interference, there was no knowing what mischief might have been done by a person so dangerous as the prisoner. The general opinion that he meant to proceed in the matter of his own rescue, *par voie du fait*, was indeed so deeply impressed on all present, that Julian saw it would be in vain to offer any defence, especially being but too conscious that the alarming, and probably the fatal consequences of his rencontre with the bully, rendered his commitment inevitable. He contented himself with asking into what prison he was to be thrown; and when the formidable word Newgate was returned as full answer, he had at least the satisfaction to reflect, that, stern and dangerous as was the shelter of that roof, he should at least enjoy it in company with his father; and that, by some means or other, they might perhaps obtain the satisfaction of a melancholy meeting, under the circumstances of mutual calamity, which seemed impending over their house.

Assuming the virtue of more patience than he actually possessed, Julian gave the magistrate, (to whom all the mildness of his demeanour could not, however, reconcile him,) the direction to the house where he lodged, together with a request that his servant, Lance Outram might be permitted to send him his money and wearing apparel; adding, that all which might be in his possession, either of arms or writings,—the former amounting to a pair of travelling pistols, and the last to a few memoranda of little consequence, he willingly consented to place at the disposal of the magistrate. It was in that moment that he entertained, with sincere satisfaction, the comforting reflection, that the important papers of Lady Derby were already in the possession of the Sovereign.

The Justice promised attention to his requests; but reminded him, with great dignity, that his present complacent and submissive behaviour ought, for his own sake, to have been adopted from the beginning, instead of disturbing the presence of magistracy with such atrocious marks of the malignant, rebellious, and murderous spirit of Popery, as he had at first exhibited. " Yet," he said, " as he was a goodly young man, and of honourable quality, he would not suffer him to be dragged through the streets as a felon, but had ordered a coach for his accommodation."

His honour, Master Maulstatute, uttered the word " coach " with the importance of one who, as Dr. Johnson saith of later date, is conscious of the dignity of

putting horses to his chariot. The worshipful Master
Maulstatute did not, however, on this occasion, do Julian
the honour of yoking to his huge family caroche the two
"frampal jades," (to use the term of the period,) which
were wont to drag that ark to the meeting-house of pure
and precious Master Howlaglass, on a Thursday's evening for lecture, and on a Sunday for a four-hours' sermon.
He had recourse to a leathern convenience, then more
rare, but just introduced, with every prospect of the great
facility which has since been afforded by hackney coaches
to all manner of communication, honest and dishonest,
legal and illegal. Our friend Julian, hitherto much more
accustomed to the saddle than to any other conveyance,
soon found himself in a hackney carriage, with the constable and two assistants for his companions, armed up to
the teeth—the port of destination being, as they had
already intimated, the ancient fortress of Newgate.

CHAPTER XXXIII.

'Tis the black ban-dog of our jail—Pray look on him,
But at a wary distance—rouse him not—
He bays not till he worries.
                        THE BLACK DOG OF NEWGATE.

THE coach stopped before those tremendous gates,
which resemble those of Tartarus, save only that they
rather more frequently permit safe and honourable egress;
although at the price of the same anxiety and labour with
which Hercules, and one or two of the demi-gods, extricated themselves from the Hell of the ancient mythol-
ogy, and sometimes, it is said, by the assistance of the
golden boughs.

Julian stepped out of the vehicle, carefully supported
on either side by his companions, and also by one or two
turnkeys, whom the first summons of the deep bell at the
gate had called to their assistance.   That attention, it
may be guessed, was not bestowed lest he should make a
false step, so much as for fear of his attempting an
escape, of which he had no intentions.   A few prentices
and straggling boys of the neighbouring market, which
derived considerable advantage from increase of custom,
in consequence of the numerous committals on account of
the Popish Plot, and who therefore were zealous Protestants, saluted him on his descent with jubilee shouts of
" Whoop, Papist! whoop, Papist! D——n to the Pope,
and all his adherents! "

Under such auspices, Peveril was ushered in beneath
that gloomy gateway, where so many bid adieu on their
entrance at once to honour and to life. The dark and
dismal arch under which he soon found himself, opened
upon a large court-yard, where a number of debtors were
employed in playing at handball, pitch-and-toss, hustle-
cap, and other games, for which relaxations the rigour
of their creditors afforded them full leisure, while it de-
barred them the means of pursuing the honest labour by
which they might have redeemed their affairs, and maintained their starving and beggared families.

But with this careless and desperate group Julian was
not to be numbered, being led, or rather forced, by his
conductors, into a low arched door, which, carefully secured by bolts and bars, opened for his reception on one
side of the archway, and closed, with all its fastenings,
the moment after his hasty entrance. He was then conducted along two or three gloomy passages, which, where
they intersected each other, were guarded by as many
strong wickets, one of iron grates, and the others of stout
oak, clenched with plates, and studded with nails of the
same metal. He was not allowed to pause until he found
himself hurried into a little round vaulted room, which
several of these passages opened into, and which seemed,
with respect to the labyrinth through part of which he
had passed, to resemble the central point of a spider's
web, in which the main lines of that reptile's curious
maze are always found to terminate.

The resemblance did not end here; for in this small
vaulted apartment, the walls of which were hung round
with musketoons, pistols, cutlasses, and other weapons, as
well as with many sets of fetters and irons of different
construction, all disposed in great order, and ready for

employment, a person sat, who might not unaptly be compared to a huge bloated and bottled spider, placed there to secure the prey which had fallen into his toils.

This official had originally been a very strong and square-built man, of large size, but was now so overgrown, from over-feeding, perhaps, and want of exercise, as to bear the same resemblance to his former self which a stall-fed ox still retains to a wild bull. The look of no man is so inauspicious as a fat man, upon whose features ill-nature has marked an habitual stamp. He seems to have reversed the old proverb of " laugh and be fat," and to have thriven under the influence of the worst affections of the mind. Passionate we can allow a jolly mortal to be; but it seems unnatural to his goodly case to be sulky and brutal. Now this man's features, surly and tallow-coloured; his limbs, swelled and disproportioned; his huge paunch and unwieldy carcass, suggested the idea, that, having once found his way into this central recess, he had there battened, like the weasel in the fable, and fed largely and foully, until he had become incapable of retreating through any of the narrow paths that terminated at his cell; and was thus compelled to remain, like a toad under the cold stone, fattening amid the squalid airs of the dungeons by which he was surrounded, which would have proved pestiferous to any other than such a congenial inhabitant. Huge iron-clasped books lay before this ominous specimen of pinguitude—the records of the realm of misery, in which office he officiated as prime minister; and had Peveril come thither as an unconcerned visitor, his heart would have sunk within him at considering the mass of human wretchedness which must needs be registered in these fatal volumes. But his own distresses sat too heavy on his mind to permit any general reflections of this nature.

The constable and this bulky official whispered together, after the former had delivered to the latter the
warrant of Julian's commitment. The word *whispered*
is not quite accurate, for their communication was carried on less by words than by looks and expressive signs;
by which, in all such situations, men learn to supply the
use of language, and to add mystery to what is in itself
sufficiently terrible to the captive. The only words
which could be heard were those of the Warden, or, as
he was called then, the Captain of the Jail, " Another
bird to the cage?"——

" Who will whistle ' Pretty Pope of Rome,' with any
starling in your Knight's ward," answered the constable,
with a facetious air, checked, however, by the due respect
to the superior presence in which he stood.

The Grim Feature relaxed into something like a smile
as he heard the officer's observation; but instantly composing himself into the stern solemnity which for an instant had been disturbed, he looked fiercely at his new
guest, and pronounced with an awful and emphatic, yet
rather an under-voice, the single and impressive word,
" *Garnish!* "

Julian Peveril replied with assumed composure; for
he had heard of the customs of such places, and was resolved to comply with them, so as if possible to obtain
the favour of seeing his father, which he shrewdly guessed
must depend on his gratifying the avarice of the keeper.
" I am quite ready," he said, " to accede to the customs
of the place in which I unhappily find myself. You
have but to name your demands, and I will satisfy them." ·

So saying, he drew out his purse, thinking himself at
the same time fortunate that he had retained about him a
considerable sum of gold. The Captain remarked its

width, depth, its extension, and depression, with an involuntary smile, which had scarce contorted his hanging
under-lip, and the wiry and greasy mustache which
thatched the upper, when it was checked by the recollection that there were regulations which set bounds to his
rapacity, and prevented him from pouncing on his prey
like a kite, and swooping it all off at once.

This chilling reflection produced the following sullen
reply to Peveril :—" There were sundry rates.   Gentlemen must choose for themselves.   He asked nothing but
his fees.   But civility," he muttered, " must be paid for."

" And shall, if I can have it for payment," said Peveril ; " but the price, my good sir, the price ? "

He spoke with some degree of scorn, which he was the
less anxious to repress, that he saw, even in this jail, his
purse gave him an indirect but powerful influence over
his jailer.

The Captain seemed to feel the same ; for, as he spoke,
he plucked from his head, almost involuntarily, a sort of
scalded fur-cap, which served it for covering.   But his
fingers revolting from so unusual an act of complaisance,
began to indemnify themselves by scratching his grizzly
shock-head, as he muttered, in a tone resembling the
softened growling of a mastiff when he has ceased to bay
the intruder who shows no fear of him,—" There are
different rates.   There is the Little Ease, for common
fees of the crown—rather dark, and the common sewer
runs below it ; and some gentlemen object to the company, who are chiefly padders and michers.   Then the
Master's side—the garnish came to one piece—and none
lay stowed there but who were in for murder at the least."

" Name your highest price, sir, and take it," was Julian's concise reply.

" Three pieces for the Knight's ward," answered the governor of this terrestrial Tartarus.

" Take five, and place me with Sir Geoffrey," was again Julian's answer, throwing down the money upon the desk before him.

" Sir Geoffrey ?—Hum !—ay, Sir Geoffrey," said the jailer, as if meditating what he ought to do. " Well, many a man has paid money to see Sir Geoffrey—Scarce so much as you have, though. But then you are like to see the last of him.—Ha, ha, ha ! "

These broken muttered exclamations, which terminated with a laugh somewhat like the joyous growl of a tiger over his meal, Julian could not comprehend ; and only replied to by repeating his request to be placed in the same cell with Sir Geoffrey.

" Ay, master," said the jailer, " never fear ; I'll keep word with you, as you seem to know something of what belongs to your station and mine. And hark ye, Jem Clink will fetch you the darbies."

" Derby ! " interrupted Julian,—" Has the Earl or Countess " ——

" Earl or Countess !—Ha, ha, ha ! " again laughed, or rather growled, the warden. " What is your head running on ? You are a high fellow belike ! but all is one here. The darbies are the fetlocks—the fast-keepers, my boy—the bail for good behaviour, my darling ; and if you are not the more conforming, I can add you a steel night-cap, and a curious bosom-friend, to keep you warm of a winter night. But don't be disheartened ; you have be-haved genteel ; and you shall not be put upon. And as for this here matter, ten to one it will turn out chance medley, or manslaughter, at the worst on it ; and then it is but a singed thumb instead of a twisted neck—always if there be no Papistry about it, for then I warrant nothing.—Take the gentleman's worship away, Clink."

A turnkey, who was one of the party that had ushered Peveril into the presence of this Cerberus, now conveyed him out in silence; and, under his guidance, the prisoner was carried through a second labyrinth of passages with cells opening on each side, to that which was destined for his reception.

On the road through this sad region, the turnkey more than once ejaculated, " Why, the gentleman must be stark-mad! Could have had the best crown cell to himself for less than half the garnish, and must pay double to pig in with Sir Geoffrey! Ha, ha!—Is Sir Geoffrey akin to you, if any one may make free to ask? "

" I am his son," answered Peveril, sternly, in hopes to impose some curb on the fellow's impertinence; but the man only laughed louder than before.

" His son!—Why, that's best of all—Why, you are a strapping youth—five feet ten, if you be an inch—and Sir Geoffrey's son!—Ha, ha, ha! "

" Truce with your impertinence," said Julian. " My situation gives you no title to insult me! "

" No more I do," said the turnkey, smothering his mirth at the recollection, perhaps, that the prisoner's purse was not exhausted. " I only laughed because you said you were Sir Geoffrey's son. But no matter—'tis a wise child that knows his own father. And here is Sir Geoffrey's cell; so you and he may settle the fatherhood between you."

So saying, he ushered his prisoner into a cell, or rather a strong room of the better order, in which there were four chairs, a truckle-bed, and one or two other articles of furniture.

Julian looked eagerly around for his father; but to his surprise the room appeared totally empty. He turned with anger on the turnkey, and charged him with misleading him; but the fellow answered, "No, no, master; I have kept faith with you. Your father, if you call him so, is only tappiced in some corner. A small hole will hide him; but I'll rouse him out presently for you.— Here, hoicks!—Turn out, Sir Geoffrey!—Here is—Ha, ha, ha!—your son—or your wife's son—for I think you can have but little share in him—come to wait on you."

Peveril knew not how to resent the man's insolence; and indeed his anxiety, and apprehension of some strange mistake, mingled with, and in some degree neutralized his anger. He looked again and again, around and around the room; until at length he became aware of something rolled up in a dark corner, which rather resembled a small bundle of crimson cloth than any living creature. At the vociferation of the turnkey, however, the object seemed to acquire life and motion, uncoiled itself in some degree, and, after an effort or two, gained an erect posture; still covered from top to toe with the crimson drapery in which it was at first wrapped. Julian, at the first glance, imagined from the size that he saw a child of five years old; but a shrill and peculiar tone of voice soon assured him of his mistake.

"Warder," said this unearthly sound, "what is the meaning of this disturbance? Have you more insults to heap on the head of one who hath ever been the butt of fortune's malice? But I have a soul that can wrestle with all my misfortunes; it is as large as any of your bodies."

"Nay, Sir Geoffrey, if this be the way you welcome your own son!"—said the turnkey; "but you quality folks know your own ways best."

" My son ! " exclaimed the little figure. " Audacious "——

" Here is some strange mistake," said Peveril, in the
same breath. " I sought Sir Geoffrey "——

" And you have him before you, young man," said the
pigmy tenant of the cell, with an air of dignity ; at the
same time casting on the floor his crimson cloak, and
standing before them in his full dignity of three feet six
inches of height. " I who was the favoured servant of
three successive Sovereigns of the Crown of England,
am now the tenant of this dungeon, and the sport of its
brutal keepers. I am Sir Geoffrey Hudson."

Julian, though he had never before seen this important personage, had no difficulty in recognising, from
description, the celebrated dwarf of Henrietta Maria,
who had survived the dangers of civil war and private
quarrel—the murder of his royal master, Charles I., and
the exile of his widow—to fall upon evil tongues and evil
days, amidst the unsparing accusations connected with the
Popish Plot. He bowed to the unhappy old man, and
hastened to explain to him, and to the turnkey, that it
was Sir Geoffrey Peveril, of Martindale Castle in Derbyshire, whose prison he had desired to share.

" You should have said that before you parted with the
gold-dust, my master," answered the turnkey; " for t'other
Sir Geoffrey, that is the big, tall, gray-haired man, was
sent to the Tower last night; and the Captain will think
he has kept his word well enow with you, by lodging you
with this here Sir Geoffrey Hudson, who is the better
show of the two."

" I pray you go to your master," said Peveril; " explain the mistake; and say to him I beg to be sent to the
Tower."

" The Tower!—Ha, ha, ha ; " exclaimed the fellow.
" The Tower is for lords and knights, and not for squires
of low degree—for high treason, and not for ruffling on
the streets with rapier and dagger ; and there must go a
secretary's warrant to send you there."

" At least, let me not be a burden on this gentleman,"
said Julian. " There can be no use in quartering us together, since we are not even acquainted. Go tell your
master of the mistake."

" Why, so I should," said Clink, still grinning, " if I
were not sure that he knew it already. You paid to be
sent to Sir Geoffrey, and he sent you to Sir Geoffrey.
You are so put down in the register, and he will blot it
for no man. Come, come, be conformable, and you shall
have light and easy irons—that's all I can do for you."

Resistance and expostulation being out of the question,
Peveril submitted to have a light pair of fetters secured
on his ankles, which allowed him, nevertheless, the power
of traversing the apartment.

During this operation, he reflected that the jailer, who
had taken the advantage of the equivoque betwixt the
two Sir Geoffreys, must have acted as his assistant had
hinted, and cheated him from malice prepense, since the
warrant of committal described him as the son of Sir
Geoffrey Peveril. It was therefore in vain, as well as
degrading, to make farther application to such a man on
the subject. Julian determined to submit to his fate, as
what could not be averted by any effort of his own.

Even the turnkey was moved in some degree by his
youth, good mien, and the patience with which, after the
first effervescence of disappointment, the new prisoner
resigned himself to his situation. " You seem a brave
young gentleman," he said; " and shall at least have a

good dinner, and as good a pallet to sleep on, as is within
the walls of Newgate.—And, Master Sir Geoffrey, you
ought to make much of him, since you do not like tall
fellows; for I can tell you that Master Peveril is in for
pinking long Jack Jenkins, that was the Master of Defence—as tall a man as is in London, always excepting
the King's Porter, Master Evans, that carried you about
in his pocket, Sir Geoffrey, as all the world has heard
tell."

"Begone, fellow;" answered the dwarf.   "Fellow, I
scorn you!"

The turnkey sneered, withdrew, and locked the door
behind him.

CHAPTER XXXIV.

Degenerate youth, and not of Tydeus' kind,
Whose little body lodged a mighty mind.

ILIAD.

LEFT quiet at least, if not alone, for the first time after
the events of this troubled and varied day, Julian threw
himself on an old oaken seat, beside the embers of a sea-
coal-fire, and began to muse on the miserable situation of
anxiety and danger in which he was placed; where,
whether he contemplated the interests of his love, his
family affections, or his friendships, all seemed such a
prospect as that of a sailor who looks upon breakers on
every hand, from the deck of a vessel which no longer
obeys the helm.

As Peveril sat sunk in despondency, his companion in
misfortune drew a chair to the opposite side of the chim-
ney-corner, and began to gaze at him with a sort of solemn
earnestness, which at length compelled him, though almost in spite of himself, to pay some attention to the singular figure who seemed so much engrossed with contemplating him.

Geoffrey Hudson, (we drop occasionally the title of
knighthood, which the King had bestowed on him in a
frolic, but which might introduce some confusion into our
history,) although a dwarf of the least possible size, had
nothing positively ugly in his countenance, or actually

distorted in his limbs. His head, hands, and feet, were indeed large, and disproportioned to the height of his body, and his body itself much thicker than was consistent with symmetry, but in a degree which was rather ludicrous than disagreeable to look upon. His countenance, in particular, had he been a little taller, would have been accounted, in youth, handsome, and now, in age, striking and expressive; it was but the uncommon disproportion betwixt the head and the trunk which made the features seem whimsical and bizarre—an effect which was considerably increased by the dwarf's mustaches, which it was his pleasure to wear so large, that they almost twisted back amongst, and mingled with, his grizzled hair.

The dress of this singular wight announced that he was not entirely free from the unhappy taste which frequently induces those whom nature has marked by personal deformity, to distinguish, and at the same time to render themselves ridiculous, by the use of showy colours, and garments fantastically and extraordinarily fashioned. But poor Geoffrey Hudson's laces, embroideries, and the rest of his finery, were sorely worn and tarnished by the time which he had spent in jail, under the vague and malicious accusation that he was somehow or other an accomplice in this all-involving, all-devouring whirlpool of a Popish conspiracy—an impeachment which, if pronounced by a mouth the foulest and most malicious, was at that time sufficiently predominant to sully the fairest reputation. It will presently appear, that in the poor man's manner of thinking, and tone of conversation, there was something analogous to his absurd fashion of apparel; for, as in the latter, good stuff and valuable decorations were rendered ludicrous by the fantastic fashion in which they were made up; so, such glimmerings of good sense and honourable feeling as the little man often evinced, were made ridiculous by a restless desire to assume certain airs of importance, and a great jealousy of being despised, on account of the peculiarity of his outward form.

After the fellow-prisoners had looked at each other for some time in silence, the dwarf, conscious of his dignity as first owner of their joint apartment, thought it necessary to do the honours of it to the new-comer. "Sir," he said, modifying the alternate harsh and squeaking tones of his voice into accents as harmonious as they could attain, "I understand you to be the son of my worthy namesake, and ancient acquaintance, the stout Sir Geoffrey Peveril of the Peak. I promise you, I have seen your father where blows have been going more plenty than gold pieces; and for a tall heavy man, who lacked, as we martialists thought, some of the lightness and activity of our more slightly made Cavaliers, he performed his duty as a man might desire. I am happy to see you, his son; and, though by a mistake, I am glad we are to share this comfortless cabin together."

Julian bowed, and thanked his courtesy; and Geoffrey Hudson, having broken the ice, proceeded to question him without further ceremony. "You are no courtier, I presume, young gentleman?"

Julian replied in the negative.

"I thought so," continued the dwarf; "for although I have now no official duty at Court, the region in which my early years were spent, and where I once held a considerable office, yet I still, when I had my liberty, visited the Presence from time to time, as in duty bound for former service; and am wont, from old habit, to take some note of the courtly gallants, those choice spirits of the age, among whom I was once enrolled. You are, not

to compliment you, a marked figure, Master Peveril—
though something of the tallest, as was your father's case;
I think, I could scarce have seen you any where without
remembering you."

Peveril thought he might, with great justice, have
returned the compliment, but contented himself with
saying, " he had scarce seen the British Court."

" 'Tis pity," said Hudson; " a gallant can hardly
be formed without frequenting it. But you have been
perhaps in a rougher school; you have served, doubtless ? "

" My Maker, I hope," said Julian.

" Fie on it, you mistake. I meant," said Hudson, " *à
la Françoise*,—you have served in the army ? "

" No. I have not yet had that honour," said Julian.

" What! neither courtier nor soldier, Master Peveril ? "
said the important little man : " Your father is to blame.
By cock and pie he is, Master Peveril ! How shall a
man be known, or distinguished, unless by his bearing in
peace and war ? I tell you, sir, that at Newberry, where
I charged with my troop abreast with Prince Rupert, and
when as you may have heard, we were both beaten off by
those cuckoldly hinds the Trained Bands of London,—we
did what men could; and I think it was a matter of three
or four minutes after most of our gentlemen had been
driven off, that his Highness and I continued to cut at
their long pikes with our swords; and I think might have
broken in, but that I had a tall, long-legged brute of a
horse, and my sword was somewhat short,—in fine, at last
we were obliged to make volte-face, and then, as I was
going to say, the fellows were so glad to get rid of us,
that they set up a great jubilee cry of 'There goes Prince
Robin and Cock Robin ! '"—Ay, ay, every scoundrel

among them knew me well. But those days are over.—
And where were you educated, young gentleman?"

Peveril named the household of the Countess of Derby.

"A most honourable lady, upon my word as a gentleman," said Hudson.—"I knew the noble Countess well,
when I was about the person of my royal mistress, Henrietta Maria. She was then the very muster of all that
was noble, loyal, and lovely. She was, indeed, one of the
fifteen fair ones of the Court, whom I permitted to call
me Piccoluomini—a foolish jest on my somewhat diminutive figure, which always distinguished me from ordinary
beings, even when I was young—I have now lost much
stature by stooping; but, always the ladies had their jest
at me.—Perhaps, young man, I had my own amends of
some of them somewhere, and somehow or other—I *say*
nothing if I had or no; far less do I insinuate disrespect
to the noble Countess. She was daughter of the Duc de
la Tremouille, or, more correctly, Des Thouars. But
certainly to serve the ladies, and condescend to their
humours, even when somewhat too free, or too fantastic,
is the true decorum of gentle blood."

Depressed as his spirits were, Peveril could scarce forbear smiling when he looked at the pigmy creature, who
told these stories with infinite complacency, and appeared
disposed to proclaim, as his own herald, that he had been
a very model of valour and gallantry, though love and
arms seemed to be pursuits totally irreconcilable to his
shrivelled, weatherbeaten countenance, and wasted limbs.
Julian was, however, so careful to avoid giving his companion pain, that he endeavoured to humour him, by saying, that, "unquestionably, one bred up like Sir Geoffrey
Hudson, in courts and camps, knew exactly when to suffer
personal freedoms, and when to control them."

The little Knight, with great vivacity, though with some difficulty, began to drag his seat from the side of the fire opposite to that where Julian was seated, and at length succeeded in bringing it near him, in token of increasing cordiality.

"You say well, Master Peveril," said the dwarf; "and I have given proofs both of bearing and forbearing. Yes, sir, there was not that thing which my most royal mistress, Henrietta Maria, could have required of me, that I would not have complied with, sir; I was her sworn servant, both in war and in festival, in battle and pageant, sir. At her Majesty's particular request, I once condescended to become—ladies, you know, have strange fancies—to become the tenant, for a time, of the interior of a pie."

"Of a pie?" said Julian, somewhat amazed.

"Yes, sir, of a pie. I hope you find nothing risible in my complaisance?" replied his companion, something jealously.

"Not I, sir," said Peveril; "I have other matters than laughter in my head at present."

"So had I," said the dwarfish champion, "when I found myself imprisoned in a huge platter, of no ordinary dimensions you may be assured, since I could lie at length in it, and when I was entombed, as it were, in walls of standing crust, and a huge cover of pastry, the whole constituting a sort of sarcophagus, of size enough to have recorded the epitaph of a general officer or an archbishop on the lid. Sir, notwithstanding the conveniences which were made to give me air, it was more like being buried alive than aught else which I could think of." *

* Geoffrey or Jeffrey Hudson is often mentioned in anecdotes of Charles I.'s time. His first appearance at court was his being pre-

" I conceive it, sir," said Julian.

" Moreover, sir," continued the dwarf, " there were few
in the secret, which was contrived for the Queen's diver-
tisement; for advancing of which I would have crept into

sented, as mentioned in the text, in a pie at an entertainment given by
the Duke of Buckingham to Charles I. and Henrietta Maria. Upon
the same occasion, the Duke presented the tenant of the pasty to the
Queen, who retained him as her page. When about eight years of
age, he was but eighteen or twenty inches high; and remained station-
ary at that stature till he was thirty years old, when he grew to the
height of three feet nine inches, and there stopped.

This singular *lusus naturæ* was trusted in some negotiations of consequence. He went to France to fetch over a midwife to his mistress,
Henrietta Maria. On his return, he was taken by Dunkirk privateers,
when he lost many valuable presents sent to the Queen from France,
and about £2500 of his own. Sir William Davenant makes a real or
supposed combat between the dwarf and a turkey-cock, the subject
of a poem called Jeffreidos. The scene is laid at Dunkirk, where, as
the satire concludes—

> " Jeffrey strait was thrown, when, faint and weak,
> The cruel fowl assaults him with his beak.
> A lady midwife now he there by chance
> Espied, that came along with him from France.
> ' A heart brought up in war, that ne'er before
> This time could bow,' he said, ' doth now implore
> Thou, that *delivered* hast so many, be
> So kind of nature as deliver me.' "

We are not acquainted how far Jeffrey resented this lampoon. But
we are assured he was a consequential personage, and endured with
little temper the teasing of the domestics and courtiers, and had many
squabbles with the King's gigantic porter.

 The fatal duel with Mr. Crofts actually took place, as mentioned in
the text. It happened in France. The poor dwarf had also the misfortune to be taken prisoner by a Turkish pirate. He was, however,
probably soon set at liberty, for Hudson was a captain for the King
during the civil war. In 1644, the dwarf attended his royal mistress
to France. The Restoration recalled him, with other royalists, to
England. But this poor being, who received, it would seem, hard
measure both from nature and fortune, was not doomed to close his
days in peace. Poor Jeffrey, upon some suspicion respecting the

a filbert nut, had it been possible; and few, as I said, being private in the scheme, there was a risk of accidents. I doubted, while in my darksome abode, whether some awkward attendant might not have let me fall, as I have seen happen to a venison pasty; or whether some hungry guest might not anticipate the moment of my resurrection, by sticking his knife into my upper crust. And though I had my weapons about me, young man, as has been my custom in every case of peril, yet, if such a rash person had plunged deep into the bowels of the supposed pasty, my sword and dagger could barely have served me to avenge, assuredly not to prevent, either of these catastrophes."

"Certainly I do so understand it," said Julian, who began, however, to feel that the company of little Hudson, talkative as he showed himself, was likely rather to aggravate than to alleviate the inconveniences of a prison.

"Nay," continued the little man, enlarging on his former topic, "I had other subjects of apprehension; for it pleased my Lord of Buckingham, his Grace's father who now bears the title, in his plenitude of Court favour, to command the pasty to be carried down to the office, and committed anew to the oven, alleging preposterously that it was better to be eaten warm than cold."

"And did this, sir, not disturb your equanimity?" said Julian.

"My young friend," said Geoffrey Hudson, "I cannot deny it.—Nature will claim her rights from the best and

Popish Plot, was taken up in 1682, and confined in the Gate-house prison, Westminster, where he ended his life in the sixty-third year of his age.

Jeffrey Hudson has been immortalized by the brush of Vandyke, and his clothes are said to be preserved as articles of curiosity in Sir Hans Sloan's Museum.

boldest of us.—I thought of Nebuchadnezzar and his fiery furnace; and I waxed warm with apprehension.— But, I thank Heaven, I also thought of my sworn duty to my royal mistress; and was thereby obliged and enabled to resist all temptations to make myself prematurely known. Nevertheless, the Duke—if of malice, may Heaven forgive him—followed down into the office himself, and urged the master-cook very hard that the pasty should be heated, were it but for five minutes. But the master-cook, being privy to the very different intentions of my royal mistress, did most manfully resist the order; and I was again reconveyed in safety to the royal table."

"And in due time liberated from your confinement, I doubt not?" said Peveril.

" Yes, sir; that happy, and I may say, glorious moment, at length arrived," continued the dwarf. " The upper crust was removed—I started up to the sound of trumpet and clarion, like the soul of a warrior when the last summons shall sound—or rather, (if that simile be over audacious,) like a spell-bound champion relieved from his enchanted state. It was then that, with my buckler on my arm, and my trusty Bilboa in my hand, I executed a sort of warlike dance, in which my skill and agility then rendered me pre-eminent, displaying, at the same time, my postures, both of defence and offence, in a manner so totally inimitable, that I was almost deafened with the applause of all around me, and half-drowned by the scented waters with which the ladies of the Court deluged me from their casting bottles. I had amends of his Grace of Buckingham also; for as I tripped a hasty morris hither and thither upon the dining-table, now offering my blade, now recovering it, I made a blow at his nose—a sort of estramaçon—the dexterity of which consists in coming mighty near to the object you seem to aim at, yet not attaining it. You may have seen a barber make such a flourish with his razor. I promise you his Grace sprung back a half-yard at least. He was pleased to threaten to brain me with a chicken-bone, as he disdainfully expressed it; but the King said, ' George, you have but a Rowland for an Oliver.' And so I tripped on, showing a bold heedlessness of his displeasure, which few dared to have done at that time, albeit countenanced to the utmost like me by the smiles of the brave and the fair. But, well-a-day! sir, youth, its fashions, its follies, its frolics, and all its pomp and pride, are as idle and transitory as the crackling of thorns under a pot."

" The flower that is cast into the oven were a better simile," thought Peveril. " Good God, that a man should live to regret not being young enough to be still treated as baked meat, and served up in a pie ! "

His companion, whose tongue had for many days been as closely imprisoned as his person, seemed resolved to indemnify his loquacity, by continuing to indulge it on the present occasion at his companion's expense. He proceeded, therefore, in a solemn tone, to moralize on the adventure which he had narrated.

" Young men will no doubt think one to be envied," he said, " who was thus enabled to be the darling and admiration of the Court," (Julian internally stood self-exculpated from the suspicion)—"and yet it is better to possess fewer means of distinction, and remain free from the backbiting, the slander, and the odium, which are always the share of Court favour. Men who had no other cause, cast reflections upon me because my size varied somewhat from the common proportion; and jests were sometimes unthinkingly passed upon me by those I was bound to, who did not in that case, peradventure, sufficiently consider that the wren is made by the same hand which formed the bustard, and that the diamond, though small in size, outvalues ten thousand-fold the rude granite. Nevertheless, they proceeded in the vein of humour; and as I could not in duty or gratitude retort upon nobles and princes, I was compelled to cast about in my mind how to vindicate my honour towards those, who, being in the same rank with myself, as servants and courtiers, nevertheless bore themselves towards me as if they were of a superior class in the rank of honour, as well as in the accidental circumstance of stature. And as a lesson to my own pride, and that of others, it so happened, that the pageant which I have but just narrated—which I justly reckon the most honourable moment of my life, excepting perhaps my distinguished share in the battle of Round-way-down—became the cause of a most tragic event, in which I acknowledge the greatest misfortune of my existence."

The dwarf here paused, fetched a sigh, big at once with regret, and with the importance becoming the subject of a tragic history; then proceeded as follows:—

"You would have thought in your simplicity, young gentleman, that the pretty pageant I have mentioned could only have been quoted to my advantage, as a rare masking frolic, prettily devised, and not less deftly executed; and yet the malice of the courtiers, who maligned and envied me, made them strain their wit, and exhaust their ingenuity, in putting false and ridiculous constructions upon it. In short, my ears were so much offended with allusions to pies, puff-paste, ovens, and the like, that I was compelled to prohibit such subject of mirth, under

penalty of my instant and severe displeasure. But it
happ'd there was then a gallant about the Court, a man
of good quality, son to a knight baronet, and in high
esteem with the best in that sphere, also a familiar friend
of mine own, from whom, therefore, I had no reason to
expect any of that species of gibing which I had intimated
my purpose to treat as offensive. Howbeit, it pleased
the Honourable Mr. Crofts, so was this youth called and
designed, one night, at the Groom Porter's, being full
of wine and waggery, to introduce this threadbare subject,
and to say something concerning a goose-pie, which I
could not but consider as levelled at me. Nevertheless,·
I did but calmly and solidly pray him to choose a different subject; failing which, I let him know I should
be sudden in my resentment. Notwithstanding, he continued in the same tone, and even aggravated the offence,
by speaking of a tomtit, and other unnecessary and obnoxious comparisons; whereupon I was compelled to send
him a cartel, and we met accordingly. Now, as I really
loved the youth, it was my intention only to correct him
by a flesh wound or two; and I would willingly that he
had named the sword for his weapon. Nevertheless, he
made pistols his election; and being on horseback, he
produced by way of his own weapon, a foolish engine,
which children are wont, in their roguery, to use for
spouting water; a——a——in short I forget the name."

"A squirt, doubtless," said Peveril, who began to
recollect having heard something of this adventure.

"You are right," said the dwarf; "you have indeed
the name of the little engine, of which I have had experience in passing the yards at Westminster.—Well, sir,
this token of slight regard compelled me to give the
gentleman such language, as soon rendered it necessary

for him to take more serious arms. We fought on horseback—breaking ground, and advancing by signal; and,
as I never miss aim, I had the misadventure to kill the
Honourable Master Crofts at the first shot. I would not
wish my worst foe the pain which I felt, when I saw him
reel on his saddle, and so fall down to the earth!—and,
when I perceived that the life-blood was pouring fast, I
could not but wish to Heaven that it had been my own
instead of his. Thus fell youth, hopes, and bravery, a
sacrifice to a silly and thoughtless jest; yet, alas! wherein
had I choice, seeing that honour is, as it were, the very
breath in our nostrils; and that in no sense can we be
said to live, if we permit ourselves to be deprived of it?"

The tone of feeling in which the dwarfish hero concluded his story, gave Julian a better opinion of his
heart, and even of his understanding, than he had been
able to form of one who gloried in having, upon a grand
occasion, formed the contents of a pasty. He was indeed
enabled to conjecture that the little champion was seduced
into such exhibitions, by the necessity attached to his
condition, by his own vanity, and by the flattery bestowed
on him by those who sought pleasure in practical jokes.
The fate of the unlucky Master Crofts, however, as well
as various exploits of this diminutive person during the
Civil Wars, in which he actually, and with great gallantry, commanded a troop of horse, rendered most men
cautious of openly rallying him; which was indeed the
less necessary, as, when left alone, he seldom failed voluntarily to show himself on the ludicrous side.

At one hour after noon, the turnkey, true to his word,
supplied the prisoners with a very tolerable dinner and a
flask of well-flavoured, though light claret; which the
old man, who was something of a bon-vivant, regretted to

observe, was nearly as diminutive as himself. The evening also passed away, but not without continued symptoms of garrulity on the part of Geoffrey Hudson.

It is true these were of a graver character than he had hitherto exhibited, for when the flask was empty, he repeated a long Latin prayer. But the religious act in which he had been engaged, only gave his discourse a more serious turn than belonged to his former themes, of war, lady's love, and courtly splendour.

The little Knight harangued, at first on polemical points of divinity, and diverged from this thorny path, into the neighbouring and twilight walk of mysticism. He talked of secret warnings—of the predictions of sad-eyed prophets—of the visits of monitory spirits, and the Rosicrucian secrets of the Cabala; all which topics he treated of with such apparent conviction, nay, with so many appeals to personal experience, that one would have supposed him a member of the fraternity of gnomes, or fairies, whom he resembled so much in point of size.

In short, he persevered for a stricken hour in such a torrent of unnecessary tattle, as determined Peveril, at all events, to endeavour to procure a separate lodging. Having repeated his evening prayers in Latin, as formerly, (for the old gentleman was a Catholic, which was the sole cause of his falling under suspicion,) he set off on a new score, as they were undressing, and continued to prattle until he had fairly talked both himself and his companion to sleep.

CHAPTER XXXV.

Of airy tongues that syllable men's names.

Comus.

JULIAN had fallen asleep, with his brain rather filled with his own sad reflections, than with the mystical lore of the little Knight; and yet it seemed as if in his visions the latter had been more present to his mind than the former.

He dreamed of gliding spirits, gibbering phantoms, bloody hands, which, dimly seen by twilight, seemed to beckon him forward like errant-knight on sad adventure bound. More than once he started from his sleep, so lively was the influence of these visions on his imagination; and he always awaked under the impression that some one stood by his bedside. The chillness of his ankles, the weight and clatter of the fetters, as he turned himself on his pallet, reminded him on these occasions where he was, and under what circumstances. The extremity to which he saw all that was dear to him at present reduced, struck a deeper cold on his heart than the iron upon his limbs; nor could he compose himself again to rest without a mental prayer to Heaven for protection. But when he had been for a third time awakened from repose by these thick-stirring fancies, his distress of mind vented itself in speech, and he was unable to suppress the almost despairing ejaculation, "God have mercy upon us!"

"Amen!" answered a voice as sweet and "soft as honey dew," which sounded as if the words were spoken close by his bedside.

The natural inference was, that Geoffrey Hudson, his companion in calamity, had echoed the prayer which was so proper to the situation of both. But the tone of voice was so different from the harsh and dissonant sounds of the dwarf's enunciation, that Peveril was impressed with the certainty it could not proceed from Hudson. He was struck with involuntary terror, for which he could give no sufficient reason; and it was not without an effort that he was able to utter the question, "Sir Geoffrey, did you speak?"

No answer was returned. He repeated the question louder; and the same silver-toned voice, which had formerly said "*Amen*" to his prayers, answered to his interrogatory, "Your companion will not awake while I am here."

"And who are you?—What seek you?—How came you into this place?" said Peveril, huddling, eagerly, question upon question.

"I am a wretched being, but one who loves you well. —I come for your good.—Concern yourself no farther."

It now rushed on Julian's mind, that he had heard of persons possessed of the wonderful talent of counterfeiting sounds to such accuracy, that they could impose on their hearers the belief, that they proceeded from a point of the apartment entirely opposite to that which the real speaker occupied. Persuaded that he had now gained the depth of the mystery, he replied, "This trifling, Sir Geoffrey, is unseasonable. Say what you have to say in

your own voice and manner. These apish pleasantries
do not become midnight in a Newgate dungeon."

" But the being who speaks with you," answered the
voice, " is fitted for the darkest hour, and the most
melancholy haunts."

Impatient of suspense, and determined to satisfy his
curiosity, Julian jumped at once from his pallet, hoping
to secure the speaker, whose voice indicated he was so
near. But he altogether failed in his attempt, and
grasped nothing save thin air.

For a turn or two, Peveril shuffled at random about
the room, with his arms extended ; and then at last
recollected, that with the impediment of his shackles, and
the noise which necessarily accompanied his motions, and
announced where he was, it would be impossible for him
to lay hands on any one who might be disposed to keep
out of his reach. He therefore endeavoured to return to
his bed ; but, in groping for his way, lighted first on that
of his fellow-prisoner. The little captive slept deep and
heavy, as was evinced from his breathing ; and upon
listening a moment, Julian became again certain, either
that his companion was the most artful of ventriloquists
and of dissemblers, or that there was actually within the
precincts of that guarded chamber, some third being,
whose very presence there seemed to intimate that it
belonged not to the ordinary line of humanity.

Julian was no ready believer in the supernatural ; but
that age was very far from being so incredulous concerning ghostly occurrences as our own ; and it was no way
derogatory to his good sense, that he shared the prejudices
of his time. His hair began to bristle, and the moisture
to stand on his brow, as he called on his companion to
awake, for Heaven's sake.

The dwarf answered—but he spoke without awaking.
—" The day may dawn and be d—d. Tell the master
of the horse I will not go to the hunting, unless I have
the little black jennet."

" I tell you," said Julian, " there is some one in the
apartment. Have you not a tinder-box to strike a
light ? "

" I care not how slight my horse be," replied the slumberer, pursuing his own train of ideas, which, doubtless,
carried him back to the green woods of Windsor, and the
royal deer-hunts which he had witnessed there. " I am
not overweight.—I will not ride that great Holstein brute,
that I must climb up to by a ladder, and then sit on his
back like a pin-cushion on an elephant."

Julian at length put his hand to the sleeper's shoulder,
and shook him, so as to awake him from his dream ;
when, after two or three snorts and groans, the dwarf
asked peevishly, what the devil ailed him ?

" The devil himself, for what I know," said Peveril,
" is at this very moment in the room here beside us."

The dwarf on this information started up, crossed
himself, and began to hammer a flint and steel with all
dispatch, until he had lighted a little piece of candle,
which he said was consecrated to Saint Bridget, and as
powerful as the herb called *fuga dæmonum*, or the liver
of the fish burnt by Tobit in the house of Raguel, for
chasing all goblins, and evil or dubious spirits, from the
place of its radiance ; " if, indeed," as the dwarf carefully
guarded his proposition, " they existed any where, save
in the imagination of his fellow-prisoner."

Accordingly, the apartment was no sooner enlightened
by this holy candle's end, than Julian began to doubt the
evidence of his own ears ; for not only was there no one

in the room save Sir Geoffrey Hudson and himself, but all the fastenings of the door were so secure, that it seemed impossible that they could have been opened and again fixed, without a great deal of noise, which, on the last occasion at least, could not possibly have escaped his ears, seeing that he must have been on his feet, and employed in searching the chamber, when the unknown, if an earthly being, was in the act of retreating from it.

Julian gazed for a moment with great earnestness, and no little perplexity, first on the bolted door, then on the grated window; and began to accuse his own imagination of having played him an unpleasant trick. He answered little to the questions of Hudson, and, returning to his bed, heard, in silence, a long studied oration on the merits of Saint Bridget, which comprehended the greater part of her long-winded legend, and concluded with the assurance, that, from all accounts preserved of her, that holy saint was the least of all possible women, except those of the pigmy kind.

By the time the dwarf had ceased to speak, Julian's desire of sleep had returned; and after a few glances around the apartment, which was still illuminated by the expiring beams of the holy taper, his eyes were again closed in forgetfulness, and his repose was not again disturbed in the course of that night.

Morning dawns on Newgate, as well as on the freest mountain-turf which Welshman or wild-goat ever trode; but in so different a fashion, that the very beams of heaven's precious sun, when they penetrate into the recesses of the prison-house, have the air of being committed to jail. Still, with the light of day around him, Peveril easily persuaded himself of the vanity of his preceding night's visions; and smiled when he reflected that fancies,

similar to those to which his ear was often exposed in the
Isle of Man, had been able to arrange themselves in a
manner so impressive, when he heard them from the
mouth of so singular a character as Hudson, and in the
solitude of a prison.

Before Julian had awaked, the dwarf had already quitted his bed, and was seated in the chimney corner of the
apartment, where, with his own hands, he had arranged a
morsel of fire, partly attending to the simmering of a
small pot, which he had placed on the flame, partly occupied with a huge folio volume which lay on the table
before him, and seemed well-nigh as tall and bulky as
himself. He was wrapped up in the dusky crimson cloak
already mentioned, which served him for a morning-gown,
as well as a mantle against the cold, and which corresponded with a large montero-cap, that enveloped his
head. The singularity of his features, and of the eyes,
armed with spectacles, which were now cast on the subject of his studies, now directed towards his little caldron,
would have tempted Rembrandt to exhibit him on can-
vas, either in the character of an alchymist, or of a
necromancer, engaged in some strange experiment, under
the direction of one of the huge manuals which treat of
the theory of these mystic arts.

The attention of the dwarf was bent, however, upon a
more domestic object. He was only preparing soup, of no
unsavoury quality, for breakfast, which he invited Peveril
to partake with him. " I am an old soldier," he said,
" and, I must add, an old prisoner ; and understand how
to shift for myself better than you can do, young man.—
Confusion to the scoundrel Clink, he has put the spice-
box out of my reach !—Will you hand it me from the
mantelpiece ?—I will teach you, as the French have it,

faire la cuisine ; and then, if you please, we will divide, like brethren, the labours of our prison house."

Julian readily assented to the little man's friendly proposal, without interposing any doubt as to his continuing an inmate of the same cell. Truth is, that although, upon the whole, he was inclined to regard the whispering voice of the preceding evening as the impression of his own excited fancy, he felt, nevertheless, curiosity to see how a second night was to pass over in the same cell ; and the tone of the invisible intruder, which at midnight had been heard by him with terror, now excited, on recollection, a gentle and not unpleasing species of agitation—the combined effect of awe, and of awakened curiosity.

Days of captivity have little to mark them as they glide away. That which followed the night which we have described, afforded no circumstance of note. The dwarf imparted to his youthful companion a volume similar to that which formed his own studies, and which proved to be a tome of one of Scuderi's now forgotten romances, of which Geoffrey Hudson was a great admirer, and which were then very fashionable both at the French and English Courts ; although they contrive to unite in their immense folios all the improbabilities and absurdities of the old romances of chivalry, without that tone of imagination which pervades them, and all the metaphysical absurdities which Cowley and the poets of the age had heaped upon the passion of love, like so many load of small coal upon a slender fire, which it smothers instead of aiding.

But Julian had no alternative, saving only to muse over the sorrows of Artamenes and Mandane, or on the complicated distresses of his own situation ; and in these disagreeable divertisements, the morning crept through as it could.

Noon first, and thereafter nightfall, were successively marked by a brief visit from their stern turnkey, who, with noiseless step and sullen demeanour, did in silence the necessary offices about the meals of the prisoners, exchanging with them as few words as an official in the Spanish Inquisition might have permitted himself upon a similar occasion. With the same taciturn gravity, very different from the laughing humour into which he had been surprised on a former occasion, he struck their fetters with a small hammer, to ascertain, by the sound thus produced, whether they had been tampered with by file or otherwise. He next mounted on a table, to make the same experiment on the window-grating.

Julian's heart throbbed; for might not one of those grates have been so tampered with as to give entrance to the nocturnal visitant? But they returned to the experienced ear of Master Clink, when he struck them in turn with the hammer, a clear and ringing sound, which assured him of their security.

"It would be difficult for any one to get in through these defences," said Julian, giving vent in words to his own feelings.

"Few wish that," answered the surly groom, misconstruing what was passing in Peveril's mind; "and let me tell you, master, folks will find it quite as difficult to get out." He retired, and night came on.

The dwarf, who took upon himself for the day the whole duties of the apartment, trundled about the room, making a most important clatter as he extinguished their fire, and put aside various matters which had been in use in the course of the day, talking to himself all the while in a tone of no little consequence, occasionally grounded on the dexterity with which an old soldier could turn his hand to every thing; and at other times, on the wonder that a courtier of the first rank should condescend to turn his hand to any thing. Then came the repetition of his accustomed prayers; but his disposition to converse did not, as on the former occasion, revive after his devotions. On the contrary, long before Julian had closed an eye, the heavy breathing from Sir Geoffrey Hudson's pallet declared that the dwarf was already in the arms of Morpheus.

Amid the total darkness of the apartment, and with a longing desire, and at the same time no small fear, for the recurrence of the mysterious address of the preceding evening, Julian lay long awake without his thoughts receiving any interruption save when the clock told the passing hour from the neighbouring steeple of St. Sepulchre. At length he sunk into slumber; but had not slept to his judgment, above an hour, when he was roused by the sound which his waking ear had so long expected in vain.

" Can you sleep?—Will you sleep?—Dare you sleep?" were the questions impressed on his ear, in the same clear, soft, and melodious voice, which had addressed him on the preceding night.

"Who is it asks me the question?" answered Julian. " But be the questioner good or evil, I reply that I am a guiltless prisoner; and that innocence may wish and dare to sleep soundly."

"Ask no questions of me," said the voice; "neither attempt to discover who speaks to you; and be assured that folly alone can sleep, with fraud around and danger before him."

" Can you, who tell me of dangers, counsel me how to combat or how to avoid them?" said Julian.

" My power is limited," said the voice; "yet something I can do, as the glow-worm can show a precipice. But you must confide in me."

" Confidence must beget confidence," answered Julian. " I cannot repose trust in I know not what or whom."

" Speak not so loud," replied the voice, sinking almost into a whisper."

" Last night you said my companion would not awake," said Julian.

" To-night I warrant not that he shall sleep," said the voice. And as it spoke, the hoarse, snatching, discordant tones of the dwarf were heard, demanding of Julian why he talked in his sleep—wherefore he did not rest himself, and let other people rest—and, finally, whether his visions of last night were returned upon him again?

" Say yes," said the voice, in a whisper, so low, yet so distinct, that Julian almost doubted whether it was not an echo of his own thought,—" Say but yes—and I part to return no more!"

In desperate circumstances men look to strange and unusual remedies; and although unable to calculate the chances of advantage which this singular communication opened to him, Julian did not feel inclined to let them at once escape from him. He answered the dwarf that he had been troubled by an alarming dream.

" I could have sworn it, from the sound of your voice," said Hudson. " It is strange, now, that you overgrown men never possess the extreme firmness of nerves proper to us who are cast in a more compact mould. My own voice retains its masculine sounds on all occasions. Dr. Cockerel was of opinion, that there was the same allowance of nerve and sinew to men of every size, and that nature spun the stock out thinner or stronger, ac-

cording to the extent of surface which they were to cover.
Hence, the least creatures are oftentimes the strongest.
Place a beetle under a tall candlestick, and the insect
will move it by its efforts to get out; which is, in point of
comparative strength, as if one of us should shake his
Majesty's prison of Newgate by similar struggles. Cats
also, and weasels, are creatures of greater exertion and
endurance than dogs or sheep. And in general, you may
remark, that little men dance better, and are more un-
wearied under exertion of every kind, than those to whom
their own weight must necessarily be burdensome. I
respect you, Master Peveril, because I am told you have
killed one of those gigantic fellows, who go about swaggering as if their souls were taller than ours, because
their noses are nearer to the clouds by a cubit or two.
But do not value yourself on this as any thing very unusual. I would have you to know it hath been always
thus; and that, in the history of all ages, the clean, tight,
dapper little fellow, hath proved an overmatch for his
bulky antagonist. I need only instance out of Holy
Writ, the celebrated downfall of Goliah, and of another
lubbard, who had more fingers to his hand, and more
inches to his stature, than ought to belong to an honest
man, and who was slain by a nephew of good King
David; and of many others whom I do not remember;
nevertheless they were all Philistines of gigantic stature.
In the classics, also, you have Tydeus, and other tight,
compact heroes, whose diminutive bodies were the abode
of large minds. And indeed you may observe, in sacred
as well as profane history, that your giants are ever heretics and blasphemers, robbers and oppressors, outragers
of the female sex, and scoffers at regular authority. Such
were Gog and Magog, whom our authentic chronicles

vouch to have been slain near to Plymouth, by the good
little Knight Corineus, who gave name to Cornwall.
Ascaparte also was subdued by Bevis, and Colbrand by
Guy, as Southampton and Warwick can testify. Like
unto these was the giant Hoel, slain in Bretagne by King
Arthur. And if Ryence, King of North Wales, who was
done to death by the same worthy champion of Christen-
dom, be not actually termed a giant, it is plain he was
little better, since he required twenty-four kings' beards,
which were then worn full and long, to fur his gown;
whereby, computing each beard at eighteen inches, (and
you cannot allow less for a beard-royal,) and supposing
only the frônt of the gown trimmed therewith, as we use
ermine; and that the back was mounted and lined, instead
of cat-skins and squirrels' fur, with the beards of earls and
dukes, and other inferior dignitaries—may amount to—
But I will work the question to-morrow."

Nothing is more soporific to any (save a philosopher
or moneyed man) than the operation of figures; and when
in bed, the effect is irresistible. Sir Geoffrey fell asleep
in the act of calculating King Ryence's height, from the
supposed length of his mantle. Indeed, had he not stum-
bled on this abstruse subject of calculation, there is no
guessing how long he might have held forth upon the
superiority of men of little stature, which was so great a
favourite with him, that, numerous as such narratives
are, the dwarf had collected almost all the instances of
their victories over giants, which history or romance
afforded.

No sooner had unequivocal signs of the dwarf's sound
slumbers reached Julian's ears, than he began again to
listen eagerly for the renewal of that mysterious communication which was at once interesting and awful. Even

whilst Hudson was speaking, he had, instead of bestowing his attention upon his eulogy on persons of low stature, kept his ears on watchful guard to mark, if possible, the lightest sounds of any sort which might occur in the apartment; so that he thought it scarce possible that even a fly should have left it without its motion being over-heard. If, therefore, his invisible monitor was indeed a creature of this world—an opinion which Julian's sound sense rendered him unwilling to renounce—that being could not have left the apartment; and he waited im-patiently for a renewal of their communication. He was disappointed; not the slightest sound reached his ear; and the nocturnal visitor, if still in the room, appeared determined on silence.

It was in vain that Peveril coughed, hemmed, and gave other symptoms of being awake; at length, such became his impatience, that he resolved, at any risk, to speak first, in hopes of renewing the communication betwixt them. "Whoever thou art," he said, in a voice loud enough to be heard by a waking person, but not so high as to disturb his sleeping companion—"Whoever, or whatever thou art, that hast shown some interest in the fate of such a castaway as Julian Peveril, speak once more, I conjure thee; and be your communication for good or evil, believe me, I am equally prepared to abide the issue."

No answer of any kind was returned to this invoca-tion; nor did the least sound intimate the presence of the being to whom it was so solemnly addressed.

"I speak in vain," said Julian; "and perhaps I am but invoking that which is insensible of human feeling, or which takes a malign pleasure in human suffer-ing."

There was a gentle and half-broken sigh from a corner of the apartment, which, answering to this exclamation, seemed to contradict the imputation which it conveyed.

Julian, naturally courageous, and familiarized by this time to his situation, raised himself in bed, and stretched out his arm, to repeat his adjuration, when the voice, as if alarmed at his action and energy, whispered in a tone more hurried than that which it had hitherto used, "Be still—move not—or I am mute for ever!"

"It is then a mortal being who is present with me," was the natural inference of Julian, "and one who is probably afraid of being detected; I have then some power over my visitor, though I must be cautious how I use it.—If your intents are friendly," he proceeded, "there was never a time in which I lacked friends more, or would be more grateful for kindness. The fate of all who are dear to me is weighed in the balance, and with worlds would I buy the tidings of their safety."

"I have said my power is limited," replied the voice. " *You* I may be able to preserve—the fate of your friends is beyond my control."

"Let me at least know it," said Julian; "and, be it as it may, I will not shun to share it."

"For whom would you inquire?" said the soft, sweet voice, not without a tremulousness of accent, as if the question was put with diffident reluctance.

"My parents," said Julian, after a moment's hesitation; "how fare they?—What will be their fate?"

"They fare as the fort under which the enemy has dug a deadly mine. The work may have cost the labour of years, such were the impediments to the engineers; but Time brings opportunity upon its wings."

" And what will be the event ? " said Peveril.

" Can I read the future," answered the voice, " save by comparison with the past ?—Who has been hunted on these stern and unmitigable accusations, but has been at last brought to bay ? Did high and noble birth, honoured age, and approved benevolence, save the unfortunate Lord Stafford ? Did learning, capacity of intrigue, or high Court favour, redeem Coleman, although the confidential servant of the heir presumptive of the Crown of England ?—Did subtilty and genius, and the exertions of a numerous sect, save Fenwicke, or Whitbread, or any other of the accused priests ?—Were Groves, Pickering, or the other humble wretches who have suffered, safe in their obscurity ? There is no condition in life, no degree of talent, no form of principle, which affords protection against an accusation, which levels conditions, confounds characters, renders men's virtues their sins, and rates them as dangerous in proportion as they have influence, though attained in the noblest manner, and used for the best purposes. Call such a one but an accessory to the Plot—let him be mouthed in the evidence of Oates or Dugdale—and the blindest shall foresee the issue of their trial."

" Prophet of Evil ! " said Julian, " my father has a shield invulnerable to protect him. He is innocent."

" Let him plead his innocence at the bar of Heaven," said the voice ; " it will serve him little where Scroggs presides."

" Still I fear not," said Julian, counterfeiting more confidence than he really possessed ; " my father's cause will be pleaded before twelve Englishmen."

" Better before twelve wild beasts," answered the In-

visible, "than before Englishmen, influenced with party
prejudice, passion, and the epidemic terror of an imagi-
nary danger.   They are bold in guilt in proportion to the
number amongst whom the crime is divided."

"Ill-omened speaker," said Julian, thine is indeed a
voice fitted only to sound with the midnight bell, and the
screech-owl.   Yet speak again.   Tell me, if thou canst"
—(he would have said of Alice Bridgenorth, but the
word would not leave his tongue)—"Tell me," he said,
" if the noble house of Derby "——

" Let them keep their rock like the sea-fowl in the
tempest; and it may so fall out," answered the voice,
"that their rock may be a safe refuge.   But there is
blood on their ermine; and revenge has dogged them
for many a year, like a bloodhound that hath been dis-
tanced in the morning chase, but may yet grapple the
quarry ere the sun shall set.   At present, however, they
are safe.—Am I now to speak farther on your own
affairs, which involve little short of your life and honour?
or are there yet any whose interests you prefer to your
own?"

"There is," said Julian, "one, from whom I was
violently parted yesterday; if I knew but of her safety,
I were little anxious for my own."

"One!" returned the voice, "only *one* from whom you
were parted yesterday?"

" But in parting from whom," said Julian, I felt
separated from all happiness which the world can give
me."

"You mean Alice Bridgenorth," said the Invisible,
with some bitterness of accent; "but her you will never
see more.   Your own life and hers depend on your forgetting each other."

"I cannot purchase my own life at that price," replied Julian.

"Then DIE in your obstinacy," returned the Invisible; nor to all the entreaties which he used was he able to obtain another word in the course of that remarkable night.

CHAPTER XXXVI.

A short-hough'd man, but full of pride.

ALLAN RAMSAY.

THE blood of Julian Peveril was so much fevered by
the state in which his invisible visitor left him, that he
was unable, for a length of time, to find repose. He
swore to himself, that he would discover and expose the
nocturnal demon which stole on his hours of rest, only to
add gall to bitterness, and to pour poison into those
wounds which already smarted so severely. There was
nothing which his power extended to, that, in his rage, he
did not threaten. He proposed a closer and a more
rigorous survey of his cell, so that he might discover the
mode by which his tormentor entered, were it as un-
noticeable as an auger-hole. If his diligence should
prove unavailing, he determined to inform the jailers,
to whom it could not be indifferent to know, that their
prison was open to such intrusions. He proposed to
himself, to discover from their looks, whether they were
already privy to these visits; and if so, to denounce them
to the magistrates, to the judges, to the house of Commons, was the least that his resentment proposed. Sleep
surprised his worn-out frame in the midst of his projects
of discovery and vengeance, and, as frequently happens,
the light of the ensuing day proved favourable to calmer
resolutions.

He now reflected that he had no ground to consider
the motives of his visitor as positively malevolent, although he had afforded him little encouragement to hope
for assistance on the points he had most at heart.
Towards himself, there had been expressed a decided
feeling, both of sympathy and interest; if through means
of these he could acquire his liberty, he might, when
possessed of freedom, turn it to the benefit of those for
whom he was more interested than for his own welfare.
" I have behaved like a fool," he said; "I ought to have
temporized with this singular being, learned the motives
of its interference, and availed myself of its succour provided I could do so without any dishonourable conditions.
It would have been always time enough to reject such
when they should have been proposed to me."

So saying, he was forming projects for regulating his
intercourse with the stranger more prudently, in case their
communication should be renewed, when his meditations
were interrupted by the peremptory summons of Sir
Geoffrey Hudson, that he would, in his turn, be pleased
to perform those domestic duties of their common habitation, which the dwarf had yesterday taken upon himself.

There was no resisting a request so reasonable, and
Peveril accordingly rose and betook himself to the arrangement of their prison, while Sir Hudson, perched upon a
stool from which his legs did not by half way reach the
ground, sat in a posture of elegant languor, twangling
upon an old broken-winded guitar, and singing songs in
Spanish, Moorish, and Lingua Franca, most detestably
out of tune. He failed not, at the conclusion of each
ditty, to favour Julian with some account of what he had
sung, either in the way of translation, or historical anec-
dote, or as the lay was connected with some peculiar part

of his own eventful history, in the course of which the poor little man had chanced to have been taken by a Sallee rover, and carried captive into Morocco.

This part of his life Hudson used to make the era of many strange adventures; and, if he could himself be believed, he had made wild work among the affections of the Emperor's seraglio. But, although few were in a situation to cross-examine him on gallantries and intrigues of which the scene was so remote, the officers of the garrison of Tangier had a report current amongst them, that the only use to which the tyrannical Moors could convert a slave of such slender corporeal strength, was to employ him to lie a-bed all day and hatch turkey's eggs. The least allusion to this rumour used to drive him well-nigh frantic, and, the fatal termination of his duel with young Crofts, which began in wanton mirth, and ended in bloodshed, made men more coy than they had formerly been, of making the fiery little hero the subject of their raillery.

While Peveril did the drudgery of the apartment, the dwarf remained much at his ease, carolling in the manner we have described; but when he beheld Julian attempting the task of the cook, Sir Geoffrey Hudson sprung from the stool on which he sat *en Signor*, at the risk of breaking both his guitar and his neck, exclaiming, " That he would rather prepare breakfast every morning betwixt this and the day of judgment, than commit a task of such consequence to an inexperienced bungler like his companion."

The young man gladly resigned his task to the splenetic little Knight, and only smiled at his resentment when he added, that, to be but a mortal of middle stature, Julian was as stupid as a giant. Leaving the dwarf to prepare the meal after his own pleasure, Peveril employed himself in measuring the room with his eyes on every side, and in endeavouring to discover some private entrance, such as might admit his midnight visitant, and perhaps could be employed in case of need for effecting his own escape. · The floor next engaged a scrutiny equally minute, but more successful.

Close by his own pallet, and dropped in such a manner that he must have seen it sooner but for the hurry with which he obeyed the summons of the impatient dwarf, lay a slip of paper, sealed, and directed with the initial letters, J. P., which seemed to ascertain that it was addressed to himself. He took the opportunity of opening it while the soup was in the very moment of projection, and the full attention of his companion was occupied by what he, in common with wiser and taller men, considered as one of the principal occupations of life; so that, without incurring his observation or awaking his curiosity, Julian had the opportunity to read as follows :—

"Rash and infatuated as you are, there is one who would forfeit much to stand betwixt you and your fate. You are to-morrow to be removed to the Tower, where your life cannot be assured for a single day; for, during the few hours you have been in London, you have provoked a resentment which is not easily slaked. There is but one chance for you,—renounce A. B.—think no more of her. If that be impossible, think of her but as one whom you can never see again. If your heart can resolve to give up an attachment which it should never have entertained, and which it would be madness to cherish longer, make your acquiescence in this condition known by putting on your hat a white band, or white feather, or knot of ribbon of the same colour, whichever you may most easily come by. A boat will, in that case, run, as if by accident, on board of that which is to convey you to the Tower. Do you in the confusion jump overboard, and swim to the Southwark side of the Thames. Friends will attend there to secure your escape, and you will find yourself with one who will rather lose character and life, than that a hair of your head should fall to the ground; but who, if you reject the warning, can only think of you as of the fool who perishes in his folly. May Heaven guide you to a sound judgment of your condition! So prays one who would be your friend, if you pleased,

"UNKNOWN."

The Tower!—it was a word of terror, even more so than a civil prison; for how many passages to death did that dark structure present! The severe executions which it had witnessed in preceding reigns, were not perhaps more numerous than the secret murders which had taken place within its walls; yet Peveril did not a moment hesitate on the part which he had to perform. "I will share my father's fate," he said; "I thought but of him when they brought me hither; I will think of nothing else when they convey me to yonder still more dreadful place of confinement; it is his, and it is but meet that it should be his son's.—And thou, Alice Bridgenorth, the day that I renounce thee may I be held alike a traitor and a dastard!—Go, false adviser, and share the fate of seducers and heretical teachers!"

He could not help uttering this last expression aloud, as he threw the billet into the fire, with a vehemence which made the dwarf start with surprise. "What say you of burning heretics, young man?" he exclaimed; "by my faith, your zeal must be warmer than mine, if you talk on such a subject when the heretics are the pre-vailing number. May I measure six feet without my shoes, but the heretics would have the best of it if we came to that work. Beware of such words."

"Too late to beware of words spoken and heard," said the turnkey, who, opening the door with unusual precau-tions to avoid noise, had stolen unperceived into the room; "however, Master Peveril has behaved like a gentleman, and I am no tale-bearer, on condition he will consider I have had trouble in his matters."

Julian had no alternative but to take the fellow's hint and administer a bribe, with which Master Clink was so well satisfied, that he exclaimed, "It went to his heart to take leave of such a kind-natured gentleman, and that he could have turned the key on him for twenty years with pleasure. But the best friends must part."

"I am to be removed, then?" said Julian.

"Ay, truly, master, the warrant is come from the Council."

"To convey me to the Tower."

"Whew!" exclaimed the officer of the law—"who the devil told you that? But since you do know it, there is no harm to say ay. So make yourself ready to move immediately; and first, hold out your dew-beaters till I take off the darbies."

"Is that usual?" said Peveril, stretching out his feet as the fellow directed, while his fetters were unlocked.

"Why, ay, master, these fetters belong to the keeper; they are not a-going to send them to the Lieutenant, I trow. No, no, the warders must bring their own gear with them; they get none here, I promise them. Never-theless, if your honour hath a fancy to go in fetters, as thinking it may move compassion of your case "——

"I have no intention to make my case seem worse than it is," said Julian; whilst at the same time it crossed his mind that his anonymous correspondent must be well acquainted both with his own personal habits, since the letter proposed a plan of escape which could only be executed by a bold swimmer, and with the fashions of the prison, since it was foreseen that he would not be ironed on his passage to the Tower. The turnkey's next speech made him carry conjecture still farther.

"There is nothing in life I would not do for so brave a guest," said Clink; "I could nab one of my wife's ribbons for you, if your honour had the fancy to mount the white flag in your beaver."

"To what good purpose?" said Julian, shortly connecting, as was natural, the man's proposed civility with the advice given and the signal prescribed in the letter.

"Nay, to no good purpose I know of," said the turnkey; "only it is the fashion to seem white and harmless —a sort of token of not-guiltiness, as I may say, which folks desire to show the world, whether they be truly guilty or not; but I cannot say that guiltiness or not-guiltiness argufies much, saving they be words in the vardict."

"Strange," thought Peveril, although the man seemed to speak quite naturally, and without any double meaning, "strange that all should apparently combine to realize the plan of escape, could I but give my consent to it! And had I not better consent? Whoever does so much for me must wish me well, and a well-wisher would never enforce the unjust conditions on which I am required to consent to my liberation."

But this misgiving of his resolution was but for a moment. He speedily recollected, that whoever aided him in escaping, must be necessarily exposed to great risk, and had a right to name the stipulation on which he was willing to incur it.   He also recollected that falsehood is equally base, whether expressed in words or in dumb show ; and that he should lie as flatly by using the signal agreed upon in evidence of his renouncing Alice Bridge-north, as he would in direct terms if he made such renunciation without the purpose of abiding by it.

" If you would oblige me," he said to the turnkey, " let me have a piece of black silk or crape for the purpose you mention."

" Of crape," said the fellow ; " what should that signify ?   Why, the bien morts, who bing out to tour at you,* will think you a chimney-sweeper on Mayday."

" It will show my settled sorrow," said Julian, " as well as my determined resolution."

" As you will, sir," answered the fellow ; " I'll provide you with a black rag of some kind or other.   So, now ; let us be moving."

Julian intimated his readiness to attend him, and proceeded to bid farewell to his late companion, the stout Geoffrey Hudson.   The parting was not without emotion on both sides, more particularly on that of the poor little man, who had taken a particular liking to the companion of whom he was now about to be deprived.   " Fare ye well," he said, " my young friend," taking Julian's hand in both his own uplifted palms, in which action he somewhat resembled the attitude of a sailor pulling a rope overhead,—" Many in my situation would think himself wronged, as a soldier and servant of the king's chamber, in seeing you removed to a more honourable prison than that which I am limited unto.   But, I thank God, I

* The smart girls, who turn out to look at you.

grudge you not the Tower, nor the rocks of Scilly, nor even Carisbrooke Castle, though the latter was graced with the captivity of my blessed and martyred master. Go where you will, I wish you all the distinction of an honourable prison-house, and a safe and speedy deliverance in God's own time. For myself, my race is near a close, and that because I fall a martyr to the over-tenderness of my own heart. There is a circumstance, good Master Julian Peveril, which should have been yours, had Providence permitted our farther intimacy, but it fits not the present hour. Go, then, my friend, and bear witness in life and death, that Geoffrey Hudson scorns the insults and persecutions of fortune, as he would despise, and has often despised, the mischievous pranks of an overgrown schoolboy."

So saying, he turned away, and hid his face with his little handkerchief, while Julian felt towards him that tragi-comic sensation which makes us pity the object which excites it, not the less that we are somewhat inclined to laugh amid our sympathy. The jailer made him a signal, which Peveril obeyed, leaving the dwarf to disconsolate solitude.

As Julian followed the keeper through the various windings of this penal labyrinth, the man observed, that "he was a rum fellow, that little Sir Geoffrey, and, for gallantry, a perfect Cock of Bantam, for as old as he was. There was a certain gay wench," he said, "that had hooked him; but what she could make of him, save she carried him to Smithfield, and took money for him, as for a motion of puppets, it was," he said, "hard to gather."

Encouraged by this opening, Julian asked if his attendant knew why his prison was changed. "To teach you to become a King's post without commission," answered the fellow.

He stopped in his tattle as they approached that formidable central point, in which lay couched on his leathern elbow-chair the fat commander of the fortress, stationed apparently for ever in the midst of his citadel, as the huge Boa is sometimes said to lie stretched as a guard upon the subterranean treasures of Eastern Rajahs. This overgrown man of authority eyed Julian wistfully and sullenly, as the miser the guinea which he must part with, or the hungry mastiff the food which is carried to another kennel. He growled to himself as he turned the leaves of his ominous register, in order to make the necessary entry respecting the removal of his prisoner. " To the Tower—to the Tower—ay, ay, all must to the Tower— that's the fashion of it—free Britons to a military prison, as if we had neither bolts nor chains here!—I hope Parliament will have it up, this Towering work, that's all.— Well, the youngster will take no good by the change, and that is one comfort."

Having finished at once his official act of registration, and his soliloquy, he made a signal to his assistants to remove Julian, who was led along the same stern passages which he had traversed upon his entrance, to the gate of the prison, whence a coach, escorted by two officers of justice, conveyed him to the water-side.

A boat here waited him, with four warders of the Tower, to whose custody he was formally resigned by his late attendants. Clink, however, the turnkey, with whom he was more specially acquainted, did not take leave of him without furnishing him with the piece of black crape which he requested. Peveril fixed it on his hat amid the whispers of his new guardians. " The gentleman is in a hurry to go into mourning," said one ; " mayhap he had better wait till he has cause."

" Perhaps others may. wear mourning for him, ere he can mourn for any one," answered another of these functionaries.

Yet, notwithstanding the tenor of these whispers, their behaviour to their prisoner was more respectful than he had experienced from his former keepers, and might be termed a sullen civility. The ordinary officers of the law were in general rude, as having to do with felons of every description ; whereas these men were only employed with persons accused of state crimes—men who were from birth and circumstances usually entitled to expect, and able to reward, decent usage.

The change of keepers passed unnoticed by Julian, as did the gay and busy scene presented by the broad and beautiful river on which he was now launched. A hundred boats shot past them, bearing parties intent on business, or on pleasure. Julian only viewed them with the stern hope, that whoever had endeavoured to bribe him from his fidelity by the hope of freedom, might see, from the colour of the badge which he had assumed, how determined he was to resist the temptation presented to him.

It was about high water, and a stout wherry came up the river, with sail and oar, so directly upon that in which Julian was embarked, that it seemed as if likely to run her aboard. " Get your carabines ready," cried the principal warder to his assistants. " What the devil can these scoundrels mean ? "

But the crew in the other boat seemed to have perceived their error, for they suddenly altered their course, and struck off into the middle stream, while a torrent of mutual abuse was exchanged betwixt them and the boat whose course they had threatened to impede.

" The Unknown has kept his faith," said Julian to himself; " I too have kept mine."

It even seemed to him, as the boats neared each other, that he heard, from the other wherry, something like a stifled scream or groan; and when the momentary bustle was over, he asked the warder who sat next him, what boat that was.

" Men-of-war's-men, on a frolic, I suppose," answered the warder. " I know no one else would be so impudent as run foul of the King's boat; for I am sure the fellow put the helm up on purpose. But mayhap you, sir, know more of the matter than I do."

This insinuation effectually prevented Julian from putting farther questions, and he remained silent until the boat came under the dusky bastions of the Tower. The tide carried them up under a dark and lowering arch, closed at the upper end by the well-known Traitor's Gate,* formed like a wicket of huge intersecting bars of wood, through which might be seen a dim and imperfect view of soldiers and warders upon duty, and of the steep ascending causeway which leads up from the river into the interior of the fortress. By this gate,—and it is the well-known circumstance which assigned its name,—those accused of state crimes were usually committed to the Tower. The Thames afforded a secret and silent mode of conveyance for transporting thither such whose fallen fortunes might move the commiseration, or whose popular qualities might excite the sympathy, of the public; and even where no cause for especial secrecy existed, the peace of the city was undisturbed by the tumult attending the passage of the prisoner and his guards through the most frequented streets.

* See Note, in " Fortunes of Nigel," vol. xxviii. p. 156.

Yet this custom, however recommended by state policy, must have often struck chill upon the heart of the criminal, who thus, stolen, as it were, out of society, reached the place of his confinement, without encountering even one glance of compassion on the road; and as, from under the dusky arch, he landed on those flinty steps, worn by many a footstep anxious as his own, against which the tide lapped fitfully with small successive waves, and thence looked forward to the steep ascent into a Gothic state-prison, and backward to such part of the river as the low-brow'd vault suffered to become visible, he must often have felt that he was leaving daylight, hope, and life itself, behind him.

While the warder's challenge was made and answered, Peveril endeavoured to obtain information from his conductors where he was likely to be confined; but the answer was brief and general—"Where the Lieutenant should direct."

" Could he not be permitted to share the imprisonment of his father, Sir Geoffrey Peveril ? " He forgot not, on this occasion, to add the surname of his house.

The warder, an old man of respectable appearance, stared, as if at the extravagance of the demand, and said bluntly, " It is impossible."

" At least," said Peveril, " show me where my father is confined, that I may look upon the walls which separate us."

" Young gentleman," said the senior warder, shaking his gray head, " I am sorry for you; but asking questions will do you no service. In this place we know nothing of fathers and sons."

Yet chance seemed, in a few minutes afterwards, to offer Peveril that satisfaction which the rigour of his keepers was disposed to deny to him. As he was conveyed up the steep passage which leads under what is called the Wakefield Tower, a female voice, in a tone wherein grief and joy were indescribably mixed, exclaimed, "My son!—My dear son!"

Even those who guarded Julian seemed softened by a tone of such acute feeling. They slackened their pace. They almost paused to permit him to look up towards the casement from which the sounds of maternal agony proceeded; but the aperture was so narrow, and so closely grated, that nothing was visible save a white female hand, which grasped one of those rusty barricadoes, as if for supporting the person within, while another streamed a white handkerchief, and then let it fall. The casement was instantly deserted.

"Give it me," said Julian to the officer who lifted the handkerchief; "it is perhaps a mother's last gift."

The old warder lifted the napkin, and looked at it with the jealous minuteness of one who is accustomed to detect secret correspondence in the most trifling acts of intercourse.

"There may be writing on it with invisible ink," said one of his comrades.

"It is wetted, but I think it is only with tears," answered the senior. "I cannot keep it from the poor young gentleman."

"Ah, Master Coleby," said his comrade, in a gentle tone of reproach, "you would have been wearing a better coat than a yeoman's to-day, had it not been for your tender heart."

"It signifies little," said old Coleby, "while my heart is true to my King, what I feel in discharging my duty, or what coat keeps my old bosom from the cold weather."

Peveril, meanwhile, folded in his breast the token of his mother's affection which chance had favoured him with; and when placed in the small and solitary chamber which he was told to consider as his own during his residence in the Tower, he was soothed even to weeping by this trifling circumstance, which he could not help considering as an omen, that his unfortunate house was not entirely deserted by Providence.

But the thoughts and occurrences of a prison are too uniform for a narrative, and we must now convey our readers into a more bustling scene.

CHAPTER XXXVII.

Henceforth 'tis done—Fortune and I are friends;
And I must live, for Buckingham commends.

PLACE.

THE spacious mansion of the Duke of Buckingham, with the demesne belonging to it, originally bore the name of York House, and occupied a large portion of the ground adjacent to the Savoy.

This had been laid out by the munificence of his father, the favourite of Charles the First, in a most splendid manner, so as almost to rival Whitehall itself. But during the increasing rage for building new streets, and the creating of almost an additional town, in order to connect London and Westminster, this ground had become of very great value; and the second Duke of Buckingham, who was at once fond of scheming, and needy of money, had agreed to a plan laid before him by some adventurous architect, for converting the extensive grounds around his palace into those streets, lanes, and courts, which still perpetuate his name and titles; though those who live in Buckingham Street, Duke Street, Villiers Street, or in Of-alley, (for even that connecting particle is locally commemorated,) probably think seldom of the memory of the witty, eccentric, and licentious George Villiers, Duke of Buckingham, whose titles are preserved in the names of their residence and its neighbourhood.

This building-plan the Duke had entered upon with all the eagerness which he usually attached to novelty. His gardens were destroyed—his pavilions levelled—his splendid stables demolished—the whole pomp of his suburban demesne laid waste, cumbered with ruins, and intersected with the foundations of new buildings and cellars, and the process of levelling different lines for the intended streets. But the undertaking, although it proved afterwards both lucrative and successful, met with a check at the outset, partly from want of the necessary funds, partly from the impatient and mercurial temper of the Duke, which soon carried him off in pursuit of some more new object. So that, though much was demolished, very little, in comparison, was reared up in the stead, and nothing was completed. The principal part of the ducal mansion still remained uninjured; but the demesne in which it stood bore a strange analogy to the irregular mind of its noble owner. Here stood a beautiful group of exotic trees and shrubs, the remnant of the garden, amid yawning common-sewers, and heaps of rubbish. In one place an old tower threatened to fall upon the spectator; and in another he ran the risk of being swallowed up by a modern vault. Grandeur of conception could be discovered in the undertaking, but was almost every where marred by poverty or negligence of execution. In short, the whole place was the true emblem of an understanding and talents run to waste, and become more dangerous than advantageous to society, by the want of steady principle, and the improvidence of the possessor.

There were men who took a different view of the Duke's purpose in permitting his mansion to be thus surrounded, and his demesne occupied by modern buildings which were incomplete, and ancient which were but half demolished.

They alleged, that, engaged as he was in so many mysteries of love and of politics, and having the character of the most daring and dangerous intriguer of his time, his Grace found it convenient to surround himself with this ruinous arena, into which officers of justice could not penetrate without some difficulty and hazard; and which might afford, upon occasion, a safe and secret shelter for such tools as were fit for desperate enterprises, and a private and unobserved mode of access to those whom he might have any special reason for receiving in secret.

Leaving Peveril in the Tower, we must once more convey our readers to the Levee of the Duke, who, on the morning of Julian's transference to that fortress, thus addressed his minister-in-chief, and principal attendant:—
"I have been so pleased with your conduct in this matter, Jerningham, that if Old Nick were to arise in our presence, and offer me his best imp as a familiar in thy room, I would hold it but a poor compliment."

"A legion of imps," said Jerningham, bowing, "could not have been more busy than I in your Grace's service; but if your Grace will permit me to say so, your whole plan was well-nigh marred by your not returning home till last night, or rather this morning."

"And why, I pray you, sage Master Jerningham," said his Grace, "should I have returned home an instant sooner than my pleasure and convenience served?"

"Nay, my Lord Duke," replied the attendant, "I know not; only, when you sent us word by Empson, in Chiffinch's apartment, to command us to make sure of the girl at any rate, and at all risks, you said you would be here so soon as you could get freed of the King."

"Freed of the King, you rascal! What sort of phrase is that?" demanded the Duke.

"It was Empson who used it, my lord, as coming from your Grace."

"There is much very fit for my Grace to say, that misbecomes such mouths as Empson's or yours to repeat," answered the Duke, haughtily, but instantly resumed his tone of familiarity, for his humour was as capricious as his pursuits. "But I know what thou wouldst have; first, your wisdom would know what became of me since thou hadst my commands at Chiffinch's; and next, your valour would fain sound another flourish of trumpets on thine own most artificial retreat, leaving thy comrade in the hands of the Philistines."

"May it please your Grace," said Jerningham, "I did but retreat for the preservation of the baggage."

"What! do you play at crambo with me?" said the Duke. "I would have you know that the common parish fool should be whipt, were he to attempt to pass pun or quodlibet as a genuine jest, even amongst ticket-porters and hackney chairmen."

"And yet I have heard your Grace indulge in the *jeu de mots*," answered the attendant.

"Sirrah Jerningham," answered the patron, "discard thy memory, or keep it under correction, else it will hamper thy rise in the world. Thou mayst perchance have seen me also have a fancy to play at trap-ball, or to kiss a serving-wench, or to guzzle ale and eat toasted cheese in a porterly whimsy; but is it fitting thou shouldst remember such follies? No more on't.—Hark you; how came the long lubberly fool, Jenkins, being a master of the noble science of defence, to suffer himself to be run through the body so simply by a rustic swain like this same Peveril?"

"Please your Grace, this same Corydon is no such

novice. I saw the onset; and, except in one hand, I never saw a sword managed with such life, grace, and facility."

"Ay, indeed?" said the Duke, taking his own sheathed rapier in his hand, "I could not have thought that. I am somewhat rusted, and have need of breathing. Peveril is a name of note. As well go to the Barns-elms, or behind Montagu-House, with him as with another. His father a rumoured plotter, too. The public would have noted it in me as becoming a zealous Protestant. Needful I do something to maintain my good name in the city, to atone for non-attendance on prayer and preaching. But your Laertes is fast in the Fleet; and I suppose his blundering blockhead of an antagonist is dead or dying."

"Recovering, my lord, on the contrary," replied Jerningham; "the blade fortunately avoided his vitals."

"D——n his vitals!" answered the Duke. "Tell him to postpone his recovery, or I will put him to death in earnest."

"I will caution his surgeon," said Jerningham," which will answer equally well."

"Do so; and tell him he had better be on his own deathbed as cure his patient till I send him notice.—That young fellow must be let loose again at no rate."

"There is little danger," said the attendant. "I hear some of the witnesses have got their net flung over him on account of some matters down in the north; and that he is to be translated to the Tower for that, and for some letters of the Countess of Derby, as rumour goes."

"To the Tower let him go, and get out as he can," replied the Duke; "and when you hear he is fast there, let the fencing fellow recover as fast as the surgeon and he can mutually settle it."

The Duke, having said this, took two or three turns in the apartment, and appeared to be in deep thought. His attendant waited the issue of his meditations with patience, being well aware that such moods, during which his mind was strongly directed in one point, were never of so long duration with his patron as to prove a severe burden to his own patience.

Accordingly, after the silence of seven or eight minutes, the Duke broke through it, taking from the toilette a large silk purse, which seemed full of gold. "Jerningham," he said, "thou art a faithful fellow, and it would be sin not to cherish thee. I beat the King at Mall on his bold defiance. The honour is enough for me; and thou, my boy, shalt have the winnings."

Jerningham pocketed the purse with due ackowledgments.

"Jerningham," his Grace continued, "I know you blame me for changing my plans too often; and on my soul I have heard you so learned on the subject, that I have become of your opinion, and have been vexed at myself for two or three hours together, for not sticking as constantly to one object, as doubtless I shall, when age (touching his forehead) shall make this same weather-cock too rusty to turn with the changing breeze. But as yet, while I have spirit and action, let it whirl like the vane at the mast-head, which teaches the pilot how to steer his course; and when I shift mine, think I am bound to follow fortune, and not to control her."

"I can understand nothing from all this, please your Grace," replied Jerningham, "save that you have been pleased to change some purposed measures, and think that you have profited by doing so."

"You shall judge yourself," replied the Duke. "I

have seen the Duchess of Portsmouth.—You start. It is
true, by Heaven! I have seen her, and from sworn enemies we have become sworn friends. The treaty between
such high and mighty powers had some weighty articles;
besides, I had a French negotiator to deal with; so that
you will allow a few hours' absence was but a necessary
interval to make up our matters of diplomacy."

"Your Grace astonishes me," said Jerningham.
"Christian's plan of supplanting the great lady is then
entirely abandoned? I thought you had but desired to
have the fair successor here, in order to carry it on under
your own management."

"I forget what I meant at the time," said the Duke;
"unless that I was resolved she should not jilt me as she
did the good-natured man of royalty; and so I am still
determined, since you put me in mind of the fair Dowsa-
belle. But I had a contrite note from the Duchess while
we were at the Mall. I went to see her, and found her
a perfect Niobe.—On my soul, in spite of red eyes and
swelled features, and dishevelled hair, there are, after all,
Jerningham, some women, who do, as the poets say, look
lovely in affliction. Out came the cause; and with such
humility, such penitence, such throwing herself on my
mercy, (she the proudest devil, too, in the whole Court,)
that I must have had heart of steel to resist it all. In
short, Chiffinch in a drunken fit had played the babbler,
and let young Saville into our intrigue. Saville plays
the rogue, and informs the Duchess by a messenger, who
luckily came a little late into the market. She learned,
too, being a very devil for intelligence, that there had
been some jarring between the master and me about this
new Phillis; and that I was most likely to catch the bird,
—as any one may see who looks on us both. It must

have been Empson who fluted all this into her Grace's ear ; and thinking she saw how her ladyship and I could hunt in couples, she entreats me to break Christian's scheme, and keep the wench out of the King's sight, especially if she were such a rare. piece of perfection as fame has reported her."

"And your Grace has promised her your hand to up-hold the influence which you have so often threatened to ruin ? " said Jerningham.

"Ay, Jerningham ; my turn was as much served when she seemed to own herself in my power, and cry me mercy.—And observe, it is all one to me by which ladder I climb into the King's cabinet. That of Portsmouth is ready fixed—better ascend by it than fling it down to put up another—I hate all unnecessary trouble."

"And Christian ? " said Jerningham.

" May go to the devil for a self-conceited ass. One pleasure of this twist of intrigue is, to revenge me of that villain, who thought himself so essential, that, by Heaven! he forced himself on my privacy, and lectured me like a schoolboy. Hang the cold-blooded hypocritical vermin ! If he mutters, I will have his nose slit as wide as Coventry's.*—Hark ye, is the Colonel come ? "

" I expect him every moment, your Grace."

" Send him up when he arrives," said the Duke.—— " Why do you stand looking at me ? What would you have ? "

" Your Grace's direction respecting the young lady," said Jerningham.

---

* The ill usage of Sir John Coventry by some of the Life Guards-men, in revenge of something said in Parliament concerning the King's theatrical amours, gave rise to what was called Coventry's Act, against cutting and maiming the person.

"Odd zooks," said the Duke, "I had totally forgotten her.—Is she very tearful?—Exceedingly afflicted?"

"She does not take on so violently as I have seen some do," said Jerningham; "but for a strong, firm, concentrated indignation, I have seen none to match her."

"Well, we will permit her to cool. I will not face the affliction of a second fair one immediately. I am tired of snivelling, and swelled eyes, and blubbered cheeks, for some time; and, moreover, must husband my powers of consolation. Begone, and send the Colonel."

"Will your Grace permit me one other question?" demanded his confidant.

"Ask what thou wilt, Jerningham, and then be gone."

"Your Grace has determined to give up Christian," said the attendant. "May I ask what becomes of the kingdom of Man?"

"Forgotten, as I have a Christian soul!" said the Duke; "as much forgotten as if I had never nourished that scheme of royal ambition.—D—n it, we must knit up the ravelled skean of that intrigue.—Yet it is but a miserable rock, not worth the trouble I have been bestowing on it; and for a kingdom—it has a sound indeed; but, in reality, I might as well stick a cock-chicken's feather into my hat, and call it a plume. Besides, now I think upon it, it would scarce be honourable to sweep that petty royalty out of Derby's possession. I won a thousand pieces of the young Earl when he was last here, and suffered him to hang about me at Court. I question if the whole revenue of his kingdom is worth twice as much. Easily I could win it of him, were he here, with less trouble than it would cost me to carry on these troublesome intrigues of Christian's."

"If I may be permitted to say so, please your Grace,"

answered Jerningham, " although your Grace is perhaps
somewhat liable to change your mind, no man in England
can afford better reasons for doing so."

" I think so myself, Jerningham," said the Duke; " and
it may be it is one reason for my changing. One likes to
vindicate his own conduct, and to find out fine reasons for
doing what one has a mind to.—And now, once again,
begone. Or, hark ye—hark ye—I shall need some loose
gold. You may leave the purse I gave you; and I will
give you an order for as much, and two years' interest, on
old Jacob Doublefee."

" As your Grace pleases," said Jerningham, his whole
stock of complaisance scarcely able to conceal his mortification at exchanging for a distant order, of a kind which
of late had not been very regularly honoured, the sunny
contents of the purse which had actually been in his
pocket. Secretly, but solemnly did he make a vow, that
two years' interest alone should not be the compensation
for this involuntary exchange in the form of his remuneration.

As the discontented dependant left the apartment, he
met, at the head of the grand staircase, Christian himself,
who, exercising the freedom of an ancient friend of the
house, was making his way, unannounced, to the Duke's
dressing apartment. Jerningham, conjecturing that his
visit at this crisis would be any thing but well-timed, or
well-taken, endeavoured to avert his purpose, by asserting
that the Duke was indisposed, and in his bedchamber;
and this he said so loud that his master might hear him,
and, if he pleased, realize the apology which he offered
in his name, by retreating into the bedroom as his last
sanctuary, and drawing the bolt against intrusion.

But, far from adopting a stratagem to which he had

had recourse on former occasions, in order to avoid those who came upon him, though at an appointed hour, and upon business of importance, Buckingham called, in a loud voice, from his dressing apartment, commanding his chamberlain instantly to introduce his good friend Master Christian, and censuring him for hesitating for an instant to do so.

"Now," thought Jerningham within himself, "if Christian knew the Duke as well as I do, he would sooner stand the leap of a lion, like the London 'prentice bold, than venture on my master at this moment, who is even now in a humour nearly as dangerous as the animal."

He then ushered Christian into his master's presence, taking care to post himself within ear-shot of the door.

CHAPTER XXXVIII.

"Speak not of niceness. when there's chance of wreck,"
The captain said, as ladies writhed their neck
To see the dying dolphin flap the deck :
"If we go down, on us these gentry sup;.
We dine upon them, if we haul them up.
Wise men applaud us when we eat the eaters,
As the devil laughs when keen folks cheat the cheaters."

THE SEA VOYAGE.

THERE was nothing in the Duke's manner towards
Christian, which could have conveyed to that latter personage, experienced as he was in the worst possible ways
of the world, that Buckingham would, at that particular
moment, rather have seen the devil than himself; unless it
was that Buckingham's reception of him, being rather
extraordinarily courteous towards so old an acquaintance, might have excited some degree of suspicion.

Having escaped with some difficulty from the vague
region of general compliments, which bears the same relation to that of business that Milton informs us the
Limbo Patrum has to the sensible and material earth,
Christian asked his Grace of Buckingham, with the same
blunt plainness with which he usually veiled a very deep
and artificial character, whether he had lately seen Chiffinch or his helpmate ?

"Neither of them lately," answered Buckingham.
"Have not you waited on them yourself?—I thought

you would have been more anxious about the great scheme."

"I have called once and again," said Christian, "but I can gain no access to the sight of that important couple. I begin to be afraid they are paltering with me."

"Which, by the welkin and its stars, you would not be slow in avenging, Master Christian. I know your puritanical principles on that point well," said the Duke. "Revenge may be well said to be sweet, when so many grave and wise men are ready to exchange for it all the sugar-plums which pleasures offer to the poor sinful people of the world, besides the reversion of those which they talk of expecting in the way of *post obit.*"

"You may jest, my lord," said Christian, "but still "——

"But still you will be revenged on Chiffinch, and his little commodious companion. And yet the task may be difficult—Chiffinch has so many ways of obliging his master—his little woman is such a convenient pretty sort of a screen, and has such winning little ways of her own, that, in faith, in your case, I would not meddle with them. What is this refusing their door, man? We all do it to our best friends now and then, as well as to duns and dull company."

"If your Grace is in a humour of rambling thus wildly in your talk," said Christian, "you know my old faculty of patience—I can wait till it be your pleasure to talk more seriously."

"Seriously!" said his Grace—"Wherefore not?—I only wait to know what your serious business may be."

"In a word, my lord, from Chiffinch's refusal to see me, and some vain calls which I have made at your

Grace's mansion, I am afraid either that our plan has miscarried, or that there is some intention to exclude me from the farther conduct of the matter." Christian pronounced these words with considerable emphasis.

"That were folly as well as treachery," returned the Duke, "to exclude from the spoil the very engineer who conducted the attack. But hark ye, Christian—I am sorry to tell bad news without preparation ; but as you insist on knowing the worst, and are not ashamed to suspect your best friends, out it must come—Your niece left Chiffinch's house the morning before yesterday."

Christian staggered, as if he had received a severe blow ; and the blood ran to his face in such a current of passion, that the Duke concluded he was struck with an apoplexy. But, exerting the extraordinary command which he could maintain under the most trying circumstances, he said, with a voice, the composure of which had an unnatural contrast with the alteration of his countenance, "Am I to conclude, that in leaving the protection of the roof in which I placed her, the girl has found shelter under that of your Grace ?"

"Sir," replied Buckingham, gravely, "the supposition does my gallantry more credit than it deserves."

"Oh, my Lord Duke," answered Christian, "I am not one whom you can impose on by this species of courtly jargon. I know of what your Grace is capable ; and that to gratify the caprice of a moment you would not hesitate to disappoint even the schemes at which you yourself have laboured most busily.—Suppose this jest played off. Take your laugh at those simple precautions by which I intended to protect your Grace's interest, as well as that of others. Let us know the extent of your frolic, and consider how far its consequences can be repaired."

" On my word, Christian," said the Duke, laughing, "you are the most obliging of uncles and of guardians. Let your niece pass through as many adventures as Boccaccio's bride of the King of Garba, you care not. Pure or soiled, she will still make the footstool of your fortune."

An Indian proverb says, that the dart of contempt will even pierce through the shell of the tortoise; but this is more peculiarly the case when conscience tells the subject of the sarcasm that it is justly merited. Christian, stung with Buckingham's reproach, at once assumed a haughty and threatening mien, totally inconsistent with that in which sufferance seemed to be as much his badge as that of Shylock. " You are a foul-mouthed and most unworthy lord," he said; " and as such I will proclaim you, unless you make reparation for the injury you have done me."

" And what," said the Duke of Buckingham, " shall I proclaim *you*, that can give you the least title to notice from such as I am? What name shall I bestow on the little transaction which has given rise to such unexpected misunderstanding? "

Christian was silent, either from rage or from mental conviction.

" Come, come, Christian," said the Duke, smiling, " we know too much of each other to make a quarrel safe. Hate each other we may—circumvent each other—it is the way of Courts—but proclaim!—a fico for the phrase."

" I used it not," said Christian, " till your Grace drove me to extremity. You know, my lord, I have fought both at home and abroad; and you should not rashly think that I will endure any indignity which blood can wipe away."

"On the contrary," said the Duke, with the same civil and sneering manner, "I can confidently assert, that the life of half a score of your friends would seem very light to you, Christian, if their existence interfered, I do not say with your character, as being a thing of much less consequence, but with any advantage which their existence might intercept.—Fie upon it, man, we have known each other long. I never thought you a coward; and am only glad to see I could strike a few sparkles of heat out of your cold and constant disposition. I will now, if you please, tell you at once the fate of the young lady, in which I pray you to believe that I am truly interested."

"I hear you, my Lord Duke," said Christian. "The curl of your upper lip, and your eyebrow, does not escape me. Your Grace knows the French proverb, 'He laughs best who laughs last.' But I hear you."

"Thank Heaven you do," said Buckingham; "for your case requires haste, I promise you, and involves no laughing matter. Well then, hear a simple truth, on which (if it became me to offer any pledge for what I assert to be such) I could pledge life, fortune, and honour. It was the morning before last, when meeting with the King at Chiffinch's unexpectedly—in fact I had looked in to fool an hour away, and to learn how your scheme advanced—I saw a singular scene. Your niece terrified little Chiffinch—(the hen Chiffinch, I mean)—bid the King defiance to his teeth, and walked out of the presence triumphantly, under the guardianship of a young fellow of little mark or likelihood, excepting a tolerable personal presence, and the advantage of a most unconquerable impudence. Egad, I can hardly help laughing to think how the King and I were both baffled; for I will not deny, that I had tried to trifle for a moment with the fair Indamora. But, egad, the young fellow swooped her off from under our noses, like my own Drawcansir clearing off the banquet from the two Kings of Brentford. There was a dignity in the gallant's swaggering retreat which I must try to teach Mohun; * it will suit his part admirably."

"This is incomprehensible, my Lord Duke," said Christian, who by this time had recovered all his usual coolness; "you cannot expect me to believe this. Who dared be so bold as to carry off my niece in such a manner, and from so august a presence? And with whom, a stranger, as he must have been, would she, wise and cautious as I know her, have consented to depart in such a manner?—My lord, I cannot believe this."

"One of your priests, my most devout Christian," replied the Duke, "would only answer, Die, infidel, in thine unbelief; but I am only a poor worldling sinner, and will add what mite of information I can. The young fellow's name, as I am given to understand, is Julian, son of Sir Geoffrey, whom men call Peveril of the Peak."

"Peveril of the Devil, who hath his cavern there!" said Christian, warmly; "for I know that gallant, and believe him capable of any thing bold and desperate. But how could he intrude himself into the royal presence? Either Hell aids him, or Heaven looks nearer into mortal dealings than I have yet believed. If so, may God forgive us, who deemed he thought not on us at all!"

* Then a noted actor.

"Amen, most Christian Christian," replied the Duke.
"I am glad to see thou hast yet some touch of grace that
leads thee to augur so.   But Empson, the hen Chiffinch,
and half a dozen more, saw the swain's entrance and
departure.   Please examine these witnesses with your
own wisdom, if you think your time may not be better
employed in tracing the fugitives.   I believe he gained
entrance as one of some dancing or masking party.
Rowley, you know, is accessible to all who will come
forth to make him sport.   So in stole this termagant
tearing gallant, like Samson among the Philistines, to
pull down our fine scheme about our ears."

"I believe you, my lord," said Christian; "I cannot
but believe you; and I forgive you, since it is your
nature, for making sport of what is ruin and destruction.
But which way did they take?"

"To Derbyshire, I should presume, to seek her father,"
said the Duke.   "She spoke of going into the paternal
protection, instead of yours, Master Christian.   Something had chanced at Chiffinch's, to give her cause to
suspect that you had not altogether provided for his
daughter in the manner which her father was likely to
approve of."

"Now, Heaven be praised," said Christian, "she knows
not her father is come to London! and they must be gone
down either to Martindale Castle, or to Moultrassie Hall;
in either case they are in my power—I must follow them
close.   I will return instantly to Derbyshire—I am un-
done if she meet her father until these errors are
amended.   Adieu, my lord.   I forgive the part which I
fear your Grace must have had in baulking our enterprise—it is no time for mutual reproaches."

"You speak truth, Master Christian," said the Duke,

"and I wish you all success. Can I help you with men, or horses, or money?"

"I thank your Grace," said Christian, and hastily left the apartment.

The Duke watched his descending footsteps on the staircase, until they could be heard no longer, and then exclaimed to Jerningham, who entered, "*Victoria! victoria! magna est veritas et prævalebit!*—Had I told the villain a word of a lie, he is so familiar with all the regions of falsehood—his whole life has been such an absolute imposture, that I had stood detected in an instant; but I told him truth, and that was the only means of deceiving him. Victoria! my dear Jerningham, I am prouder of cheating Christian, than I should have been of circumventing a minister of state."

"Your Grace holds his wisdom very high," said the attendant.

"His cunning, at least, I do, which, in Court affairs, often takes the weather-gage of wisdom,—as in Yarmouth Roads a herring-buss will baffle a frigate. He shall not return to London if I can help it, until all these intrigues are over."

As his Grace spoke, the Colonel, after whom he had repeatedly made inquiry, was announced by a gentleman of his household. "He met not Christian, did he?" said the Duke hastily.

"No, my lord," returned the domestic, "the Colonel came by the old garden staircase."

"I judged as much," replied the Duke; "'tis an owl that will not take wing in daylight, when there is a thicket left to skulk under. Here he comes from threading lane, vault, and ruinous alley, very near as ominous a creature as the fowl of ill augury which he resembles."

The Colonel, to whom no other appellation seemed to be given, than that which belonged to his military station, now entered the apartment. He was tall, strongly built, and past the middle period of life, and his countenance, but for the heavy cloud which dwelt upon it, might have been pronounced a handsome one. While the Duke spoke to him, either from humility or some other cause, his large serious eye was cast down upon the ground; but he raised it when he answered, with a keen look of earnest observation. His dress was very plain, and more allied to that of the Puritans than of the Cavaliers of the time; a shadowy black hat, like the Spanish sombrero; a large black mantle or cloak, and a long rapier, gave him something the air of a Castilione, to which his gravity and stiffness of demeanour added considerable strength.

"Well, Colonel," said the Duke, "we have been long strangers—how have matters gone with you?"

"As with other men of action in quiet times," answered the Colonel, "or as a good war-caper * that lies high and dry in a muddy creek, till seams and planks are rent and riven."

"Well, Colonel," said the Duke, "I have used your valour before now, and I may again; so that I shall speedily see that the vessel is careened, and undergoes a thorough repair."

"I conjecture, then," said the Colonel, "that your Grace has some voyage in hand?"

"No, but there is one which I want to interrupt," replied the Duke.

"'Tis but another stave of the same tune.—Well, my lord, I listen," answered the stranger.

* A privateer.

"Nay," said the Duke, "it is but a trifling matter after all.—You know Ned Christian?"

"Ay, surely, my lord," replied the Colonel, "we have been long known to each other."

"He is about to go down to Derbyshire to seek a certain niece of his, whom he will scarcely find there. Now, I trust to your tried friendship to interrupt his return to London. Go with him, or meet him, cajole him, or assail him, or do what thou wilt with him—only keep him from London for a fortnight at least, and then I care little how soon he comes."

"For by that time, I suppose," replied the Colonel, "any one may find the wench that thinks her worth the looking for."

"Thou mayst think her worth the looking for thyself, Colonel," rejoined the Duke; "I promise you she hath many a thousand stitched to her petticoat; such a wife would save thee from skeldering on the public."

"My lord, I sell my blood and my sword, but not my honour," answered the man sullenly; "if I marry, my bed may be a poor, but it shall be an honest one."

"Then thy wife will be the only honest matter in thy possession, Colonel—at least since I have known you," replied the Duke.

"Why, truly, your Grace may speak your pleasure on that point. It is chiefly your business which I have done of late; and if it were less strictly honest than I could have wished, the employer was to blame as well as the agent. But for marrying a cast-off mistress, the man (saving your Grace, to whom I am bound) lives not who dares propose it to me."

The Duke laughed loudly. "Why, this is mine Ancient Pistol's vein," he replied.

—— " Shall I Sir Pandarus of Troy become,
And by my side wear steel?—then Lucifer take all! "

" My breeding is too plain to understand ends of playhouse verse, my lord," said the Colonel sullenly.   " Has
your Grace no other service to command me? "

" None—only I am told you have published a Narrative concerning the Plot." *

" What should ail me, my lord? " said the Colonel;
" I hope I am a witness as competent as any that has yet
appeared ? "

" Truly, I think so to the full," said the Duke; "and
it would have been hard, when so much profitable mischief was going, if so excellent a Protestant as yourself
had not come in for a share."

" I came to take your Grace's commands, not to be the
object of your wit," said the Colonel.

" Gallantly spoken, most resolute and most immaculate
Colonel!   As you are to be on full pay in my service for
a month to come, I pray your acceptance of this purse,
for contingents and equipments, and you shall have my
instructions from time to time."

" They shall be punctually obeyed, my lord," said the
Colonel; " I know the duty of a subaltern officer.   I wish
your Grace a good morning."

* Of Blood's Narrative, Roger North takes the following notice.
" There was another sham plot of one Netterville.——And here the
good Colonel Blood, that stole the Duke of Ormond, and, if a timely
rescue had not come in, had hanged him at Tyburn, and afterwards
stole the crown, though he was not so happy as to carry it off; no
player at small games, he, even he, the virtuous Colonel, as this sham
plot says, was to have been destroyed by the Papists.   It seems these
Papists would let no eminent Protestant be safe.   But some amends
were made to the Colonel by sale of the narrative licensed Thomas
Blood.   It would have been strange if so much mischief were stirring,
and he had not come in for a snack."—*Examen*, edit. 1711, p. 811.

So saying, he pocketed the purse, without either affecting hesitation, or expressing gratitude, but merely as a part of a transaction in the regular way of business, and stalked from the apartment with the same sullen gravity which marked his entrance. " Now, there goes a scoundrel after my own heart," said the Duke ; " a robber from his cradle, a murderer since he could hold a knife, a profound hypocrite in religion, and a worse and deeper hypocrite in honour,—would sell his soul to the devil to accomplish any villainy, and would cut the throat of his brother, did he dare to give the villainy he had so acted its right name.—Now, why stand you amazed, good Master Jerningham, and look on me as you would on some monster of Ind, when you had paid your shilling to see it, and were staring out your pennyworth with your eyes as round as a pair of spectacles? Wink, man, and save them, and then let thy tongue untie the mystery."

" On my word, my Lord Duke," answered Jerningham, " since I am compelled to speak, I can only say, that the longer I live with your Grace, I am the more at a loss to fathom your motives of action. Others lay plans, either to attain profit or pleasure by their execution ; but your Grace's delight is to counteract your own schemes, when in the very act of performance ; like a child—forgive me —that breaks its favourite toy, or a man who should set fire to the house he has half built."

" And why not, if he wanted to warm his hands at the blaze ? " said the Duke.

" Ay, my lord," replied his dependant ; " but what if, in doing so, he should burn his fingers ?—My lord, it is one of your noblest qualities, that you will sometimes listen to the truth without taking offence ; but were it otherwise, I could not, at this moment, help speaking out at every risk."

"Well, say on, I can bear it," said the Duke, throwing himself into an easy-chair, and using his toothpick with graceful indifference and equanimity; "I love to hear what such potsherds as thou art, think of the proceedings of us who are of the pure porcelain clay of the earth."

"In the name of Heaven, my lord, let me then ask you," said Jerningham, "what merit you claim, or what advantage you expect, from having embroiled every thing in which you are concerned to a degree which equals the chaos of the blind old Roundhead's poem which your Grace is so fond of? To begin with the King. In spite of good-humour, he will be incensed at your repeated rivalry."

"His Majesty defied me to it."

"You have lost all hopes of the Isle, by quarrelling with Christian."

"I have ceased to care a farthing about it," replied the Duke.

"In Christian himself, whom you have insulted, and to whose family you intend dishonour, you have lost a sagacious, artful, and cool-headed instrument and adherent," said the monitor.

"Poor Jerningham!" answered the Duke; "Christian would say as much for thee, I doubt not, wert thou discarded to-morrow. It is the common error of such tools as you and he to think themselves indispensable. As to his family, what was never honourable cannot be dishonoured by any connexion with my house."

"I say nothing of Chiffinch," said Jerningham, "offended as he will be when he learns why, and by whom, his scheme has been ruined, and the lady spirited away— He and his wife, I say nothing of them."

"You need not," said the Duke; "for were they even fit persons to speak to me about, the Duchess of Portsmouth has bargained for their disgrace."

"Then this bloodhound of a Colonel, as he calls himself, your Grace cannot even lay *him* on a quest which is to do you service, but you must do him such indignity at the same time, as he will not fail to remember, and be sure to fly at your throat should he ever have an opportunity of turning on you."

"I will take care he has none," said the Duke; "and yours, Jerningham, is a low-lived apprehension. Beat your spaniel heartily if you would have him under command. Ever let your agents see you know what they are, and prize them accordingly. A rogue, who must needs be treated as a man of honour, is apt to get above his work. Enough, therefore, of your advice and censure, Jerningham; we differ in every particular. Were we both engineers, you would spend your life in watching some old woman's wheel, which spins flax by the ounce; I must be in the midst of the most varied and counteracting machinery, regulating checks and counter-checks, balancing weights, proving springs and wheels, directing and controlling a hundred combined powers."

"And your fortune, in the meanwhile?" said Jerningham; "pardon this last hint, my lord."

"My fortune," said the Duke, "is too vast to be hurt by a petty wound; and I have, as thou knowest, a thousand salves in store for the scratches and scars which it sometimes receives in greasing my machinery."

"Your Grace does not mean Dr. Wilderhead's powder of projection?"

"Pshaw! he is a quacksalver, and mountebank, and beggar."

" Or Solicitor Drowndland's plan for draining the fens ? "

" He is a cheat,—*videlicet,* an attorney."

" Or the Laird of Lackpelf's sale of Highland woods ? "

" He is a Scotsman," said the Duke,—" *videlicet,* both cheat and beggar."

" These streets here, upon the site of your noble mansion-house ? " said Jerningham.

" The architect's a bite, and the plan's a bubble. I am sick of the sight of this rubbish, and I will soon replace our old alcoves, alleys, and flower-pots, by an Italian garden and a new palace."

" That, my lord, would be to waste, not to improve your fortune," said his domestic.

" Clodpate, and muddy spirit that thou art, thou hast forgot the most hopeful scheme of all—the South Sea Fisheries—their stock is up 50 per cent. already. Post down to the Alley, and tell old Manasses to buy £20,000 for me.—Forgive me, Plutus, I forgot to lay my sacrifice on thy shrine, and yet expected thy favours !—Fly posthaste, Jerningham—for thy life, for thy life, for thy life ! " *

With hands and eyes uplifted, Jerningham left the apartment ; and the Duke, without thinking a moment farther on old or new intrigues—on the friendship he had formed, or the enmity he had provoked—on the beauty whom he had carried off from her natural protectors, as well as from her lover—or on the monarch against whom

---

* Stock-jobbing, as it is called, that is, dealing in shares of monopolies, patents, and joint-stock companies of every description, was at least as common in Charles II.'s time as our own ; and as the exercise of ingenuity in this way promised a road to wealth without the necessity of industry, it was then much pursued by dissolute courtiers.

he had placed himself in rivalship,—sat down to calculate chances with all the zeal of Demoivre, tired of the drudgery in half an hour, and refused to see the zealous agent whom he had employed in the city, because he was busily engaged in writing a new lampoon.

CHAPTER XXXIX.

Ah! changeful head, and fickle heart!
PROGRESS OF DISCONTENT.

No event is more ordinary in narratives of this nature, than the abduction of the female on whose fate the interest is supposed to turn; but that of Alice Bridgenorth was thus far particular, that she was spirited away by the Duke of Buckingham, more in contradiction than in the rivalry of passion; and that, as he made his first addresses to her at Chiffinch's, rather in the spirit of rivalry to his Sovereign, than from any strong impression which her beauty had made on his affections, so he had formed the sudden plan of spiriting her away by means of his dependents, rather to perplex Christian, the King, Chiffinch, and all concerned, than because he had any particular desire for her society at his own mansion. Indeed, so far was this from being the case, that his Grace was rather surprised than delighted with the success of the enterprise which had made her an inmate there, although it is probable he might have thrown himself into an uncontrollable passion, had he learned its miscarriage instead of its success.

Twenty-four hours passed over since he had returned to his own roof, before, notwithstanding sundry hints from Jerningham, he could even determine on the exertion

necessary to pay his fair captive a visit; and then it
was with the internal reluctance of one who can only be
stirred from indolence by novelty.

"I wonder what made me plague myself about this
wench," said he, " and doom myself to encounter all the
hysterical rhapsodies of a country Phillis, with her head
stuffed with her grandmother's lessons about virtue and
the Bible-book, when the finest and best-bred women in
town may be had upon more easy terms. It is a pity one
cannot mount the victor's car of triumph without having
a victory to boast of; yet, faith, it is what most of our
modern gallants do, though it would not become Buckingham.—Well, I must see her," he concluded, "though
it were but to rid the house of her. The Portsmouth
will not hear of her being set at liberty near Charles, so
much is she afraid of a new fair seducing the old sinner
from his allegiance. So how the girl is to be disposed of
—for I shall have little fancy to keep her here, and she
is too wealthy to be sent down to Cliefden as a housekeeper—is a matter to be thought on."

He then called for such a dress as might set off his natural good mien—a compliment which he considered as
due to his own merit; for as to any thing farther, he went
to pay his respects to his fair prisoner with almost as little
zeal in the cause, as a gallant to fight a duel in which
he has no warmer interest than the maintenance of his
reputation as a man of honour.

The set of apartments consecrated to the use of those
favourites who occasionally made Buckingham's mansion
their place of abode, and who were, so far as liberty was
concerned, often required to observe the regulations of a
convent, were separated from the rest of the Duke's extensive mansion. He lived in the age when what was

called gallantry warranted the most atrocious actions of deceit and violence; as may be best illustrated by the catastrophe of an unfortunate actress, whose beauty attracted the attention of the last De Vere, Earl of Oxford. While her virtue defied his seductions, he ruined her under colour of a mock marriage, and was rewarded for a success which occasioned the death of his victim, by the general applause of the men of wit and gallantry who filled the drawing-room of Charles.

Buckingham had made provision in the interior of his ducal mansion for exploits of a similar nature; and the set of apartments which he now visited were alternately used to confine the reluctant, and to accommodate the willing.

Being now destined for the former purpose, the key was delivered to the Duke by a hooded and spectacled old lady, who sat reading a devout book in the outer hall which divided these apartments (usually called the Nunnery) from the rest of the house. This experienced dowager acted as mistress of the ceremonies on such occasions, and was the trusty depositary of more intrigues than were known to any dozen of her worshipful calling besides.

"As sweet a linnet," she said, as she undid the outward door, "as ever sung in a cage."

"I was afraid she might have been more for moping than for singing, Dowlas," said the Duke.

"Till yesterday she was so, please your Grace," answered Dowlas; "or, to speak sooth, till early this morning, we heard of nothing but Lachrymæ. But the air of your noble Grace's house is favourable to singing-birds; and to-day matters have been a-much mended."

"'Tis sudden, dame," said the Duke; "and 'tis something strange, considering that I have never visited her, that the pretty trembler should have been so soon reconciled to her fate."

" Ah, your Grace has such magic, that it communicates itself to your very walls; as wholesome Scripture says, Exodus, first and seventh, ' It cleaveth to the walls and the door-posts.' "

" You are too partial, Dame Dowlas," said the Duke of Buckingham.

" Not a word but truth," said the dame ; " and I wish I may be an outcast from the fold of the lambs, but I think this damsel's very frame has changed since she was under your Grace's roof. Methinks she hath a lighter form, a finer step, a more displayed ankle—I cannot tell, but I think there is a change. But, lack-a-day, your Grace knows I am as old as I am trusty, and that my eyes wax something uncertain."

" Especially when you wash them with a cup of canary, Dame Dowlas," answered the Duke, who was aware that temperance was not amongst the cardinal virtues which were most familiar to the old lady's practice.

" Was it canary, your Grace said ?—Was it indeed with canary, that your Grace should have supposed me to have washed my eyes ? " said the offended matron. " I am sorry that your Grace should know me no better."

" I crave your pardon, dame," said the Duke, shaking aside, fastidiously, the grasp which, in the earnestness of her exculpation, Madam Dowlas had clutched upon his sleeve. " I crave your pardon. Your nearer approach has convinced me of my erroneous imputation—I should have said nantz—not canary."

So saying, he walked forward into the inner apartments, which were fitted up with an air of voluptuous magnificence.

" The dame said true, however," said the proud deviser and proprietor of the splendid mansion—" A country Phillis might well reconcile herself to such a prison as this, even without a skilful bird-fancier to touch a bird-call. But I wonder where she can be, this rural Phidele. Is it possible she can have retreated, like a despairing commandant, into her bedchamber, the very citadel of the place, without even an attempt to defend the out-works ? "

As he made this reflection, he passed through an ante-chamber and little eating parlour, exquisitely furnished, and hung with excellent paintings of the Venetian school.

Beyond these lay a withdrawing-room, fitted up in a style of still more studied elegance. The windows were darkened with painted glass, of such a deep and rich colour, as made the midday beams, which found their way into the apartment, imitate the rich colours of sunset ; and, in the celebrated expression of the poet, " taught light to counterfeit a gloom."

Buckingham's feelings and taste had been too much, and too often, and too readily gratified, to permit him, in the general case, to be easily accessible, even to those pleasures which it had been the business of his life to pursue. The hackneyed voluptuary is like the jaded epicure, the mere listlessness of whose appetite becomes at length a sufficient penalty for having made it the principal object of his enjoyment and cultivation. Yet novelty has always some charms, and uncertainty has more.

The doubt how he was to be received—the change of mood which his prisoner was said to have evinced—the

curiosity to know how such a creature as Alice Bridgenorth had been described, was likely to bear herself under
the circumstances in which she was so unexpectedly
placed, had upon Buckingham the effect of exciting unusual interest. On his own part, he had none of those
feelings of anxiety with which a man, even of the most
vulgar mind, comes to the presence of the female whom
he wishes to please, far less the more refined sentiments
of love, respect, desire, and awe, with which the more
refined lover approaches the beloved object. He had
been, to use an expressive French phrase, too completely
blasé even from his earliest youth, to permit him now to
experience the animal eagerness of the one, far less the
more sentimental pleasure of the other. It is no small
aggravation of this jaded and uncomfortable state of mind,
that the voluptuary cannot renounce the pursuits with
which he is satiated, but must continue, for his character's
sake, or from the mere force of habit, to take all the toil,
fatigue, and danger of the chase, while he has so little real
interest in the termination.

Buckingham, therefore, felt it due to his reputation as
a successful hero of intrigue, to pay his addresses to Alice
Bridgenorth with dissembled eagerness; and, as he opened
the door of the inner apartment, he paused to consider,
whether the tone of gallantry, or that of passion, was
fittest to use on the occasion. This delay enabled him to
hear a few notes of a lute touched with exquisite skill, and
accompanied by the still sweeter strains of a female voice,
which, without executing any complete melody, seemed
to sport itself in rivalship of the silver sound of the
instrument.

" A creature so well educated," said the Duke, " with
the sense she is said to possess, would, rustic as she is,

laugh at the assumed rants of Oroondates. It is the vein
of Dorimont—once, Buckingham, thine own—that must
here do the feat, besides that the part is easier."

So thinking, he entered the room with that easy grace
which characterized the gay courtiers among whom he
flourished, and approached the fair tenant, whom he found
seated near a table covered with books and music, and
having on her left hand the large half-open casement, dim
with stained glass, admitting only a doubtful light into this
lordly retiring-room, which, hung with the richest tapestry
of the Gobelines, and ornamented with piles of china and
splendid mirrors, seemed like a bower built for a prince
to receive his bride.

The splendid dress of the inmate corresponded with the
taste of the apartment which she occupied, and partook of
the Oriental costume which the much-admired Roxalana
had then brought into fashion. A slender foot and ankle,
which escaped from the wide trowser of richly ornamented and embroidered blue satin, was the only part of
her person distinctly seen; the rest was enveloped, from
head to foot, in a long veil of silver gauze, which, like a
feathery and light mist on a beautiful landscape, suffered
you to perceive that what it concealed was rarely lovely,
yet induced the imagination even to enhance the charms
it shaded. Such part of the dress as could be discovered,
was, like the veil and the trowsers, in the Oriental taste;
a rich turban, and splendid caftan, were rather indicated
than distinguished through the folds of the former. The
whole attire argued at least coquetry on the part of a fair
one, who must have expected, from her situation, a visitor
of some pretension; and induced Buckingham to smile
internally at Christian's account of the extreme simplicity
and purity of his niece.

He approached the lady *en cavalier*, and addressed her with the air of being conscious, while he acknowledged his offences, that his condescending to do so formed a sufficient apology for them. "Fair Mistress Alice," he said, "I am sensible how deeply I ought to sue for pardon for the mistaken zeal of my servants, who, seeing you deserted and exposed without protection during an un-lucky affray, took it upon them to bring you under the roof of one who would expose his life rather than suffer you to sustain a moment's anxiety. Was it my fault that those around me should have judged it neces-sary to interfere for your preservation; or that, aware of the interest I must take in you, they have detained you till I could myself, in personal attendance, receive your commands?"

"That attendance has not been speedily rendered, my lord," answered the lady. "I have been a prisoner for two days—neglected, and left to the charge of menials."

"How say you, lady?—Neglected!" exclaimed the Duke. "By Heaven, if the best in my household has failed in his duty, I will discard him on the instant!"

"I complain of no lack of courtesy from your servants, my lord," she replied; "but methinks it had been but complaisant in the Duke himself to explain to me earlier wherefore he has had the boldness to detain me as a state prisoner."

"And can the divine Alice doubt," said Buckingham, "that, had time and space, those cruel enemies to the flight of passion, given permission, the instant in which you crossed your vassal's threshold had seen its devoted master at your feet, who hath thought, since he saw you, of nothing but the charms which that fatal morning placed before him at Chiffinch's?"

" I understand, then, my lord," said the lady, " that you have been absent, and have had no part in the restraint which has been exercised upon me ? "

"Absent on the King's command, lady, and employed in the discharge of his duty," answered Buckingham, without hesitation. " What could I do?—The moment you left Chiffinch's, his Majesty commanded me to the saddle in such haste, that I had no time to change my satin buskins for riding-boots.* If my absence has occasioned you a moment of inconvenience, blame the inconsiderate zeal of those, who, seeing me depart from London, half distracted at my separation from you, were willing to contribute their unmannered, though well-meant exertions, to preserve their master from despair, by retaining the fair Alice within his reach. To whom, indeed, could they have restored you? He whom you selected as your champion is in prison, or fled—your father absent from town—your uncle in the north. To Chiffinch's house you had expressed your well-founded aversion; and what fitter asylum remained than that of your devoted slave, where you must ever reign a queen ? "

"An imprisoned one," said the lady. "I desire not such royalty."

"Alas ! how wilfully you misconstrue me ! " said the Duke, kneeling on one knee; " and what right can you have to complain of a few hours' gentle restraint—you, who destine so many to hopeless captivity ? Be merciful for once, and withdraw that envious veil; for the divinities are ever most cruel when they deliver their oracles

* This case is not without precedent. Among the jealousies and fears expressed by the Long Parliament, they insisted much upon an agent for the King departing for the continent so abruptly, that he had not time to change his court dress—white buskins, to wit, and black silk pantaloons—for an equipment more suitable to travel with.

from such clouded recesses. Suffer at least my rash hand "——

"I will save your Grace that unworthy trouble," said the lady, haughtily ; and rising up, she flung back over her shoulders the veil which shrouded her, saying at the same time, "Look on me, my Lord Duke, and see if these be indeed the charms which have made on your Grace an impression so powerful."

Buckingham did look ; and the effect produced on him by surprise was so strong, that he rose hastily from his knee, and remained for a few seconds as if he had been petrified. The figure that stood before him had neither the height nor the rich shape of Alice Bridgenorth ; and, though perfectly well made, was so slightly formed, as to seem almost infantine. Her dress was three or four short vests of embroidered satin, disposed one over the other, of different colours, or rather different shades of similar colours ; for strong contrast was carefully avoided. These opened in front, so as to show part of the throat and neck, partially obscured by an inner covering of the finest lace ; over the uppermost vest was worn a sort of mantle, or coat of rich fur. A small but magnificent turban was carelessly placed on her head, from under which flowed a profusion of coal-black tresses, which Cleopatra might have envied. The taste and splendour of the Eastern dress corresponded with the complexion of the lady's face, which was brunette, of a shade so dark as might almost have served an Indian.

Amidst a set of features, in which rapid and keen expression made amends for the want of regular beauty, the essential points of eyes as bright as diamonds, and teeth as white as pearls, did not escape the Duke of Buckingham, a professed connoisseur in female charms.

In a word, the fanciful and singular female who thus unexpectedly produced herself before him, had one of those faces which are never seen without making an impression; which, when removed, are long after remembered; and for which, in our idleness, we are tempted to invent a hundred histories, that we may please our fancy by supposing the features under the influence of different kinds of emotion. Every one must have in recollection countenances of this kind, which, from a captivating and stimulating originality of expression, abide longer in the memory, and are more seductive to the imagination, than even regular beauty.

"My Lord Duke," said the lady, "it seems the lifting of my veil has done the work of magic upon your Grace. Alas, for the captive princess, whose nod was to command a vassal so costly as your Grace! She runs, methinks, no slight chance of being turned out of doors, like a second Cinderella, to seek her fortune among lackeys and lightermen."

"I am astonished!" said the Duke. "That villain, Jerningham—I will have the scoundrel's blood!"

"Nay, never abuse Jerningham for the matter," said the Unknown; "but lament your own unhappy engagements. While you, my Lord Duke, were posting northward, in white satin buskins, to toil in the King's affairs, the right and lawful princess sat weeping in sables in the uncheered solitude to which your absence condemned her. Two days she was disconsolate in vain; on the third came an African enchantress to change the scene for her, and the person for your Grace. Methinks, my lord, this adventure will tell but ill, when some faithful squire shall recount or record the gallant adventures of the second Duke of Buckingham."

" Fairly bit and bantered to boot," said the Duke—
" the monkey has a turn for satire, too, by all that is
piquante.—Hark ye, fair Princess, how dared you adventure on such a trick as you have been accomplice
to?"

" Dare, my lord," answered the stranger; " put the
question to others, not to one who fears nothing."

" By my faith, I believe so; for thy front is bronzed
by nature.—Hark ye, once more, mistress—What is your
name and condition?"

" My condition I have told you—I am a Mauritanian
sorceress by profession, and my name is Zarah," replied
the Eastern maiden.

" But methinks that face, shape, and eyes "—said the
Duke—" when didst thou pass for a dancing fairy?—
Some such imp thou wert not many days since."

" My sister you may have seen—my twin sister; but
not me, my lord," answered Zarah.

" Indeed," said the Duke, " that duplicate of thine, if it
was not thy very self, was possessed with a dumb spirit,
as thou with a talking one. I am still in the mind that
you are the same; and that Satan, always so powerful
with your sex, had art enough on our former meeting, to
make thee hold thy tongue."

" Believe what you will of it, my lord," replied Zarah,
" it cannot change the truth.—And now, my lord, I bid
you farewell.   Have you any commands to Mauri-
tania?"

" Tarry a little, my Princess," said the Duke; " and
remember, that you have voluntarily entered yourself as
pledge for another; and are justly subjected to any
penalty which it is my pleasure to exact. None must
brave Buckingham with impunity."

" I am in no hurry to depart, if your Grace hath any commands for me."

" What! are you neither afraid of my resentment, nor of my love, fair Zarah?" said the Duke.

" Of neither, by this glove," answered the lady. " Your resentment must be a petty passion indeed, if it could stoop to such a helpless object as I am; and for your love —good lack! good lack!"

" And why good lack with such a tone of contempt, lady?" said the Duke, piqued in spite of himself. " Think you Buckingham cannot love, or has never been beloved in return?"

" He may have thought himself beloved," said the maiden; " but by what slight creatures!—things whose heads could be rendered giddy by a playhouse rant— whose brains were only filled with red-heeled shoes and satin buskins—and who run altogether mad on the argument of a George and a star."

" And are there no such frail fair ones in your climate, most scornful Princess?" said the Duke.

" There are," said the lady; " but men rate them as parrots and monkeys—things without either sense or soul, head or heart. The nearness we bear to the sun has purified, while it strengthens, our passions. The icicles of your frozen climate shall as soon hammer hot bars into ploughshares, as shall the foppery and folly of your pretended gallantry make an instant's impression on a breast like mine."

" You speak like one who knows what passion is," said the Duke. " Sit down, fair lady, and grieve not that I detain you. Who can consent to part with a tongue of so much melody, or an eye of such expressive eloquence!— You have known then what it is to love?"

"I know—no matter if by experience, or through the report of others—but I do know, that to love, as I would love, would be to yield not an iota to avarice, not one inch to vanity, not to sacrifice the slightest feeling to interest or to ambition; but to give up ALL to fidelity of heart and reciprocal affection."

"And how many women, think you, are capable of feeling such disinterested passion?"

"More, by thousands, than there are men who merit it," answered Zarah. "Alas! how often do you see the female, pale, and wretched, and degraded, still following with patient constancy the footsteps of some predominating tyrant, and submitting to all his injustice with the endurance of a faithful and misused spaniel, which prizes a look from his master, though the surliest groom that ever disgraced humanity, more than all the pleasure which the world besides can furnish him? Think what such would be to one who merited and repaid her devotion."

"Perhaps the very reverse," said the Duke; "and for your simile, I can see little resemblance. I cannot charge my spaniel with any perfidy; but for my mistresses—to confess truth, I must always be in a cursed hurry if I would have the credit of changing them before they leave me."

"And they serve you but rightly, my lord," answered the lady; "for what are you?—Nay, frown not; for you must hear the truth for once. Nature has done its part, and made a fair outside, and courtly education hath added its share. You are noble, it is the accident of birth—handsome, it is the caprice of Nature—generous, because to give is more easy than to refuse—well-apparelled, it is to the credit of your tailor—well-natured in the main, because you have youth and health—brave, because to be otherwise were to be degraded—and witty, because you cannot help it."

The Duke darted a glance on one of the large mirrors. "Noble, and handsome, and court-like, generous, well-attired, good-humoured, brave, and witty!—You allow me more, madam, than I have the slightest pretension to, and surely enough to make my way, at some point at least, to female favour."

"I have neither allowed you a heart nor a head," said Zarah, calmly.—"Nay, never redden as if you would fly at me. I say not but nature may have given you both; but folly has confounded the one, and selfishness perverted the other. The man whom I call deserving the name, is one whose thoughts and exertions are for others, rather than himself,—whose high purpose is adopted on just principles, and never abandoned while heaven or earth affords means of accomplishing it. He is one who will neither seek an indirect advantage by a specious road, nor take an evil path to gain a real good purpose. Such a man were one for whom a woman's heart should beat constant while he breathes, and break when he dies."

She spoke with so much energy that the water sparkled in her eyes, and her cheek coloured with the vehemence of her feelings.

"You speak," said the Duke, "as if you had yourself a heart which could pay the full tribute to the merit which you describe so warmly."

"And have I not?" said she, laying her hand on her bosom. "Here beats one that would bear me out in what I have said, whether in life or in death."

"Were it in my power," said the Duke, who began to

get farther interested in his visitor than he could at first have thought possible—" Were it in my power to deserve such faithful attachment, methinks it should be my care to requite it."

" Your wealth, your titles, your reputation as a gallant —all you possess, were too little to merit such sincere affection."

" Come, fair lady," said the Duke, a good deal piqued, " do not be quite so disdainful. Bethink you, that if your love be as pure as coined gold, still a poor fellow like myself may offer you an equivalent in silver.—The quantity of my affection must make up for its quality."

" But I am not carrying my affection to market, my lord; and therefore I need none of the base coin you offer in change for it."

" How do I know that, my fairest?" said the Duke. " This is the realm of Paphos—You have invaded it, with what purpose you best know; but I think with none consistent with your present assumption of cruelty. Come, come—eyes that are so intelligent can laugh with delight, as well as gleam with scorn and anger. You are here a waif on Cupid's manor, and I must seize on you in name of the deity."

" Do not think of touching me, my lord," said the lady. " Approach me not, if you would hope to learn the purpose of my being here. Your Grace may suppose yourself a Solomon if you please; but I am no travelling princess, come from distant climes, either to flatter your pride, or wonder at your glory."

" A defiance, by Jupiter!" said the Duke.

" You mistake the signal," said the 'dark ladye;' " I came not here without taking sufficient precautions for my retreat."

"You mouth it bravely," said the Duke; "but never fortress so boasted its resources but the garrison had some thoughts of surrender. Thus I open the first parallel."

They had been hitherto divided from each other by a long narrow table, which, placed in the recess of the large casement we have mentioned, had formed a sort of barrier on the lady's side, against the adventurous gallant. The Duke went hastily to remove it as he spoke; but, attentive to all his motions, his visitor instantly darted through the half-open window. Buckingham uttered a cry of horror and surprise, having no doubt, at first, that she had precipitated herself from a height of at least fourteen feet; for so far the window was distant from the ground. But when he sprung to the spot, he perceived to his astonishment, that she had effected her descent with equal agility and safety.

The outside of this stately mansion was decorated with a quantity of carving, in the mixed state, betwixt the Gothic and Grecian styles, which marks the age of Elizabeth and her successor; and though the feat seemed a surprising one, the projections of these ornaments were sufficient to afford footing to a creature so light and active, even in her hasty descent.

Inflamed alike by mortification and curiosity, Buckingham at first entertained some thought of following her by the same dangerous route, and had actually got upon the sill of the window for that purpose; and was contemplating what might be his next safe movement, when, from a neighbouring thicket of shrubs, amongst which his visitor had disappeared, he heard her chant a verse of a comic song, then much in fashion, concerning a despairing lover who had recourse to a precipice—

> " But when he came near,
>   Beholding how steep
> The sides did appear,
>   And the bottom how deep;
> Though his suit was rejected,
>   He sadly reflected,
> That a lover forsaken
>   A new love may get;
> But a neck that's once broken
>   Can never be set."

The Duke could not help laughing, though much against his will, at the resemblance which the verses bore to his own absurd situation, and, stepping back into the apartment, desisted from an attempt which might have proved dangerous as well as ridiculous. He called his attendants, and contented himself with watching the little thicket, unwilling to think that a female, who had thrown herself in a great measure into his way, meant absolutely to mortify him by a retreat.

That question was determined in an instant. A form, wrapped in a mantle, with a slouched hat and shadowy plume, issued from the bushes, and was lost in a moment amongst the ruins of ancient and of modern buildings, with which, as we have already stated, the demesne formerly termed York House, was now encumbered in all directions.

The Duke's servants, who had obeyed his impatient summons, were hastily directed to search for this tantalizing siren in every direction. Their master, in the meantime, eager and vehement in every new pursuit, but especially when his vanity was piqued, encouraged their diligence by bribes, and threats, and commands. All was in vain. They found nothing of the Mauritanian Princess, as she called herself, but the turban and the veil;

both of which she had left in the thicket, together with her satin slippers ; which articles, doubtless, she had thrown aside as she exchanged them for others less remarkable.

Finding all his search in vain, the Duke of Buckingham, after the example of spoiled children of all ages and stations, gave a loose to the frantic vehemence of passion ; and fiercely he swore vengeance on his late visitor, whom he termed by a thousand opprobrious epithets, of which the elegant phrase " Jilt " was most frequently repeated.

Even Jerningham, who knew the depths and shallows of his master's mood, and was bold to fathom them at almost every state of his passions, kept out of his way on the present occasion ; and, cabineted with the pious old housekeeper, declared to her, over a bottle of ratafia, that, in his apprehension, if his Grace did not learn to put some control on his temper, chains, darkness, straw, and Bedlam, would be the final doom of the gifted and admired Duke of Buckingham.

CHAPTER XL.

—— Contentions fierce,
Ardent, and dire, spring from no petty cause.
ALBION.

THE quarrels between man and wife are proverbial ;
but let not these honest folks think that connexions of a
less permanent nature are free from similar jars.   The
frolic of the Duke of Buckingham, and the subsequent
escape of Alice Bridgenorth, had kindled fierce dissension
in Chiffinch's family, when, on his arrival in town, he
learned these two stunning events : " I tell you," he said
to his obliging helpmate, who seemed but little moved by
all that he could say on the subject, " that your d—d
carelessness has ruined the work of years."

" I think it is the twentieth time you have said so,"
replied the dame ; " and without such frequent assurance,
I was quite ready to believe that a very trifling matter
would overset any scheme of yours, however long thought
of."

" How on earth could you have the folly to let the
Duke into the house when you expected the King ? "
said the irritated courtier.

" Lord, Chiffinch," answered the lady, " ought not you
to ask the porter rather than me, that sort of question ?—
I was putting on my cap to receive his Majesty."

" With the address of a madge-howlet," said Chiffinch,

·"and in the meanwhile you gave the cat the cream to keep."

"Indeed, Chiffinch," said the lady, "these jaunts to the country do render you excessively vulgar! there is a brutality about your very boots! nay, your muslin ruffles, being somewhat soiled, give to your knuckles a sort of rural rusticity, as I may call it."

"It were a good deed," muttered Chiffinch, "to make both boots and knuckles bang the folly and affectation out of thee." Then speaking aloud, he added, like a man who would fain break off an argument, by extorting from his adversary a confession that he has reason on his side, "I am sure, Kate, you must be sensible that our all depends on his Majesty's pleasure."

"Leave that to me," said she; "I know how to pleasure his Majesty better than you can teach me. Do you think his Majesty is booby enough to cry like a schoolboy because his sparrow has flown away? His Majesty has better taste. I am surprised at you, Chiffinch," she added, drawing herself up, "who were once thought to know the points of a fine woman, that you should have made such a roaring about this country wench. Why, she has not even the country quality of being plump as a barn-door fowl, but is more like a Dunstable lark, that one must crack bones and all if you would make a mouthful of it. What signifies whence she came, or where she goes? There will be those behind that are much more worthy of his Majesty's condescending attention, even when the Duchess of Portsmouth takes the frumps."

"You mean your neighbour, Mistress Nelly," said her worthy helpmate; "but Kate, her date is out. Wit she has, let her keep herself warm with it in worse company, for the cant of a gang of strollers is not language for a prince's chamber." *

"It is no matter what I mean, or whom I mean," said Mrs. Chiffinch; "but I tell you, Tom Chiffinch, that you will find your master quite consoled for loss of the piece of prudish puritanism that you would needs saddle him with; as if the good man were not plagued enough with them in Parliament, but you must, forsooth, bring them into his very bedchamber."

"Well, Kate," said Chiffinch, "if a man were to speak all the sense of the seven wise masters, a woman would find nonsense enough to overwhelm him with; so I shall say no more, but that I would to Heaven I may find the King in no worse humour than you describe him. I am commanded to attend him down the river to the Tower to-day, where he is to make some survey of arms and stores. They are clever fellows who contrive to keep Rowley from engaging in business, for, by my word, he has a turn for it."

"I warrant you," said Chiffinch the female, nodding, but rather to her own figure, reflected from a mirror, than to her politic husband,—"I warrant you we will find means of occupying him that will sufficiently fill up his time."

"On my honour, Kate," said the male Chiffinch, "I find you strangely altered, and, to speak truth, grown

---

* In Evelyn's Memoirs is the following curious passage respecting Nell Gwyn, who is hinted at in the text:—"I walked with him [King Charles II.] through Saint James Park to the garden, where I both saw and heard a very familiar discourse between . . . [the King] and Mrs. Nelly, as they called her, an intimate comedian, she looking out of her garden on a terrace at the top of the wall, and [the King] standing on the green walk under it. I was heartily sorry at this scene."— EVELYN'S Memoirs, vol. i. p. 413.

most extremely opinionative. I shall be happy if you
have good reason for your confidence."

The dame smiled superciliously, but deigned no other
answer, unless this were one,—" I shall order a boat to
go upon the Thames to-day with the royal party."

" Take care what you do, Kate ; there are none dare
presume so far but women of the first rank.   Duchess of
Bolton—of Buckingham—of "——

" Who cares for a list of names ? why may not I be
as forward as the greatest B. amongst your string of
them ? "

" Nay, faith, thou mayst match the .greatest B. in
Court already," answered Chiffinch ; " so e'en take thy
own course of it.   But do not let Chaubert forget to get
some collation ready, and a *souper au petit couvert*, in
case it should be commanded for the evening."

" Ay, there your boasted knowledge of Court matters
begins and ends.—Chiffinch, Chaubert, and Company ;—
dissolve that partnership, and you break Tom Chiffinch
for a courtier."

" Amen, Kate," replied Chiffinch ; " and let me tell
you it is as safe to rely on another person's fingers as on
our own wit.   But I must give orders for the water.—If
you will take the pinnace, there are the cloth-of-gold
cushions in the chapel may serve to cover the benches for
the day.   They are never wanted where they lie, so you
may make free with them too."

Madam Chiffinch accordingly mingled with the flotilla
which attended the King on his voyage down the Thames,
amongst whom was the Queen, attended by some of the
principal ladies of the Court.   The little plump Cleopatra, dressed to as much advantage as her taste could
devise, and seated upon her embroidered cushions like

Venus in her shell, neglected nothing that effrontery and minauderie could perform to draw upon herself some portion of the King's observation; but Charles was not in the vein, and did not even pay her the slightest passing attention of any kind, until her boatmen having ventured to approach nearer to the Queen's barge than etiquette permitted, received a peremptory order to back their oars, and fall out of the royal procession. Madam Chiffinch cried for spite, and transgressed Solomon's warning, by cursing the King in her heart; but had no better course than to return to Westminster, and direct Chaubert's preparations for the evening.

In the meantime, the royal barge paused at the Tower; and, accompanied by a laughing train of ladies and of courtiers, the gay Monarch made the echoes of the old prison-towers ring with the unwonted sounds of mirth and revelry. As they ascended from the river side to the centre of the building, where the fine old keep of William the Conqueror, called the White Tower, predominates over the exterior defences, Heaven only knows how many gallant jests, good or bad, were run on the comparison of his Majesty's state-prison to that of Cupid, and what killing similes were drawn between the ladies' eyes and the guns of the fortress, which, spoken with a fashionable congée, and listened to with a smile from a fair lady, formed the fine conversation of the day.

This gay swarm of flutterers did not, however, attend close on the King's person, though they had accompanied him upon his party on the river. Charles, who often formed manly and sensible resolutions, though he was too easily diverted from them by indolence or pleasure, had some desire to make himself personally acquainted with the state of the military stores, arms, &c. of which the

Tower was then, as now, the magazine; and, although he had brought with him the usual number of his courtiers, only three or four attended him on the scrutiny which he intended. Whilst, therefore, the rest of the train amused themselves as they might in other parts of the Tower, the King, accompanied by the Dukes of Buckingham, Ormond, and one or two others, walked through the well-known hall, in which is preserved the most splendid magazine of arms in the world, and which, though far from exhibiting its present extraordinary state of perfection, was even then an arsenal worthy of the great nation to which it belonged.

The Duke of Ormond, well known for his services during the Great Civil War, was, as we have elsewhere noticed, at present rather on cold terms with his Sovereign, who nevertheless asked his advice on many occasions, and who required it on the present amongst others, when it was not a little feared that the Parliament in their zeal for the Protestant religion, might desire to take the magazines of arms and ammunition under their own exclusive orders. While Charles sadly hinted at such a termination of the popular jealousies of the period, and discussed with Ormond the means of resisting, or evading it, Buckingham, falling a little behind, amused himself with ridiculing the antiquated appearance and embarrassed demeanour of the old warder who attended on the occasion, and who chanced to be the very same that escorted Julian Peveril to his present place of confinement. The Duke prosecuted his raillery with the greater activity, that he found the old man, though restrained by the place and presence, was rather upon the whole testy, and disposed to afford what sportsmen call *play* to his persecutor. The various pieces of ancient armour, with

which the wall was covered, afforded the principal source
of the Duke's wit, as he insisted upon knowing from the
old man, who, he said, could best remember matters from
the days of King Arthur downwards at the least, the history of the different warlike weapons, and anecdotes of
the battles in which they had been wielded. The old
man obviously suffered when he was obliged, by repeated
questions, to tell the legends (often sufficiently absurd)
which the tradition of the place had assigned to particular
relics. Far from flourishing his partisan, and augment-
ing the emphasis of his voice, as was and is the prevailing
fashion of these warlike Ciceroni, it was scarcely possible
to extort from him a single word concerning those topics
on which their information is usually overflowing.

" Do you know, my friend," said the Duke to him at
last, " I begin to change my mind respecting you. I supposed you must have served as a Yeoman of the Guaru
since bluff King Henry's time, and expected to hear
something from you about the Field of the Cloth of Gold,
—and I thought of asking you the colour of Anne Bullen's
breastknot, which cost the Pope three kingdoms; but I
am afraid you are but a novice in such recollections of
love and chivalry. Art sure thou didst not creep into
thy warlike office from some dark shop in the Tower-
Hamlets, and that thou hast not converted an unlawful
measuring-yard into that glorious halberd?—I warrant
thou canst not even tell one whom this piece of antique
panoply pertained to ? "

The Duke pointed at random to a cuirass which hung
amongst others, but was rather remarkable from being
better cleansed.

" I should know that piece of iron," said the warder
bluntly, yet with some change in his voice; " for I have

known a man within side of it who would not have endured half the impertinence I have heard spoken to-day."

The tone of the old man, as well as the words, attracted the attention of Charles and the Duke of Ormond, who were only two steps before the speaker. They both stopped and turned round; the former saying at the same time,—" How now, sirrah !—what answers are these ?— What man do you speak of?"

" Of one who is none now," said the warder, "whatever he may have been."

" The old man surely speaks of himself," said the Duke of Ormond, closely examining the countenance of the warder, which he in vain endeavoured to turn away. " I am sure I remember these features—Are not you my old friend, Major Coleby ?"

" I wish your Grace's memory had been less accurate," said the old man, colouring deeply, and fixing his eyes on the ground.

The King was greatly shocked.—" Good God ! " he said, " the gallant Major Coleby, who joined us with his four sons and a hundred and fifty men at Warring-ton !—And is this all we could do for an old Worcester friend?"

The tears rushed thick into the old man's eyes as he said in broken accents, " Never mind me, sire ; I am well enough here—a worn-out soldier rusting among old armour. Where one old cavalier is better, there are twenty worse. I am sorry your Majesty should know any thing of it, since it grieves you."

With that kindness, which was a redeeming point of his character, Charles, while the old man was speaking, took the partisan from him with his own hand, and put it

into that of Buckingham, saying, " What Coleby's hand
has borne, can disgrace neither yours nor mine,—and
you owe him this atonement. Time has been with him,
that, for less provocation, he would have laid it about
your ears."

The Duke bowed deeply, but coloured with resentment,
and took an immediate opportunity to place the weapon
carelessly against a pile of arms. The King did not observe a contemptuous motion, which, perhaps, would not
have pleased him, being at the moment occupied with the
veteran, whom he exhorted to lean upon him, as he conveyed him to a seat, permitting no other person to assist
him. " Rest there," he said, " my brave old friend ; and
Charles Stewart must be poor indeed, if you wear that
dress an hour longer.—You look very pale, my good
Coleby, to have had so much colour a few minutes since.
Be not vexed at what Buckingham says, no one minds
his folly.—You look worse and worse. Come, come, you
are too much hurried by this meeting. Sit still—do not
rise—do not attempt to kneel. I command you to repose
yourself till I have made the round of these apartments."

The old cavalier stooped his head in token of acquiescence in the command of his Sovereign, but he raised it
not again. The tumultuous agitation of the moment had
been too much for spirits which had been long in a state
of depression, and health which was much decayed.
When the King and his attendants, after half an hour's
absence, returned to the spot where they had left the
veteran, they found him dead, and already cold, in the
attitude of one who has fallen easily asleep. The King
was dreadfully shocked ; and it was with a low and fal-
tering voice that he directed the body, in due time, to be

honourably buried in the chapel of the Tower.*   He was
then silent, until he attained the steps in front of the
arsenal, where the party in attendance upon his person
began to assemble at his approach, along with some other
persons of respectable appearance, whom curiosity had
attracted.

" This is dreadful," said the King.   " We must find
some means of relieving the distresses, and rewarding the
fidelity of our suffering followers, or posterity will cry fie
upon our memory."

" Your Majesty has had often such plans agitated in
your council," said Buckingham.

" True, George," said the King.   " I can safely say it
is not my fault.   I have thought of it for years."

" It cannot be too well considered," said Buckingham ;
" besides, every year makes the task of relief easier."

" True," said the Duke of Ormond, " by diminishing
the number of sufferers.   Here is poor old Coleby will no
longer be a burden to the Crown."

" You are too severe, my Lord of Ormond," said the
King, " and should respect the feelings you trespass on.
You cannot suppose that we would have permittèd this
poor man to hold such a situation, had we known of the
circumstance ? "

" For God's sake, then, sire," said the Duke of Ormond, " turn your eyes, which have just rested on the
corpse of one old friend, upon the distresses of others.
Here is the valiant old Sir Geoffrey Peveril of the Peak,
who fought through the whole war, wherever blows were

* A story of this nature is current in the legends of the Tower.
The affecting circumstances are, I believe, recorded in one of the little
manuals which are put into the hands of visitors, but are not to be
found in the later editions.

going, and was the last man, I believe, in England, who
laid down his arms—Here is his son, of whom I have
the highest accounts, as a gallant of spirit, accomplish-
ments, and courage—Here is the unfortunate House of
Derby—for pity's sake, interfere in behalf of these vic-
tims, whom the folds of this hydra-plot have entangled,
in order to crush them to death—rebuke the fiends that
are seeking to devour their lives, and disappoint the har-
pies that are gaping for their property.   This very day
seven-night the unfortunate family, father and son, are to
be brought upon trial for crimes of which they are as
guiltless, I boldly pronounce, as any who stand in this
presence.   For God's sake, sire, let us hope that, should
the prejudices of the people condemn them, as it has
done others, you will at last step in between the blood-
hunters and their prey."

The King looked, as he really was, exceedingly per-
plexed.

Buckingham, between whom and Ormond there existed
a constant and almost mortal quarrel, interfered to effect
a diversion in Charles's favour.   "Your Majesty's royal
benevolence," he said, "needs never want exercise, while
the Duke of Ormond is near your person.   He has his
sleeve cut in the old and ample fashion, that he may always have store of ruined cavaliers stowed in it to produce at demand, rare old raw-boned boys, with Malmsey
noses, bald heads, spindle shanks, and merciless histories
of Edgehill and Naseby."

"My sleeve is, I dare say, of an antique cut," said
Ormond, looking full at the Duke; "but I pin neither
bravoes nor ruffians upon it, my Lord of Buckingham,
as I see fastened to coats of the new mode."

"That is a little too sharp for our presence, my lord,"
said the King.

"Not if I make my words good," said Ormond.—"My Lord of Buckingham, will you name the man you spoke to as you left the boat?"

"I spoke to no one," said the Duke, hastily—"nay, I mistake, I remember a fellow whispered in my ear, that one, who I thought had left London, was still lingering in town. A person whom I had business with."

"Was yon the messenger?" said Ormond, singling out from the crowd who stood in the court-yard, a tall dark-looking man, muffled in a large cloak, wearing a broad shadowy black beaver hat, with a long sword of the Spanish fashion—the very Colonel, in short, whom Buckingham had dispatched in quest of Christian, with the intention of detaining him in the country.

When Buckingham's eyes had followed the direction of Ormond's finger, he could not help blushing so deeply as to attract the King's attention.*

* The conspirator Blood even fought or made his way into good society, and sat at good men's feasts. Evelyn's Diary bears, 10th May, 1671,—"Dined at Mr. Treasurer's, where dined Monsieur de Grammont and several French noblemen, and one Blood, that impudent, bold fellow, that had not long ago attempted to steal the Imperial crown itself out of the Tower, pretending curiosity of seeing the Regalia, when, stabbing the keeper, though not mortally, he boldly went away with it through all the guards, taken only by the accident of his horse falling down. How he came to be pardoned, and even received into favour, not only after this, but several other exploits almost as daring, both in Ireland and here, I could never come to understand. Some believed he became a spy of several parties, being well with the sectaries and enthusiasts, and did his Majesty service that way, which none alive could do so well as he. But it was certainly, as the boldest attempt, so the only treason of the sort that was ever pardoned. The man had not only a daring, but a villainous unmerciful look, a false countenance, but very well spoken and dangerously insinuating."—EVELYN'S *Memoirs*, vol. i. p. 413.

This is one of the many occasions on which we might make curious remarks on the disregard of our forefathers for appearances, even in

" What new frolic is this, George?" he said. " Gentlemen, bring that fellow forward. On my life, a truculentlooking caitiff—Hark ye, friend, who are you? If an honest man, Nature has forgot to label it upon your countenance.—Does none here know him?

> ' With every symptom of a knave complete,
> If he be honest, he's a devilish cheat.' "

" He is well known to many, sire," replied Ormond; " and that he walks in this area with his neck safe, and his limbs unshackled, is an instance, amongst many, that we live under the sway of the most merciful Prince of Europe."

" Oddsfish! who is the man, my Lord Duke?" said the King. " Your Grace talks mysteries—Buckingham blushes—and the rogue himself is dumb."

" That honest gentleman, please your Majesty," replied the Duke of Ormond, " whose modesty makes him mute, though it cannot make him blush, is the notorious Colonel Blood, as he calls himself, whose attempt to possess himself of your Majesty's royal crown took place at no very distant date, in this very Tower of London."

" That exploit is not easily forgotten," said the King; " but that the fellow lives, shows your Grace's clemency as well as mine."

" I cannot deny that I was in his hands, sire," said Ormond, " and had certainly been murdered by him, had he chosen to take my life on the spot, instead of destining

the regulation of society. What should we think of a Lord of the Treasury, who, to make up a party of French nobles and English gentlemen of condition, should invite as a guest Barrington or Major Semple, or any well-known *chevalier d'industrie?* Yet Evelyn does not seem to have been shocked at the man being brought into society, but only at his remaining unhanged.

me—I thank him for the honour—to be hanged at Tyburn. I had certainly been sped, if he had thought me
worth knife or pistol, or any thing short of the cord.—
Look at him, sire! If the rascal dared, he would say at
this moment, like Caliban in the play, ' Ho, ho, I would
I had done it ! ' "

"Why, oddsfish!" answered the King, "he hath a villainous sneer, my lord, which seems to say as much; but,
my Lord Duke, we have pardoned him, and so has your
Grace."

"It would ill have become me," said the Duke of Ormond, "to have been severe in prosecuting an attempt on
my poor life, when your Majesty was pleased to remit his
more outrageous and insolent attempt upon your royal
crown. But I must conceive it as a piece of supreme
insolence on the part of this bloodthirsty bully, by whomsoever he may be now backed, to appear in the Tower,
which was the theatre of one of his villainies, or before
me, who was well-nigh the victim of another."

"It shall be amended in future," said the King.—
"Hark ye, sirrah Blood, if you again presume to thrust
yourself in the way you have done but now, I will have
the hangman's knife and your knavish ears made acquainted."

Blood bowed, and with a coolness of impudence which
did his nerves great honour, he said he had only come to
the Tower accidentally, to communicate with a particular
friend on business of importance. "My Lord Duke of
Buckingham," he said, "knew he had no other intentions."

"Get you gone, you scoundrelly cut-throat," said the
Duke, as much impatient of Colonel Blood's claim of acquaintance, as a town-rake of the low and blackguard

companions of his midnight rambles, when they accost
him in daylight amidst better company ; " if you dare to
quote my name again, I will have you thrown, into the
Thames."

Blood, thus repulsed, turned round with the most insolent composure, and walked away down from the parade,
all men looking at him, as at some strange and monstrous
prodigy, so much was he renowned for daring and desperate villainy. Some even followed him, to have a
better survey of the notorious Colonel Blood, like the
smaller tribe of birds which keep fluttering round an owl
when he appears in the light of the sun. But as, in the
latter case, these thoughtless flutterers are careful to keep
out of reach of the beak and claws of the bird of Minerva, so none of those who followed and gazed on Blood
as something ominous, cared to bandy looks with him, or
to endure and return the lowering and deadly glances,
which he shot from time to time on those who pressed
nearest to him. He stalked on in this manner, like a
daunted, yet sullen wolf, afraid to stop, yet unwilling to
fly, until he reached the Traitor's gate, and getting on
board a sculler which waited for him, he disappeared
from their eyes.

Charles would fain have obliterated all recollection of
his appearance, by the observation, " It were shame that
such a reprobate scoundrel should be the subject of dis-
cord between two noblemen of distinction ; " and he recommended to the Dukes of Buckingham and Ormond to
join hands, and forget a misunderstanding which rose on
so unworthy a subject.

Buckingham answered carelessly, " That the Duke of
Ormond's honoured white hairs were a sufficient apology
for his making the first overtures to a reconciliation,"

and he held out his hand accordingly. But Ormond only bowed in return, and said, "The King had no cause to expect that the Court would be disturbed by his personal resentments, since time would not yield him back twenty years, nor the grave restore his gallant son Ossory. As to the ruffian who had intruded himself there, he was obliged to him, since, by showing that his Majesty's clemency extended even to the very worst of criminals, he strengthened his hopes of obtaining the King's favour for such of his innocent friends as were now in prison, and in danger, from the odious charges brought against them on the score of the Popish Plot."

The King made no other answer to this insinuation, than by directing that the company should embark for their return to Whitehall; and thus took leave of the officers of the Tower who were in attendance, with one of those well-turned compliments to their discharge of duty, which no man knew better how to express; and issued at the same time strict and anxious orders for protection and defence of the important fortress confided to them, and all which it contained.

Before he parted with Ormond on their arrival at Whitehall, he turned round to him, as one who has made up his resolution, and said, " Be satisfied, my Lord Duke—our friend's case shall be looked to."

In the same evening the Attorney-General, and North, Lord Chief Justice of the Common Pleas, had orders with all secrecy, to meet his Majesty that evening on especial matters of state, at the apartments of Chiffinch, the centre of all affairs, whether of gallantry or business.

CHAPTER XLI.

Yet, Corah, thou shalt from oblivion pass;
Erect thyself, thou monumental brass,
High as the serpent of thy metal made,
While nations stand secure beneath thy shade.

ABSALOM AND ACHITOPHEL.

THE morning which Charles had spent in visiting the
Tower, had been very differently employed by those unhappy individuals, whom their bad fate, and the singular
temper of the times, had made the innocent tenants of
that state prison, and who had received official notice
that they were to stand their trial in the Court of
King's Bench at Westminster, on the seventh succeeding day. The stout old Cavalier at first only railed at
the officer for spoiling his breakfast with the news, but
evinced great feeling when he was told that Julian was
to be put under the same indictment.

We intend to dwell only very generally on the nature
of their trial, which corresponded, in the .outline, with
almost all those which took place during the prevalence
of the Popish Plot. That is, one or two infamous and
perjured evidences, whose profession of common informers had become frightfully lucrative, made oath to
the prisoners' having expressed themselves interested in
the great confederacy of the Catholics. A number of
others brought forward facts or suspicions, affecting the
character of the parties as honest Protestants and good

subjects; and betwixt the direct and presumptive evidence, enough was usually extracted for justifying, to a corrupted court and perjured jury, the fatal verdict of Guilty.

The fury of the people had, however, now begun to pass away, exhausted even by its own violence. The English nation differ from all others, indeed even from those of the sister kingdoms, in being very easily sated with punishment, even when they suppose it most merited. Other nations are like the tamed tiger, which, when once its native appetite for slaughter is indulged in one instance, rushes on in promiscuous ravages. But the English public have always rather resembled what is told of the sleuth-dog, which, eager, fierce and clamorous in pursuit of his prey, desists from it so soon as blood is sprinkled upon his path.

Men's minds were now beginning to cool—the character of the witnesses was more closely sifted—their testimonies did not in all cases tally—and a wholesome suspicion began to be entertained of men, who would never say they had made a full discovery of all they knew, but avowedly reserved some points of evidence to bear on future trials.

The King also, who had lain passive during the first burst of popular fury, was now beginning to bestir himself, which produced a marked effect on the conduct of the Crown Counsel, and even the Judges. Sir George Wakeman had been acquitted in spite of Oates's direct testimony; and public attention was strongly excited concerning the event of the next trial; which chanced to be that of the Peverils, father and son, with whom, I know not from what concatenation, little Hudson the dwarf was placed at the bar of the Court of King's Bench.

It was a piteous sight to behold a father and son, who
had been so long separated, meet under circumstances so
melancholy; and many tears were shed, when the majes-
tic old man—for such he was, though now broken with
years—folded his son to his bosom, with a mixture of joy,
affection, and a bitter anticipation of the event of the impending trial. There was a feeling in the Court that for
a moment overcame every prejudice and party feeling.
Many spectators shed tears; and there was even a low
moaning, as of those who weep aloud.

Such as felt themselves sufficiently at ease to remark
the conduct of poor little Geoffrey Hudson, who was
scarcely observed amid the preponderating interest
created by his companions in misfortune, could not but
notice a strong degree of mortification on the part of that
diminutive gentleman. He had soothed his great mind
by the thoughts of playing the character which he was
called on to sustain, in a manner which should be long
remembered in that place; and on his entrance, had
saluted the numerous spectators, as well as the Court,
with a cavalier air, which he meant should express grace,
high-breeding, perfect coolness, with a noble disregard to
the issue of their proceedings. But his little person was
so obscured and jostled aside, on the meeting of the
father and son, who had been brought in different boats
from the Tower, and placed at the bar at the same
moment, that his distress and his dignity were alike
thrown into the background, and attracted neither sympathy nor admiration.

The dwarf's wisest way to attract attention, would
have been to remain quiet, when so remarkable an exterior would certainly have received in its turn the share
of public notice which he so eagerly coveted. But when

did personal vanity listen to the suggestions of prudence?
—Our impatient friend scrambled, with some difficulty,
on the top of the bench intended for his seat; and there,
" paining himself to stand a-tiptoe," like Chaucer's gallant
Sir Chaunticlere, he challenged the notice of the audience
as he stood bowing and claiming acquaintance of his
namesake Sir Geoffrey the larger, with whose shoulders,
notwithstanding his elevated situation, he was scarcely
yet upon a level.

The taller Knight, whose mind was occupied in a very
different manner, took no notice of these advances upon
the dwarf's part, but sat down with the determination
rather to die on the spot than evince any symptoms of
weakness before Roundheads and Presbyterians; under
which obnoxious epithets, being too old-fashioned to find
out party designations of a newer date, he comprehended
all persons concerned in his present trouble.

By Sir Geoffrey the larger's change of position, his
face was thus brought on a level with that of Sir Geoffrey
the less, who had an opportunity of pulling him by the
cloak.   He of Martindale Castle, rather mechanically
than consciously, turned his head towards the large
wrinkled visage, which, struggling between an assumed
air of easy importance, and an anxious desire to be
noticed, was grimacing within a yard of him.   But
neither the singular physiognomy, the nods and smiles
of greeting and recognition into which it was wreathed,
nor the strange little form by which it was supported,
had at that moment the power of exciting any recollections in the old Knight's mind; and having stared for a
moment at the poor little man, his bulky namesake turned
away his head without farther notice.

Julian Peveril, the dwarf's more recent acquaintance,

had, even amid his own anxious feelings, room for sympathy with those of his little fellow-sufferer. As soon as he discovered that he was at the same terrible bar with himself, although he could not conceive how their causes came to be conjoined, he acknowledged him by a hearty shake of the hand, which the old man returned with affected dignity and real gratitude. "Worthy youth," he said, " thy presence is restorative, like the nepenthe of Homer even in this syncopé of our mutual fate. I am concerned to see that your father hath not the same alacrity of soul as that of ours, which are lodged within smaller compass ; and that he hath forgotten an ancient comrade and fellow-soldier, who now stands beside him to perform, perhaps, their last campaign."

Julian briefly replied, that his father had much to occupy him. But the little man—who, to do him justice, cared no more (in his own phrase) for imminent danger or death, than he did for the puncture of a flea's proboscis—did not so easily renounce the secret object of his ambition, which was to acquire the notice of the large and lofty Sir Geoffrey Peveril, who, being at least three inches taller than his son, was in so far possessed of that superior excellence, which the poor dwarf, in his secret soul, valued before all other distinctions, although, in his conversation, he was constantly depreciating it. " Good comrade and namesake," he proceeded, stretching out his hand, so as again to reach the elder Peveril's cloak, " I forgive your want of reminiscence, seeing it is long since I saw you at Naseby, fighting as if you had as many arms as the fabled Briareus."

The Knight of Martindale, who had again turned his head towards the little man, and had listened, as if endeavouring to make something out of his discourse, here interrupted him with a peevish " Pshaw ! "

" Pshaw ! " repeated Sir Geoffrey the less ; " *Pshaw* is an expression of slight esteem,—nay, of contempt,—in all languages ; and were this a befitting place "——

But the Judges had now taken their places, the criers called silence, and the stern voice of the Lord Chief Justice (the notorious Scroggs) demanded what the officers meant by permitting the accused to communicate together in open court.

It may here be observed, that this celebrated personage was, upon the present occasion, at a great loss how to proceed. A calm, dignified, judicial demeanour, was at no time the characteristic of his official conduct. He always ranted and roared either on the one side or the other ; and of late, he had been much unsettled which side to take, being totally incapable of anything resembling impartiality. At the first trials for the Plot, when the whole stream of popularity ran against the accused, no one had been so loud as Scroggs ; to attempt to impeach the character of Oates or Bedlowe, or any other leading witnesses, he treated as a crime more heinous than it would have been to blaspheme the Gospel on which they had been sworn—it was a stifling of the Plot, or discrediting of the King's witnesses—a crime not greatly, if at all, short of high treason against the King himself.

But, of late, a new light had begun to glimmer upon the understanding of this interpreter of the laws. Sagacious in the signs of the times, he began to see that the tide was turning ; and that Court favour at least, and probably popular opinion also, were likely, in a short time, to declare against the witnesses, and in favour of the accused.

The opinion which Scroggs had hitherto entertained of the high respect in which Shaftesbury, the patron of the

Plot, was held by Charles, had been definitely shaken by a whisper from his brother North to the following effect: "His Lordship has no more interest at Court than your footman."

This notice from a sure hand, and received but that morning, had put the Judge to a sore dilemma; for, however indifferent to actual consistency, he was most anxious to save appearances. He could not but recollect how violent he had been on former occasions in favour of these prosecutions; and being sensible at the same time that the credit of the witnesses, though shaken in the opinion of the more judicious, was, amongst the bulk of the people out of doors, as strong as ever, he had a difficult part to play. His conduct, therefore, during the whole trial, resembled the appearance of a vessel about to go upon another tack, when her sails are shivering in the wind, ere they have yet caught the impulse which is to send her forth in a new direction. In a word, he was so uncertain which side it was his interest to favour, that he might be said on that occasion to have come nearer a state of total impartiality than he was ever capable of attaining, whether before or afterwards. This was shown by his bullying now the accused, and now the witnesses, like a mastiff too much irritated to lie still without baying, but uncertain whom he shall first bite.

The indictment was then read; and Sir Geoffrey Peveril heard, with some composure, the first part of it, which stated him to have placed his son in the household of the Countess of Derby, a recusant Papist, for the purpose of aiding the horrible and bloodthirsty Popish Plot—with having had arms and ammunition concealed in his house—and with receiving a blank commission from the Lord Stafford, who had suffered death on account of the Plot. But when the charge went on to state that he had communicated for the same purpose with Geoffrey Hudson, sometimes called Sir Geoffrey Hudson, now, or formerly in the domestic service of the Queen Dowager, he looked at his companion as if he suddenly recalled him to remembrance, and broke out impatiently, " These lies are too gross to require a moment's consideration. I might have had enough of intercourse, though in nothing but what was loyal and innocent, with my noble kinsman, the late Lord Stafford—I will call him so in spite of his misfortunes—and with my wife's relation, the Honourable Countess of Derby. But what likelihood can there be that I should have colleagued with a decrepit buffoon, with whom I never had an instant's communication, save once at an Easter feast, when I whistled a hornpipe, as he danced on a trencher to amuse the company ? "

The rage of the poor dwarf brought tears in his eyes, while, with an affected laugh, he said, that instead of those juvenile and festive passages, Sir Geoffrey Peveril might have remembered his charging along with him at Wiggan-Lane.

" On my word," said Sir Geoffrey, after a moment's recollection, " I will do you justice, Master Hudson—I believe you were there—I think I heard you did good service. But you will allow you might have been near one without his seeing you."

A sort of titter ran through the Court at the simplicity of the larger Sir Geoffrey's testimony, which the dwarf endeavoured to control, by standing on his tiptoes, and looking fiercely around, as if to admonish the laughers that they indulged their mirth at their own peril. But perceiving that this only excited farther scorn, he composed himself into a semblance of careless contempt, observing, with a smile, that no one feared the glance of a chained lion; a magnificent simile, which rather increased than diminished the mirth of those who heard it.

Against Julian Peveril there failed not to be charged the aggravated fact, that he had been bearer of letters between the Countess of Derby and other Papists and priests, engaged in the universal treasonable conspiracy of the Catholics; and the attack of the house at Moul-trassie-Hall,—with his skirmish with Chiffinch, and his assault, as it was termed, on the person of John Jenkins, servant to the Duke of Buckingham, were all narrated at length, as so many open and overt acts of treasonable import. To this charge Peveril contented himself with pleading—Not Guilty.

His little companion was not satisfied with so simple a plea; for when he heard it read, as a part of the charge applying to him, that he had received from an agent of the Plot a blank commission as Colonel of a regiment of grenadiers, he replied, in wrath and scorn, that if Goliath of Gath had come to him with such a proposal, and prof-fered him the command of the whole sons of Anak in a body, he should never have had occasion or opportunity to repeat the temptation to another. " I would have slain him," said the little man of loyalty, " even where he stood."

The charge was stated anew by the Counsel for the Crown; and forth came the notorious Doctor Oates, rust-ling in the full silken canonicals of priesthood, for it was at a time when he affected no small dignity of exterior decoration and deportment.

This singular man, who, aided by the obscure intrigues of the Catholics themselves, and the fortuitous circum-stance of Godfrey's murder, had been able to cram down the public throat such a mass of absurdity as his evidence amounts to, had no other talent for imposture than an impudence which set conviction and shame alike at defiance. A man of sense or reflection, by trying to give his plot an appearance of more probability, would most likely have failed, as wise men often do in addressing the multitude, from not daring to calculate upon the prodigious extent of their credulity, especially where the figments presented to them involve the fearful and the terrible.

Oates was by nature choleric; and the credit he had acquired made him insolent and conceited. Even his exterior was portentous. A fleece of white periwig showed a most uncouth visage, of great length, having the mouth, as the organ by use of which he was to rise to eminence, placed in the very centre of the countenance, and exhibiting to the astonished spectator as much chin below as there was nose and brow above the aperture. His pronunciation, too, was after a conceited fashion of his own, in which he accented the vowels in a manner altogether peculiar to himself.

This notorious personage, such as we have described him, stood forth on the present trial, and delivered his astonishing testimony concerning the existence of a Catholic Plot for the subversion of the government and murder of the King, in the same general outline in which it may be found in every English history. But as the Doctor always had in reserve some special piece of evidence affecting those immediately on trial, he was pleased, on the present occasion, deeply to inculpate the Countess of Derby. "He had seen," as he said, "that honourable lady when he was at the Jesuits' College at Saint Omer's. She had sent for him to an inn, or *auberge*, as it was there termed—the sign of the Golden Lamb; and had

ordered him to breakfast in the same room with her
ladyship; and afterwards told him, that, knowing he was
trusted by the Fathers of the Society, she was determined
that he should have a share of her secrets also; and there-
withal, that she drew from her bosom a broad sharp-
pointed knife, such as butchers kill sheep with, and
demanded of him what he thought of it for *the purpose;*
and when he, the witness, said for what purpose, she rapt
him on the fingers with her fan, called him a dull fellow,
and said it was designed to kill the King with."

Here Sir Geoffrey Peveril could no longer refrain his
indignation and surprise. " Mercy of Heaven!" he said,
" did ever one hear of ladies of quality carrying butchering
knives about them, and telling every scurvy companion she
meant to kill the King with them?—Gentlemen of the
Jury, do but think if this is reasonable—though, if the villain could prove by any honest evidence, that my Lady
of Derby ever let such a scum as himself come to speech
of her, I would believe all he can say."

" Sir Geoffrey," said the Judge, " rest you quiet—You
must not fly out—passion helps you not here—the Doctor
must be suffered to proceed."

Doctor Oates went on to state, how the lady complained
of the wrongs the House of Derby had sustained from
the King, and the oppression of her religion, and boasted
of the schemes of the Jesuits and seminary priests; and
how they would be furthered by her noble kinsman of the
House of Stanley. He finally averred that both the
Countess and the Fathers of the seminary abroad, founded
much upon the talents and courage of Sir Geoffrey Peveril and his son—the latter of whom was a member of
her family. Of Hudson, he only recollected of having
heard one of the Fathers say, that although but a dwarf

in stature, he would prove a giant in the cause of the Church."

When he had ended his evidence, there was a pause, until the Judge, as if the thought had suddenly occurred to him, demanded of Dr. Oates, whether he had ever mentioned the name of the Countess of Derby in any of the previous informations which he had lodged before the Privy Council, and elsewhere, upon this affair.

Oates seemed rather surprised at the question, and coloured with anger, as he answered, in his peculiar mode of pronunciation, " Whoy, no, maay laard."

"And pray, Doctor," said the Judge, " how came so great a revealer of mysteries as you have lately proved, to have suffered so material a circumstance as the accession of this powerful family to the Plot to have remained undiscovered ? "

" Maay laard," said Oates, with much effrontery, " aye do not come here to have my evidence questioned as touching the Plaat."

" I do not question your evidence, Doctor," said Scroggs, for the time was not arrived that he dared treat him roughly ; " nor do I doubt the existence of the *Plaat*, since it is your pleasure to swear to it. I would only have you, for your own sake, and the satisfaction of all good Protestants, to explain why you have kept back such a weighty point of information from the King and country."

" Maay laard," said Oates, " I will tell you a pretty fable."

" I hope," answered the Judge, " it may be the first and last which you shall tell in this place."

" Maay laard," continued Oates, " there was once a faux, who having to carry a goose over a frazen river, and being afraid the aice would not bear him and his booty, did caarry aaver a staane, my laard, in the first instance, to prove the strength of the aice."

"So your former evidence was but the stone, and now, for the first time, you have brought us the goose?" said Sir William Scroggs; "to tell us this, Doctor, is to make geese of the Court and Jury."

"I desoire your laardship's honest construction," said Oates, who saw the current changing against him, but was determined to pay the score with effrontery. "All men knaw at what coast and praice I have given my evidence, which has been always, under Gaad, the means of awakening this poor naation to the dangerous state in which it staunds. Many here knaw that I have been obliged to faartify my ladging at Whitehall against the bloody Papists. It was not to be thought that I should have brought all the story out at aance. I think your wisdom would have advised me otherwise." *

"Nay, Doctor," said the Judge, "it is not for me to direct you in this affair; and it is for the Jury to believe you or not; and as for myself, I sit here to do justice to both—the Jury have heard your answer to my question."

Doctor Oates retired from the witness-box reddening like a turkey-cock, as one totally unused to have such accounts questioned as he chose to lay before the courts of justice; and there was, perhaps, for the first time, amongst the counsel and solicitors, as well as the templars and students of law there present, a murmur, distinct

* It was on such terms that Dr. Oates was pleased to claim the extraordinary privilege of dealing out the information which he chose to communicate to a court of justice. The only sense in which his story of the fox, stone, and goose, could be applicable, is by supposing, that he was determined to ascertain the extent of his countrymen's credulity before supplying it with a full meal.

and audible, unfavourable to the character of the great
father of the Popish Plot.

Everett and Dangerfield, with whom the reader is already acquainted, were then called in succession to sustain the accusation. They were subordinate informers—
a sort of underspur-leathers, as the cant term went—who
followed the path of Oates, with all deference to his superior genius and invention, and made their own fictions
chime in and harmonize with his, as well as their talents
could devise. But as their evidence had at no time received the full credence into which the impudence of
Oates had cajoled the public, so they now began to fall
into discredit rather more hastily than their prototype, as
the superadded turrets of an ill-constructed building are
naturally the first to give way.

It was in vain that Everett, with the precision of a
hypocrite, and Dangerfield, with the audacity of a bully,
narrated, with added circumstances of suspicion and
criminality, their meeting with Julian Peveril in Liverpool, and again at Martindale Castle. It was in vain
they described the arms and accoutrements which they
pretended to have discovered in old Sir Geoffrey's possession; and that they gave a most dreadful account of
the escape of the younger Peveril from Moultrassie-Hall,
by means of an armed force.

The Jury listened coldly, and it was visible that they
were but little moved by the accusation; especially as
the Judge, always professing his belief in the Plot, and
his zeal for the Protestant religion, was ever and anon
reminding them that presumptions were no proofs—that
hearsay was no evidence—that those who made a trade
of discovery were likely to aid their researches by invention—and that, without doubting the guilt of the unfor-

tunate persons at the bar, he would gladly hear some evidence brought against them of a different nature. "Here we are told of a riot, and an escape achieved by the younger Peveril, at the house of a grave and worthy magistrate, known, I think, to most of us. Why, Master Attorney, bring ye not Master Bridgenorth himself to prove the fact, or all his household, if it be necessary?— A rising in arms is an affair over public to be left on the hearsay tale of these two men—though Heaven forbid that I should suppose they speak one word more than they believe! They are the witnesses for the King—and, what is equally dear to us, the Protestant religion—and witnesses against a most foul and heathenish Plot. On the other hand, here is a worshipful old knight, for such I must suppose him to be, since he has bled often in battle for the King,—such, I must say, I suppose him to be, until he is proved otherwise. And here is his son, a hopeful young gentleman—we must see that they have right, Master Attorney."

"Unquestionably, my lord," answered the Attorney. "God forbid else! But we will make out these matters against these unhappy gentlemen in a manner more close, if your lordship will permit us to bring in our evidence."

"Go on, Master Attorney," said the Judge, throwing himself back in his seat. "Heaven forbid I hinder proving the King's accusation! I only say, what you know as well as I, that *de non apparentibus et non existentibus eadem est ratio.*"

"We shall then call Master Bridgenorth, as your lordship advises, who I think is in waiting."

"No!" answered a voice from the crowd, apparently that of a female; "he is too wise and too honest to be here."

The voice was distinct as that of Lady Fairfax, when she expressed herself to a similar effect on the trial of Charles the First; but the researches which were made on the present occasion to discover the speaker were unsuccessful.

After the slight confusion occasioned by this circumstance was abated, the Attorney, who had been talking aside with the conductors of the prosecution, said, " Whoever favoured us with that information, my lord, had good reason for what they said.   Master Bridgenorth has become, I am told, suddenly invisible since this morning."

" Look you there now, Master Attorney," said the Judge—" This comes of not keeping the crown witnesses together and in readiness—I am sure I cannot help the consequences."

" Nor I either, my lord," said the Attorney, pettishly. " I could have proved by this worshipful gentleman, Master Justice Bridgenorth, the ancient friendship betwixt this party, Sir Geoffrey Peveril, and the Countess of Derby, of whose doings and intentions Dr. Oates has given such a deliberate evidence.   I could have proved his having sheltered her in his Castle against a process of law, and rescued her, by force of arms, from this very Justice Bridgenorth, not without actual violence.   Moreover, I could have proved against young Peveril the whole affray charged upon him by the same worshipful evidence."

Here the Judge stuck his thumbs into his girdle, which was a favourite attitude of his on such occasions, and exclaimed, " Pshaw, pshaw, Master Attorney !—Tell me not that you *could* have proved this, and you *could* have proved that, or that, or this—Prove what you will, but let it be through the mouths of your evidence.   Men are

not to be licked out of their lives by the rough side of a
lawyer's tongue."

" Nor is a foul Plot to be smothered," said the Attorney, " for all the haste your lordship is in. I cannot call
Master Chiffinch neither, as he is employed on the King's
especial affairs, as I am this instant certiorated from the
Court at Whitehall."

" Produce the papers, then, Master Attorney, of which
this young man is said to be the bearer," said the Judge.

" They are before the Privy Council, my Lord."

" Then why do you found on them here ? " said the
Judge—" This is something like trifling with the Court."

" Since your lordship gives it that name," said the
Attorney, sitting down in a huff, " you may manage the
cause as you will."

" If you do not bring more evidence, I pray you to
charge the Jury," said the Judge.

" I shall not take the trouble to do so," said the Crown
Counsel.   " I see plainly how the matter is to go."

" Nay, but be better advised," said Scroggs. " Consider, your case is but half proved respecting the two
Peverils, and doth not pinch on the little man at all,
saving that Doctor Oates said that he was in a certain
case to prove a giant, which seems no very probable
Popish miracle."

This sally occasioned a laugh in the Court, which the
Attorney-General seemed to take in great dudgeon.

" Master Attorney," said Oates, who always interfered
in the management of these lawsuits, " this is a plain and
absolute giving away of the cause—I must needs say it,
a mere stoifling of the Plaat."

" Then the devil who bred it may blow wind into it
again, if he lists," answered the Attorney-General ; and,

flinging down his brief, he left the Court, as in a huff
with all who were concerned in the affair.

The Judge having obtained silence,—for a murmur
arose in the Court when the Counsel for the prosecution
threw up his brief,—began to charge the Jury, balancing,
as he had done throughout the whole day, the different
opinions by which he seemed alternately swayed. He
protested on his salvation that he had no more doubt of
the existence of the horrid and damnable conspiracy
called the Popish Plot, than he had of the treachery of
Judas Iscariot; and that he considered Oates as the instrument under Providence of preserving the nation from
all the miseries of his Majesty's assassination, and of a
second Saint Bartholomew, acted in the streets of London.
But then he stated it was the candid construction of the
law of England, that the worse the crime, the more
strong should be the evidence. Here was the case of
accessories tried, whilst their principal—for such he
should call the Countess of Derby—was unconvicted and
at large; and for Doctor Oates, he had but spoke of
matters which personally applied to that noble lady,
whose words, if she used such in passion, touching aid
which she expected in some treasonable matters from
these Peverils, and from her kinsmen, or her son's kinsmen, of the House of Stanley, may have been but a burst
of female resentment—*dulcis Amaryllidis ira*, as the poet
hath it. Who knoweth but Doctor Oates did mistake—
he being a gentleman of a comely countenance and easy
demeanour—this same rap with the fan as a chastisement
for lack of courage in the Catholic cause, when, peradventure, it was otherwise meant, as Popish ladies will put, it
is said, such neophytes and youthful candidates for orders,
to many severe trials. " I speak these things jocularly,"

said the Judge, "having no wish to stain the reputation
either of the Honourable Countess or the Reverend Doctor; only I think the bearing between them may have
related to something short of high treason. As for what
the Attorney-General hath set forth of rescues and force,
and I wot not what, sure I am, that in a civil country,
when such things happen, such things may be proved;
and that you and I, gentlemen, are not to take them for
granted gratuitously. Touching this other prisoner, this
Galfridus minimus, he must needs say," he continued,
" he could not discover even a shadow of suspicion against
him. Was it to be thought so abortive a creature would
thrust himself into depths of policy, far less into stratagems of war? They had but to look at him to conclude
the contrary—the creature was, from his age, fitter for
the grave than a conspiracy—and by his size and appearance, for the inside of a raree-show, than the myste-
teries of a plot."

The dwarf here broke in upon the Judge by force of
screaming, to assure him that he had been, simple as he
sat there, engaged in seven plots in Cromwell's time;
and, as he proudly added, with some of the tallest men
of England. The matchless look and air with which Sir
Geoffrey Hudson made this vaunt, set all a-laughing, and
increased the ridicule with which the whole trial began to
be received; so that it was amidst shaking sides and
watery eyes that a general verdict of Not Guilty was
pronounced, and the prisoners dismissed from the bar.

But a warmer sentiment awakened among those who
saw the father and son throw themselves into each other's
arms, and, after a hearty embrace, extend their hands to
their poor little companion in peril, who, like a dog, when
present at a similar scene, had at last succeeded, by

stretching himself up to them and whimpering at the
same time, to secure to himself a portion of their sympathy and gratulation.

Such was the singular termination of this trial. Charles
himself was desirous to have taken considerable credit
with the Duke of Ormond for the evasion of the law,
which had been thus effected by his private connivance ;
and was both surprised and mortified at the coldness with
which his Grace replied, that he was rejoiced at the poor
gentlemen's safety, but would rather have had the King
redeem them like a prince, by his royal prerogative of
mercy, than that his Judge should convey them out of
the power of the law, like a juggler with his cups and
balls.

CHAPTER XLII.

——— On fair ground
I could beat forty of them!
CORIOLANUS.

IT doubtless occurred to many that were present at the
trial we have described, that it was managed in a singular
manner, and that the quarrel, which had the appearance
of having taken place between the Court and the Crown
Counsel, might proceed from some private understanding
betwixt them, the object of which was the miscarriage of
the accusation. Yet though such underhand dealing was
much suspected, the greater part of the audience, being
well educated and intelligent, had already suspected the
bubble of the Popish Plot, and were glad to see that
accusations, founded on what had already cost so much
blood, could be evaded in any way. But the crowd,
who waited in the Court of Requests, and in the hall,
and without doors, viewed in a very different light the
combination, as they interpreted it, between the Judge
and the Attorney-General, for the escape of the prisoners.

Oates, whom less provocation than he had that day
received often induced to behave like one frantic with
passion, threw himself amongst the crowd, and repeated
till he was hoarse, "Theay are stoifling the Plaat!—
theay are straangling the Plaat!—My Laard Justice and

Maaster Attarney are in league to secure the escape of
the plaaters and Paapists ! "

" It is the device of the Papist whore of Portsmouth,"
said one.

" Of old Rowley himself," said another.

" If he could be murdered by himself, why hang those
that would hinder it ! " exclaimed a third.

" He should be tried," said a fourth, " for conspiring his
own death, and hanged *in terrorem.*"

In the meanwhile, Sir Geoffrey, his son, and their little
companion, left the hall, intending to go to Lady Peveril's lodgings, which had been removed to Fleet Street.
She had been relieved from considerable inconvenience,
as Sir Geoffrey gave Julian hastily to understand, by an
angel, in the shape of a young friend, and she now expected them doubtless with impatience. Humanity, and
some indistinct idea of having unintentionally hurt the
feelings of the poor dwarf, induced the honest Cavalier to
ask this unprotected being to go with them. " He knew
Lady Peveril's lodgings were but small," he said; " but
it would be strange, if there was not some cupboard large
enough to accommodate the little gentleman."

The dwarf registered this well-meant remark in his
mind, to be the subject of a proper explanation, along
with the unhappy reminiscence of the trencher-hornpipe,
whenever time should permit an argument of such nicety.

And thus they sallied from the hall, attracting general
observation, both from the circumstances in which they
had stood so lately, and from their resemblance, as a wag
of the Inner Temple expressed it, to the three degrees
of comparison, Large, Lesser, Least. But they had not
passed far along the street, when Julian perceived, that
more malevolent passions than mere curiosity began to

actuate the crowd, which followed, and, as it were, dogged their motions.

"There go the Papist cut-throats, tantivy for Rome!" said one fellow.

"Tantivy to Whitehall, you mean!" said another.

"Ah! the bloodthirsty villains!" cried a woman: "Shame, one of them should be suffered to live, after poor Sir Edmondsbury's cruel murder."

"Out upon the mealy-mouthed jury, that turned out the blood-hounds on an innocent town!" cried a fourth.

In short, the tumult thickened, and the word began to pass among the more desperate, "Lambe them, lads; lambe them!"—a cant phrase of the time, derived from the fate of Dr. Lambe, an astrologer and quack, who was knocked on the head by the rabble in Charles the First's time.

Julian began to be much alarmed at these symptoms of violence, and regretted that they had not gone down to the city by water. It was now too late to think of that mode of retreating, and he therefore requested his father in a whisper to walk steadily forward towards Charing-Cross, taking no notice of the insults which might be cast upon them, while the steadiness of their pace and appearance might prevent the rabble from resorting to actual violence. The execution of this prudent resolution was prevented after they had passed the palace, by the hasty disposition of the elder Sir Geoffrey, and the no less choleric temper of Galfridus Minimus, who had a soul which spurned all odds, as well of numbers as of size.

"Now a murrain take the knaves, with their hollowing and whooping," said the larger knight; "by this day, if I could but light on a weapon, I would cudgel reason and loyalty into some of their carcasses!"

" And I also," said the dwarf, who was toiling to keep
up with the longer strides of his companions, and therefore spoke in a very phthisical tone.—" I also will cudgel
the plebeian knaves beyond measure—he !—hem ! "

Among the crowd who thronged around them, impeded,
and did all but assault them, was a mischievous shoe-
maker's apprentice, who, hearing this unlucky vaunt of
the valorous dwarf, repaid it by flapping him on the head
with a boot which he was carrying home to the owner, so
as to knock the little gentleman's hat over his eyes. The
dwarf, thus rendered unable to discover the urchin that
had given him the offence, flew with instinctive ambition
against the biggest fellow in the crowd, who received the
onset with a kick on the stomach, which made the poor
little champion reel back to his companions. They were
now assaulted on all sides ; but fortune complying with
the wish of Sir Geoffrey the larger, ordained that the
scuffle should happen near the booth of a cutler, from
amongst whose wares, as they stood exposed to the public,
Sir Geoffrey Peveril snatched a broadsword, which he
brandished with the formidable address of one who had
for many a day been in the familiar practice of using
such a weapon. Julian, while at the same time he called
loudly for a peace-officer, and reminded the assailants that
they were attacking inoffensive passengers, saw nothing
better for it than to imitate his father's example, and
seized also one of the weapons thus opportunely offered.

When they displayed these demonstrations of defence,
the rush which the rabble at first made towards them was
so great as to throw down the unfortunate dwarf, who
would have been trampled to death in the scuffle, had not
his stout old namesake cleared the rascal crowd from
about him with a few flourishes of his weapon, and

seizing on the fallen champion, put him out of danger, (except from missiles,) by suddenly placing him on the bulk-head, that is to say, the flat wooden roof of the cutler's projecting booth. From the rusty ironware, which was displayed there, the dwarf instantly snatched an old rapier and target, and covering himself with the one, stood making passes with the other, at the faces and eyes of the people in the street ; so much delighted with his post of vantage, that he called loudly to his friends who were skirmishing with the rioters on more equal terms as to position, to lose no time in putting themselves under his protection. But far from being in a situation to need his assistance, the father and son might easily have extricated themselves from the rabble by their own exertions, could they have thought of leaving the mannikin in the forlorn situation, in which, to every eye but his own, he stood like a diminutive puppet, tricked out with sword and target as a fencing-master's sign.

Stones and sticks began now to fly very thick, and the crowd, notwithstanding the exertions of the Peverils to disperse them with as little harm as possible, seemed determined on mischief, when some gentlemen who had been at the trial, understanding that the prisoners who had been just acquitted were in danger of being murdered by the populace, drew their swords, and made forward to effect their rescue, which was completed by a small party of the King's Life-Guards, who had been dispatched from their ordinary post of alarm, upon intelligence of what was passing. When this unexpected reinforcement arrived, the old jolly Knight at once recognised, amidst the cries of those who then entered upon action, some of the sounds which had animated his more active years.

"Where be these cuckoldly Roundheads," cried some. —"Down with the sneaking knaves!" cried others.—"The King and his friends, and the devil a one else!" exclaimed a third set, with more oaths and d—n me's, than, in the present more correct age, it is necessary to commit to paper.

The old soldier, pricking up his ears like an ancient hunter at the cry of the hounds, would gladly have scoured the Strand, with the charitable purpose, now he saw himself so well supported, of knocking the London knaves, who had insulted him, into twiggen bottles; but he was withheld by the prudence of Julian, who, though himself extremely irritated by the unprovoked ill usage which they had received, saw himself in a situation in which it was necessary to exercise more caution than vengeance. He prayed and pressed his father to seek some temporary place of retreat from the fury of the populace, while that prudent measure was yet in their power. The subaltern officer who commanded the party of the Life-Guards, exhorted the old Cavalier eagerly to the same sage counsel, using, as a spice of compulsion, the name of the King; while Julian strongly urged that of his mother. The old Knight looked at his blade, crimsoned with cross-cuts and slashes which he had given to the most forward of the assailants, with the eye of one not half sufficed.

"I would I had pinked one of the knaves at least—but I know not how it was, when I looked on their broad round English faces, I shunned to use my point, and only sliced the rogues a little."

"But the King's pleasure," said the officer, "is, that no tumult be prosecuted."

"My mother," said Julian, "will die with fright, if

the rumour of this scuffle reaches her ere we see her."

"Ay, ay," said the Knight, "the King's Majesty and my good dame—well, their pleasure be done, that's all I can say—Kings and ladies must be obeyed. But which way to retreat, since retreat we needs must?"

Julian would have been at some loss to advise what course to take, for every body in the vicinity had shut up their shops, and chained their doors, upon observing the confusion become so formidable. The poor cutler, however, with whose goods they made so free, offered them an asylum on the part of his landlord, whose house served as a rest for his shop, and only intimated gently, he hoped the gentlemen would consider him for the use of his weapons.

Julian was hastily revolving whether they ought, in prudence, to accept this man's invitation, aware, by experience, how many trepans, as they were then termed, were used betwixt two contending factions, each too inveterate to be very scrupulous of the character of fair play to an enemy, when the dwarf, exerting his cracked voice to the uttermost, and shrieking like an exhausted herald, from the exalted station which he still occupied on the bulk-head, exhorted them to accept the offer of the worthy man of the mansion. "He himself," he said, as he reposed himself after the glorious conquest in which he had some share, "had been favoured with a beatific vision, too splendid to be described to common and mere mortal ears, but which had commanded him, in a voice to which his heart had bounded as to a trumpet sound, to take refuge with the worthy person of the house, and cause his friends to do so."

"Vision!" said the Knight of the Peak,—sound of a trumpet!—the little man is stark mad."

But the cutler, in great haste, intimated to them that their little friend had received an intimation from a gentlewoman of his acquaintance, who spoke to him from the window, while he stood on the bulk-head, that they would find a safe retreat in his landlord's ; and desiring them to attend to two or three deep though distant huzzas, made them aware that the rabble were up still, and would soon be upon them with renewed violence, and increased numbers.

The father and son, therefore, hastily thanked the officer and his party, as well as the other gentlemen who had volunteered in their assistance, lifted little Sir Geoffrey Hudson from the conspicuous post which he had so creditably occupied during the skirmish, and followed the footsteps of the tenant of the booth, who conducted them down a blind alley and through one or two courts, in case, as he said, any one might have watched where they burrowed, and so into a back-door. This entrance admitted them to a staircase carefully hung with straw mats to exclude damp, from the upper step of which they entered upon a tolerably large withdrawing-room, hung with coarse green serge edged with gilded leather, which the poorer or more economical citizens at that time used instead of tapestry or wainscoting.

Here the poor cutler received from Julian such a gratuity for the loan of the swords, that he generously abandoned the property to the gentlemen who had used them so well; " the rather," he said, " that he saw, by the way they handled their weapons, that they were men of mettle, and tall fellows."

Here the dwarf smiled on him courteously, and bowed, thrusting, at the same time, his hand into his pocket, which, however, he withdrew carelessly, probably because

he found he had not the means of making the small dona-
tion which he had meditated.

The cutler proceeded to say, as he bowed and was
about to withdraw, that he saw there would be merry
days yet in Old England, and that Bilboa blades would
fetch as good a price as ever. " I remember," he said,
"gentlemen, though I was then but a prentice, the
demand for weapons in the years forty-one and forty-
two; sword blades were more in request than toothpicks,
and Old Ironsides, my master, took more for rascally
Provant rapiers, than I dare ask now-a-days for a Toledo.
But, to be sure, a man's life then rested on the blade he
carried; the Cavaliers and Roundheads fought every day
at the gates of Whitehall, as it is like, gentlemen, by
your good example, they may do again, when I shall be
enabled to leave my pitiful booth, and open a shop of
better quality. I hope you will recommend me, gentlemen, to your friends. I am always provided with ware
which a gentleman may risk his life on."

" Thank you, good friend," said Julian, " I prithee
begone. I trust we shall need thy ware no more for
some time at least."

The cutler retired, while the dwarf hollowed after him
down stairs, that he would call on him soon, and equip
himself with a longer blade, and one more proper for
action; although, he said, the little weapon he had did
well enough for a walking-sword, or in a skirmish with
such canaille as they had been engaged with.

The cutler returned at this summons, and agreed to
pleasure the little man with a weapon more suitable to
his magnanimity; then, as if the thought had suddenly
occurred to him, he said, " But, gentlemen, it will be but
wild work to walk with your naked swords through the

Strand, and it can scarce fail to raise the rabble again.
If you please, while you repose yourselves here, I can
fit the blades with sheaths."

The proposal seemed so reasonable, that Julian and his
father gave up their weapons to the friendly cutler, an
example which the dwarf followed, after a moment's
hesitation, not caring, as he magnificently expressed it,
to part so soon with the trusty friend which fortune
had but the moment before restored to his hand. The
man retired with the weapons under his arm; and, in
shutting the door behind him, they heard him turn the
key.

" Did you hear that," said Sir Geoffrey to his son—
" and we are disarmed ! "

Julian, without reply, examined the door, which was
fast secured; and then looked at the casements, which
were at a story's height from the ground, and grated
besides with iron. "I cannot think," he said, after a
moment's pause, " that the fellow means to trepan us;
and, in any event, I trust we should have no difficulty
in forcing the door, or otherwise making an escape.
But, before resorting to such violent measures, I think
it is better to give the rabble leisure to disperse, by waiting this man's return with our weapons within a reasonable time, when, if he does not appear, I trust we shall
find little difficulty in extricating ourselves." As he
spoke thus, the hangings were pulled aside, and from a
small door which was concealed behind them, Major
Bridgenorth entered the room.

CHAPTER XLIII.

He came amongst them like a new raised spirit
To speak of dreadful judgments that impend,
And of the wrath to come.

THE REFORMER.

THE astonishment of Julian at the unexpected apparition of Bridgenorth, was instantly succeeded by apprehension of his father's violence, which he had every reason to believe would break forth against one, whom he himself could not but reverence on account of his own merits, as well as because he was the father of Alice. The appearance of Bridgenorth was not, however, such as to awaken resentment. His countenance was calm, his step slow and composed, his eye not without the indication of some deep-seated anxiety, but without any expression either of anger or of triumph. "You are welcome," he said, "Sir Geoffrey Peveril, to the shelter and hospitality of this house; as welcome as you would have been in other days, when we called each other neighbours and friends."

"Odzooks," said the old Cavalier; "and had I known it was thy house, man, I would sooner had my heart's blood run down the kennel, than my foot should have crossed your threshold—in the way of seeking safety, that is."

"I forgive your inveteracy," said Major Bridgenorth, "on account of your prejudices."

"Keep your forgiveness," answered the Cavalier, "until you are pardoned yourself. By Saint George, I have sworn, if ever I got my heels out of yon rascally prison, whither I was sent much through your means, Master Bridgenorth,—that you should pay the reckoning for my bad lodging.—I will strike no man in his own house; but if you will cause the fellow to bring back my weapon, and take a turn in that blind court there below, along with me, you shall soon see what chance a traitor hath with a true man, and a kennel-blooded Puritan with Peveril of the Peak."

Bridgenorth smiled with much composure. "When I was younger and more warm-blooded," he replied, "I refused your challenge, Sir Geoffrey; it is not likely I should now accept it, when each is within a stride of the grave. I have not spared, and will not spare, my blood, when my country wants it."

"That is when there is any chance of treason against the King," said Sir Geoffrey.

"Nay, my father," said Julian, "let us hear Master Bridgenorth! We have been sheltered in his house; and although we now see him in London, we should remember that he did not appear against us this day, when perhaps his evidence might have given a fatal turn to our situation."

"You are right, young man," said Bridgenorth; "and it should be some pledge of my sincere good-will, that I was this day absent from Westminster, when a few words from my mouth had ended the long line of Peveril of the Peak: It needed but ten minutes to walk to Westminster Hall, to have ensured your condemnation. But could I have done this, knowing, as I now know, that to thee, Julian Peveril, I owe the extrication of my daughter—

of my dearest Alice—the memory of her departed mother —from the snares which hell and profligacy had opened around her?"

"She is, I trust, safe," said Peveril, eagerly, and almost forgetting his father's presence; "she is, I trust, safe, and in your own wardship?"

"Not in mine," said the dejected father; "but in that of one in whose protection, next to that of Heaven, I can most fully confide."

"Are you sure—are you very sure of that?" repeated Julian eagerly. "I found her under the charge of one to whom she had been trusted, and who yet "——

"And who yet was the basest of women," answered Bridgenorth; "but he who selected her for the charge was deceived in her character."

"Say rather you were deceived in his; remember that when we parted at Moultrassie, I warned you of that Ganlesse—that "——

"I know your meaning," said Bridgenorth; "nor did you err in describing him as a worldly-wise man. But he has atoned for his error by recovering Alice from the dangers into which she was plunged when separated from you; and besides, I have not thought meet again to intrust him with the charge that is dearest to me."

"I thank God your eyes are thus far opened!" said Julian.

"This day will open them wide, or close them for ever," answered Bridgenorth.

During this dialogue, which the speakers hurried through without attending to the others who were present, Sir Geoffrey listened with surprise and eagerness, endeavouring to catch something which should render their conversation intelligible; but as he totally failed in gain-

ing any such key to their meaning, he broke in with,—
" 'Sblood and thunder, Julian, what unprofitable gossip is
this? What hast thou to do with this fellow, more than
to bastinado him, if you should think it worth while to
beat so old a rogue?"

" My dearest father," said Julian, "you know not this
gentleman—I am certain you do him injustice. My own
obligations to him are many; and I am sure when you
come to know them "——

" I hope I shall die ere that moment come," said Sir
Geoffrey; and continued with increasing violence, "I
hope in the mercy of Heaven, that I shall be in the grave
of my ancestors, ere I learn that my son—my only son—
the last hope of my ancient house—the last remnant of
the name of Peveril—hath consented to receive obligations from the man on earth I am most bound to hate,
were I not still more bound to contemn him!—Degenerate dog-whelp!" he repeated with great vehemence,
" You colour without replying! Speak, and disown such
disgrace ; or, by the God of my fathers "——

The dwarf suddenly stepped forward, and called out,
" Forbear!" with a voice at once so discordant and commanding, that it sounded supernatural. " Man of sin and
pride," he said, "forbear; and call not the name of a
holy God, to witness thine unhallowed resentments."

The rebuke so boldly and decidedly given, and the
moral enthusiasm with which he spoke, gave the despised
dwarf an ascendency for the moment over the fiery spirit
of his gigantic namesake. Sir Geoffrey Peveril eyed
him for an instant askance and shyly, as he might have
done a supernatural apparition, and then muttered, " What
knowest thou of my cause of wrath?"

" Nothing," said the dwarf;—" nothing but this—that

no cause can warrant the oath thou wert about to swear.
Ungrateful man! thou wert to-day rescued from the de-
vouring wrath of the wicked, by a marvellous conjunction
of circumstances—Is this a day, thinkest thou, on which
to indulge thine own hasty resentments?"

"I stand rebuked," said Sir Geoffrey, "and by a singular monitor—the grasshopper, as the prayer-book saith,
hath become a burden to me.—Julian, I will speak to
thee of these matters hereafter;—and for you, Master
Bridgenorth, I desire to have no farther communication
with you, either in peace or in anger. Our time passes
fast, and I would fain return to my family. Cause our
weapons to be restored; unbar the doors, and let us part
without farther altercation, which can but disturb and aggravate our spirits."

"Sir Geoffrey Peveril," said Bridgenorth, "I have no
desire to vex your spirit or my own; but, for thus soon
dismissing you, that may hardly be, it being a course
inconsistent with the work which I have on hand."

"How, sir! Do you mean that we should abide here,
whether with or against our inclinations?" said the
dwarf. "Were it not that I am laid under charge to
remain here, by one who hath the best right to command
this poor microcosm, I would show thee that bolts and
bars are unavailing restraints on such as I am."

"Truly," said Sir Geoffrey, "I think, upon an emergency, the little man might make his escape through the
keyhole."

Bridgenorth's face was moved into something like a
smile at the swaggering speech of the pigmy hero, and
the contemptuous commentary of Sir Geoffrey Peveril;
but such an expression never dwelt on his features for
two seconds together, and he replied in these words :—

" Gentlemen, each and all of you must be fain to content yourselves. Believe me, no hurt is intended towards you; on the contrary, your remaining here will be a means of securing your safety, which would be otherwise deeply endangered. It will be your own fault if a hair of your heads is hurt. But the stronger force is on my side; and, whatever harm you may meet with should you attempt to break forth by violence, the blame must rest with yourselves. If you will not believe me, I will permit Master Julian Peveril to accompany me, where he shall see that I am provided fully with the means of repressing violence."

" Treason !—treason ! " exclaimed the old Knight— " Treason against God and King Charles !—Oh, for one half hour of the broadsword which I parted with like an ass ! "

" Hold, my father, I conjure you ! " said Julian. " I will go with Master Bridgenorth, since he requests it. I will satisfy myself whether there be danger, and of what nature. It is possible I may prevail on him to desist from some desperate measure, if such be indeed in agitation. Should it be necessary, fear not that your son will behave as he ought to do."

" Do your pleasure, Julian," said his father; " I will confide in thee. But if you betray my confidence, a father's curse shall cleave to you."

Bridgenorth now motioned to Peveril to follow him, and they passed through the small door by which he had entered.

The passage led to a vestibule or anteroom, in which several other doors and passages seemed to centre. Through one of these Julian was conducted by Bridgenorth, walking with silence and precaution, in obedience to a signal made by his guide to that effect. As they advanced, he heard sounds, like those of the human voice, engaged in urgent and emphatic declamation. With slow and light steps Bridgenorth conducted him through a door which terminated this passage ; and as he entered a little gallery, having a curtain in front, the sound of the preacher's voice—for such it now seemed—became distinct and audible.

Julian now doubted not that he was in one of those conventicles, which, though contrary to the existing laws, still continued to be regularly held in different parts of London and the suburbs. Many of these, as frequented by persons of moderate political principles, though dissenters from the church for conscience' sake, were connived at by the prudence or timidity of the government. But some of them, in which assembled the fiercer and more exalted sects of Independents, Anabaptists, Fifth-Monarchy men, and other sectaries, whose stern enthusiasm had contributed so greatly to effect the overthrow of the late King's throne, were sought after, suppressed, and dispersed, whenever they could be discovered.

Julian was soon satisfied that the meeting into which he was thus secretly introduced, was one of the latter class ; and, to judge by the violence of the preacher, of the most desperate character. He was still more effectually convinced of this, when, at a sign from Bridgenorth, he cautiously unclosed a part of the curtain which hung before the gallery, and thus, unseen himself, looked down on the audience, and obtained a view of the preacher.

About two hundred persons were assembled beneath, in an area filled up with benches, as if for the exercise of worship ; and they were all of the male sex, and well armed with pikes and muskets, as well as swords and pis-

tols. Most of them had the appearance of veteran soldiers, now past the middle of life, yet retaining such an
appearance of strength as might well supply the loss of
youthful agility. They stood, or sat, in various attitudes
of stern attention ; and, resting on their spears and muskets, kept their eyes firmly fixed on the preacher, who
ended the violence of his declamation by displaying from
the pulpit a banner, on which was represented a lion, with
the motto, " *Vicit Leo ex tribu Judæ.*"

The torrent of mystical yet animating eloquence of the
preacher—an old gray-haired man, whom zeal seemed to
supply with the powers of voice and action, of which
years had deprived him—was suited to the taste of his
audience, but could not be transferred to these pages
without scandal and impropriety. He menaced the rulers
of England with all the judgments denounced on those
of Moab and Assyria—he called upon the saints to be
strong, to be up and doing ; and promised those miracles
which, in the campaigns of Joshua, and his successors, the
valiant Judges of Israel, supplied all odds against the
Amorites, Midianites, and Philistines. He sounded
trumpets, opened vials, broke seals, and denounced approaching judgments under all the mystical signs of the
Apocalypse. The end of the world was announced, accompanied with all its preliminary terrors.

Julian, with deep anxiety, soon heard enough to make
him aware, that the meeting was likely to terminate in
open insurrection, like that of the Fifth-Monarchy men,
under Venner, at an earlier period of Charles's reign ;
and he was not a little concerned at the probability of
Bridgenorth being implicated in so criminal and desperate
an undertaking. If he had retained any doubts of the
issue of the meeting, they must have been removed when

the preacher called on his hearers to renounce all expectation which had hitherto been entertained of safety to the nation, from the execution of the ordinary laws of the land. This, he said, was at best but a carnal seeking after earthly aid—a going down to Egypt for help, which the jealousy of their Divine Leader would resent as a fleeing to another rock, and a different banner, from that which was this day displayed over them.—And here he solemnly swung the bannered lion over their heads, as the only sign under which they ought to seek for life and safety. He then proceeded to insist, that recourse to ordinary justice was vain as well as sinful.

"The event of that day at Westminster," he said, "might teach them that the Man at Whitehall was even as the Man his father;" and closed a long tirade against the vices of the Court, with assurance "that Tophet was ordained of old—for the King it was made hot."

As the preacher entered on a description of the approaching theocracy, which he dared to prophesy, Bridgenorth, who appeared for a time to have forgotten the presence of Julian, whilst with stern and fixed attention he drank in the words of the preacher, seemed suddenly to collect himself, and, taking Julian by the hand, led him out of the gallery, of which he carefully closed the door, into an apartment at no great distance.

When they arrived there, he anticipated the expostulations of Julian, by asking him, in a tone of severe triumph, whether these men he had seen were likely to do their work negligently, or whether it would not be perilous to attempt to force their way from a house, when all the avenues were guarded by such as he had now seen—men of war from their childhood upwards.

"In the name of Heaven," said Julian, without reply-

ing to Bridgenorth's question, "for what desperate purpose have you assembled so many desperate men? I am
well aware that your sentiments of religion are peculiar;
but beware how you deceive yourself—No views of religion can sanction rebellion and murder; and such are the
natural and necessary consequences of the doctrine we
have just heard poured into the ears of fanatical and violent enthusiasts."

"My son," said Bridgenorth, calmly, "in the days of
my non-age, I thought as you do. I deemed it sufficient
to pay my tithes of cummin and anise-seed—my poor petty
moral observances of the old law; and I thought I was
heaping up precious things, when they were in value no
more than the husks of the swine-trough. Praised be
Heaven, the scales are fallen from mine eyes; and after
forty years' wandering in the desert of Sinai, I am at
length arrived in the Land of Promise—My corrupt
human nature has left me—I have cast my slough, and
can now with some conscience put my hand to the plough,
certain that there is no weakness left in me wherethrough
I may look back. The furrows," he added, bending his
brows, while a gloomy fire filled his large eyes, "must be
drawn long and deep, and watered by the blood of the
mighty."

There was a change in Bridgenorth's tone and manner,
when he used these singular expressions, which convinced
Julian, that his mind, which had wavered for so many
years between his natural good sense and the insane enthusiasm of the time, had finally given way to the latter;
and, sensible of the danger in which the unhappy man
himself, the innocent and beautiful Alice, and his own
father, were likely to be placed—to say nothing of the
general risk of the community by a sudden insurrection,

he at the same time felt that there was no chance of rea-
soning effectually with one, who would oppose spiritual
conviction to all arguments which reason could urge
against his wild schemes. To touch his feelings seemed
a more probable resource ; and Julian therefore conjured
Bridgenorth to think how much his daughter's honour
and safety were concerned in his abstaining from the dangerous course which he meditated. " If you fall," he
said, " must she not pass under the power and guardianship of her uncle, whom you allow to have shown himself
capable of the grossest mistake in the choice of her female
protectress ; and whom I believe, upon good grounds, to
have made that infamous choice with his eyes open ? "

" Young man," answered Bridgenorth, " you make me
feel like the poor bird, around whose wing some wanton
boy has fixed a line, to pull the struggling wretch to earth
at his pleasure. Know, since thou wilt play this cruel
part, and drag me down from higher contemplations, that
she with whom Alice is placed, and who hath in future
full power to guide her motions, and decide her fate, despite of Christian and every one else, is—I will not tell
thee who she is—Enough—no one—thou least of all,
needs to fear for her safety."

At this moment a side-door opened, and Christian himself came into the apartment. He started and coloured
when he saw Julian Peveril ; then turning to Bridgenorth
with an assumed air of indifference, asked, " Is Saul
among the prophets ?—Is a Peveril among the saints ? "

" No, brother," replied Bridgenorth, " his time is not
come more than thine own—thou art too deep in the ambitious intrigues of manhood, and he in the giddy passions
of youth, to hear the still calm voice—You will both hear
it, as I trust and pray."

"Master Ganlesse, or Christian, or by whatever name you are called," said Julian, "by whatever reasons you guide yourself in this most perilous matter, *you* at least are not influenced by any idea of an immediate divine command for commencing hostilities against the state. Leaving, therefore, for the present, whatever subjects of discussion may be between us, I implore you, as a man of shrewdness and sense, to join with me in dissuading Master Bridgenorth from the fatal enterprise which he now meditates."

" Young gentleman," said Christian, with great composure, " when we met in the west, I was willing to have made a friend of you, but you rejected the overture. You might, however, even then have seen enough of me to be assured, that I am not likely to rush too rashly on any desperate undertaking. As to this which lies before us, my brother Bridgenorth brings to it the simplicity, though not the harmlessness of the dove, and I the subtilty of the serpent. He hath the leading of saints who are moved by the spirit; and I can add to their efforts a powerful body, who have for their instigators, the world, the devil, and the flesh."

" And can you," said Julian, looking at Bridgenorth, " accede to such an unworthy union ? "

" I unite not with them," said Bridgenorth; " but I may not, without guilt, reject the aid which Providence sends to assist his servants. We are ourselves few, though determined—Those whose swords come *to* help the cutting down of the harvest, must be welcome— When their work is wrought, they will be converted or scattered.—Have you been at York-Place, brother, with that unstable epicure ? We must have his last resolution, and that within an hour."

Christian looked at Julian, as if his presence prevented him from returning an answer; upon which Bridgenorth arose, and taking the young man by the arm, led him out of the apartment, into that in which they had left his father; assuring him by the way, that determined and vigilant guards were placed in every different quarter by which escape could be effected, and that he would do well to persuade his father to remain a quiet prisoner for a few hours.

Julian returned him no answer, and Bridgenorth presently retired, leaving him alone with his father and Hudson. To their questions he could only briefly reply, that he feared they were trepanned, since they were in the house with at least two hundred fanatics, completely armed, and apparently prepared for some desperate enterprise. Their own want of arms precluded the possibility of open violence; and however unpleasant it might be to remain in such a condition, it seemed difficult, from the strength of the fastenings at doors and windows, to attempt any secret escape without instantaneous detection.

The valiant dwarf alone nursed hopes, with which he in vain endeavoured to inspire his companions in affliction. "The fair one, whose eyes," he said, "were like the twin stars of Leda"—for the little man was a great admirer of lofty language—"had not invited him, the most devoted, and, it might be, not the least favoured of her servants, into this place, as a harbour, in order that he might therein suffer shipwreck; and he generously assured his friends, that in his safety they also should be safe."

Sir Geoffrey, little cheered by this intimation, expressed his despair at not being able to get the length of Whitehall, where he trusted to find as many jolly Cavaliers as would help him to stifle the whole nest of wasps in their hive; while Julian was of opinion that the best service he could now render Bridgenorth, would be timeously to disclose his plot, and, if possible, to send him at the same time warning to save his person.

But we must leave them to meditate over their plans at leisure; no one of which, as they all depended on their previous escape from confinement, seemed in any great chance of being executed.

CHAPTER XLIV.

And some for safety took the dreadful leap;
Some for the voice of Heaven seem'd calling on them;
Some for advancement, or for lucre's sake—
I leap'd in frolic.

THE DREAM.

AFTER a private conversation with Bridgenorth, Christian hastened to the Duke of Buckingham's hotel, taking at the same time such a route as to avoid meeting with any acquaintance. He was ushered into the apartment of the Duke, whom he found cracking and eating filberts, with a flask of excellent white wine at his elbow. " Christian," said his Grace, " come help me to laugh—I have bit Sir Charles Sedley—flung him for a thousand, by the gods ! "

" I am glad at your luck, my Lord Duke," replied Christian ; " but I am come here on serious business."

" Serious ?—why, I shall hardly be serious in my life again—ha, ha, ha !—and for luck, it was no such thing—sheer wit, and excellent contrivance ; and but that I don't care to affront Fortune, like the old Greek general, I might tell her to her face—In this thou hadst no share. You have heard, Ned Christian, that Mother Cresswell is dead ? "

" Yes, I did hear that the devil hath got his due," answered Christian.

"Well," said the Duke, "you are ungrateful; for I know you have been obliged to her, as well as others. Before George, a most benevolent and helpful old lady ; and that she might not sleep in an unblest grave, I betted —do you mark me—with Sedley, that I would write her funeral sermon; that it should be every word in praise of her life and conversation, that it should be all true, and yet that the diocesan should be unable to lay his thumb on Quodling, my little chaplain, who should preach it."

"I perfectly see the difficulty, my lord," said Christian, who well knew that if he wished to secure attention from this volatile nobleman, he must first suffer, nay, encourage him, to exhaust the topic, whatever it might be, that had got temporary possession of his pineal gland.

"Why," said the Duke, "I had caused my little Quodling to go through his oration thus—'That whatever evil reports had passed current during the lifetime of the worthy matron whom they had restored to dust that day, malice itself could not deny that she was born well, married well, lived well, and died well; since she was born in Shadwell, married to Cresswell, lived in Camberwell, and died in Bridewell.' Here ended the oration, and with it Sedley's ambitious hopes of overreaching Buckingham—ha, ha, ha!—And now, Master Christian, what are your commands for me to-day?"

"First, to thank your Grace for being so attentive as to send so formidable a person as Colonel Blood, to wait upon your poor friend and servant. Faith, he took such an interest in my leaving town, that he wanted to compel me to do it at point of fox, so I was obliged to spill a little of his malapert blood. Your Grace's swordsmen have had ill luck of late; and it is hard, since you al-

ways choose the best hands, and such scrupleless knaves
too."

"Come now, Christian," said the Duke, "do not thus
exult over me; a great man, if I may so call myself, is
never greater than amid miscarriage. I only played
this little trick on you, Christian, to impress on you a
wholesome idea of the interest I take in your motions.
The scoundrel's having dared to draw upon you, is a
thing not to be forgiven.—What! injure my old friend
Christian?"

"And why not," said Christian, coolly, "if your old
friend was so stubborn as not to go out of town, like a
good boy, when your Grace required him to do so, for
the civil purpose of entertaining his niece in his absence?"

"How—what!—how do you mean by *my* entertaining
your niece, Master Christian?" said the Duke. She
was a personage far beyond my poor attentions, being
destined, if I recollect aright, to something like royal
favour."

"It was her fate, however, to be the guest of your
Grace's convent for a brace of days, or so. Marry, my
lord, the father confessor was not at home, and—for con-
vents have been scaled of late—returned not till the bird
was flown."

"Christian, thou art an old reynard—I see there is no
doubling with thee. It was thou, then, stole away my
pretty prize, but left me something so much prettier in
my mind, that, had it not made itself wings to fly away
with, I would have placed it in a cage of gold. Never
be downcast, man; I forgive thee—I forgive thee."

"Your Grace is of a most merciful disposition,
especially considering it is I who have had the wrong;

and sages have said, that he who doth the injury, is less apt to forgive than he who only sustains it."

"True, true, Christian," said the Duke, "which, as you say, is something quite new, and places my clemency in a striking point of view. Well, then, thou forgiven man, when shall I see my Mauritanian Princess again?"

"Whenever I am certain that a quibble, and a carwhichit, for a play or a sermon, will not banish her from your Grace's memory."

"Not all the wit of South, or of Etherege," said Buckingham, hastily, "to say nothing of my own, shall in future make me oblivious of what I owe the Morisco Princess."

"Yet, to leave the fair lady out of thought for a little while—a very little while," said Christian, "since I swear that in due time your Grace shall see her, and know in her the most extraordinary woman that the age has produced—to leave her, I say, out of sight for a little while, has your Grace had late notice of your Duchess's health?"

"Health," said the Duke. "Umph—no—nothing particular. She has been ill—but "——

"She is no longer so," subjoined Christian; "she died in Yorkshire forty-eight hours since."

"Thou must deal with the devil," said the Duke.

"It would ill become one of my name to do so," replied Christian. "But in the brief interval, since your Grace hath known of an event which hath not yet reached the public ear, you have, I believe, made proposals to the King for the hand of the Lady Anne, second daughter of the Duke of York, and your Grace's proposals have been rejected."

"Fiends and firebrands, villain!" said the Duke, starting up and seizing Christian by the collar; "who hath told thee that?"

"Take your hand from my cloak, my Lord Duke, and I may answer you," said Christian. "I have a scurvy touch of old puritanical humour about me. I abide not the imposition of hands—take off your grasp from my cloak, or I will find means to make you unloose it."

The Duke, who had kept his right hand on his dagger-hilt while he held Christian's collar with his left, unloosed it as he spoke, but slowly, and as one who rather suspends than abandons the execution of some hasty impulse; while Christian, adjusting his cloak with perfect composure, said, " Soh—my cloak being at liberty, we speak on equal terms. I come not to insult your Grace, but to offer you vengeance for the insult you have received."

"Vengeance!" said the Duke—"It is the dearest proffer man can present to me in my present mood. I hunger for vengeance—thirst for vengeance—could die to ensure vengeance!—'Sdeath!" he continued, walking up and down the large apartment with the most unrestrained and violent agitation; "I have chased this repulse out of my brain with ten thousand trifles, because I thought no one knew it. But it is known, and to thee, the very common-sewer of Court secrets—the honour of Villiers is in thy keeping, Ned Christian! Speak, thou man of wiles and of intrigue—on whom dost thou promise the vengeance? Speak! and if thy answers meet my desires, I will make a bargain with thee as willingly as with thy master, Satan himself."

"I will not be," said Christian, "so unreasonable in my terms as stories tell of the old apostate; I will offer your Grace, as he might do, temporal prosperity and revenge, which is his frequent recruiting money, but I leave it to yourself to provide, as you may be pleased, for your future salvation."

The Duke, gazing upon him fixedly and sadly, replied, "I would to God, Christian, that I could read what purpose of damnable villainy thou hast to propose to me in thy countenance, without the necessity of thy using words!"

"Your Grace can but try a guess," said Christian, calmly smiling.

"No," replied the Duke, after gazing at him again for the space of a minute; "thou art so deeply dyed an hypocrite, that thy mean features, and clear gray eye, are as likely to conceal treason, as any petty scheme of theft or larceny more corresponding to your degree."

"Treason, my lord!" echoed Christian; "you may have guessed more nearly than you were aware of. I honour your Grace's penetration."

"Treason!" echoed the Duke. "Who dare name such a crime to me?"

"If a name startles your Grace, you may call it vengeance—vengeance on the cabal of councillors, who have ever countermined you, in spite of your wit and your interest with the King.—Vengeance on Arlington, Ormond—on Charles himself."

"No, by Heaven," said the Duke, resuming his disordered walk through the apartment—"Vengeance on these rats of the Privy Council,—come at it as you will. But the King!—never—never. I have provoked him a hundred times, where he has stirred me once. I have crossed his path in state intrigue—rivalled him in love— had the advantage in both,—and, d—n it, he has forgiven me! If treason would put me in his throne, I have no apology for it—it were worse than bestial ingratitude."

"Nobly spoken, my lord," said Christian; "and consistent alike with the obligations under which your Grace lies to Charles Stewart, and the sense you have ever shown of them.—But it signifies not. If your Grace patronize not our enterprise, there is Shaftesbury —there is Monmouth"——

"Scoundrel!" exclaimed the Duke, even more vehemently agitated than before, "think you that you shall carry on with others an enterprise which I have refused? —No, by every heathen and every Christian god!— Hark ye, Christian, I will arrest you on the spot—I will, by gods and devils, and carry you to unravel your plot at Whitehall."

"Where the first words I speak," answered the imperturbable Christian, "will be to inform the Privy Council in what place they may find certain letters, wherewith your Grace has honoured your poor vassal, containing, as I think, particulars which his Majesty will read with more surprise than pleasure."

"'Sdeath, villain!" said the Duke, once more laying his hand on his poniard-hilt, "thou hast me again at advantage. I know not why I forbear to poniard you where you stand!"

"I might fall, my Lord Duke," said Christian, slightly colouring, and putting his right hand into his bosom, "though not, I think, unavenged—for I have not put my person into this peril altogether without means of defence. I might fall, but, alas! your Grace's correspondence is in hands, which, by that very act, would be rendered sufficiently active in handing them to the King and the Privy

Council. What say you to the Moorish Princess, my Lord Duke? What if I have left her executrix of my will, with certain instructions how to proceed if I return not unharmed from York-Place? O, my lord, though my head is in the wolf's mouth, I was not goose enough to place it there without settling how many carabines should be fired on the wolf, so soon as my dying cackle was heard.—Pshaw, my Lord Duke! you deal with a man of sense and courage, yet you speak to him as a child and a coward."

The Duke threw himself into a chair, fixed his eyes on the ground, and spoke without raising them. " I am about to call Jerningham," he said ; " but fear nothing—it is only for a draught of wine—That stuff on the table may be a vehicle for filberts and walnuts, but not for such communications as yours.—Bring me champagne," he said to the attendant who answered on his summons.

The domestic returned, and brought a flask of champagne, with two large silver cups. One of them he filled for Buckingham, who, contrary to the usual etiquette, was always served first at home, and then offered the other to Christian, who declined to receive it.

The Duke drank off the large goblet which was presented to him, and for a moment covered his forehead with the palm of his hand ; then instantly withdrew it, and said, " Christian, speak your errand plainly. We know each other. If my reputation be in some degree in your hands, you are well aware that your life is in mine. Sit down," he said, taking a pistol from his bosom and laying it on the table—" Sit down, and let me hear your proposal."

"My lord," said Christian, smiling, "I shall produce no such ultimate argument on my part, though possibly, in time of need, I may not be found destitute of them. But my defence is in the situation of things, and in the composed view which, doubtless, your Majesty will take of them."

"Majesty!" repeated the Duke—"My good friend Christian, you have kept company with the Puritans so long, that you confuse the ordinary titles of the Court."

"I know not how to apologize," said Christian, "unless your Grace will suppose that I spoke by prophecy."

"Such as the devil delivered to Macbeth," said the Duke—again paced the chamber, and again seated himself, and said, "Be plain, Christian—speak out at once, and manfully, what is it you intend?"

"*I*," said Christian—"What should I do?—I can do nothing in such a matter; but I thought it right that your Grace should know that the godly of this city"—(he spoke the word with a kind of ironical grin)—"are impatient of inactivity, and must needs be up and doing. My brother Bridgenorth is at the head of all old Weiver's congregation; for you must know, that, after floundering from one faith to another, he hath now got beyond ordinances, and is become a Fifth-Monarchy man. He has nigh two hundred of Weiver's people, fully equipped, and ready to fall on; and, with slight aid from your Grace's people, they must carry Whitehall, and make prisoners of all within it."

"Rascal!" said the Duke, "and is it to a Peer of England you make this communication?"

"Nay," answered Christian, "I admit it would be extreme folly in your Grace to appear until all is over. But let me give Blood and the others a hint on your part. There are the four Germans also—right Knipperdolings and Anabaptists—will be specially useful. You are wise,

my lord, and know the value of a corps of domestic gladiators, as well as did Octavius, Lepidus, and Anthony, when, by such family forces, they divided the world by indenture tripartite."

" Stay, stay," said the Duke. " Even if these bloodhounds were to join with you—not that I would permit it without the most positive assurances for the King's personal safety—but say the villains were to join, what hope have you of carrying the Court ? "

" Bully Tom Armstrong,* my lord, hath promised his interest with the Life-Guards. Then there are my Lord Shaftesbury's brisk boys in the city—thirty thousand on the holding up a finger."

" Let him hold up both hands, and if he count a hundred for each finger," said the Duke, " it will be more than I expect. You have not spoken to him ? "

" Surely not till your Grace's pleasure was known. But, if he is not applied to, there is the Dutch train, Hans Snorehout's congregation in the Strand—there are the French Protestants in Piccadilly—there are the family of Levi in Lewkenor's Lane—the Muggletonians in Thames Street "——

" Ah, faugh !—Out upon them—out upon them !—How the knaves will stink of cheese and tobacco when they come upon action !—they will drown all the perfumes in Whitehall. Spare me the detail ; and let me know, my dearest Ned, the sum total of thy most odoriferous forces."

---

* Thomas, or Sir Thomas Armstrong, a person who had distinguished himself in youth by duels and drunken exploits. He was particularly connected with the Duke of Monmouth, and was said to be concerned in the Rye-House Plot, for which he suffered capital punishment, 20th June, 1684.

"Fifteen hundred men, well armed," said Christian, "besides the rabble that will rise to a certainty—they have already nearly torn to pieces the prisoners who were this day acquitted on account of the Plot."

"All, then, I understand.—And now, hark ye, most Christian Christian," said he, wheeling his chair full in front of that on which his agent was seated, "you have told me many things to-day—Shall I be equally communicative? Shall I show you that my accuracy of information matches yours? Shall I tell you, in a word, why you have at once resolved to push every one, from the Puritan to the free-thinker, upon a general attack of the Palace at Whitehall, without allowing me, a peer of the realm, time either to pause upon or to prepare for a step so desperate? Shall I tell you why you would lead or drive, seduce or compel me, into countenancing your measures?"

"My lord, if you please to form a guess," said Christian, "I will answer with all sincerity, if you have assigned the right cause."

"The Countess of Derby is this day arrived, and attends the Court this evening, with hopes of the kindest reception. She may be surprised amid the mêlée?—Ha! said I not right, Master Christian? You, who pretend to offer me revenge, know yourself its exquisite sweetness."

"I would not presume," said Christian, half smiling, "to offer your Grace a dish without acting as your taster as well as purveyor."

"That's honestly said," said the Duke. "Away then, my friend. Give Blood this ring—he knows it, and knows how to obey him who bears it. Let him assemble my gladiators, as thou dost most wittily term my *coup jarrets.* The old scheme of the German music may be resorted to, for I think thou hast the instruments ready. But take notice, I know nothing on't; and Rowley's person must be safe—I will hang and burn on all hands if a hair of his black periwig* be but singed.—Then what is to follow—a Lord Protector of the realm—or stay—Cromwell has made the word somewhat slovenly and unpopular—a Lord Lieutenant of the Kingdom?—The patriots who take it on themselves to avenge the injustice done to the country, and to remove evil counsellors from before the King's throne, that it may be henceforward established in righteousness—so I think the rubric runs —cannot fail to make a fitting choice."

"They cannot, my Lord Duke," said Christian, "since there is but one man in the three kingdoms on whom that choice can possibly fall."

"I thank you, Christian," said his Grace; "and I trust you. Away, and make all ready. Be assured your services shall not be forgot. We will have you near to us."

"My Lord Duke," said Christian, "you bind me doubly to you. But remember that as your Grace is spared any obnoxious proceedings which may befall in the way of military execution, or otherwise, so it will be advisable that you hold yourself in preparation, upon a moment's notice, to put yourself at the head of a band of honourable friends and allies, and come presently to the palace, where you will be received by the victors as a commander, and by the vanquished as a preserver."

---

* Charles, to suit his dark complexion, always wore a black peruke. He used to say of the players, that if they wished to represent a villain on the stage, "Oddsfish, they always clapp'd on him a black periwig, whereas the greatest rogue in England [meaning, probably, Dr. Oates] wears a white one."—*See* CIBBER'S *Apology.*

"I conceive you—I conceive you. I will be in prompt readiness," said the Duke.

"Ay, my lord," continued Christian; "and for Heaven's sake, let none of those toys, which are the very Delilahs of your imagination, come across your Grace this evening, and interfere with the execution of this sublime scheme."

"Why, Christian, dost think me mad?" was his Grace's emphatic reply. "It is you who linger, when all should be ordered for a deed so daring. Go then.—But hark ye, Ned; ere you go, tell me when I shall again see yonder thing of fire and air—yon Eastern Peri, that glides into apartments by the key-hole, and leaves them through the casement—yon black-eyed houri of the Mahometan paradise—when, I say, shall I see her once more?"

"When your Grace has the truncheon of Lord Lieutenant of the Kingdom," said Christian, and left the apartment.

Buckingham stood fixed in contemplation for a moment after he was gone. "Should I have done this?" he said, arguing the matter with himself; "or had I the choice rather of doing aught else? Should I not hasten to the Court, and make Charles aware of the treason which besets him? I will, by Heaven?—Here, Jerningham, my coach, with the dispatch of light!—I will throw myself at his feet, and tell him of all the follies which I have dreamed of with this Christian.—And then he will laugh at me, and spurn me.—No, I have kneeled to him to-day already, and my repulse was nothing gentle. To be spurned once in the sun's daily round is enough for Buckingham."

Having made this reflection, he seated himself, and

began hastily to mark down the young nobles and gentlemen of quality, and others, their very ignoble companions,
who he supposed might be likely to assume him for their
leader in any popular disturbance.   He had nearly completed it, when Jerningham entered, to say the coach
would be ready in an instant, and to bring his master's
sword, hat, and cloak.

"Let the coachman draw off," said the Duke, "but
be in readiness.   And send to the gentlemen thou wilt
find named in this list; say I am but ill at ease, and wish
their company to a slight collation.   Let instant expedition be made, and care not for expense; you will find
most of them at the Club-House in Fuller's Rents." *

The preparations for festivity were speedily made, and
the intended guests, most of them persons who were at
leisure for any call that promised pleasure, though sometimes more deaf to those of duty, began speedily to assemble.   There were many youths of the highest rank,
and with them, as is usual in those circles, many of a
different class, whom talents, or impudence, or wit, or a
turn for gambling, had reared up into companions for the
great and the gay.   The Duke of Buckingham was a
general patron of persons of this description; and a
numerous attendance took place on the present occasion.

The festivity was pursued with the usual appliances of
wine, music, and games of hazard; with which, however,

---

* The place of meeting of the Green Ribbon Club. "Their place
of meeting," says Roger North, "was in a sort of Carrefour at Chan-
cery Lane, in a centre of business and company most proper for such
anglers of fools. The house was double balconied in front, as may yet
be seen, for the clubbers to issue forth *in fresco,* with hats and no
perukes, pipes in their mouths, merry faces, and dilated throats for
vocal encouragement of the canaglia below on usual and unusual
occasions."

there mingled in that period much more wit, and a good deal more gross profligacy of conversation, than the talents of the present generation can supply, or their taste would permit.

The Duke himself proved the complete command which he possessed over his versatile character, by maintaining the frolic, the laugh, and the jest, while his ear caught up, and with eagerness, the most distant sounds, as intimating the commencement of Christian's revolutionary project. Such sounds were heard from time to time, and from time to time they died away, without any of those consequences which Buckingham expected.

At length, and when it was late in the evening, Jerningham announced Master Chiffinch from the Court; and that worthy personage followed the annunciation.

" Strange things have happened, my Lord Duke," he said; " your presence at Court is instantly required by his Majesty."

" You alarm me," said Buckingham, standing up. " I hope nothing has happened—I hope there is nothing wrong—I hope his Majesty is well? "

" Perfectly well," said Chiffinch; " and desirous to see your Grace without a moment's delay."

" This is sudden," said the Duke. " You see I have had merry fellows about me, and am scarce in case to appear, Chiffinch."

" Your Grace seems to be in very handsome plight," said Chiffinch; " and you know his Majesty is gracious enough to make allowances."

" True," said the Duke, not a little anxious in his mind, touching the cause of this unexpected summons— " True—his Majesty is most gracious—I will order my coach."

"Mine is below," replied the royal messenger; "it will save time, if your Grace will condescend to use it."

Forced from every evasion, Buckingham took a goblet from the table, and requested his friends to remain at his palace so long as they could find the means of amusement there. He expected, he said, to return almost immediately; if not, he would take farewell of them with his usual toast, "May all of us that are not hanged in the interval, meet together again here on the first Monday of next month."

This standing toast of the Duke bore reference to the character of several of his guests; but he did not drink it on the present occasion without some anticipation concerning his own fate, in case Christian had betrayed him. He hastily made some addition to his dress, and attended Chiffinch in the chariot to Whitehall.

CHAPTER XLV.

High feasting was there there—the gilded roofs
Rung to the wassail-health—the dancer's step
Sprung to the chord responsive—the gay gamester
To fate's disposal flung his heap of gold,
And laugh'd alike when it increased or lessen'd:
Such virtue hath court-air to teach us patience
Which schoolmen preach in vain.

WHY COME YE NOT TO COURT?

UPON the afternoon of this eventful day, Charles held
his Court in the Queen's apartments, which were opened
at a particular hour to invited guests of a certain lower
degree, but accessible without restriction to the higher
classes of nobility who had from birth, and to the courtiers who held by office, the privilege of the *entrée*.

It was one part of Charles's character, which unquestionably rendered him personally popular, and postponed
to a subsequent reign the precipitation of his family from
the throne, that he banished from his Court many of the
formal restrictions with which it was in other reigns surrounded.   He was conscious of the good-natured grace
of his manners, and trusted to it, often not in vain, to
remove evil impressions arising from actions, which he
was sensible could not be justified on the grounds of
liberal or national policy.

In the daytime the King was commonly seen in the
public walks alone, or only attended by one or two per-

sons; and his answer to the remonstrance of his brother, on the risk of thus exposing his person, is well known ;— "Believe me, James," he said, "no one will murder *me*, to make *you* King."

In the same manner, Charles's evenings, unless such as were destined to more secret pleasures, were frequently spent amongst all who had any pretence to approach a courtly circle; and thus it was upon the night which we are treating of. Queen Catherine, reconciled or humbled to her fate, had long ceased to express any feelings of jealousy, nay, seemed so absolutely dead to such a passion, that she received at her drawing-room, without scruple, and even with encouragement, the Duchesses of Portsmouth and Cleveland, and others, who enjoyed, though in a less avowed character, the credit of having been royal favourites. Constraint of every kind was banished from a circle so composed, and which was frequented at the same time, if not by the wisest, at least by the wittiest courtiers, who ever assembled round a monarch, and who, as many of them had shared the wants, and shifts, and frolics of his exile, had then acquired a sort of prescriptive license, which the good-natured prince, when he attained his period of prosperity, could hardly have restrained had it suited his temper to do so. This, however, was the least of Charles's thoughts. His manners were such as secured him from indelicate obtrusion; and he sought no other protection from over-familiarity, than what these and his ready wit afforded him.

On the present occasion, he was peculiarly disposed to enjoy the scene· of pleasure which had been prepared. The singular death of Major Coleby, which, taking place in his own presence, had proclaimed, with the voice of a passing bell, the ungrateful neglect of the Prince for whom he had sacrificed every thing, had given Charles much pain. But, in his own opinion at least, he had completely atoned for this negligence, by the trouble which he had taken for Sir Geoffrey Peveril and his son, whose liberation he looked upon not only as an excellent good deed in itself, but, in spite of the grave rebuke of Ormond, as achieved in a very pardonable manner, considering the difficulties with which he was surrounded. He even felt a degree of satisfaction on receiving intelligence from the city that there had been disturbances in the streets, and that some of the more violent fanatics had betaken themselves to their meeting-houses, upon sudden summons, to inquire, as their preachers phrased it, into the causes of Heaven's wrath, and into the backsliding of the Court, lawyers, and jury, by whom the false and bloody favourers of the Popish Plot were screened and cloaked from deserved punishment.

The King, we repeat, seemed to hear these accounts with pleasure, even when he was reminded of the dangerous and susceptible character of those with whom such suspicions originated. "Will any one now assert," he said, with self-complacence, "that I am so utterly negligent of the interest of friends?—You see the peril in which I place myself, and even the risk to which I have exposed the public peace, to rescue a man whom I have scarce seen for twenty years, and then only in his buff-coat and bandoleers, with other Train-Band officers who kissed hands upon the Restoration. They say kings have long hands—I think they have as much occasion for long memories, since they are expected to watch over and reward every man in England, who hath but shown his good-will by crying 'God save the King!'"

" Nay, the rogues are even more unreasonable still," said Sedley ; "for every knave of them thinks himself entitled to your Majesty's protection in a good cause, whether he has cried God save the King or no."

The King smiled, and turned to another part of the stately hall, where every thing was assembled which could, according to the taste of the age, make the time glide pleasantly away.

In one place, a group of the young nobility, and of the ladies of the Court, listened to the reader's acquaintance Empson, who was accompanying with his unrivalled breathings on the flute, a young siren, who, while her bosom palpitated with pride and with fear, warbled to the courtly and august presence the beautiful air beginning,

> " Young I am, and yet unskill'd,
> How to make a lover yield," &c.

She performed her task in a manner so corresponding with the strains of the amatory poet, and the voluptuous air with which the words had been invested by the celebrated Purcel, that the men crowded around in ecstasies, while most of the ladies thought it proper either to look extremely indifferent to the words she sung, or to withdraw from the circle as quietly as possible. To the song succeeded a concerto, performed by a select band of most admirable musicians, which the King, whose taste was indisputable, had himself selected.

At other tables in the apartment, the elder courtiers worshipped Fortune, at the various fashionable games of ombre, quadrille, hazard, and the like ; while heaps of gold which lay before the players, augmented or dwindled with every turn of a card or cast of a die. Many a year's rent of fair estates was ventured upon the main or the odds ; which, spent in the old deserted manor-house, had repaired the ravages of Cromwell upon its walls, and replaced the sources of good housekeeping and hospitality, that, exhausted in the last age by fine and sequestration, were now in a fair way of being annihilated by careless prodigality. Elsewhere, under cover of observing the gamester, or listening to the music, the gallantries of that all-licensed age were practised among the gay and fair, closely watched the whilst by the ugly or the old, who promised themselves at least the pleasure of observing, and it may be that of proclaiming, intrigues in which they could not be sharers.

From one table to another glided the merry Monarch, exchanging now a glance with a Court beauty, now a jest with a Court wit, now beating time to the music, and anon losing or winning a few pieces of gold on the chance of the game to which he stood nearest ;—the most amiable of voluptuaries—the gayest and best-natured of companions—the man that would, of all others, have best sustained his character, had life been a continued banquet, and its only end to enjoy the passing hour, and send it away as pleasantly as might be.

But Kings are least of all exempted from the ordinary lot of humanity ; and Seged of Ethiopia is, amongst monarchs, no solitary example of the vanity of reckoning on a day or an hour of undisturbed serenity. An attendant on the Court announced suddenly to their Majesties that a lady, who would only announce herself as a Peeress of England, desired to be admitted into the presence.

The Queen said, hastily, it was *impossible*. No peeress, without announcing her title, was entitled to the privilege of her rank.

" I could be sworn," said a nobleman in attend-

ance, "that it is some whim of the Duchess of Newcastle."

The attendant who brought the message, said that he
did indeed believe it to be the Duchess, both from the singularity of the message, and that the lady spoke with
somewhat a foreign accent.

"In the name of madness, then," said the King, "let
us admit her. Her Grace is an entire raree-show in her
own person—a universal masquerade—indeed a sort of
private Bedlam-hospital, her whole ideas being like so
many patients crazed upon the subjects of love and liter-
ature, who act nothing in their vagaries, save Minerva,
Venus, and the nine Muses."

"Your Majesty's pleasure must always supersede
mine," said the Queen. "I only hope I shall not be
expected to entertain so fantastic a personage. The last
time she came to Court, Isabella,"—(she spoke to one of
her Portuguese ladies of honour)—" you had not returned
from our lovely Lisbon !—her Grace had the assurance
to assume a right to bring a train-bearer into my apartment; and when this was not allowed, what then, think
you, she did ?—even caused her train to be made so long,
that three mortal yards of satin and silver remained in
the antechamber, supported by four wenches, while the
other end was attached to her Grace's person, as she paid
her duty at the upper end of the presence-room. Full
thirty yards of the most beautiful silk did her Grace's
madness employ in this manner."

"And most beautiful damsels they were who bore this
portentous train," said the King—" a train never equalled
save by that of the great comet in sixty-six. Sedley and
Etherege told us wonders of them; for it is one advantage of this new fashion brought up by the Duchess, that

a matron may be totally unconscious of the coquetry of her train and its attendants."

" Am I to understand, then, your Majesty's pleasure is, that the lady is to be admitted?" said the usher.

" Certainly," said the King; " that is, if the incognito be really entitled to the honour.—It may be as well to inquire her title—there are more madwomen abroad than the Duchess of Newcastle. I will walk into the anteroom myself, and receive your answer."

But ere Charles had reached the lower end of the apartment in his progress to the anteroom, the usher surprised the assembly by announcing a name which had not for many a year been heard in these courtly halls—" the Countess of Derby!"

Stately and tall, and still, at an advanced period of life, having a person unbroken by years, the noble lady advanced towards her Sovereign, with a step resembling that with which she might have met an equal. There was indeed nothing in her manner that indicated either haughtiness or assumption unbecoming that presence; but her consciousness of wrongs, sustained from the administration of Charles, and of the superiority of the injured party over those from whom, or in whose name, the injury had been offered, gave her look dignity, and her step firmness. She was dressed in widow's weeds, of the same fashion which were worn at the time her husband was brought to the scaffold; and which, in the thirty years subsequent to that event, she had never permitted her tirewoman to alter.

The surprise was no pleasing one to the King; and cursing in his heart the rashness which had allowed the lady entrance on the gay scene in which they were engaged, he saw at the same time the necessity of receiving her in a manner suitable to his own character, and her rank in the British Court. He approached her with an air of welcome, into which he threw all his natural grace, while he began, " *Chère Comptesse de Derby, puissante Reine de Man, notre très auguste sœur* "——

" Speak English, sire, if I may presume to ask such a favour," said the Countess. " I am a Peeress of this nation—mother to one English Earl, and widow, alas, to another! In England I have spent my brief days of happiness, my long years of widowhood and sorrow. France and its language are but to me the dreams of an uninteresting childhood. I know no tongue save that of my husband and my son. Permit me, as the widow and mother of Derby, thus to render my homage."

She would have kneeled, but the King gracefully prevented her, and, saluting her cheek, according to the form, led her towards the Queen, and himself performed the ceremony of introduction. " Your Majesty," he said, " must be informed that the Countess has imposed a restriction on French—the language 'of gallantry and compliment. I trust your Majesty will, though a foreigner, like herself, find enough of honest English to assure the Countess of Derby, with what pleasure we see her at Court, after the absence of so many years."

" I will endeavour to do so, at least," said the Queen, on whom the appearance of the Countess of Derby made a more favourable impression than that of many strangers, whom, at the King's request, she was in the habit of receiving with courtesy.

Charles himself again spoke. " To any other lady of the same rank I might put the question, why she was so long absent from the circle? I fear I can only ask the

Countess of Derby, what fortunate cause produces the pleasure of seeing her here?"

"No fortunate cause, my liege, though one most strong and urgent."

The King augured nothing agreeable from this commencement; and in truth, from the Countess's first entrance, he had anticipated some unpleasant explanation, which he therefore hastened to parry, having first composed his features into an expression of sympathy and interest.

"If," said he, "the cause is of a nature in which we can render assistance, we cannot expect your ladyship should enter upon it at the present time; but a memorial addressed to our secretary, or, if it is more satisfactory, to ourselves directly, will receive our immediate, and I trust I need not add, our favourable construction."

The Countess bowed with some state, and answered, "My business, sire, is indeed important; but so brief, that it need not for more than a few minutes withdraw your ear from what is more pleasing;—yet it is so urgent, that I am afraid to postpone it even for a moment."

"This is unusual," said Charles. "But you, Countess of Derby, are an unwonted guest, and must command my time. Does the matter require my private ear?"

"For my part," said the Countess, "the whole Court might listen; but your Majesty may prefer hearing me in the presence of one or two of your counsellors."

"Ormond," said the King, looking around, "attend us for an instant—and do you, Arlington, do the same."

The King led the way into an adjoining cabinet, and, seating himself, requested the Countess would also take a chair. "It needs not, sire," she replied; then pausing for a moment, as if to collect her spirits, she proceeded with firmness.

"Your Majesty well said that no light cause had drawn me from my lonely habitation. I came not hither when the property of my son—that property which descended to him from a father who died for your Majesty's rights—was conjured away from him under pretext of justice, that it might first feed the avarice of the rebel Fairfax, and then supply the prodigality of his son-in-law, Buckingham."

"These are over harsh terms, lady," said the King. "A legal penalty was, as we remember, incurred by an act of irregular violence—so our courts and our laws term it, though personally I have no objection to call it, with you, an honourable revenge. But admit it were such, in prosecution of the laws of honour, bitter legal consequences are often necessarily incurred."

"I come not to argue for my son's wasted and forfeited inheritance, sire," said the Countess; "I only take credit for my patience, under that afflicting dispensation. I now come to redeem the honour of the House of Derby, more dear to me than all the treasures and lands which ever belonged to it."

"And by whom is the honour of the House of Derby impeached?" said the King; "for on my word you bring me the first news of it."

"Has there one Narrative, as these wild fictions are termed, been printed with regard to the Popish Plot— this pretended Plot as I will call it—in which the honour of our house has not been touched and tainted? And are there not two noble gentlemen, father and son, allies of the House of Stanley, about to be placed in jeopardy of their lives, on account of matters in which we are the parties first impeached?"

The King looked around, and smiled to Arlington and Ormond. " The Countess's courage, methinks, shames ours. What lips dared have called the immaculate Plot *pretended*, or the Narrative of the witnesses, our preservers from Popish knives, a wild fiction?—But, madam," he said, " though I admire the generosity of your interference in behalf of the two Peverils, I must acquaint you, that your interference is unnecessary—they are this morning acquitted."

" Now may God be praised! " said the Countess, folding her hands. " I have scarce slept since I heard the news of their impeachment; and have arrived here to surrender myself to your Majesty's justice, or to the prejudices of the nation, in hopes, by so doing, I might at least save the lives of my noble and generous friends, enveloped in suspicion only, or chiefly, by their connexion with us.—Are they indeed acquitted?"

" They are, by my honour," said the King. "I marvel you heard it not."

" I arrived but last night, and remained in the strictest seclusion," said the Countess, " afraid to make any inquiries that might occasion discovery ere I saw your Majesty."

" And now that we *have* met," said the King, taking her hand kindly—" a meeting which gives me the greatest pleasure—may I recommend to you speedily to return to your royal island with as little eclat as you came hither? The world, my dear Countess, has changed since we were young. Men fought in the Civil War with good swords and muskets; but now we fight with indictments and oaths, and such like legal weapons. You are no adept in such warfare; and though I am well aware you know how to hold out a castle, I doubt much if you have the art to parry off an impeachment. This Plot has come upon us like a land storm—there is no steering the vessel in the teeth of the tempest—we must run for the nearest haven, and happy if we can reach one."

"This is cowardice, my liege," said the Countess—"Forgive the word!—it is but a woman who speaks it. Call your noble friends around you, and make a stand like your royal father. There is but one right and one wrong—one honourable and forward course; and all others which deviate are oblique and unworthy."

"Your language, my venerated friend," said Ormond, —who saw the necessity of interfering betwixt the dignity of the actual Sovereign and the freedom of the Countess, who was generally accustomed to receive, not to pay observance,—"your language is strong and decided, but it applies not to the times. It might occasion a renewal of the Civil War, and of all its miseries, but could hardly be attended with the effects you sanguinely anticipate."

"You are too rash, my Lady Countess," said Arlington, "not only to rush upon this danger yourself, but to desire to involve his Majesty. Let me say plainly, that, in this jealous time, you have done but ill to exchange the security of Castle Rushin for the chance of a lodging in the Tower of London."

"And were I to kiss the block there," said the Countess, "as did my husband at Bolton-on-the-Moors, I would do so willingly, rather than forsake a friend!—and one, too, whom, as in the case of the younger Peveril, I have thrust upon danger."

"But have I not assured you that both of the Peverils, elder and younger, are freed from peril?" said the King; "and, my dear Countess, what can else tempt you to thrust *yourself* on danger, from which, doubtless, you expect to be relieved by my intervention? Methinks a lady of your judgment should not voluntarily throw herself into a river, merely that her friends might have the risk and merit of dragging her out."

The Countess reiterated her intention to claim a fair trial.—The two counsellors again pressed their advice that she should withdraw, though under the charge of absconding from justice, and remain in her own feudal kingdom.

The King, seeing no termination to the debate, gently reminded the Countess that her Majesty would be jealous if he detained her ladyship longer, and offered her his hand to conduct her back to the company. This she was under the necessity of accepting, and returned accordingly to the apartments of state, where an event occurred immediately afterwards, which must be transferred to the next chapter.

.

CHAPTER XLVI.

Here stand I tight and trim,
Quick of eye, though little of limb;
He who denieth the word I have spoken,
Betwixt him and me shall lances be broken.

LAY OF THE LITTLE JOHN DE SAINTRÉ.

WHEN Charles had reconducted the Countess of Derby into the presence-chamber, before he parted with her, he entreated her, in a whisper, to be governed by good counsel, and to regard her own safety; and then turned easily from her, as if to distribute his attentions equally among the other guests.

These were a good deal circumscribed at the instant, by the arrival of a party of five or six musicians; one of whom, a German, under the patronage of the Duke of Buckingham, was particularly renowned for his performance on the violoncello, but had been detained in inactivity in the antechamber by the non-arrival of his instrument, which had now at length made its appearance.

The domestic who placed it before the owner, shrouded as it was within its wooden case, seemed heartily glad to be rid of his load, and lingered for a moment, as if interested in discovering what sort of instrument was to be produced that could weigh so heavily. His curiosity was satisfied, and in a most extraordinary manner; for, while the musician was fumbling with the key, the case being for his greater convenience placed upright against the wall, the case and instrument itself at once flew open, and out started the dwarf, Geoffrey Hudson,—at sight of whose unearthly appearance, thus suddenly introduced, the ladies shrieked, and ran backwards; the gentlemen started, and the poor German, on seeing the portentous delivery of his fiddle-case, tumbled on the floor in an agony, supposing, it might be, that his instrument was metamorphosed into the strange figure which supplied its place. So soon, however, as he recovered, he glided out of the apartment, and was followed by most of his companions.

"Hudson!" said the King—"My little old friend, I am not sorry to see you; though Buckingham, who I suppose is the purveyor of this jest, hath served us up but a stale one."

"Will your Majesty honour me with one moment's attention?" said Hudson.

"Assuredly, my good friend," said the King. "Old acquaintances are springing up in every quarter to-night; and our leisure can hardly be better employed than in listening to them.—It was an idle trick of Buckingham," he added, in a whisper to Ormond, "to send the poor thing hither, especially as he was to-day tried for the affair of the Plot. At any rate he comes not to ask protection from us, having had the rare fortune to come off *Plot-free*. He is but fishing, I suppose, for some little present or pension."

The little man, precise in Court etiquette, yet impatient of the King's delaying to attend to him, stood in the midst of the floor, most valorously pawing and prancing, like a Scots pony assuming the airs of a war-horse, waving meanwhile his little hat with the tarnished feather, and bowing from time to time, as if impatient to be heard.

" Speak on, then, my friend," said Charles; " if thou hast some poetical address penned for thee, out with it, that thou mayst have time to repose these flourishing little limbs of thine."

" No poetical speech have I, most mighty Sovereign," answered the dwarf; " but, in plain and most loyal prose, I do accuse, before this company, the once noble Duke of Buckingham of high treason ! "

" Well spoken, and manfully—Get on, man," said the King, who never doubted that this was the introduction to something burlesque or witty, not conceiving that the charge was made in solemn earnest.

A great laugh took place among such courtiers as heard, and among many who did not hear, what was uttered by the dwarf; the former entertained by the extravagant emphasis and gesticulation of the little champion, and the others laughing not the less loud that they laughed for example's sake, and upon trust.

" What matter is there for all this mirth?" said he, very indignantly—" Is it fit subject for laughing, that I, Geoffrey Hudson, Knight, do, before King and nobles, impeach George Villiers, Duke of Buckingham, of high treason?"

" No subject of mirth, certainly," said Charles, composing his features; " but great matter of wonder.—Come, cease this mouthing, and prancing, and mummery.—If there be a jest, come out with it, man; and if not, even get thee to the beauffet, and drink a cup of wine to refresh thee after thy close lodging."

" I tell you, my liege," said Hudson, impatiently, yet in a whisper, intended only to be audible by the King, " that if you spend over much time in trifling, you will be convinced by dire experience of Buckingham's treason. I tell you,—I asseverate to your Majesty,—two hundred armed fanatics will be here within the hour, to surprise the guards."

" Stand back, ladies," said the King, " or you may hear more than you will care to listen to. My Lord of Buckingham's jests are not always, you know, quite fitted for female ears; besides, we want a few words in private with our little friend. You, my Lord of Ormond—you, Arlington," (and he named one or two others,) " may remain with us."

The gay crowd bore back, and dispersed through the apartment—the men to conjecture what the end of this mummery, as they supposed it, was likely to prove ; and what jest, as Sedley said, the bass-fiddle had been brought to bed of—and the ladies to admire and criticise the antique dress, and richly embroidered ruff and hood of the Countess of Derby, to whom the Queen was showing particular attention.

" And now, in the name of Heaven, and amongst friends," said the King to the dwarf, " what means all this ? "

" Treason, my lord the King !—Treason to his Majesty of England !—When I was chambered in yonder instrument, my lord, the High-Dutch fellows who bore me, carried me into a certain chapel, to see, as they said to each other, that all was ready. Sire, I went where bass-fiddle never went before, even into a conventicle of Fifth-Monarchists ; and when they brought me away, the preacher was concluding his sermon, and was within a ' Now to apply ' of setting off like the bell-weather at the head of his flock, to surprise your Majesty in your royal

Court! I heard him through the sound-holes of my instrument, when the fellow set me down for a moment to profit by this precious doctrine."

"It would be singular," said Lord Arlington, "were there some reality at the bottom of this buffoonery; for we know these wild men have been consulting together to-day, and five conventicles have held a solemn fast."

"Nay," said the King, "if that be the case, they are certainly determined on some villainy."

"Might I advise," said the Duke of Ormond, "I would summon the Duke of Buckingham to this presence. His connexions with the fanatics are well known, though he affects to conceal them."

"You would not, my lord, do his Grace the injustice to treat him as a criminal on such a charge as this?" said the King. "However," he added, after a moment's consideration, "Buckingham is accessible to every sort of temptation, from the flightiness of his genius. I should not be surprised if he nourished hopes of an aspiring kind —I think we had some proof of it but lately.—Hark ye, Chiffinch; go to him instantly, and bring him here on any fair pretext thou canst devise. I would fain save him from what lawyers call an overt act. The Court would be dull as a dead horse, were Buckingham to miscarry."

"Will not your Majesty order the Horse Guards to turn out?" said young Selby, who was present, and an officer.

"No, Selby," said the King, "I like not horse-play. But let them be prepared; and let the High Bailiff collect his civil officers, and command the Sheriffs to summon their worshipful attendants, from javelin-men to hang-

men,* and have them in readiness, in case of any sudden
tumult—double the sentinels on the doors of the palace—
and see no strangers get in."

" Or *out*," said the Duke of Ormond. " Where are
the foreign fellows who brought in the dwarf ? "

* It can hardly be forgotten that one of the great difficulties of
Charles II.'s reign was to obtain for the crown the power of choosing
the sheriffs of London. Roger North gives a lively account of his
brother, Sir Dudley North, who agreed to serve for the court. " I omit
the share he had in composing the tumults about burning the Pope,
because that is accounted for in the Examen, and the Life of the Lord
Keeper North. Neither is there occasion to say any thing of the rise
and discovery of the Rye Plot, for the same reason. Nor is my subject
much concerned with this latter, farther than that the conspirators
had taken especial care of Sir Dudley North. For he was one of those
who, if they had succeeded, was to have been knocked on the head,
and his skin to be stuffed, and hung up in Guildhall. But, all that
apart, he reckoned it a great unhappiness, that so many trials for high
treason, and executions, should happen in his year. However, in these
affairs, the sheriffs were passive; for all returns of panels, and other
despatches of the law, were issued and done by under-officers; which
was a fair screen for them. They attended at the trials and executions, to coerce the crowds, and keep order, which was enough for
them to do. I have heard Sir Dudley North say, that, striking with
his cane, he wondered to see what blows his countrymen would take
upon their bare heads, and never look up at it. And indeed, nothing
can match the zeal of the common people to see executions. The
worst grievance was the executioner coming to him for orders, touching the abscinded members, and to know where to dispose of them.
Once, while he was abroad, a cart, with some of them, came into the
court-yard of his house, and frighted his lady almost out of her wits;
and she could never be reconciled to the dog hangman's saying he
came to speak with his master. These are inconveniences that attend
the stations of public magistracy, and are necessary to be borne with,
as magistracy itself is necessary. I have now no more to say of any
incidents during the shrievalty; but that, at the year's end, he delivered up his charges to his successors in like manner as he had received
them from his predecessor; and, having reinstated his family, he lived
well and easy at his own house, as he did before these disturbances
put him out of order."

They were sought for, but they were not to be found. They had retreated, leaving their instruments—a circumstance which seemed to bear hard on the Duke of Buckingham, their patron.

Hasty preparations were made to provide resistance to any effort of despair which the supposed conspirators might be driven to ; and in the meanwhile, the King, withdrawing with Arlington, Ormond, and a few other counsellors, into the cabinet where the Countess of Derby had had her audience, resumed the examination of the little discoverer. His declaration, though singular, was quite coherent ; the strain of romance intermingled with it, being in fact a part of his character, which often gained him the fate of being laughed at, when he would otherwise have been pitied, or even esteemed.

He commenced with a flourish about his sufferings for the Plot, which the impatience of Ormond would have cut short, had not the King reminded his Grace, that a top, when it is not flogged, must needs go down of itself at the end of a definite time, while the application of the whip may keep it up for hours.

Geoffrey Hudson was, therefore, allowed to exhaust himself on the subject of his prison-house, which he informed the King was not without a beam of light—an emanation of loveliness—a mortal angel—quick of step and beautiful of eye, who had more than once visited his confinement with words of cheering and comfort.

"By my faith," said the King, "they fare better in Newgate than I was aware of. Who would have thought of the little gentleman being solaced with female society in such a place ? "

"I pray your Majesty," said the dwarf, after the manner of a solemn protest, " to understand nothing amiss. My

devotion to this fair creature is rather like what we poor
Catholics pay to the blessed saints, than mixed with any
grosser quality. Indeed, she seems rather a sylphid of
the Rosicrucian system, than aught more carnal; being
slighter, lighter, and less than the females of common life,
who have something of that coarseness of make which is
doubtless derived from the sinful and gigantic race of the
antediluvians."

"Well, say on, man," quoth Charles. "Didst thou not
discover this sylph to be a mere mortal wench after all?"

"Who?—I, my liege?—O, fie!"

"Nay, little gentleman, do not be so particularly scan-
dalized," said the King; "I promise you I suspect you
of no audacity of gallantry."

"Time wears fast," said the Duke of Ormond, impatiently, and looking at his watch. "Chiffinch hath been
gone ten minutes, and ten minutes will bring him back."

"True," said Charles, gravely. "Come to the point,
Hudson; and tell us what this female has to do with
your coming hither in this extraordinary manner."

"Every thing, my lord," said little Hudson. "I saw
her twice during my confinement in Newgate, and, in my
thought, she is the very angel who guards my life and
welfare; for, after my acquittal, as I walked towards the
city with two tall gentlemen, who had been in trouble
along with me, and just while we stood to our defence
against a rascally mob, and just as I had taken possession
of an elevated situation, to have some vantage against the
great odds of numbers, I heard a heavenly voice sound,
as it were, from a window behind me, counselling me to
take refuge in a certain house; to which measure I
readily persuaded my gallant friends the Peverils, who
have always shown themselves willing to be counselled
by me."

" Showing therein their wisdom at once and modesty,"
said the King.   " But what chanced next ?   Be brief—
be like thyself, man."

" For a time, sire," said the dwarf, " it seemed as if I
were not the principal object of attention.   First, the
younger Peveril was withdrawn from us by a gentleman
of venerable appearance, though somewhat smacking of a
Puritan, having boots of neat's leather, and wearing his
weapon without a sword-knot.   When Master Julian
returned, he informed us, for the first time, that we were
in the power of a body of armed fanatics, who were, as
the poet says, prompt for direful act.   And your Majesty
will remark, that both father and son were in some measure desperate, and disregardful from that moment of the
assurances which I gave them, that the star which I was
bound to worship, would, in her own time, shine forth in
signal of our safety.   May it please your Majesty, in
answer to my hilarious exhortations to confidence, the
father did but say *tush*, and the son *pshaw*, which showed
how men's prudence and manners are disturbed by affliction.   Nevertheless, these two gentlemen, the Peverils,
forming a strong opinion of the necessity there was to
break forth, were it only to convey a knowledge of these
dangerous passages to your Majesty, commenced an
assault on the door of the apartment, I also assisting with
the strength which Heaven hath given, and some threescore years have left me.   We could not, as it unhappily
proved, manage our attempt so silently, but that our
guards overheard us, and, entering in numbers, separated
us from each other, and compelled my companions, at
point of pike and poniard, to go to some other and more
distant apartment, thus separating our fair society.   I was
again enclosed in the now solitary chamber, and I will

own that I felt a certain depression of soul. But when bale is at highest, as the poet singeth, boot is at nighest, for a door of hope was suddenly opened "——

"In the name of God, my liege," said the Duke of Ormond, "let this poor creature's story be translated into the language of common sense by some of the scribblers of romances about Court, and we may be able to make meaning of it."

Geoffrey Hudson looked with a frowning countenance of reproof upon the impatient old Irish nobleman, and said, with a very dignified air, " That one Duke upon a poor gentleman's hand was enough at a time, and that, but for his present engagement and dependency with the Duke of Buckingham, he would have endured no such terms from the Duke of Ormond."

"Abate your valour, and diminish your choler, at our request, most puissant Sir Geoffrey Hudson," said the King; "and forgive the Duke of Ormond for my sake; but at all events go on with your story."

Geoffrey Hudson laid his hand on his bosom, and bowed in proud and dignified submission to his Sovereign; then waved his forgiveness gracefully to Ormond, accompanied with a horrible grin, which he designed for a smile of gracious forgiveness and conciliation. "Under the Duke's favour, then," he proceeded, "when I said a door of hope was opened to me, I meant a door behind the tapestry, from whence issued that fair vision—yet not so fair as lustrously dark, like the beauty of a continental night, where the cloudless azure sky shrouds us in a veil more lovely than that of day !—but I note your Majesty's impatience ;—enough. I followed my beautiful guide into an apartment, where there lay, strangely intermingled, warlike arms and musical instruments. Amongst

these I saw my own late place of temporary obscurity—
a violoncello. To my astonishment, she turned around
the instrument, and opening it behind by pressure of a
spring, showed that it was filled with pistols, daggers,
and ammunition made up in bandoleers. 'These,' she
said, 'are this night destined to surprise the Court of the
unwary Charles'—your Majesty must pardon my using
her own words; 'but if thou darest go in their stead,
thou mayst be the saviour of king and kingdoms; if thou
art afraid, keep secret, I will myself try the adventure.'
Now may Heaven forbid, that Geoffrey Hudson were
craven enough, said I, to let thee run such a risk! You
know not—you cannot know, what belongs to such am-
buscades and concealments—I am accustomed to them—
have lurked in the pocket of a giant, and have formed
the contents of a pasty. 'Get in then,' she said, 'and
lose no time.' Nevertheless, while I prepared to obey, I
will not deny that some cold apprehensions came over my
hot valour, and I confessed to her, if it might be so, I
would rather find my way to the palace on my own feet.
But she would not listen to me, saying hastily, ' I would
be intercepted, or refused admittance, and that I must
embrace the means she offered me of introduction into
the presence, and when there, tell the King to be on his
guard—little more is necessary ; for once the scheme is
known, it becomes desperate.' Rashly and boldly, I bid
adieu to the daylight which was then fading away. She
withdrew the contents of the instrument destined for my
concealment, and having put them behind the chimney-
board, introduced me in their room. As she clasped me
in, I implored her to warn the men who were to be intrusted with me, to take heed and keep the neck of the
violoncello uppermost; but ere I had completed my re-

quest, I found I was left alone, and in darkness. Presently, two or three fellows entered, whom, by their language, which I in some sort understood, I perceived to be Germans, and under the influence of the Duke of Buckingham. I heard them receive from the leader a charge how they were to deport themselves, when they should assume the concealed arms—and—for I will do the Duke no wrong—I understood their orders were precise, not only to spare the person of the King, but also those of the courtiers, and to protect all who might be in the presence against an irruption of the fanatics. In other respects, they had charge to disarm the Gentlemen-pensioners in the guard-room, and, in fine, to obtain the command of the Court."

The King looked disconcerted and thoughtful at this communication, and bade Lord Arlington see that Selby quietly made search into the contents of the other cases which had been brought as containing musical instruments. He then signed to the dwarf to proceed in his story, asking him again and again, and very solemnly, whether he was sure that he heard the Duke's name mentioned, as commanding or approving this action.

The dwarf answered in the affirmative.

"This," said the King, "is carrying the frolic somewhat far."

The dwarf proceeded to state, that he was carried after his metamorphosis into the chapel, where he heard the preacher seemingly about the close of his harangue, the tenor of which he also mentioned. Words, he said, could not express the agony which he felt when he found that his bearer, in placing the instrument in the corner, was about to invert its position, in which case, he said, human frailty might have proved too great for love, for loyalty, for true obedience, nay, for the fear of death, which was like to ensue on discovery; and he concluded, that he greatly doubted he could not have stood on his head for many minutes without screaming aloud.

"I could not have blamed you," said the King; "placed in such a posture in the royal oak, I must needs have roared myself.—Is this all you have to tell us of this strange conspiracy?" Sir Geoffrey Hudson replied in the affirmative, and the King presently subjoined—"Go, my little friend, your services shall not be forgotten. Since thou hast crept into the bowels of a fiddle for our service, we are bound, in duty and conscience, to find you a more roomy dwelling in future."

"It was a violoncello, if your Majesty is pleased to remember," said the little jealous man, "not a common fiddle; though, for your Majesty's service, I would have crept even into a kit."

"Whatever of that nature could have been performed by any subject of ours, thou wouldst have enacted in our behalf—of that we hold ourselves certain. Withdraw for a little; and hark ye, for the present, beware what you say about this matter. Let your appearance be considered—do you mark me—as a frolic of the Duke of Buckingham; and not a word of conspiracy."

"Were it not better to put him under some restraint, sire?" said the Duke of Ormond, when Hudson had left the room.

"It is unnecessary," said the King. "I remember the little wretch of old. Fortune, to make him the model of absurdity, has closed the most lofty soul within that little miserable carcass. For wielding his sword and keeping his word, he is a perfect Don Quixote in decimo-octavo. He shall be taken care of.—But, oddsfish, my lords, is not this freak of Buckingham too villainous and ungrateful?"

"He had not had the means of being so, had your Majesty," said the Duke of Ormond, "been less lenient on other occasions."

"My lord, my lord," said Charles, hastily—"your lordship is Buckingham's known enemy—we will take other and more impartial counsel—Arlington, what think you of all this?"

"May it please your Majesty," said Arlington, "I think the thing is absolutely impossible, unless the Duke has had some quarrel with your Majesty, of which we know nothing. His Grace is very flighty, doubtless, but this seems actual insanity."

"Why, faith," said the King, "some words passed betwixt us this morning—his Duchess it seems is dead—and to lose no time, his Grace had cast his eyes about for means of repairing the loss, and had the assurance to ask our consent to woo my niece Lady Anne."

"Which your Majesty of course rejected?" said the statesman.

"And not without rebuking his assurance," added the King.

"In private, sire, or before any witnesses?" said the Duke of Ormond.

"Before no one," said the King,—"excepting, indeed, little Chiffinch; and he, you know, is no one."

"*Hinc illæ lachrymæ*," said Ormond. "I know his Grace well. While the rebuke of his aspiring petulance was a matter betwixt your Majesty and him, he might have let it pass by; but a check before a fellow from whom it was likely enough to travel through the Court, was a matter to be revenged."

Here Selby came hastily from the other room, to say, that his Grace of Buckingham had just entered the presence chamber.

The King rose. "Let a boat be in readiness, with a party of the yeomen," said he. "It may be necessary to attach him of treason, and send him to the Tower."

"Should not a Secretary of State's warrant be prepared?" said Ormond.

"No, my Lord Duke," said the King, sharply. "I still hope that the necessity may be avoided."

CHAPTER XLVII.

High reaching Buckingham grows circumspect.

RICHARD III.

BEFORE giving the reader an account of the meeting betwixt Buckingham and his injured Sovereign, we may mention a trifling circumstance or two which took place betwixt his Grace and Chiffinch, in the short drive betwixt York-Place and Whitehall.

In the outset, the Duke endeavoured to learn from the courtier the special cause of his being summoned so hastily to the Court. Chiffinch answered, cautiously, that he believed there were some gambols going forward, at which the King desired the Duke's presence.

This did not quite satisfy Buckingham, for, conscious of his own rash purpose, he could not but apprehend discovery. After a moment's silence, " Chiffinch," he said, abruptly, " did you mention to any one what the King said to me this morning touching the Lady Anne ? "

" My Lord Duke," said Chiffinch, hesitating, " surely my duty to the King—my respect to your Grace "——

" You mentioned it to no one, then ? " said the Duke, sternly.

" To no one," replied Chiffinch, faintly, for he was intimidated by the Duke's increasing severity of manner.

" Ye lie, like a scoundrel ! " said the Duke—" You told Christian ! "

" Your Grace," said Chiffinch—" your Grace—your Grace ought to remember that I told you Christian's secret; that the Countess of Derby was come up."

" And you think the one point of treachery may balance for the other? But no. I must have a better atonement. Be assured I will blow your brains out, ere you leave this carriage, unless you tell me the truth of this message from Court."

As Chiffinch hesitated what reply to make, a man, who, by the blaze of the torches, then always borne, as well by the lackeys who hung behind the carriage, as by the footmen who ran by the side, might easily see who sat in the coach, approached, and sung in a deep manly voice, the burden of an old French song on the battle of Marignan, in which is imitated the German French of the defeated Swiss.

> " *Tout est verlore*
> *La tintelore,*
> *Tout est verlore*
> Bei Got."

" I am betrayed," said the Duke, who instantly conceived that this chorus, expressing " all is lost," was sung by one of his faithful agents, as a hint to him that their machinations were discovered.

He attempted to throw himself from the carriage, but Chiffinch held him with a firm, though respectful grasp. " Do not destroy yourself, my lord," he said, in a tone of deep humility—" there are soldiers and officers of the peace around the carriage, to enforce your Grace's coming to Whitehall, and to prevent your escape. To attempt it would be to confess guilt; and I advise you strongly against that—the King is your friend—be your own."

The Duke, after a moment's consideration, said sullenly, "I believe you are right. Why should I am guilty of nothing but sending some fireworks to entertain the Court, instead of a concert of music?"

"And the dwarf, who came so unexpectedly out of the bassviol"——

"Was a masking device of my own, Chiffinch," said the Duke, though the circumstance was then first known to him. "Chiffinch, you will bind me for ever, if you will permit me to have a minute's conversation with Christian."

"With Christian, my lord?—Where could you find him?—You are aware we must go straight on to the Court."

"True," said the Duke, "but I think I cannot miss finding him; and you, Master Chiffinch, are no officer, and have no warrant either to detain me prisoner, or prevent my speaking to whom I please."

Chiffinch replied, "My Lord Duke, your genius is so great, and your escapes so numerous, that it will be from no wish of my own if I am forced to hurt a man so skilful and so popular."

"Nay, then, there is life in it yet," said the Duke, and whistled; when, from beside the little cutler's booth, with which the reader is acquainted, appeared, suddenly, Master Christian, and was in a moment at the side of the coach. "*Ganz ist verloren*," said the Duke.

"I know it," said Christian; "and all our godly friends are dispersed upon the news. Lucky the Colonel and these German rascals gave a hint. All is safe—You go to Court—Hark ye, I will follow."

"You, Christian? that would be more friendly than wise."

"Why, what is there against me?" said Christian. "I am innocent as the child unborn—so is your Grace. There is but one creature who can bear witness to our guilt; but I trust to bring her on the stage in our favour —besides, if I went not, I should presently be sent for."

"The familiar of whom I have heard you speak, I warrant?"

"Hark in your ear again."

"I understand," said the Duke, "and will delay Master Chiffinch,—for he, you must know, is my conductor, —no longer.—Well, Chiffinch, let them drive on.— *Vogue la Galère!*" he exclaimed, as the carriage went onward; "I have sailed through worse perils than this yet."

"It is not for me to judge," said Chiffinch; "your Grace is a bold commander; and Christian hath the cunning of the devil for a pilot; but——However, I remain your Grace's poor friend, and will heartily rejoice in your extrication."

"Give me a proof of your friendship," said the Duke. "Tell me what you know of Christian's familiar, as he calls her."

"I believe it to be the same dancing wench who came with Empson to my house on the morning that Mistress Alice made her escape from us. But you have seen her, my lord?"

"I?" said the Duke; "when did I see her?"

"She was employed by Christian, I believe, to set his niece at liberty, when he found himself obliged to gratify his fanatical brother-in-law, by restoring his child; besides being prompted by a private desire, as I think, of bantering your Grace."

"Umph! I suspected so much. I will repay it," said
the Duke. "But first to get out of this dilemma.—That
little Numidian witch, then, was his familiar ; and she
joined in the plot to tantalize me?—But here we reach
Whitehall.—Now, Chiffinch, be no worse than thy word,
and—now, Buckingham, be thyself!"

But ere we follow Buckingham into the presence,
where he had so difficult a part to sustain, it may not
be amiss to follow Christian after his brief conversation
with him. On re-entering the house, which he did by a
circuitous passage, leading from a distant alley, and
through several courts, Christian hastened to a low
matted apartment, in which Bridgenorth sat alone, reading the Bible by the light of a small brazen lamp, with
the utmost serenity of countenance.

"Have you dismissed the Peverils?" said Christian,
hastily.

"I have," said the Major.

"And upon what pledge—that they will not carry information against you to Whitehall?"

"They gave me their promise voluntarily, when I
showed them our armed friends were dismissed. To-
morrow, I believe, it is their purpose to lodge informations."

"And why not to-night, I pray you?" said Christian.

"Because they allow us that time for escape."

"Why, then, do you not avail yourself of it? Wherefore are you here?" said Christian.

"Nay, rather, why do *you* not fly?" said Bridgenorth.
"Of a surety, you are as deeply engaged as I."

"Brother Bridgenorth, I am the fox, who knows a
hundred modes of deceiving the hounds; you are the
deer, whose sole resource is in hasty flight. Therefore

lose no time—begone to the country—or rather, Zede-
kiah Fish's vessel, the Good Hope, lies in the river,
bound for Massachusetts—take the wings of the morning,
and begone—she can fall down to Gravesend with the
tide."

"And leave to thee, brother Christian," said Bridgenorth, "the charge of my fortune and my daughter? No,
brother; my opinion of your good faith must be re-
established ere I again trust thee."

"Go thy ways, then, for a suspicious fool," said Christian, suppressing his strong desire to use language more
offensive; "or rather stay where thou art, and take thy
chance of the gallows!"

"It is appointed to all men to die once," said Bridgenorth; "my life hath been ·a living death. My fairest
boughs have been stripped by the axe of the forester—
that which survives must, if it shall blossom, be grafted
elsewhere, and at a distance from my aged trunk. The
sooner, then, the root feels the axe, the stroke is more
welcome. I had been pleased, indeed, had I been called
to bringing yonder licentious Court to a purer character,
and relieving the yoke of the suffering people of God.
That youth too—son to that precious woman, to whom I
owe the last tie that feebly links my wearied spirit to
humanity—could I have travailed with *him* in the good
cause!—But that, with all my other hopes, is broken for
ever; and since I am not worthy to be an instrument in
so great a work, I have little desire to abide longer in
this vale of sorrow."

"Farewell, then, desponding fool!" said Christian, unable, with all his calmness, any longer to suppress his
contempt for the resigned and hopeless predestinarian.
"That fate should have clogged me with such confeder-

ates!" he muttered, as he left the apartment—" this bigoted fool is now nearly irreclaimable—I must to Zarah;
for she, or no one, must carry us through these straits.
If I can but soothe her sullen temper, and excite her
vanity to action,—betwixt her address, the King's par-
tiality for the Duke, Buckingham's matchless effrontery,
and my own hand upon the helm, we may yet weather
the tempest that darkens around us.   But what we do
must be hastily done."

In another apartment he found the person he sought—
the same who visited the Duke of Buckingham's harem,
and, having relieved Alice Bridgenorth from her confinement there, had occupied her place as has been already
narrated, or rather intimated.   She was now much more
plainly attired than when she had tantalized the Duke
with her presence; but her dress had still something of
the Oriental character, which corresponded with the dark
complexion and quick eye of the wearer.   She had the
kerchief at her eyes as Christian entered the apartment,
but suddenly withdrew it, and, flashing on him a glance
of scorn and indignation, asked him what he meant by
intruding where his company was alike unsought for and
undesired.

"A proper question," said Christian, "from a' slave to
her master!"

"Rather say, a proper question, and of all questions the
most proper, from a mistress to her slave!   Know you
not, that from the hour in which you discovered your in-
effable baseness, you have made me mistress of your lot?
While you seemed but a demon of vengeance, you commanded terror, and to good purpose; but such a foul
fiend as thou hast of late shown thyself—such a very
worthless, base trickster of the devil—such a sordid grov-

elling imp of perdition, can gain nothing but scorn from a soul like mine."

"Gallantly mouthed," said Christian, "and with good emphasis."

"Yes," answered Zarah, "I can speak—sometimes— I can also be mute; and that no one knows better than thou."

"Thou art a spoiled child, Zarah, and dost but abuse the indulgence I entertain for your freakish humour," replied Christian; "thy wits have been disturbed since ever you landed in England, and all for the sake of one who cares for thee no more than for the most worthless object who walks the streets, amongst whom he left you to engage in a brawl for one he loved better."

"It is no matter," said Zarah, obviously repressing very bitter emotion; "it signifies not that he loves another better; there is none—no, none—that ever did, or can, love him so well."

"I pity you, Zarah!" said Christian, with some scorn.

"I deserve your pity," she replied, "were your pity worth my accepting. Whom have I to thank for my wretchedness but you?—You bred me up in thirst of vengeance, ere I knew that good and evil were any thing better than names;—to gain your applause, and to gratify the vanity you had excited, I have for years undergone a penance, from which a thousand would have shrunk."

"A thousand, Zarah!" answered Christian; "ay, a hundred thousand, and a million to boot; the creature is not on earth, being mere mortal woman, that would have undergone the thirtieth part of thy self-denial."

"I believe it," said Zarah, drawing up her slight but elegant figure; "I believe it—I have gone through a trial that few indeed could have sustained. I have renounced the dear intercourse of my kind ; compelled my tongue only to utter, like that of a spy, the knowledge which my ear had only collected as a base eavesdropper. This I have done for years—for years—and all for the sake of your private applause—and the hope of vengeance on a woman, who, if she did ill in murdering my father, has been bitterly repaid by nourishing a serpent in her bosom, that had the tooth, but not the deafened ear, of the adder."

" Well—well—well," reiterated Christian ; " and had you not your reward in my approbation—in the consciousness of your own unequalled dexterity—by which, superior to any thing of thy sex that history has ever known, you endured what woman never before endured, insolence without notice, admiration without answer, and sarcasm without reply ? "

" Not without reply !" said Zarah, fiercely. " Gave not Nature to my feelings a course of expression more impressive than words ? and did not those tremble at my shrieks, who would have little minded my entreaties or my complaints ? And my proud lady, who sauced her charities with the taunts she thought I heard not—she was justly paid by the passing of her dearest and most secret concerns into the hands of her mortal enemy ; and the vain Earl—yet he was a thing as insignificant as the plume that nodded in his cap ;—and the maidens and ladies who taunted me—I had, or can easily have, my revenge upon them.   But there is *one*," she added, looking upward, " who never taunted me ; one whose generous feelings could treat the poor dumb girl even as his sister ; who never spoke word of her but it was to excuse or defend—and you tell me I must not love him, and that it is madness to love him !—I *will* be mad then, for I will love him till the latest breath of my life ! "

" Think but an instant, silly girl—silly but in one respect, since in all others thou mayst brave the world of
women. Think what I have proposed to thee, for the
loss of this hopeless affection, a career so brilliant !—
Think only that it rests with thyself to be the wife—the
wedded wife—of the princely Buckingham ! With my
talents—with thy wit and beauty—with his passionate
love of these attributes—a short space might rank you
among England's princesses.—Be but guided by me—he
is now at a deadly pass—needs every assistance to retrieve
his fortunes—above all, that which we alone can render
him. Put yourself under my conduct, and not fate itself
shall prevent your wearing a Duchess's coronet." '

" A coronet of thistle-down, entwined with thistle-
leaves," said Zarah.—" I know not a slighter thing than
your Buckingham ! I saw him at your request—saw
him when, as a man, he should have shown himself generous and noble—I stood the proof at your desire, for I
laugh at those dangers from which the poor blushing
wailers of my sex shrink and withdraw themselves.
What did I find him ?—a poor wavering voluptuary—
his nearest attempt to passion like the fire on a wretched
stubble-field, that may singe, indeed, or smoke, but can
neither warm nor devour. Christian ! were his coronet
at my feet this moment, I would sooner take up a crown
of gilded gingerbread, than extend my hand to raise it."

" You are mad, Zarah—with all your taste and talent,
you are utterly mad ! But let Buckingham pass—Do
you owe *me* nothing on this emergency ?—Nothing to
one who rescued you from the cruelty of your owner, the
posture-master, to place you in ease and affluence ? "

" Christian," she replied, " I owe you much. Had I
not felt I did so, I would, as I have been often tempted to

do, have denounced thee to the fierce Countess, who would have gibbeted you on her feudal walls of Castle-Rushin, and bid your family seek redress from the eagles, that would long since have thatched their nest with your hair, and fed their young ospreys with your flesh."

" I am truly glad you have had so much forbearance for me," answered Christian.

" I have it, in truth and in sincerity," replied Zarah— " Not for your benefits to me—such as they were, they were every one interested, and conferred from the most selfish considerations. I have overpaid them a thousand times by the devotion to your will, which I have displayed at the greatest personal risk. But till of late I respected your powers of mind—your inimitable command of passion—the force of intellect which I have ever seen you exercise over all others, from the bigot Bridgenorth to the debauched Buckingham—in that, indeed, I have recognised my master."

" And those powers," said Christian, " are unlimited as ever; and with thy assistance, thou shalt see the strongest meshes that the laws of civil society ever wove to limit the natural dignity of man, broke asunder like a spider's web."

She paused and answered, " While a noble motive fired thee—ay, a noble motive, though irregular—for I was born to gaze on the sun which the pale daughters of Europe shrink from—I could serve thee—I could have followed, while revenge or ambition had guided thee— but love of *wealth*, and by what means acquired !—What sympathy can I hold with that ?—Wouldst thou not have pandered to the lust of the King, though the object was thine own orphan niece ?—You smile ?—Smile again when I ask you whether you meant not my own prostitution, when you charged me to remain in the house of that wretched Buckingham?—Smile at that question, and by Heaven I stab you to the heart!" And she thrust her hand into her bosom, and partly showed the hilt of a small poniard.

"And if I smile," said Christian, "it is but in scorn of so odious an accusation. Girl, I will not tell thee the reason, but there exists not on earth the living thing over whose safety and honour I would keep watch as over thine. Buckingham's wife, indeed, I wished thee ; and, through thy own beauty and thy wit, I doubted not to bring the match to pass."

"Vain flatterer," said Zarah, yet seeming soothed even by the flattery which she scoffed at, "you would persuade me that it was honourable love which you expected the Duke was to have offered me. How durst you urge so gross a deception, to which time, place, and circumstance, gave the lie?—How dare you now again mention it, when you well know, that at the time you mention, the Duchess was still in life?"

"In life, but on her deathbed," said Christian; "and for time, place, and circumstance, had your virtue, my Zarah, depended on these, how couldst thou have been the creature thou art? I knew thee all-sufficient to bid him defiance—else—for thou art dearer to me than thou thinkest—I had not risked thee to win the Duke of Buckingham; ay, and the kingdom of England to boot.—So now, wilt thou be ruled and go on with me?"

Zarah, or Fenella, for our readers must have been long aware of the identity of these two personages, cast down her eyes, and was silent for a long time. "Christian," she said at last, in a solemn voice, "if my ideas of right and of wrong be wild and incoherent, I owe it, first, to the wild fever which my native sun communicated to my veins; next, to my childhood, trained amidst the shifts, tricks, and feats of jugglers and mountebanks; and then, to a youth of fraud and deception, through the course thou didst prescribe me, in which, I might, indeed, hear every thing, but communicate with no one. The last cause of my wild errors, if such they are, originates, O Christian, with you alone; by whose intrigues I was placed with yonder lady, and who taught me, that to revenge my father's death, was my first great duty on earth, and that I was bound by nature to hate and injure her by whom I was fed and fostered, though as she would have fed and caressed a dog, or any other mute animal. I also think—for I will deal fairly with you—that you had not so easily detected your niece, in the child whose surprising agility was making yonder brutal mountebank's fortune; nor so readily induced him to part with his bond-slave, had you not, for your own purposes, placed me under his charge, and reserved the privilege of claiming me when you pleased. I could not, under any other tuition, have identified myself with the personage of a mute, which it has been your desire that I should perform through life."

"You do me injustice, Zarah," said Christian—"I found you capable of discharging, to an uncommon degree, a task necessary to the avenging of your father's death—I consecrated you to it, as I consecrated my own life and hopes; and you held the duty sacred, till these mad feelings towards a youth who loves your cousin"——

"Who—loves—my—cousin," repeated Zarah, (for we

will continue to call her by her real name,) slowly, and
as if the words dropped unconsciously from her lips.
"Well—be it so!—Man of many wiles, I will follow
thy course for a little, a very little farther; but take
heed—tease me not with remonstrances against the
treasure of my secret thoughts—I mean my most hopeless affection to Julian Peveril—and bring me not as an
assistant to any snare which you may design to cast
around him. You and your Duke shall rue the hour
most bitterly, in which you provoke me. You may suppose you have me in your power; but remember, the
snakes of my burning climate are never so fatal as when
you grasp them."

"I care not for these Peverils," said Christian—"I
care not for their fate a poor straw, unless where it bears
on that of the destined woman, whose hands are red in
your father's blood. Believe me, I can divide her fate
and theirs. I will explain to you how. And for the
Duke, he may pass among men of the town for wit, and
among soldiers for valour, among courtiers for manners
and for form; and why, with his high rank and immense
fortune, you should throw away an opportunity, which,
as I could now improve it"——

"Speak not of it," said Zarah, "if thou wouldst have
our truce—remember it is no peace—if, I say, thou
wouldst have our truce grow to be an hour old!"

"This, then," said Christian, with a last effort to work
upon the vanity of this singular being, "is she who pretended such superiority to human passion, that she could
walk indifferently and unmoved through the halls of the
prosperous, and the prison cells of the captive, unknow-
ing and unknown, sympathizing neither with the pleasures of the one, nor the woes of the other, but advancing

with sure, though silent steps, her own plans, in despite and regardless of either!"

"My own plans!" said Zarah—" *Thy* plans, Christian—thy plans of extorting from the surprised prisoners, means whereby to convict them—thine own plans, formed with those more powerful than thyself, to sound men's secrets, and, by using them as matter of accusation, to keep up the great delusion of the nation."

"Such access was indeed given you as my agent," said Christian, "and for advancing a great national change. But how did you use it?—to advance your own insane passion."

"Insane!" said Zarah—"Had he been less than insane whom I addressed, he and I had ere now been far from the toils which you have pitched for us both. I had means prepared for every thing; and ere this, the shores of Britain had been lost to our sight for ever."

"The miserable dwarf, too," said Christian—"Was it worthy of you to delude that poor creature with flattering visions—lull him asleep with drugs! Was *that* my doing?"

"He was my destined tool," said Zarah, haughtily. "I remembered your lessons too well not to use him as such. Yet scorn him not too much. I tell you, that yon very miserable dwarf, whom I made my sport in the prison—yon wretched abortion of nature, I would select for a husband, ere I would marry your Buckingham;—the vain and imbecile pigmy has yet the warm heart and noble feelings, that a man should hold his highest honour."

"In God's name, then, take your own way," said Christian; "and, for my sake, let never man hereafter limit a woman in the use of her tongue, since he must make it amply up to her, in allowing her the privilege of her own will. Who would have thought it? But the colt has slipped the bridle, and I must needs follow, since I cannot guide her."

Our narrative returns to the Court of King Charles at Whitehall.

CHAPTER XLVIII.

——— But O !
What shall I say to thee, Lord Scroop; thou cruel,
Ingrateful, savage, and inhuman creature!
Thou that didst bear the key of all my counsels,
That knew'st the very bottom of my soul,
That almost might'st have coined me into gold,
Wouldst thou have practised on me for thy use?

HENRY V.

AT no period of his life, not even when that life was
in imminent danger, did the constitutional gaiety of
Charles seem more overclouded, than when waiting for
the return of Chiffinch with the Duke of Buckingham.
His mind revolted at the idea, that the person to whom
he had been so particularly indulgent, and whom he had
selected as the friend of his lighter hours and amuse-
ments, should prove capable of having tampered with a
plot apparently directed against his liberty and life.   He
more than once examined the dwarf anew, but could ex-
tract nothing more than his first narrative contained.   The
apparition of the female to him in the cell of Newgate, he
described in such fanciful and romantic colours, that the
King could not help thinking the poor man's head a little
turned ; and, as nothing was found in the kettledrum, and
other musical instruments brought for the use of the
Duke's band of foreigners, he nourished some slight hope
that the whole plan might be either a mere jest, or that
the idea of an actual conspiracy was founded in mistake.

The persons who had been dispatched to watch the motions of Mr. Weiver's congregation, brought back word that they had quietly dispersed. It was known, at the same time, that they had met in arms, but this augured no particular design of aggression, at a time when all true Protestants conceived themselves in danger of immediate massacre ; when the fathers of the city had repeatedly called out the Train-Bands, and alarmed the citizens of London, under the idea of an instant insurrection of the Catholics; and when, to sum the whole up, in the emphatic words of an alderman of the day, there was a general belief that they would all waken some unhappy morning with their throats cut. Who was to do these dire deeds, it was more difficult to suppose ; but all admitted the possibility that they might be achieved, since one Justice of the Peace was already murdered. There was, therefore, no inference of hostile intentions against the State, to be decidedly derived from a congregation of Protestants *par excellence,* military from old associations, bringing their arms with them to a place of worship, in the midst of a panic so universal.

Neither did the violent language of the minister, supposing that to be proved, absolutely infer meditated violence. The favourite parables of the preachers, and the metaphors and ornaments which they selected, were at all times of a military cast; and the taking the kingdom of heaven by storm, a strong and beautiful metaphor, when used generally as in Scripture, was detailed in their sermons in all the technical language of the attack and defence of a fortified place. The danger, in short, whatever might have been its actual degree, had disappeared as suddenly as a bubble upon the water, when broken by a casual touch, and had left as little trace behind it. It became, therefore, matter of much doubt, whether it had ever actually existed.

While various reports were making from without, and while their tenor was discussed by the King, and such nobles and statesmen as he thought proper to consult on the occasion, a gradual sadness and anxiety mingled with, and finally silenced, the mirth of the evening. All became sensible that something unusual was going forward ; and the unwonted distance which Charles maintained from his guests, while it added greatly to the dulness that began to predominate in the presence-chamber, ' gave intimation that something unusual was labouring in the King's mind.

Thus play was neglected—the music was silent, or played without being heard—gallants ceased to make compliments, and ladies to expect them; and a sort of apprehensive curiosity pervaded the circle. Each asked the others why they were grave; and no answer was returned, any more than could have been rendered by a herd of cattle instinctively disturbed by the approach of a thunder-storm.

To add to the general apprehension, it began to be whispered, that one or two of the guests, who were desirous of leaving the palace, had been informed no one could be permitted to retire until the general hour of dismissal. And these, gliding back into the hall, communicated in whispers that the sentinels at the gates were doubled, and that there was a troop of the Horse Guards drawn up in the court—circumstances so unusual, as to excite the most anxious curiosity.

Such was the state of the Court, when wheels were heard without, and the bustle which took place denoted the arrival of some person of consequence."

"Here comes Chiffinch," said the King, "with his prey in his clutch."

It was indeed the Duke of Buckingham; nor did he approach the royal presence without emotion. On entering the court, the flambeaux which were borne around the carriage gleamed on the scarlet coats, laced hats, and drawn broadswords of the Horse Guards—a sight unusual, and calculated to strike terror into a conscience which was none of the clearest.

The Duke alighted from the carriage, and only said to the officer, whom he saw upon duty, "You are late under arms to-night, Captain Carleton."

"Such are our orders, sir," answered Carleton, with military brevity; and then commanded the four dismounted sentinels at the under gate to make way for the Duke of Buckingham. His Grace had no sooner entered, than he heard behind him the command, "Move close up, sentinels—closer yet to the gate." And he felt as if all chance of rescue were excluded by the sound.

As he advanced up the grand staircase, there were other symptoms of alarm and precaution. The Yeomen of the Guard were mustered in unusual numbers, and carried carabines instead of their halberds; and the Gentlemen Pensioners, with their partisans, appeared also in proportional force. In short, all that sort of defence which the royal household possesses within itself, seemed, for some hasty and urgent reason, to have been placed under arms, and upon duty.

Buckingham ascended the royal staircase with an eye attentive to these preparations, and a step steady and slow, as if he counted each step on which he trode. "Who," he asked himself, "shall ensure Christian's fidelity? Let him but stand fast and we are secure. Otherwise "——

As he shaped the alternative, he entered the presence-chamber.

The King stood in the midst of the apartment, surrounded by the personages with whom he had been consulting. The rest of the brilliant assembly, scattered into groups, looked on at some distance. All were silent when Buckingham entered, in hopes of receiving some explanation of the mysteries of the evening. All bent forward, though etiquette forbade them to advance, to catch, if possible, something of what was about to pass betwixt the King and his intriguing statesman. At the same time, those counsellors who stood around Charles, drew back on either side, so as to permit the Duke to pay his respects to his Majesty in the usual form. He went through the ceremonial with his accustomed grace, but was received by Charles with much unwonted gravity.

" We have waited for you for some time, my Lord Duke. It is long since Chiffinch left us, to request your attendance here. I see you are elaborately dressed. Your toilette was needless on the present occasion."

" Needless to the splendour of your Majesty's Court," said the Duke, " but not needless on my part. This chanced to be Black Monday at York-Place, and my club of *Pendables* were in full glee when your Majesty's summons arrived. I could not be in the company of Ogle, Maniduc, Dawson, and so forth, but what I must needs make some preparation, and some ablution ere entering the circle here."

" I trust the purification will be complete," said the King, without any tendency to the smile which always softened features, that, ungilded by its influence, were dark, harsh, and even severe. " We wished to ask your Grace concerning the import of a sort of musical mask which you designed us here, but which miscarried, as we are given to understand."

" It must have been a great miscarriage indeed," said the Duke, " since your Majesty looks so serious on it. I thought to have done your Majesty a pleasure, (as I have seen you condescend to be pleased with such passages,) by sending the contents of that bass-viol; but I fear the jest has been unacceptable—I fear the fireworks may have done mischief."

" Not the mischief they were designed for, perhaps," said the King, gravely; "you see, my lord, we are all alive, and unsinged."

" Long may your Majesty remain so," said the Duke; " yet I see there is something misconstrued on my part —it must be a matter unpardonable, however little intended, since it hath displeased so indulgent a master."

" Too indulgent a master, indeed, Buckingham," replied the King; "and the fruit of my indulgence has been to change loyal men into traitors."

" May it please your Majesty, I cannot understand this," said the Duke.

" Follow us, my lord," answered Charles, " and we will endeavour to explain our meaning."

Attended by the same lords who stood around him, and followed by the Duke of Buckingham, on whom all eyes were fixed, Charles retired into the same cabinet which had been the scene of repeated consultations in the course of the evening. There, leaning with his arms crossed on the back of an easy-chair, Charles proceeded to interrogate the suspected nobleman.

" Let us be plain with each other. Speak out, Buckingham. What, in one word, was to have been the regale intended for us this evening?"

"A petty mask, my lord. I had destined a little dancing-girl to come out of that instrument, who, I thought, would have performed to your Majesty's liking—a few Chinese fireworks there were, which, thinking the entertainment was to have taken place in the marble hall, might, I hoped, have been discharged with good effect, and without the slightest alarm, at the first appearance of my little sorceress, and were designed to have masked, as it were, her entrance upon the stage. I hope there have been no perukes singed—no ladies frightened—no hopes of noble descent interrupted by my ill-fancied jest."

"We have seen no such fireworks, my lord; and your female dancer, of whom we now hear for the first time, came forth in the form of our old acquaintance Geoffrey Hudson, whose dancing days are surely ended."

"Your Majesty surprises me! I beseech you, let Christian be sent for—Edward Christian—he will be found lodging in a large old house near Sharper the cutler's, in the Strand. As I live by bread, sire, I trusted him with the arrangement of this matter, as indeed the dancing-girl was his property. If he has done aught to dishonour my concert, or disparage my character, he shall die under the baton."

"It is singular," said the King, "and I have often observed it, that this fellow Christian bears the blame of all men's enormities—he performs the part which, in a great family, is usually assigned to that mischief-doing personage, Nobody. When Chiffinch blunders, he always quotes Christian. When Sheffield writes a lampoon, I am sure to hear of Christian having corrected, or copied, or dispersed it—he is the *ame damnée* of every one about my Court—the scapegoat, who is to carry away all their iniquities; and he will have a cruel load to bear into the wilderness. But for Buckingham's sins, in particular, he is the regular and uniform sponsor; and I am convinced his Grace expects Christian should suffer every penalty which he has incurred, in this world or the next."

" Not so," with the deepest reverence replied the Duke. " I have no hope of being either hanged or damned by proxy; but it is clear some one hath tampered with and altered my device. If I am accused of aught, let me at least hear the charge, and see my accuser."

" That is but fair," said the King. " Bring our little friend from behind the chimney-board. [Hudson being accordingly produced, he continued.] There stands the Duke of Buckingham. Repeat before him the tale you told us. Let him hear what were those contents of the bass-viol which were removed that you might enter it. Be not afraid of any one, but speak the truth boldly."

" May it please your Majesty," said Hudson, " fear is a thing unknown to me."

" His body has no room to hold such a passion ; or there is too little of it to be worth fearing for," said Buckingham.—" But let him speak."

Ere Hudson had completed his tale, Buckingham interrupted him by exclaiming, " Is it possible that I can be suspected by your Majesty on the word of this pitiful variety of the baboon tribe ? "

" Villain-Lord, I appeal thee to the combat!" said the little man, highly offended at the appellation thus bestowed on him.

" La you there now!" said the Duke—" The little animal is quite crazed, and defies a man who need ask no other weapon than a corking-pin to run him through the lungs, and whose single kick could hoist him from Dover to Calais without yacht or wherry. And what

can you expect from an idiot, who is *engoué* of a common
rope-dancing girl, that capered on a packthread at Ghent
in Flanders, unless they were to club their talents to set
up a booth at Bartholomew-Fair?—Is it not plain, that
supposing the little animal is not malicious, as indeed his
whole kind bear a general and most cankered malice
against those who have the ordinary proportions of humanity—Grant, I say, that this were not a malicious
falsehood of his, why, what does it amount to?—That he
has mistaken squibs and Chinese crackers for arms! He
says not he himself touched or handled them; and judging by the sight alone, I question if the infirm old creature, when any whim or preconception hath possession
of his noddle, can distinguish betwixt a blunderbuss and a
black-pudding."

The horrible clamour which the dwarf made so soon
as he heard this disparagement of his military skill—the
haste with which he blundered out a detail of his warlike
experiences—and the absurd grimaces which he made in
order to enforce his story, provoked not only the risibility
of Charles, but even of the statesmen around him, and
added absurdity to the motley complexion of the scene.
The King terminated this dispute, by commanding the
dwarf to withdraw.

A more regular discussion of his evidence was then
resumed, and Ormond was the first who pointed out, that
it went farther than had been noticed, since the little man
had mentioned a certain extraordinary and treasonable
conversation held by the Duke's dependents, by whom
he had been conveyed to the palace.

"I am sure not to lack my lord of Ormond's good
word," said the Duke, scornfully; " but I defy him alike,
and all my other enemies, and shall find it easy to show

that this alleged conspiracy, if any grounds for it at all exist, is a mere sham-plot, got up to turn the odium justly attached to the Papists upon the Protestants. Here is a half-hanged creature, who, on the very day he escapes from the gallows, which many believe was his most deserved destiny, comes to take away the reputation of a Protestant Peer—and, on what?—on the treasonable conversation of three or four German fiddlers, heard through the sound-holes of a violoncello, and that, too, when the creature was incased in it, and mounted on a man's shoulders! The urchin, too, in repeating their language, shows he understands German as little as my horse does; and if he did rightly hear, truly comprehend, and accurately report what they said, still, is my honour to be touched by the language held by such persons as these are, with whom I have never communicated, otherwise than men of my rank do with those of their calling and capacity?—Pardon me, sire, if I presume to say, that the profound statesmen who endeavoured to stifle the Popish conspiracy by the pretended Meal-tub Plot, will take little more credit by their figments about fiddles and concertos."

The assistant counsellors looked at each other; and Charles turned on his heel, and walked through the room with long steps.

At this period the Peverils, father and son, were announced to have reached the palace, and were ordered into the royal presence.

These gentlemen had received the royal mandate at a moment of great interest. After being dismissed from their confinement by the elder Bridgenorth, in the manner and upon the terms which the reader must have gathered from the conversation of the latter with Chris-

tian, they reached the lodgings of Lady Peveril, who
awaited them with joy, mingled with terror and uncertainty. The news of the acquittal had reached her by
the exertions of the faithful Lance Outram, but her mind
had been since harassed by the long delay of their appearance, and rumours of disturbances which had taken
place in Fleet Street and in the Strand.

When the first rapturous meeting was over, Lady
Peveril, with an anxious look towards her son, as if recommending caution, said she was now about to present to
him the daughter of an old friend, whom he had *never*
(there was an emphasis on the word) seen before. "This
young lady," she continued, "was the only child of Colonel Mitford, in North Wales, who had sent her to remain
under her guardianship for an interval, finding himself
unequal to attempt the task of her education."

"Ay, ay," said Sir Geoffrey, "Dick Mitford must be
old now—beyond the threescore and ten, I think. He
was no chicken, though a cock of the game, when he
joined the Marquis of Hertford at Namptwich with two
hundred wild Welshmen.—Before George, Julian, I love
that girl as if she was my own flesh and blood ! Lady
Peveril would never have got through this work without
her ; and Dick Mitford sent me a thousand pieces, too, in
excellent time, when there was scarce a cross to keep the
devil from dancing in our pockets, much more for these
law-doings. I used it without scruple, for there is wood
ready to be cut at Martindale when we get down there,
and Dick Mitford knows I would have done the like for
him. Strange that he should have been the only one of
my friends to reflect I might want a few pieces."

Whilst Sir Geoffrey thus run on, the meeting betwixt
Alice and Julian Peveril was accomplished, without any

particular notice on his side, except to say, " Kiss her,
Julian—kiss her.   What the devil! is that the way you
learned to accost a lady at the Isle of Man, as if her lips
were a red-hot horseshoe ?—And do not you be offended,
my pretty one ; Julian is naturally bashful, and has been
bred by an old lady, but you will find him, by and by, as
gallant as thou hast found me, my princess.—And now,
Dame Peveril, to dinner, to dinner ! the old fox must
have his belly-timber, though the hounds have been after
him the whole day."

Lance, whose joyous congratulations were next to be
undergone, had the consideration to cut them short, in
order to provide a plain but hearty meal from the next
cook's shop, at which Julian sat like one enchanted, betwixt his mistress and his mother. He easily conceived
that the last was the confidential friend to whom Bridgenorth had finally committed the charge of his daughter,
and his only anxiety now was, to anticipate the confusion
that was likely to arise when her real parentage was
made known to his father.   Wisely, however, he suffered
not these anticipations to interfere with the delight of his
present situation, in the course of which, many slight but
delightful tokens of recognition were exchanged, without
censure, under the eye of Lady Peveril, under cover of
the boisterous mirth of the old Baronet, who spoke for
two, ate for four, and drank wine for half a dozen.   His
progress in the latter exercise might have proceeded rather
too far, had he not been interrupted by a gentleman bearing the King's orders, that he should instantly attend upon
the presence at Whitehall, and bring his son along with
him.

Lady Peveril was alarmed, and Alice grew pale with
sympathetic anxiety ; but the old Knight, who never saw

more than what lay straight before him, set it down to the
King's hasty anxiety to congratulate him on his escape;
an interest on his Majesty's part which he considered by
no means extravagant, conscious that it was reciprocal on
his own side. It came upon him, indeed, with the more
joyful surprise that he had received a previous hint, ere
he left the court of justice, that it would be prudent in
him to go down to Martindale before presenting himself
at Court,—a restriction which he supposed as repugnant
to his Majesty's feelings as it was to his own.

While he consulted with Lance Outram about cleaning
his buff-belt and sword-hilt, as well as time admitted,
Lady Peveril had the means to give Julian more distinct
information, that Alice was under her protection by her
father's authority, and with his consent to their union, if
it could be accomplished. She added that it was her determination to employ the mediation of the Countess of
Derby, to overcome the obstacles which might be foreseen
on the part of Sir Geoffrey.

CHAPTER XLIX.

In the King's name,
Let fall your swords and daggers!
CRITIC.

WHEN the father and son entered the cabinet of audience, it was easily visible that Sir Geoffrey had obeyed
the summons as he would have done the trumpet's call to
horse; and his dishevelled gray locks and half-arranged
dress, though they showed zeal and haste, such as he would
have used when Charles I. called him to attend a council
of war, seemed rather indecorous in a pacific drawing-
room. He paused at the door of the cabinet, but when
the King called on him to advance, came hastily forward,
with every feeling of his earlier and later life afloat and
contending in his memory, threw himself on his knees
before the King, seized his hand, and, without even an
effort to speak, wept aloud. Charles, who generally felt
deeply so long as an impressive object was before his
eyes, indulged for a moment the old man's rapture.—
"My good Sir Geoffrey," he said, "you have had some
hard measure; we owe you amends, and will find time to
pay our debt."

"No suffering—no debt," said the old man; "I cared
not what the rogues said of me—I knew they could
never get twelve honest fellows to believe a word of their
most damnable lies. I did long to beat them when they

called me traitor to your Majesty—that I confess—But to have such an early opportunity of paying my duty to your Majesty, overpays it all. The villains would have persuaded me I ought not to come to court—aha! "

The Duke of Ormond perceived that the King coloured much; for in truth it was from the Court that the private intimation had been given to Sir Geoffrey to go down to the country, without appearing at Whitehall; and he, moreover, suspected that the jolly old Knight had not risen from his dinner altogether dry-lipped, after the fatigues of a day so agitating.—" My old friend," he whispered, " you forget that your son is to be presented—permit me to have that honour."

" I crave your Grace's pardon humbly," said Sir Geoffrey, "but it is an honour I design for myself, as I apprehend no one can so utterly surrender and deliver him up to his Majesty's service as the father that begot him is entitled to do.—Julian, come forward, and kneel.—Here he is, please your Majesty—Julian Peveril—a chip of the old block—as stout, though scarce so tall a tree, as the old trunk, when at the freshest. Take him to you, sir, for a faithful servant, *à vendre et à pendre*, as the French say; if he fears fire or steel, axe or gallows, in your Majesty's service, I renounce him—he is no son of mine—I disown him, and he may go to the Isle of Man, the Isle of Dogs, or the Isle of Devils, for what I care."

Charles winked to Ormond, and having, with his wonted courtesy, expressed his thorough conviction that Julian would imitate the loyalty of his ancestors, and especially of his father, added, that he believed his Grace of Ormond had something to communicate which was of consequence to his service. Sir Geoffrey made his military reverence at this hint, and marched off in the rear of the Duke, who proceeded to inquire of him concerning the events of the day. Charles, in the meanwhile, having, in the first place, ascertained that the son was not in the same genial condition with the father, demanded and received from him a precise account of all the proceedings subsequent to the trial.

Julian, with the plainness and precision which such a subject demanded, when treated in such a presence, narrated all that had happened down to the entrance of Bridgenorth; and his Majesty was so much pleased with his manner, that he congratulated Arlington on their having gained the evidence of at least one man of sense to these dark and mysterious events. But when Bridgenorth was brought upon the scene, Julian hesitated to bestow a name upon him; and although he mentioned the chapel which he had seen filled with men in arms, and the violent language of the preacher, he added, with earnestness, that, notwithstanding all this, the men departed without coming to any extremity, and had all left the place before his father and he were set at liberty.

"And you retired quietly to your dinner in Fleet Street, young man," said the King, severely, "without giving a magistrate notice of the dangerous meeting which was held in the vicinity of our palace, and who did not conceal their intention of proceeding to extremities?"

Peveril blushed, and was silent. The King frowned, and stepped aside to communicate with Ormond, who reported that the father seemed to have known nothing of the matter.

"And the son, I am sorry to say," said the King, "seems more unwilling to speak the truth than I should have expected. We have all variety of evidence in this singular investigation—a mad witness like the dwarf, a drunken witness like the father, and now a dumb witness. —Young man," he continued, addressing Julian, " your behaviour is less frank than I expected from your father's son. I must know who this person is with whom you held such familiar intercourse—you know him, I presume ? "

Julian acknowledged that he did, but, kneeling on one knee, entreated his Majesty's forgiveness for concealing his name; " he had been freed," he said, " from his confinement, on promising to that effect."

" That was a promise made, by your own account, under compulsion," answered the King. " and I cannot authorize your keeping it; it is your duty to speak the truth—if you are afraid of Buckingham, the Duke shall withdraw."

" I have no reason to fear the Duke of Buckingham," said Peveril; " that I had an affair with one of his household, was the man's own fault and not mine."

" Oddsfish !" said the King, " the light begins to break in on me—I thought I remembered thy physiognomy. Wert thou not the very fellow whom I met at Chiffinch's yonder morning ?—The matter escaped me since ; but now I recollect thou saidst then, that thou wert the son of that jolly old three-bottle Baronet yonder."

" It is true," said Julian, " that I met your Majesty at Master Chiffinch's, and I am afraid had the misfortune to displease you ; but "——

" No more of that, young man—no more of that—But I recollect you had with you that beautiful dancing siren. —Buckingham, I will hold you gold to silver, that she was the intended tenant of that bass-fiddle ? "

" Your Majesty has rightly guessed it," said the Duke;

"and I suspect she has put a trick upon me, by substituting the dwarf in her place; for Christian thinks "——

"Damn Christian!" said the King hastily—"I wish they would bring him hither, that universal referee."— And as the wish was uttered, Christian's arrival was announced. "Let him attend," said the King: "But hark —a thought strikes me.—Here, Master Peveril—yonder dancing maiden that introduced you to us by the singular agility of her performance, is she not, by your account, a dependent on the Countess of Derby?"

"I have known her such for years," answered Julian.

"Then will we call the Countess hither," said the King: "It is fit we should learn who this little fairy really is; and if she be now so absolutely at the beck of Buckingham, and this Master Christian of his—why I think it would be but charity to let her ladyship know so much, since I question if she will wish, in that case, to retain her in her service. Besides," he continued, speaking apart, "this Julian, to whom suspicion attaches in these matters from his obstinate silence, is also of the Countess's household. We will sift this matter to the bottom, and do justice to all."

The Countess of Derby, hastily summoned, entered the royal closet at one door, just as Christian and Zarah, or Fenella, were ushered in by the other. The old Knight of Martindale, who had ere this returned to the presence, was scarce controlled, even by the signs which she made, so much was he desirous of greeting his old friend; but as Ormond laid a kind restraining hand upon his arm, he was prevailed on to sit still.

The Countess, after a deep reverence to the King, acknowledged the rest of the nobility present by a slighter reverence, smiled to Julian Peveril, and looked with sur-

prise at the unexpected apparition of Fenella. Buckingham bit his lip, for he saw the introduction of Lady Derby
was likely to confuse and embroil every preparation which
he had arranged for his defence; and he stole a glance at
Christian, whose eye, when fixed on the Countess, assumed
the deadly sharpness which sparkles in the adder's, while
his cheek grew almost black under the influence of strong
emotion.

" Is there any one in this presence whom your ladyship
recognises," said the King, graciously, " besides your old
friends of Ormond and Arlington ? "

" I see, my liege, two worthy friends of my husband's
house," replied the Countess ; " Sir Geoffrey Peveril and
his son—the latter a distinguished member of my son's
household."

" Any one else ? " continued the King.

" An unfortunate female of my family, who disappeared
from the Island of Marr at the same time when Julian
Peveril left it upon business of importance. She was
thought to have fallen from the cliff into the sea."

" Had your ladyship any reason to suspect—pardon
me," said the King, " for putting such a question—any
improper intimacy between Master Peveril and this same
female attendant ? "

" My liege," said the Countess, colouring indignantly,
" my household is of reputation."

" Nay, my lady, be not angry," said the King ; " I did
but ask—such things will befall in the best regulated
families."

" Not in mine, sire," said the Countess. " Besides that,
in common pride and in common honesty, Julian Peveril
is incapable of intriguing with an unhappy creature,
removed by her misfortune almost beyond the limits of
humanity."

Zarah looked at her, and compressed her lips, as if to keep in the words that would fain break from them.

" I know not how it is," said the King—"What your ladyship says may be true in the main, yet men's tastes have strange vagaries. This girl is lost in Man so soon as the youth leaves it, and is found in Saint James's Park, bouncing and dancing like a fairy, so soon as he appears in London."

" Impossible ! " said the Countess ; "she cannot dance."

" I believe," said the King, " she can do more feats than your ladyship either suspects or would approve of."

The Countess drew up, and was indignantly silent.

The King proceeded—"No sooner is Peveril in Newgate, than, by the account of the venerable little gentleman, this merry maiden is even there also for company. Now, without inquiring how she got in, I think charitably that she had better taste than to come there on the dwarf's account.—Ah ha! I think Master Julian is touched in conscience ! "

Julian did indeed start as the King spoke, for it reminded him of the midnight visit in his cell.

The King looked fixedly at him, and then proceeded— " Well, gentlemen, Peveril is carried to his trial, and is no sooner at liberty, than we find him in the house where the Duke of Buckingham was arranging what he calls a musical mask.—Egad, I hold it next to certain, that this wench put the change on his Grace, and popt the poor dwarf into the bass-viol, reserving her own more precious hours to be spent with Master Julian Peveril.—Think you not so, Sir Christian, you, the universal referee ?   Is there any truth in this conjecture ? "

Christian stole a glance on Zarah, and read that in her eye which embarrassed him.   " He did not know," he

said; " he had indeed engaged this unrivalled performer
to take the proposed part in the mask ; and she was to
have come forth in the midst of a shower of lambent fire,
very artificially prepared with perfumes, to overcome the
smell of the powder ; but he knew not why—excepting
that she was wilful and capricious, like all great geniuses
—she had certainly spoiled the concert by cramming in
that more bulky dwarf."

" I should like," said the King, " to see this little maiden
stand forth, and bear witness, in such manner as she can
express herself, on this mysterious matter. Can any one
here understand her mode of communication ? "

Christian said, he knew something of it since he had
become acquainted with her in London. The Countess
spoke not till the King asked her, and then owned dryly,
that she had necessarily some habitual means of intercourse with one who had been immediately about her
person for so many years.

" I should think," said Charles, " that this same Master
Julian Peveril has the more direct key to her language,
after all we have heard."

The King looked first at Peveril, who blushed like a
maiden at the inference which the King's remark implied,
and then suddenly turned his eyes on the supposed mute,
on whose cheek a faint colour was dying away. A moment afterwards, at a signal from the Countess, Fenella,
or Zarah, stepped forward, and having kneeled down and
kissed her lady's hand, stood with her arms folded on her
breast, with an humble air, as different from that which
she wore in the harem of the Duke of Buckingham, as that
of a Magdalene from a Judith. Yet this was the least
show of her talent of versatility, for so well did she play
the part of the dumb girl, that Buckingham, sharp as his

discernment was, remained undecided whether the creature which stood before him could possibly be the same
with her, who had, in a different dress, made such an
impression on his imagination, or indeed was the imperfect creature she now represented. She had at once all
that could mark the imperfection of hearing, and all that
could show the wonderful address by which nature so
often makes up for the deficiency. There was the lip
that trembled not at any sound—the seeming insensibility
to the conversation which passed around ; while, on the
other hand, was the quick and vivid glance, that seemed
anxious to devour the meaning of those sounds, which
she could gather no otherwise than by the motion of
the lips.

Examined after her own fashion, Zarah confirmed the
tale of Christian in all its points, and admitted that she
had deranged the project laid for a mask, by placing the
dwarf in her own stead; the cause of her doing so she
declined to assign, and the Countess pressed her no
farther.

"Every thing tells to exculpate my Lord of Buckingham," said Charles, "from so absurd an accusation ; the
dwarf's testimony is too fantastic, that of the two Peverils does not in the least affect the Duke; that of the
dumb damsel completely contradicts the possibility of his
guilt. Methinks, my lords, we should acquaint him that
he stands acquitted of a complaint, too ridiculous to have
ever been subjected to a more serious scrutiny than we
have hastily made upon this occasion."

Arlington bowed in acquiescence, but Ormond spoke
plainly.—" I should suffer, sire, in the opinion of the
Duke of Buckingham, brilliant as his talents are known
to be, should I say that I am satisfied in my own mind on

this occasion.   But I subscribe to the spirit of the times ;
and I agree it would be highly dangerous, on such accusations as we have been able to collect, to impeach the character of a zealous Protestant like his Grace—Had he
been a Catholic, under such circumstances of suspicion,
the Tower had been too good a prison for him."

Buckingham bowed to the Duke of Ormond, with a
meaning which even his triumph could not disguise.—
" *Tu me la pagherai !* " he muttered, in a tone of deep
and abiding resentment ; but the stout old Irishman, who
had long since braved his utmost wrath, cared little for
this expression of his displeasure.

The King then, signing to the other nobles to pass into
the public apartments, stopped Buckingham as he was
about to follow them ; and when they were alone, asked,
with a significant tone, which brought all the blood in the
Duke's veins into his countenance, " When was it,
George, that your useful friend Colonel Blood * became

* This person, who was capable of framing and carrying into execution the most desperate enterprises, was one of those extraordinary
characters, who can only arise amid the bloodshed, confusion, destruction of morality, and wide-spreading violence, which take place during civil war.   We cannot, perhaps, enter upon a subject more extraordinary or entertaining, than the history of this notorious desperado,
who exhibited all the elements of a most accomplished ruffian.   As
the account of these adventures is scattered in various and scarce pub-
lications, it will probably be a service to the reader to bring the most
remarkable of them under his eye, in a simultaneous point of view.
  Blood's father is reported to have been a blacksmith; but this was
only a disparaging mode of describing a person who had a concern in
iron-works, and had thus acquired independence.   He entered early
in life into the Civil War, served as a lieutenant in the Parliament
forces, and was put by Henry Cromwell, Lord Deputy of Ireland, into
the commission of the peace, when he was scarcely two-and-twenty.
This outset in life decided his political party for ever; and however
unfit the principles of such a man rendered him for the society of
those who professed a rigidity of religion and morals, so useful was

a musician?—You are silent," he said; " do not deny the charge, for yonder villain, once seen, is remembered for ever.   Down, down on your knees, George, and acknowledge that you have abused my easy temper.—Seek for

Blood's rapidity of invention, and so well was he known, that he was held capable of framing with sagacity, and conducting with skill, the most desperate undertakings, and in a turbulent time, was allowed to associate with the non-jurors, who affected a peculiar austerity of conduct and sentiments. In 1663, the Act of Settlement in Ireland, and the proceedings thereupon, affected Blood deeply in his fortune, and from that moment he appears to have nourished the most inveterate hatred to the Duke of Ormond, the Lord Lieutenant of Ireland, whom he considered as the author of the measures under which he suffered. There were at this time many malecontents of the same party with himself, so that Lieutenant Blood, as the most daring among them, was able to put himself at the head of a conspiracy which had for its purpose the exciting a general insurrection, and, as a preliminary step, the surprising of the castle of Dublin. The means proposed for the last purpose, which was to be the prelude to the rising, augured the desperation of the person by whom it was contrived, and yet might probably have succeeded, from its very boldness. A declaration was drawn up by the hand of Blood himself, calling upon all persons to take arms for the liberty of the subject, and the restoration of the Solemn League and Covenant. For the surprise of the castle, it was provided, that several persons with petitions in their hands, were to wait within the walls, as if they staid to present them to the Lord Lieutenant, while about fourscore of the old daring disbanded soldiers were to remain on the outside, dressed like carpenters, smiths, shoemakers, and other ordinary mechanics. As soon as the Lord Lieutenant went in, a baker was to pass by the main guard with a large basket of white bread on his back. By making a false step, he was to throw down his burden, which might create a scramble among the soldiers, and offer the fourscore men before mentioned an opportunity of disarming them, while the others with petitions in their hands secured all within; and being once master of the castle and the Duke of Ormond's person, they were to publish their declaration. But some of the principal conspirators were apprehended about twelve hours before the time appointed for the execution of the design, in which no less than seven members of the House of Commons (for the Parliament of Ireland was then sitting) were concerned. Leckie, a minister, the brother-in-law of Blood, was with several others tried, no apology—none will serve your turn. I saw the man myself, among your Germans as you call them; and you know what I must needs believe from such a circumstance."

condemned, and executed. Blood effected his escape, but was still so much the object of public apprehension, that a rumour having arisen during Leckie's execution, that Major Blood was at hand with a party to rescue the prisoner, every one of the guards, and the executioner himself, shifted for themselves, leaving Leckie, with the halter about his neck, standing alone under the gallows; but as no rescue appeared, the sheriff-officers returned to their duty, and the criminal was executed. Meantime Blood retired among the mountains of Ireland, where he herded alternately with fanatics and Papists, provided only they were discontented with the government. There were few persons better acquainted with the intrigues of the time than this active partisan, who was alternately Quaker, Anabaptist, or Catholic, but always a rebel, and revolutionist; he shifted from place to place, and from kingdom to kingdom; became known to the Admiral de Ruyter, and was the soul of every desperate plot.

In particular, about 1665, Mr. Blood was one of a revolutionary committee, or secret council, which continued its sittings, notwithstanding that government knew of its meetings. For their security, they had about thirty stout fellows posted around the place where they met in the nature of a *corps de garde*. It fell out, that two of the members of the council, to save themselves, and perhaps for the sake of a reward, betrayed all their transactions to the ministry, which Mr. Blood soon suspected, and in a short time got to the bottom of the whole affair. He appointed these two persons to meet him at a tavern in the city, where he had his guard ready, who secured them without any noise, and carried them to a private place provided for the purpose, where he called a kind of court-martial, before whom they were tried, found guilty, and sentenced to be shot two days after in the same place. When the time appointed came, they were brought out, and all the necessary preparations made for putting the sentence in execution; and the poor men, seeing no hopes of escape, disposed themselves to suffer as well as they could. At this critical juncture, Mr. Blood was graciously pleased to grant them his pardon, and at the same time advised them to go to their new master, tell him all that had happened, and request him, in the name of their old confederates, to be as favourable to such of them as should at any time stand in need of his mercy. Whether these unfortunate people carried Mr.

"Believe that I have been guilty—most guilty, my liege and King," said the Duke, conscience-struck, and kneeling down ;—"believe that I was misguided— that I was mad—Believe any thing but that I was

Blood's message to the King, does not any where appear. It is however certain, that not long after the whole conspiracy was discovered; in consequence of which, on the 26th of April, 1666, Col. John Rathbone, and some other officers of the late disbanded army, were tried and convicted at the Old Bailey for a plot to surprise the Tower, and to kill General Monk.

After his concern with this desperate conclave, who were chiefly fanatics and Fifth-Monarchy men, Blood exchanged the scene for Scotland, where he mingled among the Cameronians, and must have been a most acceptable associate to John Balfour of Burley, or any other who joined the insurgents more out of spleen or desire of plunder, than from religious motives. The writers of the sect seem to have thought his name a discredit, or perhaps did not know it; nevertheless, it is affirmed in a pamphlet written by a person who seems to have been well acquainted with the incidents of his life, that he shared the dangers of the defeat at Pentland Hills, 27th November, 1666, in which the Cameronians were totally routed. After the engagement, he found his way again to Ireland, but was hunted out of Ulster by Lord Dungannon, who pursued him very closely. On his return to England, he made himself again notorious by an exploit, of which the very singular particulars are contained in the pamphlet already mentioned.* The narrative runs as follows:—"Among the persons apprehended for the late fanatic conspiracy, was one Captain Mason, a person for whom Mr. Blood had a particular affection and friendship. This person was to be removed from London to one of the northern counties, in order to his trial at the assizes; and to that intent was sent down with eight of the Duke's troop to guard him, being reckoned to be a person bold and courageous. Mr. Blood having notice of this journey, resolves by the way to rescue his friend. The prisoner and his guard went away in the morning, and Mr. Blood having made choice of three more of his acquaintance, set forward the same day at night, without boots, upon small horses, and their pistols in their trowsers, to prevent suspicion. But opportunities are not so easily had, neither were all places convenient, so that the convoy and their prisoner were gone a good way beyond Newark, before Mr. Blood and his friends had any scent of their prisoner. At

* Remarks on the Life of the famed Mr. Blood. London, 1680. Folio.

capable of harming, or being accessory to harm, your person."

"I do not believe it," said the King; "I think of you, Villiers, as the companion of my dangers and my exile,

one place, they set a sentinel to watch his coming by; but whether it was out of fear, or that the person was tired with a tedious expectation, the sentinel brought them no tidings either of the prisoner or his guard, insomuch that Mr. Blood and his companions began to think their friend so far before them upon the road, that it would be in vain to follow him. Yet not willing to give over an enterprise so generously undertaken, upon Mr. Blood's encouragement, they rode on, though despairing of success, till finding it grow towards evening, and meeting with a convenient inn upon the road, in a small village not far from Doncaster, they resolved to lie there all night, and return for London the next morning. In that inn they had not sat long in a room next the street, condoling among themselves the ill success of such a tedious journey, and the misfortune of their friend, before the convoy came thundering up to the door of the said inn with their prisoner, Captain Mason having made choice of that inn, as being best known to him, to give his guardians the refreshment of a dozen of drink. There Mr. Blood, unseen, had a full view of his friend, and of the persons he had to deal with. He had bespoke a small supper, which was at the fire, so that he had but very little time for consultation; finding that Captain Mason's party did not intend to alight. On this account he only gave general directions to his associates to follow his example in whatever they saw him do. In haste, therefore, they called for their horses, and threw down their money for their reckoning, telling the woman of the house, that since they had met with such good company, they were resolved to go forward. Captain Mason went off first upon a sorry beast, and with him the commander of the party, and four more; the rest staid behind to make an end of their liquor. Then away marched one more single, and in a very small time after, the last two. By this time, Mr. Blood and one of his friends being horsed, followed the two that were hindmost, and soon overtook them. These four rode some little time together, Mr. Blood on the right hand of the two soldiers, and his friend on the left. But upon a sudden, Mr. Blood laid hold of the reins of the horse next him, while his friend, in observation to his directions, did the same on the other hand; and having presently by surprise dismounted the soldiers, pulled off their bridles, and sent their horses to pick their grass where they pleased. These two being thus made sure of, Mr. Blood pursues

and am so far from supposing you mean worse than you
say, that I am convinced you acknowledge more than
you ever meant to attempt."

" By all that is sacred," said the Duke, still kneeling,

his game, intending to have reached the single trooper; but he being
got to the rest of his fellows, now reduced to six, and a barber of York,
that travelled in their company, Mr. Blood made up, heads the whole
party, and stops them; of which some of the foremost, looking upon
him to be either drunk or mad, thought the rebuke of a switch to be
a sufficient chastisement of such a rash presumption, which they
exercised with more contempt than fury, till, by the rudeness of his
compliments in return, he gave them to understand he was not in jest,
but in very good earnest. He was soon seconded by his friend that
was with him in his first exploit; but there had been several rough
blows dealt between the unequal number of six to two, before Mr.
Blood's two other friends came up to their assistance ; nay, I may
safely say six to two; for the barber of York, whether out of his natural
propensity to the sport, or that his pot-valiantness had made him so
generous as to help his fellow-travellers, would needs show his valour
at the beginning of the fray; but better had he been at the latter end
of a feast; for though he showed his prudence to take the stronger
side, as he guessed by the number, yet because he would take no
warning, which was often given him, not to put himself to the hazard
of losing a guitar-finger by meddling in a business that nothing concerned him, he lost his life, as they were forced to despatch him, in
the first place, for giving them a needless trouble. The barber, being
become an useless instrument, and the other of Mr. Blood's friends
being come up, the skirmish began to be very smart, the four
assailants having singled out their champions as fairly and equally
as they could. All this while, Captain Mason, being rode before
upon his thirty-shilling steed, wondering his guard came not with
him, looked back, and observing a combustion, and that they were
altogether by the ears, knew not what to think. He conjectured it at
first to have been some intrigue upon him, as if the troopers had a
design to tempt him to an escape, which might afterwards prove
more to his prejudice; just like cats, that, with regardless scorn,
seem to give the distressed mouse all the liberty in the world to get
away out of their paws, but soon recover their prey again at one
jump. Thereupon, unwilling to undergo the hazard of such a trial,
he comes back, at which time Mr. Blood cried out to him, ' Horse,
horse, quickly ! ' an alarm so amazing at first, that he could not

" had I not been involved to the extent of life and fortune with the villain Christian "——

" Nay, if you bring Christian on the stage again," said the King, smiling, " it is time for me to withdraw.

believe it to be his friend's voice when he heard it; but as the thoughts of military men are soon summoned together, and never hold Spanish councils, the Captain presently settled his resolution, mounts the next horse that wanted a rider, and puts it in for a share of his own self-preservation. In this bloody conflict, Mr. Blood was three times unhorsed, occasioned by his forgetfulness, as having omitted to new girt his saddle, which the ostler had unloosed upon the wadding at his first coming into the inn. Being then so often dis-. mounted, and not knowing the reason, which the occasion would not give him leave to consider, he resolved to fight it out on foot; of which two of the soldiers taking the advantage, singled him out, and drove him into a court-yard, where he made a stand with a full body, his sword in one hand, and his pistol in the other. One of the soldiers taking that advantage of his open body, shot him near the shoulder-blade of his pistol-arm, at which time he had four other bullets in his . body, that he had received before; which the soldier observing, flung his discharged pistol at him with that good aim and violence, that he hit him a stunning blow just under the forehead, upon the upper part of the nose between the eyes, which for the present so amazed him, that he gave himself over for a dead man; yet resolving to give one sparring blow before he expired, such is the strange provocation and success of despair, with one vigorous stroke of his sword, he brought his adversary with a vengeance from his horse, and laid him in a far worse condition than himself at his horse's feet. At that time, full of anger and revenge, he was just going to make an end of his conquest, by giving him the fatal stab, but that in the very nick of time, Captain Mason, having, by the help of his friends, done his business where they had fought, by the death of some, and the disabling of others that opposed them, came in, and bid him, hold and spare the life of one that had been the civilest person to him upon the road,—a fortunate piece of kindness in the one, and of gratitude in the other; which Mr. Blood easily condescending to, by the joint assistance of the Captain, the other soldier was soon mastered, and the victory, after a sharp fight, that lasted above two hours, was at length completed. You may be sure the fight was well maintained on both sides, while two of the soldiers, besides the barber, were slain upon the place, three unhorsed, and the rest wounded. And it was ob-

Come, Villiers, rise—I forgive thee, and only recommend one act of penance—the curse you yourself bestowed on the dog who bit you—marriage, and retirement to your country-seat."

servable, that though the encounter happened in a village, where a great number of people were spectators of the combat, yet none would adventure the rescue of either party, as not knowing which was in the wrong, or which in the right, and were therefore wary of being arbitrators in such a desperate contest, where they saw the reward of assistance to be nothing but present death. After the combat was over, Mr. Blood and his friends divided themselves, and parted several ways."

Before he had engaged in this adventure, Blood had placed his wife and son in an apothecary's shop at Rumford, under the name of Weston. He himself afterwards affected to practise as a physician under that of Ayliffe, under which guise he remained concealed until his wounds were cured, and the hue and cry against him and his accomplices was somewhat abated.

In the meantime, this extraordinary man, whose spirits toiled in framing the most daring enterprises, had devised a plot which, as it respected the person at whom it was aimed, was of a much more ambitious character than that for the delivery of Mason. It had for its object the seizure of the person of the Duke of Ormond, his ancient enemy, in the streets of London. In this some have thought he only meant to gratify his resentment, while others suppose that he might hope to extort some important advantages by detaining his Grace in his hands as a prisoner. The Duke's historian, Carte, gives the following account of this extraordinary enterprise:—" The Prince of Orange came this year (1670) into England, and being invited, on Dec. 6, to an entertainment in the city of London, his Grace attended him thither. As he was returning homewards in a dark night, and going up St. James's Street, at the end of which, facing the palace, stood Clarendon House, where he then lived, he was attacked by Blood and five of his accomplices. The Duke always used to go attended with six footmen; but as they were too heavy a load to ride upon a coach, he always had iron spikes behind it to keep them from getting up; and continued this practice to his dying day, even after this attempt of assassination. These six footmen used to walk on both sides of the street, over against the coach; but by some contrivance or other, they were all stopped and out of the way, when the Duke was taken out of his coach by Blood and his

The Duke rose abashed, and followed the King into the circle, which Charles entered, leaning on the shoulder of his repentant peer; to whom he showed so much countenance, as led the most acute observers present, to

son, and mounted on horseback, behind one of the horsemen in his company. The coachman drove on to Clarendon House, and told the porter that the Duke had been seized by two men, who had carried him down Pickadilly. The porter immediately ran that way, and Mr. James Clarke chancing to be at that time in the court of the house, followed with all possible haste, having first alarmed the family, and ordered the servants to come after him as fast as they could. Blood, it seems, either to gratify the humour of his patron, who had set him upon this work, or to glut his own revenge by putting his Grace to the same ignominious death, which his accomplices in the treasonable design upon Dublin Castle had suffered, had taken a strong fancy into his head to hang the Duke at Tyburn. Nothing could have saved his Grace's life, but that extravagant imagination and passion of the villain, who, leaving the Duke mounted and buckled to one of his comrades, rode on before, and (as is said) actually tied a rope to the gallows, and then rode back to see what was become of his accomplices, whom he met riding off in a great hurry. The horseman to whom the Duke was tied, was a person of great strength, but being embarrassed by his Grace's struggling, could not advance as fast as he desired. He was, however, got a good way beyond Berkeley (now Devonshire) House, towards Knightsbridge, when the Duke, having got his foot under the man's, unhorsed him, and they both fell down together in the mud, where they were struggling, when the porter and Mr. Clarke came up. The villain then disengaged himself, and seeing the neighbourhood alarmed, and numbers of people running towards them, got on horseback, and having, with one of his comrades, fired their pistols at the Duke, (but missed him, as taking their aim in the dark, and in a hurry,) rode off as fast as they could to save themselves. The Duke (now sixty years of age) was quite spent with struggling, so that when Mr. Clarke and the porter came up, they knew him rather by feeling his star, than by any sound of voice he could utter; and they were forced to carry him home, and lay him on a bed to recover his spirits. He received some wounds and bruises in the struggle, which confined him within doors for some days. The King, when he heard of this intended assassination of the Duke of Ormond, expressed a great resentment on that occasion, and issued out a proclamation for

doubt the possibility of there existing any real cause for
the surmises to the Duke's prejudice.

The Countess of Derby had in the meanwhile consulted
with the Duke of Ormond, with the Peverils, and with

the discovery and apprehension of the miscreants concerned in the
attempt."

Blood, however, lay concealed, and, with his usual success, escaped
apprehension. While thus lurking, he entertained and digested an
exploit, evincing the same atrocity which had characterized the
undertakings he had formerly been engaged in; there was also to
be traced in his new device something of that peculiar disposition
which inclined him to be desirous of adding to the murder of the
Duke of Ormond, the singular infamy of putting him to death at
Tyburn. With something of the same spirit, he now resolved to
show his contempt of monarchy, and all its symbols, by stealing the
crown, sceptre, and other articles of the regalia out of the office in
which they were deposited, and enriching himself and his needy
associates with the produce of the spoils. This feat, by which Blood
is now chiefly remembered, is, like all his transactions, marked with
a daring strain of courage and duplicity, and like most of his undertakings, was very likely to have proved successful. John Bayley,
Esq., in his History and Antiquities of the Tower of London, gives
the following distinct account of this curious exploit. At this period,
Sir Gilbert Talbot was Keeper, as it was called, of the Jewel
House.

"It was soon after the appointment of Sir Gilbert Talbot, that the
Regalia in the Tower first became objects of public inspection, which
King Charles allowed in consequence of the reduction in the emolu-
ments of the master's office. The profits which arose from showing
the jewels to strangers, Sir Gilbert assigned in lieu of a salary, to the
person whom he had appointed to the care of them. This was an old
confidential servant of his father's, one Talbot Edwards, whose name
is handed down to posterity as keeper of the regalia, when the
notorious attempt to steal the crown was made in the year 1673; the
following account of which is chiefly derived from a relation which
Mr. Edwards himself made of the transaction.

"About three weeks before this audacious villain Blood made his
attempt upon the crown, he came to the Tower in the habit of a
parson, with a long cloak, cassock, and canonical girdle, accompanied
by a woman, whom he called his wife. They desired to see the regalia, and, just as their wishes had been gratified, the lady feigned

her other friends; and, by their unanimous advice, though with considerable difficulty, became satisfied, that to have thus shown herself at Court, was sufficient to vindicate the honour of her house; and that it was her wisest

sudden indisposition; this called forth the kind offices of Mrs. Edwards, the keeper's wife, who, having courteously invited her into their house to repose herself, she soon recovered, and on their departure, professed themselves thankful for this civility. A few days after, Blood came again, bringing a present to Mrs. Edwards, of four pairs of white gloves from his pretended wife; and having thus begun the acquaintance, they made frequent visits to improve it. After a short respite of their compliments, the disguised ruffian returned again; and in conversation with Mrs. Edwards, said that his wife could discourse of nothing but the kindness of those good people in the Tower —that she had long studied, and at length bethought herself of a handsome way of requital. You have, quoth he, a pretty young gentlewoman for your daughter, and I have a young nephew, who has two or three hundred a-year in land, and is at my disposal. If your daughter be free, and you approve it, I'll bring him here to see her, and we will endeavour to make it a match. This was easily assented to by old Mr. Edwards, who invited the parson to dine with him on that day; he readily accepted the invitation; and taking upon him to say grace, performed it with great seeming devotion, and casting up his eyes, concluded it with a prayer for the King, Queen, and royal family. After dinner, he went up to see the rooms, and observing a handsome case of pistols hang there, expressed a great desire to buy them, to present to a young lord, who was his neighbour; a pretence by which he thought of disarming the house against the period intended for the execution of his design. At his departure, which was a canonical benediction of the good company, he appointed a day and hour to bring his young nephew to see his mistress, which was the very day that he made his daring attempt. The good old gentleman had got up ready to receive his guest, and the daughter was in her best dress to entertain her expected lover; when, behold Parson Blood, with three more, came to the jewel-house, all armed with rapier-blades in their canes, and every one a dagger, and a brace of pocket-pistols. Two of his companions entered in with him, on pretence of seeing the crown, and the third staid at the door, as if to look after the young lady, a jewel of a more charming description, but in reality as a watch. The daughter, who thought it not modest to come down till she was called, sent the maid to take a view of the company, and bring a description course, after having done so, to retire to her insular dominions, without farther provoking the resentment of a powerful faction. She took farewell of the King in form, and demanded his permission to carry back with her the

of her gallant; and the servant, conceiving that he was the intended bridegroom who staid at the door, being the youngest of the party, returned to soothe the anxiety of her young mistress with the idea she had formed of his person. Blood told Mr. Edwards that they would not go up stairs till his wife came, and desired him to show his friends the crown to pass the time till then; and they had no sooner entered the room, and the door, as usual, shut, than a cloak was thrown over the old man's head, and a gag put in his mouth. Thus secured, they told him that their resolution was to have the crown, globe, and sceptre; and, if he would quietly submit to it, they would spare his life; otherwise he was to expect no mercy. He thereupon endeavoured to make all the noise he possibly could, to be heard above; they then knocked him down with a wooden mallet, and told him, that, if yet he would lie quietly, they would spare his life; but if not, upon his next attempt to discover them, they would kill him. Mr. Edwards, however, according to his own account, was not intimidated by this threat, but strained himself to make the greater noise, and in consequence, received several more blows on the head with the mallet, and was stabbed in the belly; this again brought the poor old man to the ground, where he lay for some time in so senseless a state, that one of the villains pronounced him dead. Edwards had come a little to himself, and hearing this, lay quietly, conceiving it best to be thought so. The booty was now to be disposed of, and one of them, named Parrot, secreted the orb. Blood held the crown under his cloak; and the third was about to file the sceptre in two, in order that it might be placed in a bag, brought for that purpose; but, fortunately, the son of Mr. Edwards, who had been in Flanders with Sir John Talbot, and on his landing in England, had obtained leave to come away post to visit his father, happened to arrive whilst this scene was acting; and on coming to the door, the person that stood sentinel asked with whom he would speak; to which he answered, that he belonged to the house; and, perceiving the person to be a stranger, told him that if he had any business with his father, that he would acquaint him with it, and so hastened up stairs to salute his friends. This unexpected accident spread confusion amongst the party, and they instantly decamped with the crown and orb, leaving the sceptre yet unfiled. The aged keeper now raised himself upon his legs, forced helpless creature who had so strangely escaped from her protection, into a world where her condition might make her so subject to every species of misfortune.

"Will your ladyship forgive me?" said Charles. "I

the gag from his mouth, and cried, 'Treason, murder!' which being heard by his daughter, who was, perhaps, anxiously expecting far other sounds, ran out and reiterated the cry. The alarm now became general, and young Edwards and his brother-in-law, Captain Beckman, ran after the conspirators, whom a warder put himself in a position to stop, but Blood discharged a pistol at him, and he fell, although unhurt, and the thieves proceeded safely to the next post, where one Sill, who had been a soldier under Cromwell, stood sentinel; but he offered no opposition, and they accordingly passed the drawbridge. Horses were waiting for them at St. Catherine's gate; and as they ran that way along the Tower wharf, they themselves cried out, 'Stop the rogues!' by which they passed on unsuspected, till Captain Beckman overtook them. At his head Blood fired another pistol, but missed him, and was seized. Under the cloak of this daring villain was found the crown, and, although he saw himself a prisoner, he had yet the impudence to struggle for his prey; and when it was finally wrested from him, said, 'It was a gallant attempt, however unsuccessful; it was for a crown!' Parrot, who had formerly served under General Harrison, was also taken; but Hunt, Blood's son-in-law, reached his horse and rode off, as did two others of the thieves; but he was soon afterwards stopped, and likewise committed to custody. In this struggle and confusion, the great pearl, a large diamond, and several smaller stones, were lost from the crown; but the two former, and some of the latter, were afterwards found and restored; and the Ballas ruby, broken off the sceptre, being found in Parrot's pocket, nothing considerable was eventually missing.

"As soon as the prisoners were secured, young Edwards hastened to Sir Gilbert Talbot, who was then master and treasurer of the Jewel House, and gave him an account of the transaction. Sir Gilbert instantly went to the King, and acquainted his majesty with it; and his majesty commanded him to proceed forthwith to the Tower, to see how matters stood; to take the examination of Blood and the others; and to return and report it to him. Sir Gilbert accordingly went; but the King in the meantime was persuaded by some about him, to hear the examination himself, and the prisoners were in consequence sent for to Whitehall; a circumstance which is supposed to have saved these daring wretches from the gallows."

have studied your sex long—I am mistaken if your little maiden is not as capable of caring for herself as any of us."

"Impossible!" said the Countess.

On his examination under such an atrocious charge, Blood audaciously replied, "that he would never betray an associate, or defend himself at the expense of uttering a falsehood." He even averred, perhaps, more than was true against himself, when he confessed that he had lain concealed among the reeds for the purpose of killing the King with a carabine, while Charles was bathing; but he pretended that on this occasion his purpose was disconcerted by a secret awe,— appearing to verify the allegation in Shakspeare, "There's such divinity doth hedge a king, that treason can but peep to what it would, acts little of its will." To this story, true or false, Blood added a declaration that he was at the head of a numerous following, disbanded soldiers and others, who, from motives of religion, were determined to take the life of the King, as the only obstacle to their obtaining freedom of worship and liberty of conscience. These men, he said, would be determined, by his execution, to persist in the resolution of putting Charles to death; whereas, he averred that, by sparing his life, the King might disarm a hundred poniards directed against his own. This view of the case made a strong impression on Charles, whose selfishness was uncommonly acute: yet he felt the impropriety of pardoning the attempt upon the life of the Duke of Ormond, and condescended to ask that faithful servant's permission, before he would exert his authority, to spare the assassin. Ormond answered, that if the King chose to pardon the attempt to steal his crown, he himself might easily consent, that the attempt upon his own life, as a crime of much less importance, should also be forgiven. Charles, accordingly, not only gave Blood a pardon, but endowed him with a pension of £500 a-year; which led many persons to infer, not only that the King wished to preserve himself from the future attempts of this desperate man, but that he had it also in view to secure the services of so determined a ruffian, in case he should have an opportunity of employing him in his own line of business. There is a striking contrast between the fate of Blood, pensioned and rewarded for this audacious attempt, and that of the faithful Edwards, who may be safely said to have sacrificed his life in defence of the property intrusted to him! In remuneration for his fidelity and his sufferings, Edwards only obtained a grant of £200 from the Exchequer, with £100 to his son; but so little pains were taken about the regular discharge of these donatives,

"Possible, and most true," whispered the King. "I will instantly convince you of the fact, though the experiment is too delicate to be made by any but your ladyship. Yonder she stands, looking as if she heard no more than

that the parties entitled to them were glad to sell them for half the sum. After this wonderful escape from justice, Blood seems to have affected the airs of a person in favour, and was known to solicit the suits of many of the old republican party, for whom he is said to have gained considerable indulgences, when the old cavaliers, who had ruined themselves in the cause of Charles the First, could obtain neither countenance nor restitution. During the ministry called the Cabal, he was high in favour with the Duke of Buckingham; till upon their declension, his favour began also to fail, and we find him again engaged in opposition to the Court. Blood was not likely to lie idle amid·the busy intrigues and factions which succeeded the celebrated discovery of Oates. He appears to have passed again into violent opposition to the Court, but his steps were no longer so sounding as to be heard above his contemporaries. North hints at his being involved in a plot against his former friend and patron the Duke of Buckingham. The passage is quoted at length in Note, p. 274.

The Plot, it appears, consisted in an attempt to throw some scandalous imputation upon the Duke of Buckingham, for a conspiracy to effect which Edward Christian, Arthur O'Brien, and Thomas Blood, were indicted in the King's Bench, and found guilty, 25th June, 1680. The damages sued for were laid as high as ten thousand pounds, for which Colonel Blood found bail. But he appears to have been severely affected in health, as, 24th August, 1680, he departed this life in a species of lethargy. It is remarkable enough that the story of his death and funeral was generally regarded as fabricated, preparative to some exploit of his own; nay, so general was this report, that the coroner caused his body to be raised, and a jury to sit upon it, for the purpose of ensuring that the celebrated Blood had at length undergone the common fate of mankind. There was found unexpected difficulty in proving that the miserable corpse before the jury was that of the celebrated conspirator. It was at length recognised by some of his acquaintances, who swore to the preternatural size of the thumb, so that the coroner, convinced of the identity, remanded this once active, and now quiet person, to his final rest in Tothill-fields.

Such were the adventures of an individual, whose real exploits, whether the motive, the danger, or the character of the enterprises be the marble pillar against which she leans. Now, if Lady Derby will contrive either to place her hand near the region of the damsel's heart, or at least on her arm, so that she can feel the sensation of the blood when the pulse increases, then do you, my Lord of Ormond, beckon Julian Peveril out of sight—I will show you in a moment that it can stir at sounds spoken."

The Countess, much surprised, afraid of some embarrassing pleasantry on the part of Charles, yet unable to repress her curiosity, placed herself near Fenella, as she called her little mute; and, while making signs to her, contrived to place her hand on her wrist.

At this moment the King, passing near them, said, "This is a horrid deed—the villain Christian has stabbed young Peveril!"

The mute evidence of the pulse, which bounded as if a cannon had been discharged close by the poor girl's ear, was accompanied by such a loud scream of agony, as distressed, while it startled, the good-natured monarch himself. "I did but jest," he said; "Julian is well, my pretty maiden. I only used the wand of a certain blind deity, called Cupid, to bring a deaf and dumb vassal of his to the exercise of her faculties." *

considered, equal, or rather surpass, those fictions of violence and peril which we love to peruse in romance. They cannot, therefore, be deemed foreign to a work dedicated, like the present, to the preservation of extraordinary occurrences, whether real or fictitious.

* This little piece of superstition was suggested by the following incident. The Author of Waverley happened to be standing by with other gentlemen, while the captain of the Selkirk Yeomanry was purchasing a horse for the use of his trumpeter. The animal offered was a handsome one, and neither the officer, who was an excellent jockey, nor any one present, could see any imperfection in wind or limb. But a person happened to pass, who was asked to give an opinion. This man was called Blind Willie, who drove a small trade in cattle and

"I am betrayed!" she said, with her eyes fixed on the ground—"I am betrayed!—and it is fit that she, whose life has been spent in practising treason on others, should be caught in her own snare.—But where is my tutor in iniquity?—where is Christian, who taught me to play the part of spy on this unsuspicious lady, until I had well-nigh delivered her into his bloody hands?"

"This," said the King, "craves more secret examination. Let all leave the apartment who are not immediately connected with these proceedings, and let this Christian be again brought before us.—Wretched man," he continued, addressing Christian, "what wiles are these you have practised, and by what extraordinary means?"

"She has betrayed me, then!" said Christian—"Betrayed me to bonds and death, merely for an idle passion, which can never be successful!—But know, Zarah," he added, addressing her sternly, "when my life is forfeited through thy evidence, the daughter has murdered the father!"

The unfortunate girl stared on him in astonishment.

---

horses, and what seemed as extraordinary, in watches, notwithstanding his having been born blind. He was accounted to possess a rare judgment in these subjects of traffic. So soon as he had examined the horse in question, he immediately pronounced it to have something of his own complaint, and in plain words, stated it to be blind, or verging upon that imperfection, which was found to be the case on close examination. None present had suspected this fault in the animal; which is not wonderful, considering that it may frequently exist, without any appearance in the organ affected. Blind Willie being asked how he made a discovery imperceptible to so many gentlemen who had their eyesight, explained, that after feeling the horse's limbs, he laid one hand on its heart, and drew the other briskly across the animal's eyes, when finding no increase of pulsation, in consequence of the latter motion, he had come to the conclusion that the horse must be blind.

" You said," at length she stammered forth, " that I was
the daughter of your slaughtered brother? "

" That was partly to reconcile thee to the part thou
wert to play in my destined drama of vengeance—partly
to hide what men call the infamy of thy birth. But *my*
daughter thou art! and from the eastern clime, in which
thy mother was born, you derive that fierce torrent of
passion which I laboured to train to my purposes, but
which, turned into another channel, has become the cause
of your father's destruction.—My destiny is the Tower,
I suppose? "

He spoke these words with great composure, and
scarce seemed to regard the agonies of his daughter,
who, throwing herself at his feet, sobbed and wept most
bitterly.

" This must not be," said the King, moved with compassion at this scene of misery. " If you consent, Christian, to leave this country, there is a vessel in the river
bound for New England—Go, carry your dark intrigues
to other lands."

" I might dispute the sentence," said Christian, boldly;
" and if I submit to it, it is a matter of my own choice.—
One half hour had made me even with that proud woman,
but fortune hath cast the balance against me.—Rise,
Zarah, Fenella no more! Tell the Lady of Derby, that,
if the daughter of Edward Christian, the niece of her
murdered victim, served her as a menial, it was but for
the purpose of vengeance—miserably, miserably frus-
trated!—Thou seest thy folly now—thou wouldst follow
yonder ungrateful stripling—thou wouldst forsake all
other thoughts to gain his slightest notice ; and now, thou
art a forlorn outcast, ridiculed and insulted by those on
whose necks you might have trod, had you governed

yourself with more wisdom!—But come, thou art still my daughter—there are other skies than that which canopies Britain."

" Stop him," said the King ; " we must know by what means this maiden found access to those confined in our prisons."

" I refer your Majesty to your most Protestant jailer, and to the most Protestant Peers, who, in order to obtain perfect knowledge of the depth of the Popish Plot, have contrived these ingenious apertures for visiting them in their cells by night or day. His Grace of Buckingham can assist your Majesty, if you are inclined to make the inquiry." *

" Christian," said the Duke, " thou art the most barefaced villain who ever breathed."

" Of a commoner, I may," answered Christian, and led his daughter out of the presence.

" See after him, Selby," said the King ; " lose not sight of him till the ship sail ; if he dare return to Britain, it shall be at his peril. Would to God we had as good riddance of others as dangerous ! And I would also," he added, after a moment's pause, " that all our ·political intrigues and feverish alarms could terminate as harmlessly as now. Here is a plot without a drop of blood ; and all the elements of a romance, without its conclusion. Here we have a wandering island princess, (I pray my Lady of Derby's pardon,) a dwarf, a Moorish sorceress, an impenitent rogue, and a repentant man of rank, and yet all ends without either hanging or marriage."

" Not altogether without the latter," said the Countess,

---

* It was said that very unfair means were used to compel the prisoners, committed on account of the Popish Plot, to make disclosures, and that several of them were privately put to the torture.

who had an opportunity, during the evening, of much private conversation with Julian Peveril. "There is a certain Major Bridgenorth, who, since your Majesty relinquishes farther inquiry into these proceedings, which he had otherwise intended to abide, designs, as we are informed, to leave England forever. Now, this Bridgenorth, by dint of the law, hath acquired strong possession over the domains of Peveril, which he is desirous to restore to the ancient owners, with much fair land besides, conditionally, that our young Julian will receive them as the dowry of his only child and heir."

"By my faith," said the King, "she must be a foul-favoured wench, indeed, if Julian requires to be pressed to accept her on such fair conditions."

"They love each other like lovers of the last age," said the Countess; "but the stout old Knight likes not the roundheaded alliance."

"Our royal recommendation shall put that to rights," said the King; "Sir Geoffrey Peveril has not suffered hardship so often at our command, that he will refuse our recommendation when it comes to make him amends for all his losses."

It may be supposed the King did not speak without being fully aware of the unlimited ascendency which he possessed over the spirit of the old Tory; for within four weeks afterwards, the bells of Martindale-Moultrassie were ringing for the union of the families, from whose estates it takes its compound name, and the beacon-light of the Castle blazed high over hill and dale, and summoned all to rejoice who were within twenty miles of its gleam."

END OF PEVERIL OF THE PEAK.

LIST OF THE WAVERLEY NOVELS.

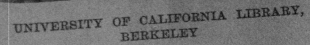
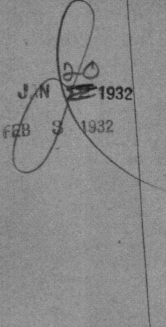

CPSIA information can be obtained
at www.ICGtesting.com
Printed in the USA
BVHW041201120819
555674BV00009B/108/P